On Time

The publisher gratefully acknowledges the generous support of the Ahmanson Foundation Humanities Endowment Fund of the University of California Press Foundation.

On Time

TECHNOLOGY AND TEMPORALITY IN MODERN EGYPT

On Barak

UNIVERSITY OF CALIFORNIA PRESS
BERKELEY LOS ANGELES LONDON

University of California Press, one of the most distinguished university presses in the United States, enriches lives around the world by advancing scholarship in the humanities, social sciences, and natural sciences. Its activities are supported by the UC Press Foundation and by philanthropic contributions from individuals and institutions. For more information, visit www.ucpress.edu.

University of California Press
Berkeley and Los Angeles, California

University of California Press, Ltd.
London, England

Library of Congress Cataloging-in-Publication Data

Barak, On.
On time : technology and temporality in modern Egypt / On Barak.
p. cm.
Revised version of the author's dissertation—New York University, 2009.
Includes bibliographical references and index.
ISBN 978-0-520-27613-0 (cloth : alk. paper)
ISBN 978-0-520-27614-7 (pbk. : alk. paper)
ISBN 978-0-520-95656-8 (ebook)
1. Egypt—History—British occupation, 1882–1936. 2. Egypt—Social conditions—19th century. 3. Egypt—Social conditions—20th century. 4. Time—Social aspects—Egypt. 5. Time perception—Social aspects—Egypt. 6. Technology—Social aspects—Egypt. I. Title.
DT107.B366 2013
962.04—dc23 2013010761

Manufactured in the United States of America

21 20 19 18 17 16 15 14 13
10 9 8 7 6 5 4 3 2 1

In keeping with a commitment to support environmentally responsible and sustainable printing practices, UC Press has printed this book on Rolland Enviro100, a 100% postconsumer fiber paper that is FSC certified, deinked, processed chlorine-free, and manufactured with renewable biogas energy. It is acid-free and EcoLogo certified.

To my family, old and new

CONTENTS

ILLUSTRATIONS

MAPS

FIGURES

ACKNOWLEDGMENTS

The engagement, insightfulness, and sheer number of friends, teachers and interlocutors who nourished this book in its different stages troubles conventional notions of authorship. The mentorship, and gradually also the friendship of my advisor Khaled Fahmy, Zachary Lockman, Timothy Mitchell, Michael Gilsenan, and Arvind Rajagopal turned New York University into the best place in the world for writing a dissertation in modern Egyptian history. My deepest thanks also go to Waiel Ashry, Zvi Ben-Dor Benite, James Baldwin, Omar Cheta, Leena Dallasheh, Noah Haiduc-Dale, Rania Jawad, Hanan Kholoussy, Elias Khoury, Tamer el-Leithy, David Ludden, Jeanne Miller, Molly Nolan, Chris Otter, Leslie Peirce, Everett Rowson, Sherene Seikaly, Robin Shulman, Karim Tartoussieh, Sarah Tunney, Peter Valenti, and Helena Wright, who together and apart, at times briefly and at others in a sustained fashion, made my years in New York truly inspiring and supportive.

The Society of Fellows at Princeton offered a utopian milieu to think, discuss, research and transform the dissertation into a book. My thanks go especially to Lucia Allais, Leonard Barkan, Scott Burnham, Eduardo Canedo, the late Jim Clark, Isabelle Clark-Decès, Yaacob Dweck, Mischa Gabowitsch, Simon Grote, Mary Harper, Russ Leo, Susan Stewart, and Kerim Yasar.

The interdisciplinarity of the society was supplemented by two complementing kinds of disciplinary rigor, courtesy of the History and the Near Eastern Studies Departments at Princeton. I am grateful to Michael Cook, Katharina Ivanyi, Cyrus Schayegh, Daniel Stolz (who helped me edit the manuscript), Muhammad Qasim Zaman, Max Weiss, Elizabeth Bennett, D. Graham Burnett, Angela Creager, Michael Gordin, Anthony Grafton, Molly Greene, Katja Guenther, Robert Karl, Judith Laffan, Michael Laffan,

Jonathan Levy, Yair Mintzker, Bhavani Raman, Susan Naquin, Gyan Prakash, and Keith Wailoo.

Many other friends, colleagues, and family members in the United States, Israel, Egypt, and Europe are less easily classifiable but not less supportive: the late Nasr Abu Zayd, Marc Ayms, Elif Babul, Mériam Belli, Yael Berda, Crystal Biruk, Lucrezia Botton, Lisa Cody, Yoav Di-Capua, Ed Eigen, Tomer Gardi, Israel Gershoni, Angie Heo, Wilson Chacko Jacob, Aaron Jakes, Rebecca Johnson, Abdelfattah Kilito, Noam Korin, Liat Kozma, Lital Levy, Dotan Leshem, Lisa Onaga, Wen-Chin Ouyang, Nancy Reynolds, Michal Shapira, Gilad Seliktar, Yael Schacher, Eve M. Troutt Powell, Avner Wishnitzer, Rhona and Arthur Wexler, P. S. van Koningsveld, and Gerard Wiegers.

Research in Egypt, the United Kingdom, the United States, and Israel during 2006–2007 was made possible by a National Science Foundation Dissertation Improvement Grant and a Social Science Research Council International Dissertation Research Fellowship. NYU's Graduate School of Arts and Sciences provided various research and writing scholarships, including a Henry M. MacCracken Fellowship, a Pre-Dissertation Research Award, and a Dean's Dissertation Fellowship. The Department of Middle Eastern and Islamic Studies provided summer funds and various teaching opportunities. The Princeton University Committee on Research in the Humanities and Social Sciences helped fund several research trips and editorial services. The Department for Middle Eastern and African History at Tel Aviv University helped with image production costs. I would like to thank the staffs of the Egyptian National Library, the Egyptian Geographical Society, the library of the Centre d'Études et de Documentation Économique, Juridique, et Sociale in Cairo, the American University in Cairo Library, Maktabat al-Qahira al-Kubra, the Bibliotheca Alexandrina, the Egyptian Railway Museum, the British National Archives, the British Library, the BBC Library, the London School of Economics Library, the SOAS Library, Yale University Library, Princeton University Library, New York Public Library, and the Jewish National and University Library in Jerusalem. I am especially thankful for the kindness shown to me by the staff of the periodical room of the Egyptian National Library, where I spent the longest research period. At University of California Press, I would like to thank all those who helped bring this book to press: Niels Hooper, Kim Hogeland, Elizabeth Berg, and Suzanne Knott.

My family has always been my most stimulating and supportive community. Avishai Ehrlich, Lesley Marks, Ayelet Barak, Ofir Nahum, Chen Barak, Dvora Barak, Moshe Barak, Galit Seliktar, and Tamuz Barak, this book is for you.

NOTE ON TRANSLITERATION

Arabic words are transliterated based on a modified version of the system of the *International Journal of Middle East Studies.* I omit the diacritic for the initial *hamzah* (ʾ), and use *ah* for *tāʾ marbūṭah* (in the construct form, *at*). Occasionally, to indicate colloquial Egyptian Arabic, I transcribe *qāf* (q) as *hamzah* (ʾ) and *jīm* (j) as *gīm* (g). Standard English versions of certain personal names have been preserved (e.g., Naguib Mahfouz, rather than Najīb Maḥfūẓ).

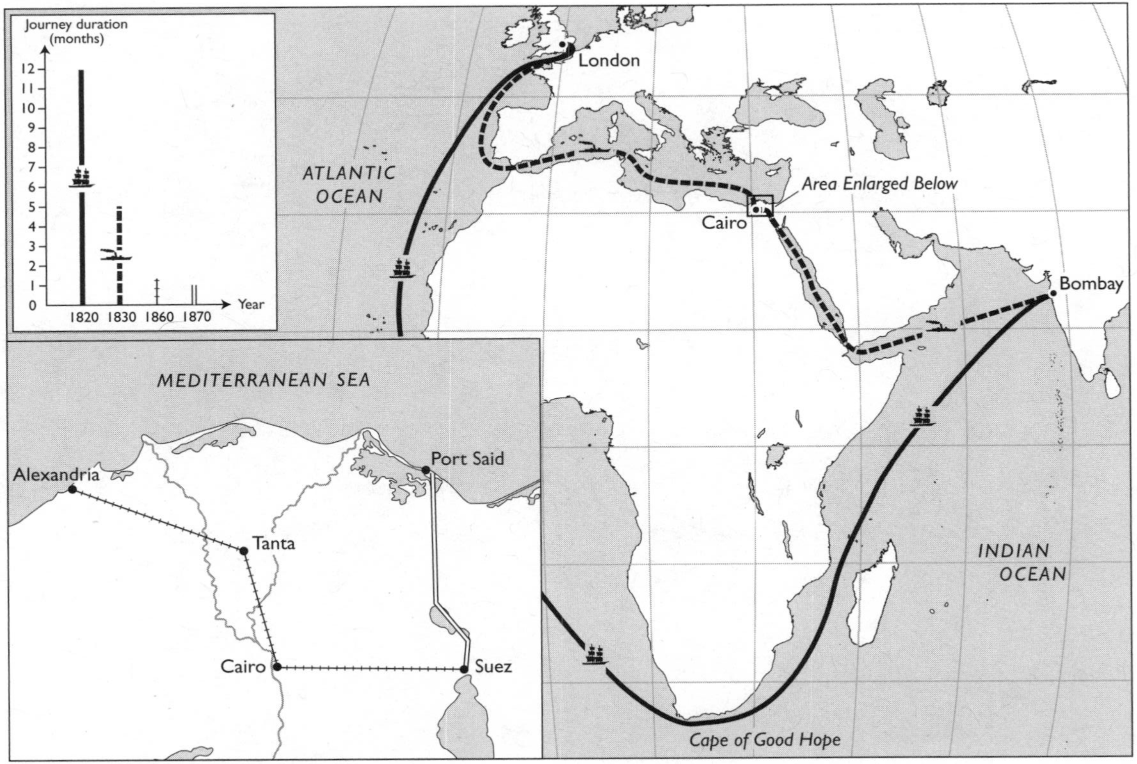

MAP 1. Routes of the British India traffic.

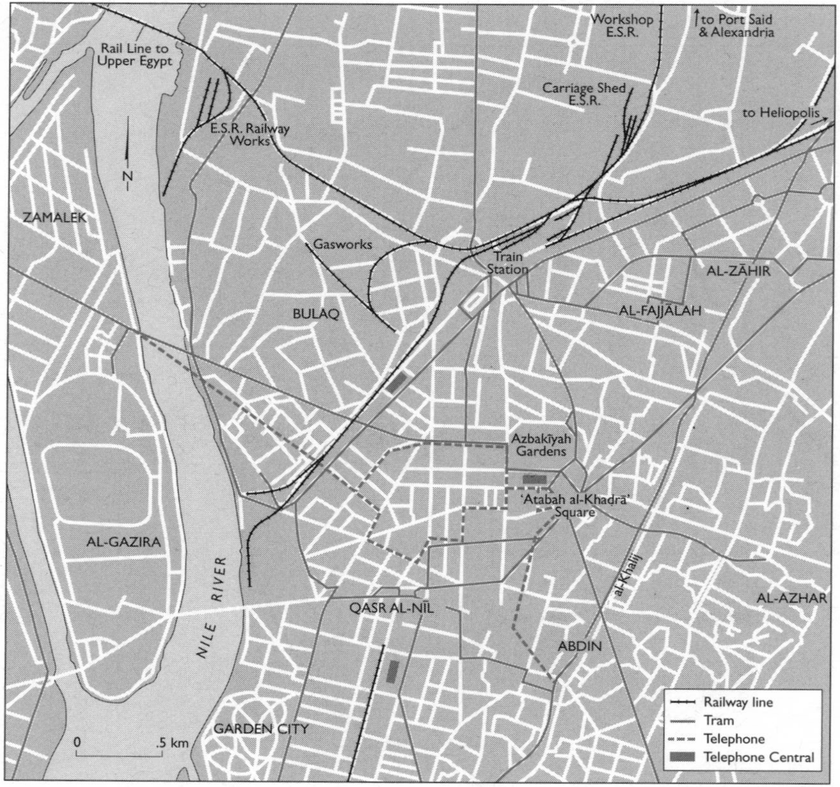

MAP 2. Cairo, c. 1930. Adapted from Alexander Nicohossof's Map of Cairo (1932) and *Miṣr al-Ḥadīthah al-Muṣawwarah* (April–May 1928).

INTRODUCTION

Another Time?

ONE AFTERNOON IN THE SUMMER of 2006, during my research in Cairo, I headed to the cinema with two Italian friends. Before entering the theater, we rushed to buy sandwiches from a nearby kofta place. "How long will it take?" asked one of my friends in heavily accented Arabic. "We have a film to catch." "Only five minutes," said the kiosk owner as he started throwing meat on the grill. Then he added, "Don't worry, five minutes American time, not Egyptian time *[waʾt maṣrī]*."

The kofta maker responded to what he recognized as the typical expectations of foreigners about Egyptian punctuality, reproduced in films and tourist guidebooks and endorsed by many Egyptians too.[1] As the popular *Rough Guide to Egypt* puts it, "Time in Egypt is a more elastic concept than Westerners are used to. In practice, 'five minutes' often means an hour or more; *bahdeen* ('later') the next day; and *bukkra* ('tomorrow') an indefinite wait for something that may never happen."[2]

The designation "in five minutes" *(baʿd khams daʾāyiʾ)* may refer to an exact duration of clock time or may denote a context-specific interval, "a little while." The sandwich vendor wanted to reassure us that the food would be prepared promptly. His comment demonstrates that punctuality entails articulating a spectrum of approximations, one of which is decreed to be standard while the rest become substandard. "Egyptian time" can be evoked only in comparison (here to "American time" or to "what Westerners are used to"). This book explores the colonial origins of this comparison, its productive powers, the history of its automatic evocation as a binary opposition, and its specific hierarchy: how did "Western time" come to be associated with standard clock time and "Egyptian time" with a substandard approximation?

"Egyptian time" appears indeed to be substandard, both lax and primordial. Westerners and Egyptians alike have tended (and still tend) to embrace culturalist and essentialist explanations for a seemingly unwavering aversion to regularity and punctuality and a proclivity for slowness.[3] Such temporal dispositions, ascribed to religion, tradition, climate, or character, are sharply contrasted with the "modern" time of new technologies of transportation and communication. But this elastic sense of temporality, supposed to characterize the colonial and postcolonial worlds from time immemorial, was in fact a nineteenth-century creation, one that was every bit as technological and modern as its Western counterpart. Modern science and technology have provided a yardstick that allowed Europe to reveal its assumed superiority vis-à-vis its colonies. Nineteenth-century European supremacy was brought into relief with technical gauges provided by the new transportation and communication networks that welded together the metropole and colonies, offering a continuum along which the East could be demonstrated to be spatially peripheral and temporally backward.[4] Difference and hierarchy often found their source in comparability, connectivity, and commensurability.[5]

This book, which focuses on the sphere of timekeeping, is a study of how commensurability operated across a colonial divide. It shows how the first modern wave of globalization (roughly from the mid-nineteenth century to World War I)—which, as most scholars agree, saw mutually reinforcing processes of industrialization and deindustrialization, development and underdevelopment, connectivity and disaggregation—also witnessed a remarkable technological quickening, accompanied by experiential slowing in the peripheralized parts of the newly interconnected world.[6] Egypt's annexation to and synchronization with the world beyond its borders was such a process. The country's modernizing classes understood the slowing down of colonial modernity as Egyptian and its acceleration as Western. They experienced modernity as moving swiftly ahead yet always remaining one step behind.

From the second quarter of the nineteenth century, Egypt became increasingly important to the rapidly accelerating British India traffic. Coach, then steamer, railway, and telegraph lines, transformed this Ottoman province into the metal setting for the jewel in the British crown. Situating Egypt alongside other emerging spatial and temporal peripheries of the British Empire and stressing the importance of technology in the empire's reconfiguration allow us to trace the contrast between "mechanical, swift,

Western time" and "cultural, slow, Egyptian time" to an underlying opposition between culture, religion, and spirituality on the one hand and technology, materiality, and instrumental rationality on the other. This set of oppositions also has a history, as scholars of colonial India were the first to point out.[7] As in the subcontinent, in Egypt too this history was contested and nonlinear. After the 1882 British occupation, which ushered in seven decades of colonial rule, and increasingly during the 1890s, Egyptians embraced the materialist language of their country's managers, turning it against the British occupiers by using technical terms to negotiate rights, reform, and equality.[8]

But if Egypt was governed as a machine, it was imagined as a poorly tuned and dysfunctional engine. The instrumentalist political theory of Egypt's British rulers (men such as Lord Cromer, the de facto engineer of Egyptian colonialism) matched the principles of "colonial engineering," a discipline that rearranged difference and multiplicity—the fact that machines worked differently in different settings—into an East/West opposition. This kind of colonial instrumentalism offered a narrow platform for anticolonial politics, and from the turn of the century onward, it pushed Egyptian activists to develop political discourses that went beyond the technical. As jurist and intellectual Qāsim Amīn (1863–1908) put it in 1900,

> We grant scientific and technical progress to Westerners, because their effects surround us wherever we look. . . . In sum, we find material proof everywhere, every day, that compels us to concede that we lag behind Western civilization in scientific and technical knowledge. But it is as though we wish to erase the shame that results from this confession, and to take our revenge. And we find no other means to do this but to claim that we have superior moral standards, and that if they excel in material developments, then we excel in spirituality and soul.[9]

To account for what they began to perceive as anomalies in their entrance into modernity, Egyptian writers of the period increasingly contested modern mechanical rapidity and productivity by citing traditions such as a famous statement by the Prophet Muḥammad, "Al-ʿAjalah min al-shayṭān waʾl-taʾānī min al-raḥmān" (Haste is from the devil and composure is from the Merciful). As Gandhi had put it in 1909 in another colonial context (one that Egyptians followed closely), "Good travels at a snail's pace—it can, therefore, have little to do with the railways. Those who want to do good are not selfish, they are not in a hurry, they know that to impregnate people with good requires a long time. But evil has wings."[10]

Modern technology was indeed a main context for the devil's appearance as an emblem of alienating swiftness and efficiency. As Nile Green has shown for Bombay,[11] in Egypt too, the devil, jinn, saints, and a host of other specters constantly made their uncanny appearances around trains, trams, and other technologies. Egyptian peasant women sometimes even stretched out between the tracks, waiting for the passing train to summon the *qarīnah,* the soul's twin in the spirit world, and induce it to plant children in their wombs. Such specters were conjured up by members of the middle class who sought to eschew vociferously popular theories about these haunted devices and publicly align themselves with new, scientific ones. These effendis, Westernized enough to know they were not modernized enough, vented their inferiority complexes by obsessively summoning and then dismissing popular epistemologies, thus keeping them in perpetual circulation.

In the process, a new cultural sphere was created, one associated with superstition, slowness, and belatedness, but also with authenticity, religion, and pure Egyptian customs. "Culture" emerged as a new object of scientific study. Foreign and, increasingly, indigenous ethnographers found popular "perceptions of time" not only fascinating in their own right but also indispensable for anthropologists interested in arriving promptly to observe festivals, rituals, manners, and customs. The study of these "time perceptions" also made possible the calculation and forecasting of religious festival dates, rituals that constituted a major source of revenue for the Egyptian railways. Technological modernity and the fetish of authenticity thus had a synergic effect that depended on maintaining their separateness.

This novel "Egyptian time" retroactively sprouted roots in the Islamic tradition and rural folklore. This wasn't simply "the invention of tradition"[12] but the emergence of a refurbished concept of tradition, involving a resequencing of time whereby phenomena could be construed at once as simultaneous and noncontemporaneous. Like culture, religion, recast as a domain for the interiorization and privatization of individual faith, was another modern invention projected into the past. Talal Asad has demonstrated the transformation of the *sharīʿah* into "religious law" from the end of the nineteenth century onward.[13] At the turn of the twentieth century, a similar transformation resulted in the emergence of the lunar *Hijrī* calendar as a mere "religious calendar," outdone by the newly introduced solar Gregorian calendar promoted by the telegraph, against which Hijrī lunar time now emerged as capricious and imprecise, but also as sacred, authentic, and profound.

. . .

In recounting the introduction of the steamer, railway, telegraph, tramway, and telephone into Egypt between 1830 and 1940, this study traces the development of these unique practices of timekeeping, recovering a time that subverts the modernist infatuation with expediency and promptness. In Egypt, these newly introduced means of transportation and communication did not drive social synchronization and standardized timekeeping, as social scientists conventionally argue.[14] Rather, they promoted what I call "countertempos" predicated on discomfort with the time of the clock and a disdain for dehumanizing European standards of efficiency, linearity, and punctuality.[15]

Modern technology is at the heart of most projects for reforming "the developing world." The more Chinese citizens have free access to Google, or the more Saudi women can drive, the story goes, the more participatory democracy, secularism, or women's liberation these societies will enjoy. Such assumptions are based on a limited set of experiences—a Western history of technology—generalized into a universal rule and in turn seen as the political essence of technology. The historical formation of this ethos during the nineteenth century paralleled and was interwoven with the development of the steam engine, making trains, steamers, and trams into emblematic driving forces of liberal modernity. As they sweep traditional societies, we expect these devices to unify time zones and enhance instrumental rationality, synchronization, and egalitarian social cohesion—or at least, as the young Karl Marx forecast, unleash the logic of capitalism (perhaps the equation of time-as-money itself) and sweep traditional societies into the progressive tide of the history of the bourgeoisie. The supposedly obligatory road to a modern secular democracy is thought to be paved with rail and tram tracks, and lined with telegraph and telephone poles.

More recently, these expectations have informed representations of the 2011 revolution in Egypt, seen by many as a social-media uprising of networked middle-class secularists who are activating the liberalizing potential of modern technology. There is much to be said for this view and its empowering effects, and it is shared by some Egyptians and many Westerners. What it occludes, however, is not only a two-century-long tradition of revolutions against the central state and its technologies of rule, including an intensification of this trend from the early 2000s. No less importantly, it prevents acknowledgment of the religious, proletarian, authoritarian, populist, and messianic dimensions of the Egyptian uprising and of technology itself—elements that crucially shaped and continue to shape the revolutionary and postrevolutionary period.

This convergence of history and recent events brings into sharp relief the stakes of writing a history of technology in Egypt, a setting that offers an alternative to the Archimedean point from which technology and its temporal effects are usually seen. From the vantage point of semicolonial Egypt, much of the received wisdom about key social dimensions of technology is called into question, revealing the need for a non-Western history of technology to refurbish the critical social sciences. Egypt's technologically induced timekeeping arrangements confound conventional conceptions of social solidarity, and indeed, of the "social" and "political" themselves.

Yet this project is not an attempt to provincialize Europe with an alternative history of technology in the non-West.[16] As numerous arguments in this book reveal, I am deeply indebted to historians and theorists such as Partha Chatterjee, Dipesh Chakrabarty, Gyan Prakash, and Nile Green, whose insights about colonial difference were generated in India. Nevertheless, by broadening the spectrum of coloniality and semicoloniality, Egyptian history pushes their insights forward and sometimes also sideways. For instance, this history can help illuminate why, paradoxically, rather than destabilizing, problematizing, or decentering the celebratory progressive narrative of technology and enlightenment, evidence to the contrary makes that narrative more durable; why, instead of promoting a reconceptualization of technology and timekeeping, counterfactuals denote cultural opposition, an anomalous divergence from Western history rather than an indication of its ungeneralizable nature. As the following chapters demonstrate, provincializing Europe entailed "spreading it thin" on the face of the globe with a network of steamer, railway, telephone, and telegraph lines in ways that forced Europeans to interact with local institutions, actors, and traditions. This was thus also the moment of Western Europe's universalization. Indeed, the colonial encounter is the context in which constructs such as the West, modernity, and capitalism acquired a new generality through a set of colonial antagonisms, tensions, accidents, comparisons, and compromises. Faced with the unintended impetuses and consequences of the rise of these constructs, it is clear that our interrogations of power must include an examination of the efficacy of weakness.

This book thus considers together power and weakness, representation and misrepresentation, hybridity and purification. It shows that technological determinism is not simply an analytical framework whose flaws can and should be exposed. It was (and still is) itself also a historical force, an instrument deployed by actors trying to tame and make sense of a fluid reality. During the nineteenth century, the idea that "everything solid melts into air"—especially space, "annihilated by time"—had an appeal on both sides of the colonial divide. To the colonized and colonizers alike, the partial realization of this modernist utopia in Egypt appeared as a glass half empty when contrasted to the glass half full of its partial fulfillment in Western Europe and North America. The convergence of the weak analytical purchase with the strong popular appeal and political import of technical determinism in the sphere of timekeeping thus forms the central concern of this study: what is the relation between the empty, homogeneous, mechanical time of modernity and the multiple, nonlinear temporalities that haunt it?

Simultaneously holding on to time's homogeneity and heterogeneity, linearity and circularity, and seeking to retrace these productive tensions to their platforms of emergence, each chapter examines how one technology intersected with one temporality—that is, a mode of organizing, schematizing, plotting, or keeping time—together producing a countertempo. The chapters tell particular stories, but whether discussing the tram's contribution to a dislike for motorized speed, the train's role in the development of elastic standards of colonial punctuality, or the telephone's role in eroticizing delay, Egyptian countertempos emerge as technological and modern. In each chapter I also seek to historicize how these mechanical temporalities were anchored in religion or tradition, making them understandable as cultural artifacts. In other words, rather than seeking to replace cultural determinism with technological determinism, I examine both determinisms as converging historical forces.

Punctuated by this thematic division, the narrative progresses chronologically, starting in the second quarter of the nineteenth century and ending in the interwar period. Beginning with the intercontinental steamer lines and submarine telegraph cables that repositioned Egypt in the British Empire from the late 1820s onward (chapter 1), the book gradually zooms in. From railway and telegraph lines deployed among Egypt's cities from the 1850s onward (chapters 2, 3, and 4), we move to examine intracity tramways introduced at the turn of the twentieth century (chapter 5) and their volatile interface with the railway during the roaring 1910s (chapter 6), ending with the introduction of domestic telephones and the shift from manual to automatic exchanges in the 1920s and 1930s (chapter 7). As technology penetrated increasingly intimate spheres of life, with growing expectations that it would facilitate ever smoother and more immediate communication, Egyptians witnessed increasing frustration with and politicization of holdup and delay. The faster things moved, the slower they appeared.

Finally, each chapter features an accident or malfunction: in the first, underwater telegraph cables are attacked by marine borers while trains repeatedly collide with camels and water buffalos; in the second and third, trains are derailed or misdirected in suspicious, even supernatural circumstances; in the fourth, the telegraph breaks down; in the fifth, trams collide with coaches. The last two chapters feature telephonic delays and even a revolution, the mother of all communication and transportation ruptures. The book's conclusion completes this theme by focusing on the image of a broken clock. Technical processes are made invisible by their own success, directing attention toward their inputs and outputs and away from their internal complexity and fragility, a process that Bruno Latour calls "blackboxing."[17] Accidents offer a peek inside this black box, a fact that makes them especially revealing moments for disclosing the logics of the systems that produce them as "accidents" within a contrasting "routine." In this respect, *On Time* itself can be seen as an opportunity to probe such a glitch on a historical scale. Accidentally proliferating in a semicolony, the countertempos explored in this study cast light on countertempos elsewhere, including at the metropole's heart: slave time, rural time, women's time, ethnic or southern times. Egyptian time thus unwinds and exposes the otherwise tightly coiled spring that renders the modern world smoothly operative.

. . .

On Time seeks to transform the acquired acumen of the colonized into such broader theoretical insights by keeping the language of analysis as close as possible to the historical actors' categories of praxis. As the following chapters focus on hardware, relating the history of timekeeping without taking up timekeeping directly (postponing this issue to the conclusion), an account of the discourse on "Egyptian time" is now in order, and what better place to start than with historicizing what appears to be its basic unit, those indeterminate five minutes with which we began? To do this, I resort to the tautological question, "How long is five minutes?" examining five very different answers that converge at this temporal vanishing point.

THE VIOLENCE OF A TRAM EVERY FIVE MINUTES

During the late nineteenth and the early twentieth centuries, Egyptian train and tram passengers fully embraced the need for punctuality and expediency. In January 1898, less than a year after the tramway was introduced into Alexandria, an article in the local newspaper *Al-Ittiḥād al-Miṣrī* supported the request of the Belgian tram company for tax reductions from the Alexandria Municipality. If the request were not approved, the newspaper warned, "the company would have to decrease the number of its streetcars. The result would be delays in the schedule of the locomotives, and it would not be possible to meet the public demand for a tram every five minutes."[18] A 1902 article complained on behalf of passengers on the Cairo-Alexandria railway line that the current train schedule caused them to waste time, "and time is silver and gold."[19]

While turn-of-the-century middle-class Egyptian railway passengers covered within a matter of hours distances their grandfathers had taken a fortnight to traverse (this was the average prerailway travel time from Cairo to Alexandria), they often experienced this acceleration as frustratingly sluggish. These second-class travelers often regarded the "time/space compression" attributed to the train by thinkers from Karl Marx to David Harvey[20] in the context of what may be called a "time/space comparison," constantly contrasting their schedules and velocities with their more rapid counterparts in France, Britain, or the United States. The swifter a society gets, the more sensitive its members become to technological delays. This was all the more true when retardation was brought into relief against a more efficient techno-political horizon.

Part of the reason Egyptian trains could not keep up, according to these comparisons, had to do with the fact that the British engineers who designed and operated them were engaged in making comparisons, too. From the second half of the nineteenth century, the racial presuppositions of these railway engineers about "indolent time-mindless Orientals" informed scheduling and management schemes, yielding a double standard of punctuality:

a colonial, lax punctuality, contrasted with a stricter metropolitan one. This way of conceptualizing punctuality percolated from the British chief mechanical engineer to the shed foremen as policy guidelines for deciding which locomotive to assign to which train, becoming a key principle of machine operation. These protocols were resisted by railway workers and passengers, but in some respects they also took root. In an early 1930s novel, one of the passengers in a second-class train carriage explains that "[in Europe], the poison of 'efficiency' had spread through the souls of Europeans. A dog-eat-dog strife prevailed with emphasis on the personal welfare of the individual. Everyone, both the turbaned and the befezzed, pondered these words and this claim. It seems he had laid bare to them a reality that had previously been concealed under the cloak of that word."[21]

Similar processes took place not only among but also inside Cairo, Alexandria, and, later, other urban centers. To keep to strict schedules and dispatch a streetcar every five minutes, Egyptian drivers—subjected to foreign supervision and fined for the slightest delay—had to move with great speed in urban spaces quite unfit for such rapid vehicles. The new risks created by their speed were unevenly distributed among different groups of citizens. Drivers tended to stop or decelerate near stations only for European passengers and for women, while local Egyptian men were forced to jump on and off moving trams. The hazard associated with the supposedly color- and gender-blind speed of the tram and the time-is-money logic that animated it was thus diagnosed in Egyptian periodicals as a political hazard, fueling an already intense unease with what were seen as European standards of dehumanizing swiftness and efficiency.

FIVE MINUTES OF ISLAMIC ETHIC AND THE SPIRIT OF CAPITALISM

The roots of the divergence of "European efficiency" from its local antitheses can be traced to the early 1880s, even before the 1882 British occupation. Telegraph-operator-turned-public-intellectual ʿAbd Allāh al-Nadīm, a vocal detractor of creeping British colonialism, pioneered the critique of efficiency when contrasting Eastern and Western customs. For example, he distinguished Egyptian solidarity from the fate of a poor English worker driven to commit suicide after being fired from his London factory for arriving a few minutes late to work. European objectifying, man-eating efficiency did not stop at death: the corpse of that wretched soul was taken by train to the English Channel, to be used as fish bait.[22]

Such anticolonial voices were muted after 1882. They were replaced—but in an inverted sense extended—by calls for reform in which timekeeping played a key role. During the 1890s, a new obsession with "the value of time" *(qīmat al-waqt)* took over the Egyptian press, as part of a larger late-Ottoman reformative discourse that developed in response to European influence.[23] Like al-Nadīm's dichotomies, and in contrast to the sanguine tone in Istanbul, where he ended his life in exile between 1893 and 1896, such discussions tended to exaggerate both the Egyptian tendency to squander time and Western impersonal time thrift: "Time is a fleeting treasure. . . . We all know time is costly, yet spend it deliberately. . . . [W]e value and save dirhams; unfortunately, we are too generous with our time."[24] The tone of self-admonition reveals the effective internalization of British claims about the general lack of time consciousness among indolent Egyptians. There was nothing subtle about this internalization. For example, one of many articles titled "The Value of Time" quoted with approval a British observation that "the Egyptians are the most observant people when it comes to setting their clocks . . . but the most time-wasteful people when it comes to their professional lives."[25] While mechanical time was steadily gaining ground in Egypt with train schedules and timepieces, its advance was accompanied by reprimands and a discourse of hierarchical difference: "How valuable time is for them and how cheap it is for us."[26]

These exercises in self-orientalizing regularly featured Western Europe and North America as standards against which Egyptian deficiency could be measured. Rather than "othering" the West, effendi intellectuals "factishized"[27] it and began to view themselves as the West's "others." In this, they resorted to oversimplifications of timekeeping in the West, anointing "Western time" as the gold standard. Europe, and increasingly also the United States, thus emerged as epitomes of mechanical punctuality, a status they enjoyed only in the colonies.

Middle-class Egyptians were clearly adopting the universalizing episteme wherein time could be squandered and economized. Yet this was not the end: it was indeed only the beginning of their engagement with monetized temporality. In 1907, a Cairo-based weekly magazine dedicated a long article to a phenomenon it deemed both widespread and damaging—the frequent misuse of the expression "wait just five minutes." Many people, the article claimed, have developed the habit of asking their friends or clients to wait "five minutes" while they quickly perform a minor task before giving them their undivided attention. However, these five minutes tend to stretch and stretch, making the waiting person anxious and often causing a loss of time and business.[28]

Two years earlier, in 1905, Max Weber had famously identified the equation of time and money as one of the characteristic features of the protestant ethic animating Western capitalism: "Remember, that 'time is money.' . . . That it is the spirit of capitalism which here speaks in characteristic fashion, no one will doubt."[29] Equally, the article "Wait Just Five Minutes" stressed the immoral dimensions of tardiness and analyzed this phenomenon in the realm of Islamic ethics *(akhlāq)*. Thus the statement "wait just five minutes" was seen in the article as a promise, the breaking of which amounted to dishonesty and corruption. Such behavior was seen to threaten the bonds most vital to a civilized society: communal reliance and mutual help.[30] Several years later, a translated advice book titled *ʿAlayka (Duty)* similarly framed timekeeping as promises to be kept: "You must keep your promise *[waʿd]*, and a set date *[mawʿid]* is a contract or pact between yourself and the other party."[31] Indeed, *promise* and *date* are conjugations of the same Arabic root *(w-ʿ-d)*, stressing the interpersonal nature of timekeeping.

This moralization of punctuality and its connection to essential modes of sociability was achieved in "Wait Just Five Minutes," *Duty,* and numerous other texts through the use of Islamic and Arabic dictums and references. In such texts, newly imported temporal conventions retroactively sprouted authentic roots. British admonitory discourses about Egyptian indolence were likewise incorporated into *akhlāq*.[32] The same applies to struggles to decolonize time, such as an early twentieth-century campaign to change the official day of rest from Sunday to Friday, despite the fact that Islamic societies customarily did not have a day of rest.[33] Even Darwinian notions of progressive evolution were claimed to have Islamic origins.[34]

This cultural translation necessarily entailed modifying the borrowed norm. As Weber recognized, the monetized time of Western capitalism had its roots in monastic functional and symbolic orders.[35] Yet in Egypt the Islamic ethics animating post-Christian clock time transformed it into a completely different social organizing principle. Clock time became responsive to a communal subject rather than an individual one. Instead of predicating timekeeping on the individualistic pursuit of profit as a calling, texts such as "Wait Just Five Minutes" connected it to Islamic conviviality and solidarity.[36]

FIVE COLONIAL MINUTES AND FIVE ANTICOLONIAL MINUTES

In the most famous historical exploration of clock time and capitalistic work discipline, E. P. Thompson claimed that nineteenth-century English industrial workers adopted their employers' equation of time and money to beat them at their own game.[37] Modern forms of power and governmentality solicit one's willing participation rather than coercing it.[38] This was especially the case with railway companies.[39] The importance of safety, the wide geographical dispersal of the labor force, and the need for synchronization all pushed these companies to develop new, merit-based methods of controlling their employees, subjecting workers to an effective discipline—their own—and thus allowing a gradual shift away from fines.[40]

Yet British understandings of indigenous agency (and assumptions about the lack thereof) made such methods unthinkable in Egypt.[41] Well into the twentieth century, fining remained the key mode of discipline in the Egyptian railways and tramways and one of the main causes of worker unrest. In 1909 the English deputy chief mechanical engineer of the Egyptian State Railways determined that a half-day's wages might be withheld for arriving five minutes late to work.[42] Such measures revealed for workers—who started unionizing that year "to reduce work hours and increase wages"[43]—the lack of any reasonable correspondence between time lost and money withheld. Colonial double standards repeatedly made it clear that in a place like Egypt, the formula "time is money" was politically fraught, well beyond mere labor politics.

The fact that workers encountered the coercive dimensions of clock discipline but were not privy to its enabling aspects had far-reaching implications. For example, in October 1910, chronometers were installed in the workers' toilets in al-ʿAnābir, the railways' central repairs facility in Cairo, to enforce a new regulation whereby a worker who spent more than five minutes in the toilet was to be fined. This attempt to apply clocks and fines bodily, to regulate task-oriented toilet time, was met with fierce resistance. After collecting their salaries, workers demolished the chronometers and the toilets, then cut the rail line to Upper Egypt.[44] Unable to internalize and embrace the logic of their subjugation, they made clear that certain tasks should not be clocked or monetized.[45]

The blatant encroachment of the chronometers on the body and the violent Egyptian response fully explicate what so far has been implicit: engaging with time was another way of engaging power. Timetables and timepieces organized different modes of distributing, suspending, legitimating, or sublimating various forms of violence. They were biopolitical artifacts, and resistance to them was likewise a political project. Whereas workers everywhere deployed work stoppages and slowdowns as means of labor militancy, in early twentieth-century Egypt slowness and tardiness could also become embodied modes of anticolonial resistance.

FIVE REVOLUTIONARY MINUTES

The 1910 railway workers' insurrection was one of several small-scale rehearsals for a widespread uprising at the end of the decade. Egypt's 1919 anticolonial revolution was mainly waged along the railway, tramway, and telegraph networks. Indeed, the "networked" nature of the colonial project in Egypt opened it up for contestation and disruption along technological lines. The uprising was ignited by middle-class students inspired by nationalist figures and ideas and disillusioned with the frustrating deferral of the promised political independence. Students were joined by rail and tram workers striving to put the time-is-money equation into an egalitarian form, and by peasants who rejected altogether the monetized time of cash-cropping in the face of postwar hardships.

While members of these groups had different and sometimes conflicting agendas, the fact that most of the revolutionary violence occurred around interconnected transportation and communication networks convinced the occupation authorities that this was actually a premeditated, collective campaign. The impact of this misconception was so powerful that by 1922 Britain granted Egypt nominal political independence. For their part, Egyptian participants tended to experience the revolt not only as unplanned and spontaneous but as an event of millenarian proportions. Time itself seemed to have stopped and started moving backward. As telephone and telegraph poles were brought down and trains and tram lines cut, the technological linear time these disseminated was arrested and even reversed.

This sentiment of a "counterclockwise revolution" was perhaps felt most strongly in the educational institutions from which the revolt spread. Not unlike railway workers subjected only to the oppressive dimensions of the equation of time and money, students were deprived of the empowering aspects of this otherwise subtle form of modern discipline. Rather than the carrot of incentive or promotion, the stick of fines or detention was used in the mid-1840s in the Egyptian school in Paris, where a regulation stipulated that "the punishment of students will be by detention in school on days of leave for one or more days, or by fines."[46] Under Mehmet ʿAli, the so-called father of modern Egypt, the school day in government schools was divided into equal sections (called *ḥiṣaṣ,* "temporal sections"), and students were paid a salary at the end of each month.[47] Time-is-money became a pedagogical, punitive protocol in British-occupied Egypt in 1891, when corporal punishment was replaced in governmental schools with detention and a corollary stipend deduction.[48] Early twentieth-century Egyptian writer and activist Salāmaḥ Mūsā remembered his sojourn in the British-run Khedival College between 1903 and 1907 as

> a succession of punishments. One [student], I remember, was punished by being kept in school every Friday throughout the year, so that for weeks on end he lost his free day. A common form of punishment was that we had to be in school at half past six in the morning, even during the winter season when it was still dark, and were not allowed to leave until an hour after class time. . . . The poor boy who had to be in at half past six in the morning would of course be late, and his punishment would thereby be doubled, every time again.[49]

The revolutionary suspension of the tyranny of the clock in 1919 was thus understandably experienced as a redemptive moment: "The school bell rang, but no one paid any attention to it. It was an amazing moment in the history of the schools. The pupils rallied in this fashion and on all their faces was the same awesome expression. . . . It was as if the Day of Resurrection had come."[50] Various other accounts of the revolution also described this event in messianic temporal terms. As Giorgio Agamben put it, developing Walter Benjamin's call to replace empty homogeneous time with a messianic, revolutionary temporality, "The original task of a genuine revolution is never merely to 'change the world,' but also—and above all—to 'change time.'"[51]

And briefly this indeed seemed possible. In August 1923, only four months after the approval of a new constitution that transformed Egypt into an independent parliamentary monarchy, the magazine *Al-Niẓām* printed a joke about a teacher asking a student to respond to an elaborate list of accusations about repeatedly being five minutes late for class in the previous three weeks. "My response, sir, is that you have an excellent memory," the student retorts with tongue in cheek. Such impudence would have been unthinkable before the revolution. What made it possible during the fleeting postrevolutionary euphoria, and—if we accept that humor indexes social tension—what made it potent, was a change in how an empowered student body challenged its elders by defying the hierarchy that promptness secured. Notably, the student not only talked back but dared congratulate his teacher on the latter's *memory*. The student not only switched roles by claiming for himself the prerogative to praise but implicitly evoked a premodern Islamic pedagogy based on memorization—the very pedagogy that temporal abstraction came to replace.

FIVE MINUTES OF LOVE

One of the best-known accounts of the 1919 Revolution and the days leading to it is the semiautobiographical novel *ʿAwdat al-Rūḥ* (*Return of the Spirit*—a title that itself captures the cyclical messianic temporality of the revolution), written in 1933 by Tawfīq al-Ḥakīm. As in many Egyptian novels before and after, the female protagonist symbolized Egypt, while a gamut of men vying for her heart represented a spectrum of possible political futures. The eruption of the revolution corresponds to the moment when Sanīyah chooses one of these suitors, Muṣṭafā, and the severed rail lines interfere with the lovers' correspondence and heighten the drama of their reunion. The following paragraph depicts the beginning of this politically charged affair.

> [Muṣṭafā] bared his left wrist and looked at his gold watch. It seemed to him that he had been waiting there a century. . . . He felt increasingly uneasy and despaired as time passed. The waiting got on his nerves. He swore he would leave in five minutes if she had not appeared. The five minutes passed but hope tempted him to renew the period and extend the deadline. She did not appear. He despaired and started to rise. Then he relented and renewed the period, extending the deadline a third, fourth, and fifth time.[52]

Waiting for his sweetheart, Muṣṭafā's usual experience of time is altered. On the one hand, longing makes short durations of five minutes seem like a century. On the other hand, waiting is fragmented into these fixed sequences of deadlines being repeatedly reset and broken (as "Wait Just Five Minutes" diagnosed). Five minutes were at once too long and too short.[53]

Conjugal relationships based on love—in Egypt a twentieth-century innovation[54]—overlapped and were intimately entangled in the development of effendi nationalism and its passions. *Return of the Spirit* was an allegory for the colonial deferral ad infinitum of the consummation of political independence. Accordingly, Sanīyah's heart was repeatedly within reach and then snatched away. (Sanīyah herself carefully deployed such arousing and calculated deferrals to enflame her suitor's desire). Muṣṭafā's nationalist masculinity depended at once on the clock and on ignoring it. If above we saw timekeeping stand for political power, here we encounter the countertempo that organized desire and its politicization.

When *Return of the Spirit* was written in 1933, it was already clear that the nominal independence granted in 1922 was a far cry from actual decolonization. With British troops still deployed in the country and the British still involved in Egypt's foreign and internal affairs, self-government was gradually seen as just another promise whose fulfillment was deferred ad infinitum. This political climate is key to understanding complaints uttered during the interwar period by middle-class men about delays caused by their wives and, even more so, by unmarried young women, most notably the figure of the female phone operator. Yet these complaints also disclosed masculine arousal in such situations, and men sometimes even associated female procrastination with creative modes of anticolonial resistance. An aesthetics of delay was in the making, one seeking to mark the interplay between the tyranny of the clock and the artistic license to carefully resist it.

Like al-Ḥakīm's Sanīyah, the singer Umm Kulthūm, hailed as "the voice of Egypt," perfected this technique in her live performances. "In the ideal performance the singer would vary one or more lines upon encouragement from the audience and thus extend a five-minute song to twenty or thirty minutes or more."[55] Umm Kulthūm could not have developed her "traditional" singing style without recourse to 78 rpm records, the modern cinema, and the radio—technologies that fixed songs to five-minute intervals to begin with. This independent and quick-witted woman was given lyrics that sought to transform her stage persona into "a character crushed by passion and dependence on an ever-absent other."[56] Subverting these materials by modifying their scales and cadences, she frequently began by singing an entire phrase, properly performing its meter and rhyme as a template later to be unraveled. Then she proceeded to shorten the lyrics while lengthening the melody. She might eventually lengthen a single vowel and even a consonant and then be silent, making silent waiting itself sing—at which point the audience would explode.

• • •

These various answers to the question "How long is five minutes?" reveal that in different historical moments and contexts "five minutes" denoted quite different referents and disclosed diverse experiences. While these accounts all presuppose a stable notion of clock time ("five minutes"), they reveal shifting and often conflicting ideas about how five minutes should be kept, performed, moralized, monetized, inscribed on the body, classed, or gendered.

Such multiplicity coalesces into a brief genealogy of timekeeping in Egypt, stretching between the closing decades of the nineteenth century and the late 1930s: from embracing strict punctuality in the beginning of this period, through intense contestation of and debate about "the value of time" in its middle, to a growing critique of efficiency and speed, and an eroticization of delay toward its end. This arc may be mapped onto other historical trajectories, which together form the skeleton of this book. Some are more familiar, like state and middle-class formation, and the resulting development of anticolonial, territorial nationalism. Some are less familiar. Indeed, following time and technology makes it possible to move beyond these overburdened research agendas and avoid anthropocentric analytical categories.

Moreover, this focus enables a historicizing of anthropocentrism and a registering of its effects. As our anecdotes suggest, the development of Egyptian time overlapped an initial, optimistic embrace of the instrumentalist language of reform, followed by a growing disillusionment with technoscientific enlightenment and disenchantment with technology's alienating temporal regimes. This is one rationale for the periodization chosen for this study, which begins with the introduction of devices that gradually coagulated, long before 1882, into the infrastructure of a "colonialism before colonialism," and which extended this embedded, semicolonial condition well after nominal independence in 1922. Technology was not subject to a priori rejection, but what were initially regarded as sources of wonder and hope had absorbed by the late 1930s much discontent and skepticism. This experience-based distrust was projected back into the past and anchored in tradition and culture, successfully masking the marks of its painful birth.

In addition to retracing the disillusionment with European, technoscientific enlightenment, the historical trajectory of "Egyptian time" also helps delineate Egypt's divergence from the rest of the Ottoman Empire. During most of the period covered in this study, Egypt, subjected to more direct forms of European interference than any other Ottoman territory, was the most "advanced" province of the empire. This was especially the case in the fields of European science and technology and the techniques of discipline, schooling, agriculture, military, and bureaucracy based on them. Here the first telegraph in the empire was built; here an Ottoman sultan took his first train ride.

Egyptians were also the first to see through the temporalities that these devices propagated. While during the second half of the nineteenth century they shared with other Ottomans the discourse of the value of time, at the beginning of the twentieth century these attitudes bifurcated. Time thrift was a key reformative agenda developing in Istanbul schools from the 1860s, culminating in the early 1890s in the formal legislation regulating Ottoman state administration. Educational and bureaucratic institutions pushed a generation of middle-class professionals away from late-Ottoman temporal "pragmatic eclecticism" and toward homogeneous Western time. After the Young Turk Revolution of 1908, this approach gained the upper hand in Istanbul.[57] That same year in the far more mechanized Egypt, middle-class nationalists (inspired by the Young Turks) started jumping on the strike wagon during a decade-long campaign of labor unrest spearheaded by rail and tram workers. These militant workers used the language of time-is-money, but they also disrupted the infrastructures that enabled and propagated it, revealing the political potential of delays and stoppages. The very elements that made Egyptian nationalism anticolonial and populist prevented it from embracing Western time lock, stock, and barrel, and put it on another course.

As these complex interactions across class, gender, ethnic, and imperial lines suggest, examining time and technology allows for a different kind of engagement with Egyptian social history, one that interrogates the alignment and harmonization of "the social" itself. If "the social" is a stand-in for the comprehensive yet uneven togetherness attainable in a particular setting, then these infrastructures and modes of synchronization and hierarchy form some of the most basic codes and frames of the Egyptian social sphere.

Together, these historical arcs—divergence from the Ottoman Empire; intensifying colonialism; and a growing dependence on, as well as disenchantment with, the Western technologies that sustained it and with the temporal arrangements these devices propagated—created the atmosphere that pushed Egyptian intellectuals in the 1930s to embrace the philosophy of Henri Bergson. Bergson's work (partly inspired by Eastern mysticism) on time and free will, multiplicity, and authenticity laid the foundations for the critique of mechanical, empty, homogeneous time subsequently taken up by Émile Durkheim and Walter Benjamin, and later by Benedict Anderson, Giorgio Agamben, and others.[58]

The intuitions of colonized Egyptians concretized and grounded the theoretical treatment of "the philosopher of intuition," as did their ethical commitment to a temporality that would privilege the communal. For Bergson, representing time as a line, thus turning it into static space, meant flattening the heterogeneity of the real. Rendering the world immobile, he claimed, facilitated mastery over it, enabling the collection of its dynamic multiplicity in a stable net or grid that organizes it for control.[59] Seen in this light, it is not surprising that a rich and widespread critique of this effective mode of domination came from those subjected to it. Exploring these Egyptian encounters and insights makes it possible to situate the critique of empty homogeneous time in the context of the critique of empire, as part of the exploration of technological modernity understood not through the celebratory prism of a triumphant march of enlightenment but as lived (often uneasily lived) experience.

Finally, denaturalizing this temporality of control and mastery by construing it as "Western time," these anecdotes demonstrate the stabilization of mechanical time and its co-emergence as an antithesis to "Egyptian time" (alongside similarly incomplete replicas around the globe). Indeed, the colonial career of modern mechanical time is not a story of its failure but the scene of its universalization. The sites where alternative temporalities developed were loci for at once its further intensification as well as its splintering and displacement. As commensurability and synchronicity became means of control and schemes of subjugation, incorporating places like Egypt as highly productive and central yet politically and culturally subsidiary sites of a global system, Egyptian time became a means of creative engagement with, extension of, and resistance to these processes. The lessons it can teach us are likewise at once context specific and broadly applicable.

ONE

En Route

They have wakened the timeless Things; they have killed their
father Time;
Joining hands in the gloom, a league from the last of the sun.
Hush! Men talk to-day o'er the waste of the ultimate slime,
And a new Word runs between: whispering, "Let us be one!"

KIPLING, *"The Deep-Sea Cables"*

THE TERM *MIDDLE EAST* WAS born in the beginning of the twentieth century.[1] It would have been unthinkable without a series of spatial transformations in the nineteenth century, including the deployment of new steamer and telegraph lines, railways, and the Suez Canal, which together constituted a new West-East route via Egypt and gradually replaced the long sea voyage to India around the Cape of Good Hope. The geography we now deem natural was produced by these technologies of transportation and communication.

The *longue durée* expansion of European trade and colonialism was shaped by the monopoly of Muslim merchants, cities, states, and empires over the major transregional trade routes to the East and their alliance with Genoa and Venice. The desire to circumvent these middlemen was a key impetus in the European search for a sea route to India and direct access to the spices and textiles coveted in Western Europe. In 1492 Columbus voyaged across the Atlantic, looking for a westward alternative to the overland trade route to the Indies. This desire was fulfilled several years later with Vasco da Gama's "discovery" of a direct sea route to India around Africa via the Cape of Good Hope. Ironically, the feat was made possible by an ensemble of Islamicate seafaring technologies, navigational knowledge, wind records, and expertise. Da Gama's 1498 Indian Ocean journey from the Cape to Goa was guided by a Muslim pilot.[2] Europe's "great divergence" at the turn of the nineteenth century has been attributed to the opening up of these New Worlds of possibility.[3]

The great distances separating the disjointed parts of the European early modern colonial empires—empires born out of such famous voyages—fragmentized their geographies, and hence their politics. Until the nineteenth century, a one-way journey between England and India along the sea route around Africa could last an entire year—a delay requiring that most decision making and administration take place "on the spot." Yet during the second quarter of the nineteenth century, the Overland Route to India via Egypt—one of the key routes whose circumvention propelled the European colonial project in the first place—was rediscovered. In less than two decades, between the late 1820s and the mid-1840s, travel time between England and India had shrunk to one month, and the distance between these two places imploded. The gradual abandonment over the next three decades of the sea route around Africa significantly contributed to a rearrangement of the eastern parts of the British Empire. This space could gradually be traversed and managed as a continuous geographical, political, and economic surface formally governed, since 1858, from London.

This reconfiguration was not simply a result of technological acceleration or the preference of one route over another. Rather, it involved a complex negotiation among people, energy sources, engineering techniques, cultural protocols, and economic forces that gradually interfaced in more and more synchronized and stable manners. This chapter explores how this process created the British route to India via Egypt, overland and also over and underwater. As far as Egypt is concerned, it examines how this country was gradually annexed into a global technological, notional, political, and economic world beyond its borders. How did Egypt emerge simultaneously as a new geographical hub and as a political and economic periphery in a refashioned British Empire? We cannot discuss time without recourse to spatial concepts. Exploring this paradoxical "Middle Eastern" spatiality and the embryonic forms of politics spawned by the temporal standardization and synchronization that created it thus lays the groundwork for the equally contradictory temporality that will come to punctuate this space—the "Egyptian time" recounted in the following chapters.

TECHNOLOGY AND GEOGRAPHY: FROM THE CAPE ROUTE TO THE EGYPTIAN ROUTE

The surfacing of Egypt as a middle ground between a Britain and an India[4] that were distinct parts of a single colonial empire can be ascribed to the very outcomes of the European success in circumventing Egypt as a central junction of East-West trade and traffic from the turn of the sixteenth century onward. The opening of the Americas and of the sea route to India intensified the gradual and uneven decline of the Mediterranean and weakened Ottoman influence over transregional trade and politics. The subsequent hegemony over trade and later the colonization of production brought unparalleled wealth to Western Europe, eventually financing its industrialization. The development of steam power in England at the end of the eighteenth century expedited technological developments in seafaring, improving communication with overseas colonies. The Industrial Revolution provided financial and political incentives for using steam power to bring England and India closer. Great profits could be made not only in the colonies but also in the growing industry of transportation and communication that linked them with Europe by moving goods, travelers, and information.

The opening of the Egyptian route was attributed (by historical actors since the early 1850s and until recently by historians) to one of these profit seekers, Thomas Waghorn (1800–1850), a pioneering son of a butcher from Chatham. Yet historians have shifted lately from their longstanding admiration of Waghorn as the route's founder to dismissing him as a self-promoter and exaggerator who unfairly claimed credit for a process that also involved many others.[5] Both admiration and criticism make Waghorn a suitable first protagonist for this chapter. (He will later be joined by a dying camel and a semiliterate sea termite.) Waghorn indeed simplified a complex and heterogeneous story into a morality tale of great men and entrepreneurial spirit. Keeping him at the center of this decentered history is a way of keeping in sight the importance of simplification as part and parcel of hybrid histories involving multiple human and nonhuman actors. (Mis)representation, as all three protagonists will demonstrate, was itself a historical force, often constituting very real environments.

To begin recounting the creation of the new Egyptian route, a process whereby geography and technology produced each other, we might start with the geotechnical coincidence that fueled the Industrial Revolution. Whereas coal and even basic steam-engine technology could also be found outside of Britain, the geographical proximity of British coal mines to mechanically skilled artisans and water transportation networks, as well as a related mining problem—the need to pump out water—may explain early nineteenth-century developments in British steam engines and the country's growing reliance on fossil fuels.[6]

A similar argument can be made about subsequent attempts to use steam engines to travel by water. Ocean steamers presented a new set of problems for shipbuilders who needed to develop new designs for vessels carrying their own energy source onboard. For example, the Dutch steamer *Atlas,* built in

1826 for the purpose of testing the practicability of steam navigation between Holland and Java, failed because it was too large and heavy for its engines and steering systems.[7] The *Atlas*'s size was a direct result of the fact that it was designed to carry a sufficient supply of coals for the entire voyage to Java, because the Dutch did not have any settlement at which they could stop for refueling along the way. By contrast, British ocean steamers could be much smaller (and therefore cheaper to build, and easier to propel and navigate) because they could stop for refueling when circling Africa. In both the Dutch and British cases, imperial geographies were mapped on the design of ships, and vice versa. Imperialism operated at the level of the engine, the size and shape of the ship, and the political map of the ocean it crossed. It was simultaneously an engineering factor and a political vector.

From the design perspective, in the ideal steamer coal occupied all free space, leaving no room for cargo or passengers. Waghorn, a young lieutenant stationed at the Bengal Pilot Service during the early days of ocean steam navigation in the 1820s, was obsessed with designing and commanding a steamer that would be able to make the journey from England to India via the Cape of Good Hope. He proposed to solve the aforementioned design problem by building small steamers whose voyages would be financed exclusively by delivering newspapers and letters between the metropolis and the potential coaling depots along the way to India. Steam power was expected to cut one-way travel time roughly in half, to six months. Waghorn aimed to translate this saved time into capital, increasing mail fares to the point at which steam navigation would become profitable.[8]

Waghorn spent the second half of the 1820s trying to gather support for his proposed steamer line via the Cape. Among his interlocutors were engineers, members of Parliament, colonial officials, and merchants, making it impossible to neatly categorize this scheme as political, economic, or technical. It can be labeled a failure, however. Existing post laws compelled all vessels on the Cape route to take letter bags on board free of any sea postage. Any change in postage fares required an act of Parliament.

Waghorn, who thus had to seek his fortune elsewhere, accepted an invitation to examine the possibility of steam navigation in the Red Sea.[9] A rapid and well-publicized trip in 1830 from London to Suez and from there to India convinced him that his destiny was as the proprietor of a private Overland Route mail agency. One of the ways he promoted this agency was to claim the discovery of a new route to India, even though other Britons were already aware of it.[10] This false advertisement proved extremely durable.

Waghorn's career trajectory reveals the acceleration of British communication with India. As late as the 1820s, sailing via the Cape could take as long as a year. Waghorn's 1829 plan for steam communication on that route was meant to reduce this time by half. During the same year, even that hypothetical record was broken by Waghorn himself in his first rapid journey to India via Suez, which lasted four months and twenty-one days. In half a decade of operating an efficient private line, he reduced this time so significantly that by 1835, after the advent of Red Sea steam navigation, a ninety-day journey was considered slow. In 1837 the journey lasted about fifty-four days in each direction, and between 1841 and 1843 Waghorn reported an average traveling time of thirty-six days. When the plan for a Cairo–Suez railway (abandoned in the late 1830s) was reconsidered in 1844, one of its goals was to reduce Indian communication to less than one month, enabling letters from India to be answered by the ensuing mail to India.[11] In less than fifteen years, the distance between India and England shrank to approximately one-twelfth of what it had been.

Aside from improving the safety and comfort of the journey, the most important endeavor was constantly expediting it. Waghorn devoted most of his efforts to synchronizing the various sections of the route, preventing time gained by technological acceleration from being lost waiting for the next means of transportation, thereby wasting the fuel, and hence money, spent in acceleration. Synchronicity optimized the equation of time and money. Time was not only a quantity to be reduced but a standard to be adhered to, speed and synchronicity thus reinforcing each other. During the 1840s, travel time between India and England was already calculated *by the minute,* and complex calculi that factored the different speeds of vehicles, weather variations, and optimal stopping times at stations were devised to match synchronicity with speed.[12] These calculi enabled unifying the multiple schedules of the different sections into a single standard timetable that came to embody the Overland Route.

Synchronicity was made possible, to a large degree, by steam navigation. Steamers began sailing in the Mediterranean and Indian Ocean in the early 1830s. But as late as 1870, they were still competing nose-to-nose with sailing ships whose driving force—the wind—was free and did not take up space onboard. Like coal, wind was wedded to a particular temporality. Not unlike coal, it could be micromanaged with translations into money, space, and time. Yet such translations, for example the word *monsoon,* derived from the Arabic word for seasons *(mawasim),* reveal the difference in scale between calculi of wind and coal. The monsoon winds did not make sailing a whimsical matter; on the contrary, since the fifteenth century, careful registration of weather conditions dictated fixed schedules and itineraries.[13] The monsoon weather system allowed sailing through the Indian Ocean in the spring and fall, compelling ships and merchants to wait in ports in between.[14] Steamers, by contrast, could move year round.

Yet there was nothing inherently superior in the incessant (and by 1870, faster) motion of the steamer, compared to the significantly cheaper and more spacious sailing ship. As we now know, the competition was settled after the 1869 inauguration of the Suez Canal, which put the Mediterranean in direct contact with the Indian Ocean. The narrow waterway could be crossed only slowly and with difficulty by sailing ships (dependent on tacking to catch the wind). Reducing average steam travel between London and Bombay to thirty-three days in 1870 (compared with eighty-seven sailing days around the Cape),[15] and significantly reducing insurance premiums, the canal eventually made steam navigation the preferable mode of sea voyage.

But the synchronizing of traffic along the new route to India cannot be reduced to the regularity of steam. It also entailed increasingly efficient interfaces among different means of transportation (steamers, animal-driven carts, and trains), and between them and human institutions (border and customs controls, hotels, tourist guides, and political authorities). What were the forms of politics, management, supervision, and culture that created the new route and were created around it?

EGYPT: A STATE WITH A ROUTE OR A ROUTE WITH A STATE?

Waghorn's remarkable success in expediting travel between England and India owes much to the fact that such acceleration complemented the interests of Egypt's ruler, Mehmet ʿAli Pasha (who eventually took on Waghorn as an ambassador and advisor), and was one of his lasting legacies. Mehmet ʿAli was the second in command of the Ottoman army (backed by a British fleet) sent in 1801 to drive Napoleon's army of occupation out of Egypt.[16] The French had occupied this eastern Mediterranean Ottoman province in 1798, implementing a plan promoted by Charles Maurice de Talleyrand several years earlier. Instead of a frontal assault on Britain, they chose to challenge British possession of the Cape of Good Hope with a French-controlled Red Sea route to India. Invoking the old Venetian model of conducting eastern trade through Egypt, French politicians dreamed of renewing their colonial empire and making the Mediterranean a French lake.[17] These dreams had already faded by the end of 1798, with Nelson's victory in the so called Battle of the Nile. After the French army evacuated Egypt three years later, Mehmet ʿAli prevailed in the ensuing struggle for power. He would rule as the Ottoman governor of Egypt until his death in 1848.

Thus the arrival on the scene of Mehmet ʿAli, hailed by British colonial administrators and later by Egyptian nationalists as "the father of modern Egypt," bears the mark of the European India traffic. And so does the centralizing state he began to establish, formally part of the Ottoman Empire but increasingly independent from Istanbul. Egypt's relative autonomy was attained by a rapid pursuit of economic development, which tied it to the global market and pushed it toward the ambit of the British Empire. Waghorn's arrival in Egypt coincided with the culmination of Mehmet ʿAli's state-building efforts, which included the introduction of long-staple cotton, the building of a modern European-trained army, and innovations in transportation and communication—of which Waghorn's Overland Route agency reaped the fruits. In turn, the influx of goods, tourists, and information along the route meant more taxable revenue for Egypt and the channeling of East-West commerce through the country.

To maintain and develop this resource, the safety, efficiency, and comfort of British travelers and mail became an important Egyptian concern. Overland Route traffic was handled by special officers in distinct warehouses in Alexandria, Cairo, and Suez. Passenger luggage was transported on the route free of tax. The Pasha paved parts of the route between Cairo and Suez and built desert lodges for the comfort of travelers, in which one could even get a haircut.[18]

Mehmet ʿAli's commitment to continuous and uninterrupted British communication with India remained unwavering even during his 1831 invasion of Syria, which put Egypt at war with Britain and led to a British blockade of Alexandria and interception of Egyptian communications.[19] When important news arrived in Egypt, the Pasha made exceptional efforts to expedite it.[20] Further, the Pasha deliberately sabotaged attempts to explore and open competing routes outside Egypt. One of the reasons for the failure of an expedition to the Euphrates during the mid-1830s, for example, was sabotage perpetrated by Egyptian agents in Syria—from denying the expedition animals and workers to actively damaging its equipment.[21]

At Waghorn's suggestion, in 1835 the Pasha started constructing a railway between Cairo and Suez—the most difficult section of the Overland Route—for the purpose of "the acceleration of the mails and passengers through

Egypt."[22] According to the plan, the extension of the Cairo-Suez line to Alexandria would have reduced the time required for crossing Egypt from between eight and ten days to only twenty-four to thirty hours.[23] The death of Alexander Galloway, the engineer in charge, and Britain's refusal to commit in advance to paying postage for conveyance of the mail, delayed the completion of this railway, the first outside Western Europe and North America.[24]

Despite these efforts, the Egyptian route was not without competitors.[25] In 1834, letters from Bombay arrived in England via an overland route through Persia in three months.[26] In 1837 the British press printed accounts of the aforementioned expedition to the Euphrates for the purpose of ascertaining the most eligible overland route to India. This route required 46 days from England to Bombay and 52 on the return. It was one of five overland routes to India at this time, all going through what came to be known as the Middle East. The same year, the route via Egypt took 53.5 days outbound and 55.5 on the return but had the advantage of including less land travel time than any other route as a result of the constant improvement and acceleration of Egyptian travel arrangements.[27]

In 1839, a new steamer line via the Cape began to compete with the Egyptian route. Its proponents claimed that the Egyptian route, dependent on a foreign ruler, was unreliable and would increase British involvement in the region, eventually forcing Britain to conquer Egypt.[28] This prophecy—repeated frequently in subsequent decades[29] and eventually fulfilled in 1882—reveals the kind of British involvement Egypt's ruler was facilitating. Mehmet ʿAli is said to have used similar words himself: "Egypt is a bridge thrown between Asia and Europe; England must have a free passage over it, or she must take possession of Egypt."[30] Indeed, Thomas Waghorn was one of the first to raise the possibility of British colonization of Egypt, as early as 1837.[31] Acceleration and synchronization had significant political implications.

The gradual development of the overland route and the extension throughout Egypt of a network of railways, roads, telegraphs, bridges, canals, and ports accelerated the shift of the Nile Valley to raw cotton production for the expanding European textile industry. According to the existing historiography, the development of these transportation networks was an offshoot of the industrialization of Egyptian agriculture and its transition to cash crops.[32] While there is much evidence that supports the opposite causality (i.e., that new kinds of transportation technologies gave rise to the cotton economy), given that ends often turn into means, it is sufficient to agree that these were mutually reinforcing processes.

Beginning in the 1830s, new coal depots on the Egyptian shores of the Mediterranean and Red Sea that serviced steamers on both sides of the Overland Route[33] started supplying mainly British coal to inland Egypt, fueling its Nile steamers, its cotton industry, and later its railway.[34] These technologies transported state officials, tax collectors, agricultural inspectors, judges, conscription officers, and policemen between Cairo and the provinces, putting the modern centralizing state in motion. This point reveals much more than simply a causal problem with the claim that the cotton industry spawned the transportation network. The Overland Route provided the infrastructure and impetus for Egypt's transition to fossil fuel. The introduction of this new energy source into a country where even wood was scarce is indispensable for understanding Egypt's great political and economic leaps in the nineteenth century.

Coal consumption grew exponentially. During the year 1842, 7,260 tons of British coal were imported into Egypt; in 1843, this quantity grew to 13,000 tons; in 1844, 23,866 tons were imported; and during 1845, 48,063 tons.[35] By 1899 the total consumption of coal in Egypt reached 825,000 tons.[36] This growth translated into accelerated production and circulation of goods, information, and control. British coal fueled the Egyptian railway, Nile steamers, and other steam engines, including those operating water pumps for irrigation and urban water supply,[37] as well as engines employed in the cotton industry (particularly cotton mills).

Cotton was the key raw material of the Industrial Revolution, and its movements were abstracted to sketch the world system itself—its market structure, monetized economies, and global division of labor.[38] But if raw Egyptian cotton was a product of British coal, the ultimate raw material,[39] can we sustain the neat division of global center and periphery corresponding to a stable opposition of raw and processed? Fueling Egypt with British coal and bringing to its shores the technologies and powers that this coal animated, the Overland Route was a tail wagging the dog.

A LETTER THAT CREATED ITS DESTINATION

In 1851, less than three years after Mehmet ʿAli's death, his grandson and successor, ʿAbbas, hired George Stephenson (the son of the pioneer of British railway engineering) to construct a railway on the Overland Route. Work began a year later on a Cairo–Alexandria line, sending clear political signals.

To the Ottomans it was an accretion of Egypt's continued autonomous and vanguard role in the empire. To the British it was a signal that the new Egyptian ruler would continue his grandfather's policy of commitment to the improvement of British communication with India.[40]

Twenty-four thousand corvée workers were put to the task, with hundreds of policemen preventing escape attempts.[41] The line connected Egypt's two key urban and commercial centers and tied the cotton-growing Delta to the Alexandria port. Indeed, the construction of this railroad (and the increasing importance of steamships to the Egyptian economy) helped Alexandria replace Dimyat as Egypt's second city, precisely in this period. The new railway covered a significant section of the Overland Route and stretched parallel to and across a major water source (the Nile). It could be presented to the Porte as an internal Egyptian matter and to the British as a compromise that distinguished Egypt's position within the otherwise hostile Ottoman Empire.[42]

The quick completion (by 1858) of the next section, between Cairo and Suez, and British support for this railway should also be seen in the context of one of the most important messages conveyed along the Overland Route: the news of the 1857 anticolonial uprising in India, a letter that created its own destination. Violence broke out in India on May 10 of that year, and the news reached London a month and a half later. Inside the Indian subcontinent, news moved along a newly introduced telegraph and railway. (The disastrous economic effects of these networks contributed to the spread of the revolt in the first place, according to some historians.)[43] The message was dispatched from Calcutta on May 18, reached Bombay by land on May 27, was transmitted by steamer to Suez, crossed Egypt overland, and was sent again by steamer from Alexandria to Trieste. Leaving Trieste on June 25, it reached London by wire on the night of June 26—about one month and twenty hours after leaving India.[44]

As soon as the news arrived, the Court of Directors of the East India Company recommended to the British cabinet the immediate dispatch of army units via the Overland Route. The cabinet decided instead to send troops in sailing vessels around the Cape—the slowest means possible. Only after the first confusion subsided were steamers used on this route, and even then, only the older and slower side-wheelers.[45] The main reason for avoiding the Egyptian route was fear that the Ottomans, Egyptians, or French would object to the transit of British troops through Egypt. But when it was suggested to ʿAbbas that small units might pass through Egypt in civilian clothes and without their weapons, he declared that he would arrange the transport of not merely two hundred men, but of twenty thousand if necessary, in uniform and armed. "I will not consider them as transit passengers, but as my own, and will carry them by my own private engines, carriages, and trucks."[46] His enthusiasm indeed translated into reduced travel fares for the passing soldiers.[47] By the end of September, troops were moving along the Egyptian route. Regiments leaving Plymouth reached India after thirty-seven days, while those departing from Malta arrived after sixteen to eighteen days. The Egyptian railway had greatly expedited their transit. The 130 miles between Alexandria and Cairo were completely bridged by rail, as was most of the distance between Cairo and Suez. The entire passage through Egypt, which previously lasted two weeks or more, took about fifty hours.[48]

After 1857 the Egyptian route was regularly used for sending reinforcements to India and considerably aided the suppression of the uprising. In turn, the passage of armed British troops in uniform became a familiar sight in Egypt.[49] In London, the "scandalous" delay in adopting the Overland Route for immediately relieving British India prompted the formation of an investigating committee in 1858. The committee's findings later that year had the effect of calling attention to the divided responsibility of the Indian administration, leading to the passing of the August 1858 "Act for Better Government of India," which terminated the raj of the East India Company.[50] The passage of information and forces via the Egyptian route, as well as the nearly disastrous bypassing of this route, clearly demonstrated the importance of imperial connectivity and the dangers of ignoring it.

These events greatly promoted the status of the Egyptian route as the fastest and most reliable passage to India. By the end of 1858, the Cairo–Suez section of the Egyptian railway was complete. The diplomatic precedent, a reconfigured imperial administration, and the material infrastructure for the colonization of Egypt were now firmly in place. England and India were officially hyphenated by Egypt. An ensemble of railways, laws, telegraphs, political alignments and institutions, waterways, coal depots, and commercial arrangements stabilized this geography and presented it as natural rather than the outcome of contingency, aggression, self-promotion, and a great deal of maintenance. The violent history that connected these different segments left hardly any trace in the timetables, maps, or guidebooks that provided a bird's-eye view of the new route to India. Already the 1846 *Waghorn & Co.'s*

Overland Guide to India: By Three Routes to Egypt, with a Map and subsequent texts naturalized the new route and allowed it to emerge as a totality. As we will see, this representation helped shape the space it supposedly merely reflected.

DRAWING ATTENTION: DISORIENTATION AND THE DESERT OF THE REAL

The Overland Route was constructed, synchronized, and promoted also in places quite far from Egypt and India. One of these sites was a theatrical adaptation of Waghorn's guidebook. Offering another example of his self-promotion skills, the "Diorama of the Route of the Overland Mail to India" was one of the last public matters in which Waghorn interested himself, and he even managed to promote it with his publicized death in 1851.[51]

Dioramas were given their definitive form by Louis Daguerre, the inventor of photography, in the early 1820s. They consisted of massive, realistic landscape paintings, suspended from a theater ceiling and moving in sequence on a wire, with shifting light effects projected from behind. Alternatively, pictures might be stationed around a revolving platform. During the midcentury "panoramania,"[52] the Egyptian Hall in Piccadilly—the central diorama venue in London—boasted millions of spectators annually,[53] marking the emergence of a new mass medium of popular entertainment.[54]

Throughout the 1850s, after the diorama of the Overland Mail debuted in London, various other dioramas and panoramas showcased Egypt. "The Great Moving Panorama of the Nile" had been exhibited in England over 2,500 times by 1852.[55] The new photographic "Cairo Panorama"[56] debuted in 1859. In 1860 "London to Hong Kong in Two Hours" took spectators to the Far East via Egypt along the Overland Route.[57] The Overland Route diorama was the emblem of a decade of anxiety about imperial integrity.[58]

Panoramas and dioramas of this period attempted to bring together entertainment and education. A typical description, taken from a review of the 1847 "City of Cairo Panorama," reveals how Eurocentrism was performed in these spectacles: "The visitor standing on the circular platform is in the very center of the locality represented, as real to the eye as if he were on the spot itself."[59] However, unlike the older and static panorama painting, whose viewers had to move their heads and eyes to observe it in full, the new dioramas removed this autonomy, enabling "incorporation of an *immobile* observer into a mechanical apparatus and a subjection to a predesigned temporal unfolding of optical experience."[60] The metaphor of a mechanical clock was regularly used to describe this nexus of observer, object, and time. In his armchair travel, the spectator was able to "enjoy an imaginary tour without stirring out of his chair, 'While Fancy, like the finger of the clock, / Runs the great circuit, and is still at home.'"[61] Spectators became centerpieces in machines made of wheels in motion. This *pseudo*panoptic centrality was predicated on the removal of visual sovereignty and the impossibility of separating a viewing subject from the object of perception.

The Route of the Overland Mail to India Diorama—thought to have elevated the medium to an art form[62]—was considered by a theater reviewer to be a superior example of such attention management. It was much longer than most other spectacles, comprising about forty tableaux. The Egyptian scenes attracted the most critical comment:

> The route over the desert from Cairo to Suez, a subject offering but few opportunities for variety of effect, is treated with great skill, every occasion being seized of keeping up the interest by the introduction of characteristic details. At the station from which the caravan starts we have a group of figures representing the various classes of personages who are usually to be met on this overland journey; and as we proceed onwards the carcass of a dead camel mourned over by its Ethiopian owner, the withering skeletons of similar victims . . . serve to diversify the dreary waste of sand over which *the eye is made to travel.*[63]

An 1882 description of the history of theatrical effects considered the Overland Route diorama as a forerunner to realistic theater. One of the manifestations of this new theatrical realism was the use of panoramic backgrounds to give the illusion of motion in a railway train during the 1870s and 1880s.[64] From the beginning of the 1850s, the Overland Route diorama was one of the first to simulate actual travel. It was thus a link in the convergence of forms of transportation with forms of representation and perception. In the history that starts with the balloon and painted panorama[65] and continues with aerial photography and cinema,[66] the relation of dioramas, travel books, and trains was an important chapter.

Many dioramas, especially those devoted to foreign travel, were painted with a camera lucida, a portable optical device invented in the first decade of the nineteenth century that allowed a painter to see simultaneously his subject, his pencil, and the drawing surface. Fusing the viewer's hand and object, sight and the illusion of touch, prosthetic devices like the camera lucida marked a turning point in the history of vision. Jonathan Crary argues that during the early nineteenth century geometrical optics, with its model of incorporeal relationship between a sovereign observer and an object of perception, was displaced by physiological optics and nerve theory, in which the body became the idiosyncratic surface on which vision is inscribed, obliterating the distinction between ("internal") sensorium and ("external") stimulation. The camera obscura embodied the older, Cartesian model of vision and subjectivity paradigmatic between the fifteenth and the late eighteenth century. Technologies such as the camera lucida were part of this early modern episteme's deterioration, eventually leading to the abandonment of representational aesthetics and naive realism.[67]

The first known camera lucida to be used in Egypt was brought there in the mid-1820s by Edward William Lane, a friend of the device's inventor.[68] His descriptive texts, written with the intention of accompanying camera lucida drawings, were later expanded and published as the 1836 *Account of the Manners and Costumes of the Modern Egyptians,* a work that Edward Said used to construct the archetypical figure of the Orientalist.[69] For Said, Lane's work demonstrated Orientalism's construction of a self-referential representational archive that came to replace the real East. Yet by defining Orientalism as a set of literary maneuvers in an insulated written corpus, a (mis)representation of a real East, Said replicated the oppositional mode of Cartesian observation he sought to critique. Camera lucidas like Lane's, the diorama panels created with them, and the landscapes viewed from the windows of trains by the many diorama-viewers-turned-tourists (like Lane himself)[70] suggest that Orientalism shaped the environments it misrepresented. Paradoxically, realistic pictures painted with camera lucidas—accurate simulations standing apart from their observer—helped reestablish the myth of the camera obscura and reincarnated the seemingly stable separation between the observer and a view standing apart (the very gap that the device demolished). Timothy Mitchell described this split as an effect of an "exhibitionary order."[71] Seen from an Egyptian train, the supposedly stable gap between reality and representation was repeatedly put in crisis and restabilized.

In 1845, half a decade before the beginning of railway works in Egypt and the debut of the Overland Route diorama, a British tourist imagined with trepidation the march of technological modernity in the ancient land he was crossing on camelback: "A railroad is about to be constructed across the desert. . . . [W]hen that day comes, all the excitement and wonder of a journey in the desert will be over. There will be no more pitching of tents, or sleeping under the starry firmament, surrounded by Arabs and camels. . . . All will be reduced to the systematic tameness of a cotton-factory."[72] But the Egyptian railway did not eradicate excitement; it aestheticized it. Only when the active, dangerous, and bouncy crossing of the desert on camelback or cart was replaced by a relatively smooth, linear, and passive movement through the landscape could the landscape be viewed *as landscape*—an image set apart from its observer.

Looking at the desert through the train's window (window seats were always in high demand)[73] revealed an Egypt that was flying past as a spectacle. Westerners were now looking at it with the kind of gaze they developed to circumvent the nausea of motion sickness:[74] fixing their eyes on a distant stable point in the landscape, through which they saw Egypt moving like a diorama. The gaze from the train's window was predicated on the incorporation of a passive observer inside the optical mechanism. A sovereign external gaze was replaced by a new episteme that regarded the eye as part of the field of vision, problematizing the neat separation of subject and object. The train was an optical device that seemed to put things in perspective, creating the distance from the object and its picturesque effect: "You only need a mosque with a minaret and a few saints' tombs with whitewashed domes, built of mud, to make a picture," one railway passenger remarked.[75] Or as another passenger put it, "[An Arab village] is hardly distinguishable from the land, certainly not in color. . . . However, a clump of palm-trees near it gives it an air of repose, and if it possesses a mosque or a minaret it has a picturesque appearance, if the observer does not go too near."[76]

Discerning the village depends on familiar features (like palm trees or mosque minarets) on which rests its picturesque *appearance* (i.e., its visibility as village). Focus also requires maintaining the "right distance" from the object. Notably, the familiarity of the view, which enabled seeing it as view, was not necessarily the result of a previous sighting. For most travelers in Egypt, crossing the country on their way between Europe and India, the train's window was the first and often the only extended encounter with the "Egyptian landscape." However, framed by the train's window, this landscape that they were freshly laying eyes on was already a familiar one: "We felt at once that we had reached the Egypt of our dreams. The palm tree—that familiar type of Eastern scenery,—the foliage of scripture illustrations, which were so dear among the pictures of our childhood . . . was before us at every stage. . . . By half-past-three, P.M., we had our first sight of the pyramids, and their long familiar forms mellowed to the view by a rosy hue which rested upon them in the distance."[77] Looking for the first time, the eye immediately identifies the already familiar. "They [the pyramids, but in another account] stand still in that purple distance in which we have seen them all our lives."[78] Actual Egypt was filtered through another Egypt brought from home.

And sometimes home erupted into Egypt. Casting a dioramic gaze in the land of the pharaohs was disturbingly uncanny. Sights of "unchanging" agricultural techniques, "ageless" pyramids, and "primordial" camel caravans seemed unreal when viewed from the windows of the most modern means of transportation: "It seems hardly natural to look from the windows of comfortable first-class carriages, rapidly whirling through so primitive a country as we pass through."[79]

The paradoxical nature of the "modern" spectator's relation to the "ancient" surroundings was not confined to the view outside the train. According to various reports, in the first years of their operation, before a steady supply of coal was secured along the railroad, Egyptian trains and Nile steamers were occasionally fueled by mummies.[80] Their dried organic substance and the bitumen used in the embalming made mummies a potent fuel, which Egyptians had used for centuries.[81] The claim that "mummies, cut into proper lengths, made a very good substitute for wood and coal"[82] was printed in English scientific journals, passed by word of mouth, and transformed into the stuff of jokes, rumors, and anxieties. It spread like wildfire among travelers, exacerbating the uncanny temporal paradox of Egyptian railway travel.[83]

Rushing across ancient surroundings on board such haunted trains gave a suspect character to the overly spectacular Egyptian landscape. While dioramas were becoming more and more "realistic," the Egyptian real was increasingly deemed "unreal," "unnatural," "uncanny," "dreamy," or "picturesque." The convergence of these processes accounts for a disorientation reported by European railway and steamer travelers in Egypt. As visitors noted in their diaries and travel accounts, sailing up the Nile,[84] crossing Egypt by rail on the overland route,[85] or viewing Cairo[86] evoked in their minds' eyes the diorama. Real Egypt transported them to the theaters of Europe. "Often, while I was amusing myself with the view of this unbroken series of foreign images," wrote one traveler, "I could fancy that I was still in Europe, and was only looking at a painted diorama of Egypt."[87]

Indeed, while viewing the hyperrealistic Overland Route diorama in London made spectators briefly believe they were actually in the East,[88] looking at the East from the window of a moving train confused passengers into thinking they were watching a diorama in the Egyptian Hall in Piccadilly. In such disorientations reality and its representations switched parts, and the temporal structure of the semiotic axis was reversed (the signifier preceding the signified). What were the forces that structured such a nebulous domain, in which reality and representation were not firmly separated? What might constitute appropriate cartography for a terrain where boundaries between the real and simulated were so porous? To answer these questions, we follow our second protagonist, a dying camel, along a macabre path running parallel to the Overland Route.

One of the highlights of the Overland Route diorama was the scene of "the dying camel," regarded as one of the spectacle's key demonstrations of verisimilitude: "Camels too are dying—which is a great proof of the picture's accuracy, for we never recollect a view of the desert yet but that there was sure to be a camel dying in it."[89] As this review suggests, one could hardly represent (i.e., see, as descriptions are always also prescriptions for how to look) the Egyptian desert without this necessary corpus. As a result (one train passenger noted typically), the image of "the artistic painting of the 'Dying Camel,' ... frequently came before me as I saw the decaying carcasses of the faithful quadrupeds scattered along the desert in all stages of decay."[90] The dioramic depiction of the dying camel was an adaptation of a popular 1840s realistic work,[91] Henry Warren's *The Dying Camel in the Desert*.[92] The diorama further popularized it so much as to warrant a writer's assumption that "most of us have seen the picture of the dying camel."[93] By the 1880s, the image was emblematic of Egypt itself.[94]

The prominence of dying camel images can be explained in two ways. First, camels tended to die near the railway, mostly because they increasingly tended to live and move near it. The camel and the train may appear to be opposites, embodiments of the clashing forces of modernity and tradition. Yet during its first years, the Egyptian railway generated a steady increase in camel caravan transportation (from 50 camels to more than 2,500 in less than three years in the early 1850s).[95] Put plainly, Egyptian trains could not move without camels. Camels carried railway tracks and telegraph poles, transported water (required for engine cooling and steam production) from the Nile to train stations, and moved leftover merchandise and passengers to destinations that were past the railway's reach or beyond its capacity to transport. The animal's split foot even inspired a track-laying system unique

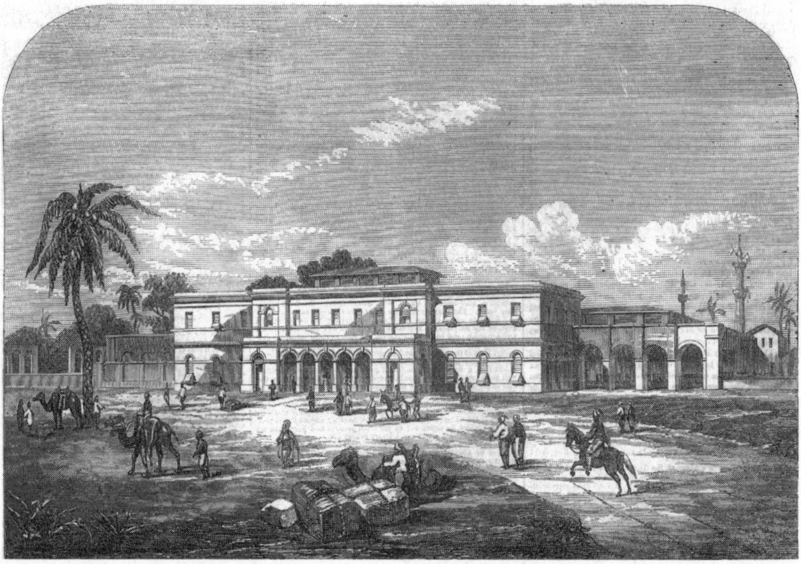

FIGURE 1. The Alexandria Railway Terminus, 1858. *Illustrated London News,* January 23, 1858. © Illustrated London News Ltd/Mary Evans.

to Egypt: instead of using expensive wood boards to tie the tracks to each other, British railway engineers devised a bell-shaped connector that tied the tracks together under the desert sand.[96] Pictorial representations of Egyptian railway stations from the 1850s reveal that camels were an indispensable part of the picture. Yet this proximity led to numerous road accidents involving camels and trains, providing fodder for the pictorial representation of the Egyptian landscape as exotic and ancient.[97] The train was literally producing Egyptian antiquity in the collateral damage of its own modernity.

The second explanation for realistic painting's attraction to dying camels has to do with the aesthetic virtues of death. As panoramas and dioramas grew more realistic, their creators started to face increasing criticism about inanimate objects in the foreground. Figures of humans and animals spoiled the realistic illusion by looking inanimate. Ploys such as foregrounding dying camels offered a solution. Dying camels satisfied various requirements of realistic accuracy: they were "typical" (establishing the correspondence between dioramic and real views) and "worthy of attention,"[98] capturing the mortal danger of crossing the desert; they provided a familiar image; and they legitimately didn't move, thereby promoting the realism of a medium that depended on controlling the temporal unfolding of the visualization of movement.

Indeed, the power of such pictures to bring the landscape into focus should be understood within the temporal structure of vision. The movement of the train did not allow extended viewing; it presented snapshots quickly flying past. In this speed the familiar—the contours of which the eye recognizes—was always the first to present itself. The dying camel was a nexus of multiple citations of texts citing images citing other images citing the real, and vice versa: of the real eliciting attention to the elements that made it *realistic,* worthy of attention and description. This process generalized the singularity of the cited images, transforming every dying camel into the Dying Camel, evoking the type as the organizing principle of the particular. The picture functioned as the standard that *comes before* its constitutive "examples." "Examples," in turn, came to attest to the image's truth in a protocol whereby essence precedes existence. And of course, drawing attention *to* always entailed also drawing attention *from;* focus is always also a procedure of blurring. If dead camels were primordial features of the desert, they could not be seen as casualties of the train.

Meanwhile, the problem of roaming camels colliding with trains on railway bridges and other parts of the track was severe enough to generate abundant correspondence between the Railway Administration, the Ministry of Interior, and other governmental departments, yielding new legislation that attempted to contain the situation.[99] Preventing such dangerous crashes required better control over human and animal movements in the countryside. As camels found it hard to internalize new notions of property, village headmen were assigned the responsibility of supervising herding in their territories. A heavy fine was levied on animal owners whose beasts were hit by a train. As a result of this fine, animal owners most likely refrained from reporting the deaths of their camels and buffaloes.

Administrative reports from places where trains and animals collided frequently included—as an unrelated event to be investigated and prevented by village headmen—incidents of train stoning by rural "riffraff." Camel and peasant unruliness emerges as instances of a similar irrationality. The anger of peasants whose camels were killed on the unfenced railroad was understood by officials, and later by Egyptian literati,[100] as pure rage against the machine, demonstrating a superstitious or traditional aversion to modern technology.[101] This standard caricature of the Egyptian peasant reorganized and resignified what were seen as specific examples of its manifestation, preventing other causal connections from becoming apparent.

Synchronization and representation held the Overland Route together, even where land was covered by water. A key component in the Overland Route was a submarine telegraph that tied together England and India via Egypt. The tale of its deployment concludes the story of a fragmented British Empire made whole, politically, technologically, and territorially, and of Egypt's emergence in it as a spatial core and political fringe.

Colonial studies has increasingly challenged the notion that an influx of Western techno-sciences transformed the colonial world while leaving Europe unchanged. Recent work on the development of new sciences—from botanic gardening to statistics—as means of governing native populations in the colonies shows that these and other techno-sciences should not be seen as purely Western products that were merely disseminated to the colonial world. Rather, they developed through the interaction of the "West" and the colonial world, and ought to be seen as the product of that interaction.[102] However, much of this literature seeks to provincialize Europe by focusing on the governance of native populations, presenting the colonies mostly as a challenge to Western hegemony, a set of problems that required path-breaking *European* solutions. If the colonies emerge as laboratories of modernity, Europeans, with their guns, germs, steel, and coal, are seen as its sole scientists, leaving the natives with the role of the fruit flies. Such models of "interaction" reinforce the inherent separateness of the categories they aim to blend.

Broadening our perspective of imperialism to include, alongside the governance of populations, also the challenges of transportation and communication between the colonies and the metropole, casts light on previously ignored arenas of knowledge production and scientific development. As we will see, indigenous knowledge, materials, and actors originating from the colonies remade the metropole in significant if unacknowledged ways.

Projects such as the deployment of a submarine telegraph line between Europe and India via Egypt generated new knowledge about the sea surface, currents, flora, and fauna, giving rise to new sciences such as ocean cartography[103] and new technologies like sounding devices.[104] While land telegraphy was advancing rapidly in Europe and its colonies, alongside railroads that required signaling systems, communication over water stalled. While attempts at tightly wrapping metal conductors with tarred jute or hemp were effective in crossing rivers and maintaining communications for short spans of time, during the first decades of the nineteenth century European materials and expertise were insufficient to traverse large bodies of water.

Successful underwater telegraphy was the result of a combination of European and colonial materials and knowledge. Effective insulation was made possible with the 1840s "discovery" of gutta-percha, a material used in Southeast Asia for centuries.[105] Gutta-percha ("Percha rubber" in Malay), a natural latex produced from the sap of tropical trees native chiefly to the Malay Archipelago, is waterproof and thermoplastic (malleable in high temperatures but solidifying under pressure and in the low temperatures of the ocean bed). These properties made it an excellent electrical insulator. Gutta-percha insulation made possible the first successful transmissions of long-distance electrical signals under water, including the 1851 connection of England with France and later with the rest of Europe. Indeed, Europe was glued together with Asian latex.

Europe's new connectivity was made possible by over a decade of experiments with underwater telegraphy, carried out mainly in India by British colonial engineers as part of the deployment of an Indian telegraph network.[106] This network—significant parts of which were completed in the mid-1850s—both precipitated the 1857 uprising and was the only successful line of defense keeping the British army from total defeat during its initial stages.[107] Marine telegraphy relied on local knowledge for the extraction of gutta-percha,[108] and on the actual stuff itself. It thus offers a case in which the colonies presented both the problem (the urgent need for long-distance communication across water) and the solution (the insulation material that made communication possible).

Rather than being the fruit of an interaction between colony and center, submarine telegraphy was one of the sites where these categories were violently inscribed. In the early days of underwater telegraphy, cables were used to ignite gunpowder from a distance.[109] Blasting things from afar has been an important dimension of the new technology ever since: though marine telegraphy has been repeatedly hailed as a technology that will promote communication, understanding, and peace between nations, it has often been utilized as a weapon.[110] The Egyptian connection with Europe is a good example of this violent history.

The Malta–Alexandria cable was diverted to the Mediterranean after being initially manufactured for serving military communications in one of the Opium Wars, which ended by the time the cable was ready. Yet the cable would soon be put to its original purpose in its new setting. In 1882 Britain occupied Egypt with the undisclosed motivation of gaining direct control of the Suez Canal, in fulfillment of earlier prophecies about the Overland Route. During the bombardment of Alexandria from the sea, the Eastern Telegraph Company's ship *Chiltern* attached itself to the Mediterranean cable and transmitted to London minute-by-minute telegraphic descriptions of the destruction of the city.[111]

It is tempting to call this the first sea assault to be transmitted in real time.[112] But telegrams between the *Chiltern* and the headquarters in London were received within *approximately* thirty-five minutes. The delay's indeterminacy is as significant as its actual duration: only two years later, in 1884, did the newly established Greenwich Mean Time allow for a claim to "real time" in the singular. And only in 1900 was the Malta–Alexandria cable used for telegraphing time signals from the "master clock" in Greenwich to the subordinated Egyptian "slave clocks."[113] Yet the desire for temporal commensurability was clearly at work already in the 1882 bombardment. On June 14, the *Chiltern* hosted an experiment that fused the scientific and military meanings of *breakthrough:* "A telephone was attached at Malta to the Alexandria cable and connection was made with the other end of the cable on board the Chiltern off Alexandria. It was found that owing either to the distance or to the vibration caused by the firing it was impracticable to send a verbal message but the firing at Alexandria was distinctly heard through the telephone at Malta, a distance of more than a thousand miles."[114]

Ricochets from Alexandria could arrive at Malta instantly, reaching the London press the following day. Yet the telegraph, hailed as the great leveler in that it put all humanity on the same line, also created centers and peripheries. Even while being submerged in water, oceanic telegraphy provided a bird's-eye view of the empire at every moment. In the 1840s land telegraphy allowed for standardizing national time zones. Four decades later, submarine cables enabled intercontinental standardization and the synchronization of steamer lines, railways, and telegraphs, connecting new geographies and creating new geopolitics. In Egypt, after taking Alexandria, British troops marched on the railroad, which marked the shortest route to Cairo and was an easier alternative to walking in the desert sand. Embedded reporters joined the units and sent their "live" reports from the battle via telegraph. The Overland Route literally laid the ground for the British occupation. The direction of flows of power between two points on a line transformed these points into a center and a periphery.

FIGURE 2. The British invasion along the Egyptian railway. *The Graphic,* October 7, 1882.

FIGURE 3. The British invasion along the Egyptian railway. *The Graphic,* September 16, 1882.

Temporal standardization can be seen as symptomatic of a more general standardization project in which telegraphy played a crucial part. During the 1850s, submarine telegraphy was a key scientific field in which electrical and engineering standards were fixed. The birth of ocean telegraphy was marked by two colossal failures in the deployment of the Red Sea (via Egypt) and Atlantic cables toward the end of that decade. Breakdowns were partly attributed to a lack of standard units for precisely measuring resistance along the cable.[115] As a result, an 1859 committee of inquiry and the 1861 British Association Standard Committee were created for establishing uniform yardsticks for telegraphy and engineering. Submarine cable failures were thus a key moment in the establishment of late Victorian metrology and its instrumentation.[116] Lessons learned from these failures translated into the emergence of the "culture of accurate and absolute measurement" and started "a train of investigation which now sends up branches into the loftiest region and subtlest ether of natural philosophy."[117]

The integrity of the cables and hence of the empire hinged on such accurate and uniform "standards" and on a set of mediatory principles for applying abstract theory to practice.[118] The institutional subordination of electrical and engineering practice to theory (i.e., physics) was another outcome of the 1861 investigation of telegraph failures.[119] In this struggle between "practical men" and "men of science," the latter emerged victorious.[120] Not all standards were stable, but standardization, the perceived necessity of a correspondence between standard and example, and the continued pursuit of better theory have proven durable. Standards were frequently replaced by other standards, theories replaced by other theories. For example, the resistance standard developed while laying the Malta–Alexandria cable became the accepted imperial standard until it was replaced by the ohm.[121] But once they were established, standards could be replaced only by other standards; standardization itself became standard.

The standard is at once a product of the empirical data and the abstract principle that precedes it. It is positioned simultaneously before and after the empirical. The efficacy of the standard therefore hinges on effacing its own messy history, on making invisible the circumstances of its production, and on presenting itself as something that precedes nature, not as something imposed on it.[122] Metrology devices measured ohms, hours, and kilometers, as if resistance, time, or space were naturally expressed in these terms. The standard established itself as the organizing principle of engagement with the real, the only avenue for accessing it.

TROPICOPOLITAN STOWAWAYS

During the 1860s, Egypt gradually became a telegraphic hub connecting Europe and India via a Malta–Alexandria cable and a Red Sea cable between Suez and Karachi. The latter connection was preceded by a failed attempt at connecting Egypt to India through the Red Sea in 1859, resulting in one of the two defining breakdowns of submarine telegraphy. Exploring this failure more closely allows us to move beyond regarding the cables as passive connectors of historical actors and to acknowledge their active role as dynamic (if invisible) sites of history making, if not actors in their own right. It is also an opportunity to introduce the third and last protagonist to the stage. Underwater, "where the blind white sea-snakes are,"[123] cables crept among other nonhuman actors through whose silent universe human words were passing. In this abyss, the "Eurocentric" structure of the cables—made of a core of European metal and insulated by gutta-percha—and the neat center-periphery division itself were severely challenged.

A major reason for the 1859 failure was the fact that the cable was submerged without adequate survey of the topography and conditions of the seabed.[124] It was released in a straight line by compass, without any attempt to select a uniform depth and with no slack that would allow the cable to adapt to irregularities of the floor. Rather than touching the bottom at all points, the cable was suspended in various places between different elevations; as a result, it collected sea growths and broke under their weight. At these and other points, the warm, salty water of the Red Sea degraded the cable's wrappings, exposing it to marine borers such as "the formidable *Teredo navalis*,"[125] a tunneling shipworm with an insatiable appetite for gutta-percha that quickly ate through the insulation.

The teredo was an active, if invisible, participant in the project of European colonialism as well as in a colonial project of its own. In an age of colonial expansion that depended on wooden ships, the teredo, whose diet was based on driftwood and submerged wood, traveled all across the globe, drilling their way through colonial fleets and establishing their own colonies in submerged wooden structures, from ships to docks and dikes, for which they were nicknamed "sea termites." After centuries of this pattern of traveling, it is hard to establish the teredo's exact origins. One assumption is that the worm originated in the Pacific and Indian Oceans, traveling to the Mediterranean with Dutch ships returning from their Southeast Asian colonial possessions (from which gutta-percha also originated) in the eighteenth century. The Dutch regarded the teredo as a plague sent by God.[126] As the Dutch fleet transported human colonists from Europe, it carried stowaway nonhuman ones back home. While the former violently changed essential

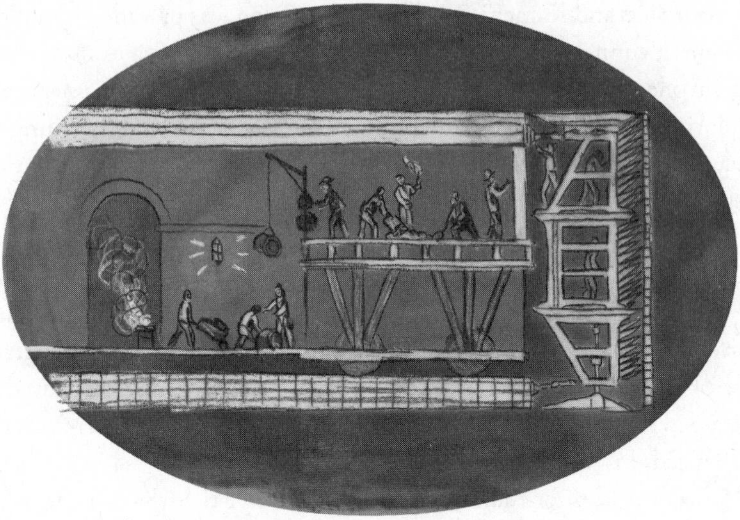

FIGURE 4. Diagram of the tunneling shield and a *Teredo Navalis (facing page).* Drawings by Gilad Seliktar after the *Illustrated London News.*

local forms of being in the colonies, the latter assaulted the most distinctive and basic infrastructure of Dutch life, the canal. In 1731 (when the worm was first recorded),[127] a teredo infestation, eating away wooden seawalls, nearly flooded the Netherlands. All the attempted solutions were like sticking a child's finger in the dike. Arguably, teredos may have been responsible for drilling the famous hole itself,[128] making the transition from wood to imported stone inevitable.

The implications of the transition to stone, from increased taxation and a growing reliance on the colonies to a later disdain of alternative means of transportation such as the railway, can only be alluded to here. Like gutta-percha, the building of stone canals supports the argument made by scholars of colonialism—so far mainly with regard to a nonmaterial realm—that colonialism reshaped the imperial center as well as the periphery. Another outcome of these events was a growing scientific interest in the teredo, whose morphology, reproduction, and eating habits became an object of research and observation.

After redesigning Dutch canals, the teredo helped solve one of the most daunting engineering problems of the Victorian era: digging the first tunnel under a body of water, a project that started the modern tunneling industry. After repeated failures and collapses while digging in the soft mud under the Thames, engineer Marc Brunel was driven to approach the task

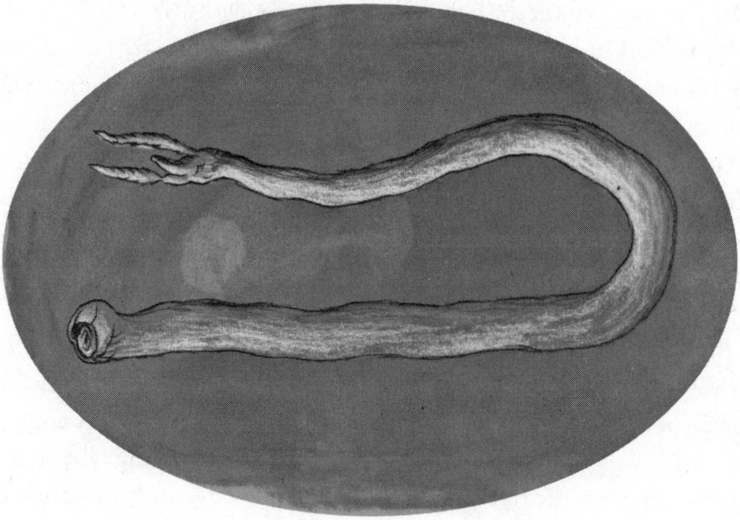

after drawing inspiration from the teredo's tactics.[129] The worm was able to eat its way through the stoutest wood while protecting its head with shells that oscillated to cut the wood at the same time, while its petrified layer of excreta formed a smooth lining for the tunnel to protect its delicate tissues. Brunel copied the teredo, replicating it in metal and at a larger scale. "A teredo navalis, or something very like it, in steel, did the great engineer make, and so the tunnel was bored. Even a nuisance like this may form a useful object lesson."[130] During the 1820s, miners were imitating the techniques of the teredo inside the "tunneling shield," cutting wormholes through the earth. The tunneling shield was a worm hosting human agency.

The Thames Tunnel, "the eighth world wonder," was a career-making project, an undertaking of unprecedented scale and public attention.[131] Its successful completion made possible the conception of and public support for even larger engineering feats.[132] Brunel's son and collaborator in the tunnel project, Isambard Kingdom Brunel, became the first railway engineer to standardize time zones in 1840, one year after he deployed a telegraph line along the track of the Great Western Railway (GWR).[133] Brunel's steamship the *Great Western* was a westward extension of the GWR from Bristol to New York. Based on this model, the Peninsular and Oriental's Liverpool–Alexandria and Suez–Karachi steamer lines were synchronized with the Egyptian railway in 1857 in a similar fashion.[134]

In 1859 Brunel built the largest ship in the world, the *Great Eastern,* with such interfaces in mind. Built on the Thames, the *Great Eastern* was the only ship big enough to carry onboard the entire Atlantic submarine telegraph cable and was one of the key factors in the eventual successful deployment of this line in 1866. Likewise, the *Great Eastern,* accompanied by the *Chiltern* (which would later become the floating communications hub of the Alexandria bombardment), deployed a second Red Sea cable—now including iron coating against teredo boring—and firmly reconnected India and Europe via Egypt.

The engineering success of the Thames Tunnel and its commercial failure were important frames of reference for even larger projects, such as the digging of the Suez Canal.[135] The canal made iron steamers more competitive than wooden sailing ships, inadvertently solving the boring problem posed by the teredo. Yet as one door closed, another one opened. The 1869 opening of the canal had put the waters of the Red Sea and Mediterranean in direct contact, gradually equalizing the salinity of the Bitter Lakes with that of the Red Sea. This initiated a process called Lessepsian Migration—named for Ferdinand de Lesseps, the canal's chief developer—which enabled colonization of the eastern Mediterranean by Red Sea species.[136]

The worm's great appetite for gutta-percha and its formidable drilling techniques thus played an important part in the failure of the first attempt at intercontinental telegraphy at the end of the 1850s. The next telegraphic connection, a decade later, factored in the teredo in various ways. Second-generation cables were much thicker and more durable, as they included teredo-proof iron coating, which also made them much more expensive. As a result of the failure of the first attempt, which was subsidized by the British government, the second Red Sea telegraph had to be privately funded. One way to finance its deployment and maintenance and underwrite the higher costs of the new cables was opening news agencies that sold telegraphic information to clients along the line. As we will see in chapter 4, new pricing structures for telegraphy (entailing higher costs per word), and the presence of news agencies such as the Reuters office in Alexandria, opened in 1865, were among the key conditions for a series of changes in the Arabic language—the emergence of what we call today modern standard Arabic and the prose written with it.

In an influential text titled "Can the Mosquito Speak?" Timothy Mitchell implicitly connected Science and Technology Studies with Subaltern and

Postcolonial Studies, playfully evoking Gayatri Spivak's famous question about the subaltern.[137] Along these lines, and in a much more literal sense, our worm may almost be able to write: the electrical throb of human words through the long throats of submarine cables transformed sea termites into key actors in a new underwater linguistic environment. During my own research in the Rare Books Reading Room in the British Library, where I picked up the trail of the teredo's story, I traveled daily to Kings Cross Station through the Thames Tunnel, which is now part of the London underground network. The teredo opened the door for my own entry into the narrative, thus participating in the writing of its own history.

Yet despite, or probably because of, all the hybridity, flux, and havoc it wreaked underwater, *Teredo navalis* eventually promoted more stable center-periphery relations onshore. The durable antiboring submarine cables, the heavy metal steamers that sunk them properly and in straight lines, and the news agencies that helped finance them by circulating information in unprecedented volume, rapidity, and variety joined Egypt tightly to Europe and facilitated more nuanced, multilayered, and hence effective imperial control. Accidents, breakdowns, and malfunctions are vital forces of technological advancement. To the extent that the train crash informed the development of the railway, with its technological safety measures, synchronization schemes, and operation protocols, and the shipwreck shaped modern sea vessels, *Teredo navalis* shaped the submarine telegraph, as a present absentee. The worms thus created the conditions wherein humans were the only ones able to claim credit for the traces they left in their wake.

THE MIDDLENESS AND PERIPHERALITY OF THE MIDDLE EAST

Critiques of anthropocentrism, seeking to expand social history (and "the social" itself) to include nonhumans, are a continuation and culmination of critiques of ethno- and Eurocentrism (such as critiques of Orientalism or efforts to provincialize Europe), as well as phalo- and logocentrism. And they appear to be the final frontier in the battle against humanism, which aims to decenter the human himself. Yet what emerges from connecting the ignored wormholes of the teredo, the invisible history of dead camels, and the fragmented history of the Overland Route is the inherent problem of centrism as such. Such linkages suggest that our anthropocentric conventions may be tied historically, and not only analytically, to other centric projects that not only divide humans from nonhumans but also introduce hierarchy inside "the human," into space, and even into the real itself. As we have seen, representation often precedes reality, it is impossible to separate a viewing subject and an object of perception, and examples come before the standard. Yet modern epistemology is predicated on blocking such multidirectionality, reducing this flux to manageable categories: "subject" and "object," "Europe" and "Egypt," "human" and "nonhuman."

The foregoing sections retraced the role of these fluctuations and their stabilization—and the importance of hybridity and its simplification—in laying the techno-political foundations of colonial Egypt. What makes Egypt a privileged locus for examining the workings of centrism per se is the fact that the very history and the same actors that transformed this country into the spatial heart of the British Empire and eventually into a "Middle East" simultaneously caused its economic and political peripheralization. Egypt offers an example in which "the middle" and "the center" are diametrically opposed and mutually incommensurable. As we have seen, Egypt's "natural" middleness and accompanying decentering were a long time in the making. The shift in British India traffic away from the Cape involved the installation of physical infrastructures (coal depots, steamer lines, railways, submarine telegraphs, and canals), political structures (a centralizing state, foreign intervention and occupation), and protocols of representation (guidebooks, timetables, dioramas, and news agencies) that joined this country as a periphery to a European center.

The tension between center and middle was reproduced inside Egypt itself, in the very mechanisms used to synchronize the different sections of the Overland Route. For example, beginning in 1831 and throughout the 1830s, Mehmet ʿAli's son Ibrahim constructed a new overland mail route to Syria to expedite communications with the headquarters of the Egyptian army in Damascus and to facilitate control over the occupied space.[138] The system included sixty-eight postal stations, built at equal distances between Cairo and Damascus,[139] with five horses, five couriers, a scribe, an inspector, and a silver watch in each.[140]

The watch seemed to bring the disciplinary and punishing institutions of the centralizing Egyptian state into each and every remote station. Careful registration of arrival and departure times of the mail bag (the reports being added to the mail) pinpointed sources of holdups, for which stationmasters were punished,[141] and slowness—for which couriers were whipped.[142] It was as if the watch adorned the Pasha's long hand, as if through it the state could see.[143]

However, despite its appearance, reminiscent of an eye (the black pupil in the center of a white sclera, the twelve eyelashes), the clock face never casts a gaze. Its English homonym "watch!" is always only an imperative. While initially the new Egyptian postal authority intended to appoint only literate scribes, officials quickly realized that there were not enough of them to man the stations. Instead, the authority had to employ people who knew only how to copy the numbers from one to twelve, and when those were scarce, to train illiterate "scribes" to do the job.[144] Scribes, stationmasters, and couriers themselves constituted the gaze of authority, by appending their own vision onto the mechanism that controlled them.[145]

Another example, also part of the evolving Egyptian communications system, is a semaphoric telegraph line, built in 1839 between Suez, Cairo, and Alexandria.[146] This system comprised "telegraph towers" consisting of upright posts or masts fifty or sixty feet high, with movable wooden arms whose position could be manipulated by means of chains. Different positions indicated different signals, which could be discerned from the next tower with the aid of powerful looking glasses.[147] The signals could be deciphered with a special dictionary, but for communication between the towers themselves, all that was required was exact reproduction of the signal so that it could be communicated to the next post. As in the case above, human vision was detached from the reflexivity with which it is conventionally associated and incorporated as a cog in a machine.

After semaphoric telegraphs were put to use on the Overland Route, passengers for India could stay in Cairo until their ship was ready to depart from Suez before they set out across the desert.[148] The Alexandria–Cairo semaphore was used to notify Alexandria, twelve hours in advance, of the arrival of the Indian mail at Suez.[149] Again, it was as if the steamers arriving at Suez and Alexandria were actually "seen" from Cairo. But vision, apparently, had a very different function in the creation of the "panoptic" central state.

Reading clock faces and engaging in semaphoric synchronization did not involve "telling time." The Egyptian telegraphers, postmen, and railway workers who harmonized the empire could remain external and peripheral to the mechanical time they helped keep. The centralizing Egyptian state that emerged in the midst of this synchronized empire—our "route with a state"—was predicated, like the dioramic performances of Eurocentrism in the Egyptian Hall in Piccadilly, on the denial of various kinds of autonomy and sovereignty: political, economic, and even visual, across the ranks, from its workers to its ruler.

These instances—in which communication and synchronicity were devoid of intentionality or autonomy—narrow the gap between scribes and telegraphers on the one hand and writing worms on the other. In this respect Brunel's teredo-inspired "tunneling shield" provides an emblem for the ways people move about in the world, devouring it while being insulated from it, producing from its messy substance their smooth passageways made from processed and petrified excreta. We have seen them do so in other metal frames wheeling forward, carrying human actors through alien terrains. Overland Route train passengers were moving along a network that generated the conditions of its own perception and legibility. The camouflage of the worms, camels, and other nonhuman, non-European, and non-elite driving forces and casualties was a crucial part of the view.

TWO

Double Standards

> The story is told of an automaton constructed in such a way that it could play a winning game of chess. . . . A puppet in Turkish attire . . . sat before a chessboard. . . . [A] little hunchback who was an expert chess player sat inside and guided the puppet's hand. . . . One can imagine a philosophical counterpart to this device. The puppet called "historical materialism" is to win all the time. It can easily be a match for anyone if it enlists the services of theology, which today, as we know, is wizened and has to keep out of sight.
>
> WALTER BENJAMIN, *"Theses on the Philosophy of History"*

THE OVERLAND ROUTE TO INDIA via Egypt, which replaced the voyage around the Cape of Good Hope, received its deathblow from the Suez Canal, which the route itself had facilitated. From its 1869 inauguration, the canal brought to realization the desire to pass quickly through the Egyptian landscape by making landing redundant: the Egyptian "land obstacle" was finally hollowed out. In 1871, the British Empire formally shifted its India traffic away from the Egyptian State Railways (ESR)—whose Alexandria–Cairo–Suez lines were the backbone of the Overland Route—to the canal. Deprived of its main source of income, the ESR had to reinvent itself as an internal means of transportation, directing its attention to local lines and weaving together previously disconnected sites into the entity we now recognize as "Modern Egypt." In the process, the Egyptian railway was transformed into a synchronized and unified system controlled from a central location.

Alongside the sleepers and junctions, beginning in the year 1870, new timekeeping and scheduling arrangements were part of this transformation, and they bore its distinctive mark. In its revamped shape, the ESR laid the foundations for a unique "Egyptian time," just as it adopted universal timetables and train schedules. As Timothy Mitchell has shown, the introduction of new spatiotemporal abstractions into schooling or city planning, resulting in "the appearance of order" at this historical moment, recast preexisting practices as "disorderly."[1] Yet rather than simply offering a novel object of reform, one revealed against new yardsticks of exactitude, the newly emergent "oriental unpunctuality" itself became a principle of machine operation. "Disorder" thus artificially produced and framed the second-rate "order" attainable in a colony, and hence the modes of accepting and resisting it. It is this simultaneous appearance and long coexistence of the standard and substandard versions of monetized mechanical time that the title of this chapter, as well as what follows it, seeks to capture.

During its first decade and a half, until 1870, the ESR ran without printed timetables. There seem to have been two main reasons for not using schedules, which by the 1850s were already standard devices in British and American railways. (The Stephensons, who built the Egyptian railway, pioneered the first timetabled railway, between Liverpool and Manchester, in 1830.) First, as part of the Overland Route, the Egyptian railway depended on the arrival of steamers in Alexandria and Suez, with two weekly trains on the Cairo–Alexandria line leaving when overland passengers disembarked and were ready to move.[2] This policy was indicative of the clear preference for European over local traffic. While it was in force, passengers at the intermediary stations would wait indefinitely for the unpredictable train, with agricultural products often rotting in stations.[3] Because of the scarcity of carriages and the preference given to Overland Route passengers, locals had to use third-class carriages even if they could afford better seats. During the pilgrimage to Mecca or a countryside festival, they often had to ride on the roof.[4]

The second reason for not using schedules had to do with the fact that the Egyptian railway was considered the private possession of the Egyptian ruler, who, in the hierarchy of passengers, was the top traveler, superior even to the tyranny of the clock. The ruler's power as master of the track was overt and ideologically articulated in a hierarchy of waiting:[5] (mainly) Egyptian local passengers had to wait for the (mainly) European Overland Route passengers and for Egyptian notables, while ordinary trains transporting these Overland Route passengers had to wait on the track as khedival trains passed them.

Because the regular movement of trains depended on the rank of the passengers, stationmasters and supervisors regularly received notices from important persons demanding that the train await them at the station, or even stop between stations to wait for notables in the countryside. The resulting delays were so habitual that a Ṭanṭā supervisor, an Englishman fed up with the grievances of his impatient countrymen, used to dress like an Egyptian and pretend not to speak English, except for one phrase that he used to ward off complaints: "God created the world in six days—be patient."[6] This anecdote reveals more than the routine delays. It discloses also how British railway officials accepted as given and made use of what they regarded to be key temporal features of the Egyptian character—tardiness, indolence, patience, and time mindlessness—in operating the line. Such practices, which at first might indeed have been anecdotal, gradually came to be the rule.

Complaints from European passengers whose train was suspended for hours to allow the viceroy's train to pass were a frequent theme in travel writing, revealing the racial vocabulary by which delays were understood. Frederick Ayrton, a civil engineer and British officer who closely followed the formation of the ESR, revealingly framed Saʿīd's (r. 1854–1863) attitude to the railway: "With the egotism of a true Turk, he will sacrifice revenue rather than subject himself to the necessity of consulting the interests of the public, when he wishes to make use of the line."[7] Accepting this state of affairs as part of Egyptian reality, Europeans made the best of the situation. Before 1870, it was the habit of foreign consuls landing in Alexandria to make the train take them to Cairo, even if this meant telegraphing an express full of passengers that was already an hour on the way and forcing it to reverse course.[8] Such practices had a systemic effect that went well beyond the waiting (or the bypassing) trains themselves. Under these circumstances, it was impossible to predict if a journey—say between Cairo and Suez—would take the expected eight hours or the not infrequent fourteen.[9]

The memoirs of Iskandar Bāshā Fahmī, a stationmaster and later ESR director, illustrate this dynamic with a startling story. One day, Saʿīd whimsically ordered his private salon connected to the middle of a sixty-car train and sent immediately to his Qaṣr al-Nīl palace on the outskirts of Cairo. There the ruler ordered his soldiers to mount the train and head to Cairo station, where he arrived by surprise, ordering the train to continue directly to Suez and to send telegrams to stationmasters along the way to clear the line. (Saʿīd was known for his obsession with a rice and chicken curry dish cooked in the Suez Hotel.) Two and a half hours later, Fahmī saw the train returning. It turned out that as the day was already hot, Saʿīd had demanded to continue without heed to Suez on the single track upon which trains were then returning to Cairo. Advancing despite the warnings of the driver, the train suddenly broke down along the way, delaying all the other trains on the line.[10]

Such typical accounts are illuminating in several respects. They were simultaneously portrayals of the Egyptian railway system and indications of how it was represented by the men who operated it. Similar horror stories were part of a demonization campaign against the viceroys Saʿīd and ʿAbbas,[11] and as far as the ESR was concerned, ill repute extended to the entire "human element" of the railway, from the ruler to the humblest laborer, albeit in different ways. British engineers designed the Egyptian railway in response to the particular features they attributed to its indigenous operators and users, whom they found lacking in initiative and foresight and regarded as puppets subjected to their capricious Turkish rulers or, better still, to rational British managers. Such understandings framed the unavoidable ensuing conflicts between these managers and engineers on the one hand, and local workers and passengers on the other, as a dialogue of the deaf, informing in turn the spectrum of attitudes toward timekeeping and discipline in the ESR.

Introducing timetables into such a system—with the limitations and inflections of these fixed schedules—was associated not only with transformations in "time consciousness," but also with reforms in local political culture, a new international matrix, and new approaches to fuel, labor, passengers, and hardware. These changes were both calculated and accidental, as they were elsewhere. In the United States, for example, printing timetables and standardizing time zones prevented train collisions, which, as Paul Verilio argues, were key driving forces for the development of the technologies that caused them.[12] Accidents were consequential also in the appearance of synchronization in the ESR. Moreover, as symptoms of the underlying (economic, political, and cultural) logics of the technological systems in which they occur, accidents help reveal these logics as well as how contemporaries deduced and understood them.[13] They thus offer a handy point of departure for an investigation of the routines and procedures put in place to prevent them, as well as the unintended consequences of these preventive stabilizing measures.

ORIENT AND ACCIDENT

Toward the end of his reign, even a notoriously "reckless" ruler such as Saʿīd was reminded of the fragility of his own body natural. An 1862 travel account linked the improvement in train punctuality on the Alexandria–Cairo line (at that time a one-hour deviation from the announced five hours) to an incident that curbed the ruler's proclivity to use the railway as he pleased: "He was cured of his whim by a slight reminder of his own danger. One day he felt sleepy and ordered the train to stop for his nap; it did so and was run into by another train, which rudely woke his highness and convinced him of the propriety of sleeping elsewhere."[14]

Already in the late 1850s, "numerous accidents" were attributed to the lack of central planning in the ESR. "The loss of life to men and animal has been such, as would have startled any community," especially given the sparse traffic on the railroad.[15] By the mid-1870s, there were already about 240 locomotives made by over 60 companies carrying more than 4,000 vehicles of different types over a thousand miles of alternating single and double tracks.[16] Despite the growing size and complexity of the system, it was mostly still managed according to a "go-as-you-please" principle, making it more and more hazardous to ordinary and royal passengers alike, as well as to peasants and animals crossing the track in the countryside. These rural actors in turn started posing a danger to trains, be it from haphazard collisions or intended violence, which was becoming more and more frequent.[17]

Many such early train accidents in Egypt can be explained not only by the lack of timetables but also by the manner in which related political assumptions were welded into the railway and its equipment. Let us introduce in this first act three such techno-political fusions, together making the loaded revolver that will go off in the following act. The most observable and vivid example of the political shaping of technology in the ESR was provided by locomotives and carriages designed for the use of members of the Egyptian viceregal family, such as the aforementioned engine salon "finished and decorated in the most gorgeous style of eastern luxury and splendor"[18] by Robert Stephenson and Company. These vehicles included unique hybrid apparatuses, such as a combined engine and carriage, customized to satisfy Saʿīd's majestic impulse to proudly drive his own train. Moreover, "his highness being corpulent," the interior of the engine was designed accordingly.[19]

More important, Stephenson's team designed an innovative hydraulic system for aligning a Nile ferry and the railroad track at the point where the Alexandria–Cairo railroad crossed the Nile at Kafr al-ʿĪṣ.[20] Designers factored in the levels of the river and the track, as well as the mental and technical levels of native operators, striving for the utmost simplicity of operation.[21] They regarded these local workers as automatons and sought to eliminate any human agency on their part. Likewise, during the creation of a telegraphic signaling and synchronization scheme, engineers factored in the "oriental despotism" of Egyptian rulers and gave them unhindered right-of-way when driving their private trains along the single-track line.

FIGURE 5. Saʿīd's Locomotive Salon, built by Stephenson in 1862. From Lionel Wiener, *L'Égypte et ses chemins de fer,* 1932.

Translating their understandings of Egypt's politics into railway apparatuses, signaling systems, or layout patterns, British engineers made these understandings durable—parts of the material landscape rather than amorphous ideologies or free-floating representations. These ironclad politics in turn framed the experiences of colonial officials, travelers, and the many passengers of the Egyptian railway. Western travelers whose journey was halted to allow a viceregal train to move ahead saw this as a typical example of Oriental despotism and tyranny.[22] As such techno-political arrangements did not allow for the use of train timetables and schedules, they reinforced the image of the unpunctual, indolent East, where even the train was never on time.

In May 1858, the two key suppositions of European railway engineers about the Egyptian political culture—the technical deficiency of the natives and the unrestrained privileges of their rulers—were put on a collision course:

> It is certainly a most unfortunate circumstance that his Highness Ahmet Pacha should happen to be the victim of the first railway accident we have had here ever since the line was opened.... The train, as usual, started and arrived safely at Kafr-Lais [Kafr al-ʿĪṣ] where passengers generally alight to cross the Nile in a steamer, but, as on all occasions when princes are on the line, the ferry is held in readiness to convey them across in their carriages. The Arabs in charge, on pushing the wagons on the ferry, very carelessly omitted to put on the shappens *[sic]*, and the four wagons, one after the other, dropped into the Nile.[23]

The death of the Egyptian crown prince may be considered the first railway accident in Egypt only if previous deaths by train of ordinary Egyptians and their animals—mentioned in travel accounts—are discounted.[24] It is nonetheless important that this was the first accident of note. Accepting for the moment the language of the above report, we may ask how the fatal failure of the manually operated hydraulic device was understood. As the text makes clear, the ensemble of railroad, native labor, British design, and ferry that made up the apparatus was disassembled into its components, faulting one element, "the Arabs in charge." The characteristic deficiency of the native operators—the original reason for simplifying the system—was the target also of other descriptions of the accident.[25]

In other versions of this account, the Arab operators, excited by the important persona in the train or encouraged by the chance of receiving handsome alms, flocked in unexpected numbers and pulled the train too fast.[26] Another version blamed the future khedive Ismāʿīl (along with his mother), whose road to the throne was paved by the accident.[27] According to yet another theory, the viceroy himself planned the accident to rid himself of his ambitious heirs, of which "there were two on the train when the accident occurred, and it is rumored that the others only saved themselves by having been too late for the departure."[28] A more plausible hypothesis in the eyes of the reporter was that the Muslim operators were careless, because the accident occurred a day after the end of Ramadan.[29] In short, Arab belatedness, negligence, religious zeal, and conniving political culture were highlighted, obfuscating other elements of the design.

For example, it was nowhere mentioned that the line had been prematurely opened for traffic before the bridge across the Nile was finished, to demonstrate for Saʿīd how lucrative it was, at a time when the viceroy was considering a moratorium on further railway works.[30] Also, British observers never assigned blame to the English engine driver. Their silence is especially glaring given that only a month before the accident, when Saʿīd appointed the first Arab engine drivers (chiefly in branch lines and luggage trains), the British acting consul general protested profusely to ESR director Nūbār Bey, reminding him of "the onerous and delicate position of English Drivers, to whose judgment and experience so many lives are entrusted."[31] (This was far from being the only time Arab functionaries were blamed for accidents or near accidents.)[32]

The Kafr al-ʿĪṣ accident was seen as emblematic of Egyptian carelessness and inexactness.[33] It had two other distinct outcomes. The first was regarded as purely technical: to eliminate altogether "the human factor" blamed for the accident, Nile ferries were replaced by railway bridges.[34] These bridges brought about a new and unexpected kind of railway accident: crossing animals (mainly water buffalos and camels) frequently found themselves in front of moving trains, occasionally leading to derailment.[35] The second outcome was seen as political: the prince's death cleared the way to the crown for Ismāʿīl (r. 1863–1879), the ruler most responsible for railway development[36] and other projects of "modernization," along with the indebtedness that eventually led to British occupation in 1882. In many counterfactual "what if" histories, Ismāʿīl's profligacy was contrasted with the frugal attitude of his dead half-brother Aḥmad.[37] The accident helped other careers, too. Nūbār Bey, ESR director in 1858, was given pasha status during Ismāʿīl's first year of reign, later becoming one of Egypt's most prominent politicians and, eventually, prime minister. In 1868, Ismāʿīl appointed his school friend ʿAlī Mubārak (1823–1893) as ESR director.

Though not as rash as his predecessor, Ismāʿīl too was accused of using the railway for his private ends. For example, during the 1860s cotton boom that financed Egyptian railway development, Ismāʿīl, the largest cotton grower and chief merchant in the country, monopolized the railway for transporting his own goods. At one time, European merchants wishing to send a consignment to the interior were told by a railway employee that "so long as there remained for transport a single package of the merchandise belonging to His Highness, the Viceroy, the goods of private persons could not go forward."[38]

Nevertheless, the new ruler was also impressed by train schedules during his education in Europe,[39] and during his reign, ʿAlī Mubārak launched a series of significant reforms in the ESR. Instead of two trains per week on the Alexandria–Cairo line, a morning train now left both cities at fixed and predictable times, meeting in Ṭanṭā and allowing the drivers and conductors to change trains and return home.[40] Further, the new ESR director, who liked to compare intricate systems to complex watches in need of winding and tuning,[41] published timetables for the Alexandria–Cairo line in 1870. In 1877 schedules were also printed for most other lines.[42] Indirectly, then, the 1858 accident indeed promoted the introduction of railway timetables in Egypt. However, allowing Mubārak's fascination with clocks and Ismāʿīl's attraction to timetables to dominate the story creates the impression that the temporality of timetables simply floated into Egypt as an abstract and generic European "conception of time."

To some extent, this was indeed the case. Timetables came from Europe, and they did so at a moment when, with the inauguration of the canal, Egypt was said to "no longer be in Africa; it is a part of Europe," as Ismāʿīl had famously put it. The first schedules were printed in Britain and India in English,[43] according to the "Frankish" European day, which started at midnight, in contrast to the Arabic day starting at sunset. Egyptians could access them in Arabic in *Wādī al-Nīl,* the first semiprivate Egyptian newspaper, which was founded by Ismāʿīl in response to a perceived lack of European-style press in Egypt.[44] European conceptions of modernity clearly cannot be dismissed. Yet to fully understand the motivations behind the appearance of railway scheduling in Egypt and appreciate its particular inflections, a more grounded explanation is required, one that takes stock of several other changes and contexts that affected the ESR.

Railways are hardly ever built en bloc (even when this was their designers' intention);[45] usually they are constructed section after section, sometimes taking years to lay the track to the next stop. This holds true even for a single railway line, such as the Cairo–Alexandria line, which consisted of twelve stations and took five years to lay.[46] In such a system, every station was once a final stop and a first stop on the return. The system was built so that trains could stop for refueling at each station, with coal storage facilities, a locomotive garage, personnel, and equipment at every stop. What made such a fragmented patchwork into a smooth and synchronized network?

To survive the displacement of the India traffic, the ESR had to undergo a dramatic restructuring, including the development of internal lines to attract local passengers and goods. The distribution of most of the Egyptian population along the Nile Valley and main railroad facilitated this transition, and between the mid-1860s—when it became clear that the canal was feasible—and the late 1870s, the ESR tripled its size.[47] Seen in this light, the 1870 introduction of timetables does not represent the dawn of railway synchronization per se, but rather a new *kind* and *focus* of synchronization: no longer an ad hoc telegraphic coordination of trains and the steamers of the Peninsular and Oriental Company, but a centrally planned harmonization of proliferating internal railway lines.

The introduction of train schedules and the appearance of the logic of time-is-money were parts of an even more profound transformation in which a new abstract configuration of power gained ground in Egypt. As described by Timothy Mitchell, beginning in 1868 (the intended year for the canal's inauguration),[48] ʿAlī Mubārak, who was also the minister of public works and schooling, instituted the so-called Haussmannization of Cairo, along with educational policies meant to produce a modern regularized subject through strict spatiotemporal discipline.[49]

Mubārak's different hats—the master city planner, educator, and railway director—sat atop a single mind. Revamping Cairo's central train station served the double purpose of railway and urban reform, wherein the railway was extended by a network of straight boulevards and thoroughfares in the European style. The question of whether this kind of urban renewal is best typified as "Haussmannization" notwithstanding, there can be little doubt that the railway significantly contributed to the transformation of Cairo and Paris in very similar ways.[50]

Railway and educational reform likewise intersected. Finding that engine drivers entered the ESR with no training or exam and that the Arabs among them were mostly illiterate and "oblivious about steam and its concerns," Mubārak established a special school for railway drivers and engineers. He also staffed the ESR with graduates of the khedival schools he directed.[51] Several months after the first train schedules were printed, in 1871, the Egyptian penal system also adopted the logic of timetables, with the hierarchy of juridical councils defined by the periods of imprisonment and corresponding fines they could impose.[52] It is not unlikely that Mubārak, who headed the Public Works Ministry, which was the largest employer of prisoners sentenced to forced labor, was also involved in this introduction of a monetized temporality.

However, these abstractions did not occur in the abstract. In several important respects, time, discipline, and money were all animated by coal, which with the opening of the canal became the most prominent global energy source. Examining how coaling informed scheduling arrangements in the ESR helps tap little-examined layers of Egyptian modernity and elucidate its particularities. The shift of India traffic to the canal pushed ESR directors to look for ways to reduce costs and increase efficiency. One of the first targets was coaling, which had always been "the largest item in a railway bill,"[53] especially in a place like Egypt, where local labor was cheap and fuel was imported from Britain at great cost. Whereas the new order reduced discipline, time, and space to a measure, the following discussion offers a complementary simplification, reducing time, discipline, and money to coal. In so doing, I propose not to replace one great equalizer with another but rather to draw attention to the multiple origins and diverse trajectories of abstract monetized time.

Until 1870, the different sections of the Egyptian railway operated independently, both technically and administratively. Administrative provinces were liable for damages to the train and the tracks in the territory under their jurisdiction, and often in practice for their repair.[54] Every station had a coal warehouse and the manpower necessary for coaling. Trains were loaded only with enough fuel to reach the next station, where they would be refueled.[55] Because of these arrangements and a lack of space in the central stations, locomotives were stored at intermediary stations, where they were used for repairs and track work, creating unexpected congestion along the railroad. Coal too was stored along the way, exposed to the elements.[56] Such arrangements did not allow a centralized registration of coal expenditure or maintenance work performed on the trains and track.[57] Because refueling times depended on local variables, such as the proficiency of the staff and the architecture of the station, they were difficult to calculate. Finally, the array of coal warehouses became a source of corruption and theft.[58]

In 1870, changes to the Alexandria–Cairo line were part of Egypt's urban renovation. The Cairo and Alexandria train stations were refurbished as coal warehouses and repair centers, allowing Mubārak to close the coaling warehouses in the intermediary stations on the line. Manning the service with school graduates made it possible to introduce new, written protocols for registering and classifying each engine, the mileage it traveled, the weight of goods it carried, and its detailed repair profile. These measures prevented loading carriages with too heavy or too light a load.[59] Drivers too were now classified and ranked according to their training and experience.[60] Finally, with all engines now parked in central stations and the new repair policies in place, a wider selection of working locomotives became available, facilitating adherence to a schedule.[61]

The centralization of coaling and of the locomotive fleet, along with the new registration protocols, also allowed careful documentation of maintenance and coal consumption for an entire journey, thereby facilitating the translation of time, distance, fuel, and money into every other category. Registration prevented theft and corruption, giving a comprehensive picture of the railway's fleet and the expenditure of its mechanics' and drivers' labor time at any given place and instant.[62] Trains could now advance nonstop along the track without stopping to refuel midway and could keep to a published schedule in a unified network supervised from Bāb al-Ḥadīd, Cairo Central Station. During the closing decades of the nineteenth century, train stations—already linked telegraphically—were connected by telephone lines that enabled reporting the whereabouts of all trains in real time. Based on these reports, clerks in central stations moved miniature trains along models providing a bird's-eye view of the entire railway.[63] So far, then, a familiar modernity unfolds—one associated with temporal abstraction, panopticism, and calculability. It might strike one as strange that in Egypt its main driving force, coal, would derail this modernity from the conventional track.

The techno-logic of steam power was opposed to that of transportation based on animal power, for which rest along the way was essential. For example, when the Egyptian postal service was created under Mehmet ʿAli, most of the time it took to convey the mail between remote places was expended on much-needed horse and courier rest.[64] By contrast, locomotives had nothing to gain from rest. On the contrary, in Egypt as elsewhere, a locomotive consumed as much as one tenth of its daily fuel supply simply heating itself to the point that it could produce steam to carry its own weight.[65] The steam engine combined thrift in time and money: the train that lingered in the different stations wasted more money than the train that did not wait. Setting fixed times for passenger pickup drew its logic from this nexus of time, fuel, and money. The new coaling arrangements and the centralized registration protocols made these connections inescapable.

Yet viewed from this perspective rather than from one presupposing a temporal abstraction, it becomes clear that railways produce "social synchronization" only as a side effect, a byproduct of coal thrift. As long as passengers and goods waited in stations rather than trains waiting for them, it mattered little how long passengers waited. In the early 1870s, it was clear that the interests of the public and those of rail companies were not always similar. In England, government intervention was frequently needed to circumscribe attempts by British railway companies to raise fares so that fewer passengers would be able to use the train. The interest of the public in "regularity, speed, safety, and economy" often contradicted the objective of the company "to obtain a good return for the capital expended."[66] And if this was the case when the above-quoted parliamentary report saw light in 1872, a year later, when competitive pressures in British railway companies and the coal industry turned into the global 1873–1896 Great Depression, railway companies around the world were forced to cut costs, sometimes prioritizing coal thrift over the public's interests.[67]

The global coal crisis struck Egypt just as the 1860s cotton boom, resulting from the Northern blockade of Southern exports during the American civil war, ended. Loans taken to underwrite large-scale projects, such as completing the canal and tripling the size of the railway, pushed Egypt toward a spiraling indebtedness to European creditors. In the mid-1870s, the annual interest payments alone reached 60 percent of the country's revenues,[68] leading to gradual sale of the government's shares in the canal beginning in 1875 and to the 1876 formation of the Caisse de la Dette, an international committee securing European financial control. In 1877, debt also brought to Egypt Evelyn Baring, the future Lord Cromer (1841–1917), the British representative in the Caisse and the architect of British colonialism in the country.[69] Under this new regime, the ESR was now forced to hand over 55 percent of its annual revenue to the Caisse, leaving it with only 45 percent for working expenses.[70] It was also subjected to an international board of three directors—an Egyptian, a Frenchman, and an Englishman—making it very difficult to manage. This was seen by many as a main cause for the railway's poor performance and frequent delays.[71]

Beyond the crippling international rivalries on the board, delays were directly related to austerity measures and coal-saving policies. There were economic reasons for keeping a schedule but not necessarily keeping to it. A good example is a policy born in the early 1870s, together with the aforementioned means of economizing spending in the ESR. We have already seen how reforms in scheduling were connected to the new need for fuel efficiency. For superintendents as well as drivers, the easiest way to estimate coal consumption has always been to use the clock. Indeed, "the efficiency of a railway may be judged by reference to statistics of its train delays."[72]

COMPRESSION AND/AS COMPARISON

But what should be classified as a delay? Looking in the early 1930s at the history of the ESR, W. D. Knight, the deputy chief mechanical engineer of the Egyptian State Railways, argued that the answer should be different for a railway whose "employees are drawn from the uncivilized population on which years of training must be devoted before they become competent workmen who realize what efficiency means."[73] In a colonial railway, he maintained, "the company would continue to employ cheap labour and shut its eyes to failures and delays until its passengers clamoured for better service."[74] Punctuality in this model depended on "the public," which became "more and more expecting with time. Thus, in the development of a railway, an inducement to eliminate failures is generated, and the incentive: an ever increasing number of fastidious passengers automatically provides the capital necessary for their elimination."[75] Different railways, writes Knight, should have different efficiency goals according to which failures and delays are to be classified as "avoidable" or "unavoidable." If two extremes are compared, a British railway and a colonial one, in the former more delays should be classified as "avoidable" and corrected.[76]

Knight's distinctions were well anchored in the conventions of colonial engineering, a discipline or "professional Diaspora"[77] that tended to understand technical difference—the fact that machines work differently in different settings and terrains—in terms of cultural or racial oppositions. Like European experts on colonial urban drainage or native physiology, railway engineers explained, for example, the puzzlingly excessive coal consumption of American boilers in turn-of-the-century Egypt by "the difference in the intelligence and muscular power of the firemen obtainable in Egypt and in the United States, respectively."[78] Likewise, the high rate of eye disease, which caused many Egyptian candidates to fail the vision exam for an engine driver's position, was attributed to natives' laziness in waving off germ-transmitting flies.[79]

The conceptualizing of "colonial punctuality" percolated from the chief mechanical engineer to the shed foremen as policy guidelines for deciding which locomotive to assign to which loads. One of the primary reasons for train delays was assigning to certain loads locomotives that could not carry them in the tabulated time.[80] This method was frequently and deliberately used during the 1870s and 1880s to save on "light mileage"—energy wasted on carrying too light a load. During these two decades, all the Egyptian Railway's five-ton goods wagons were converted into ten-ton wagons to eliminate carrying light loads.[81] In 1877, the ESR's engine fleet was composed of sixty models purchased all over the world during a period of almost three decades.[82] In the absence of spare parts, when an engine or a carriage broke down, parts from another vehicle were used to repair it.[83] These hybrid engines had very different capacities and therefore resulted in significant light mileage. Moving to heavier wagons meant reducing light mileage but also a poorer record of keeping on schedule.

British and American train manufacturers' unfamiliarity with the specific working conditions of trains abroad was seen as another key reason for delays in the ESR.[84] The coal-gulping American engines offer a good example of how such factors sometimes converged. The ESR bought twenty of these engines, produced in Philadelphia in 1899. The heavy and powerful locomotives reduced light mileage by working the heaviest Egyptian passenger trains. But they pulled them slowly, heating up as a result of the profuse Egyptian dust.[85]

Because of the 1870 reforms and the introduction of timetables, coal registration procedures, and repair profiles, Egyptian trains had the potential for punctuality, yet this potential was differentially and selectively realized. For example, as tourist guidebooks regularly warned their readers, Egyptian express trains, which consisted of first and second class only and whose fares were 20 percent higher, were not only much faster but also much more punctual than regular trains, which had three passenger classes and were notoriously late.[86] Further, punctuality and speed were unevenly distributed among different lines and even different stops along the same line: a clear preference for the Alexandria–Cairo line was evident in its monopoly of the newest and fastest trains and European drivers. In 1902, eight daily trains traveled on this line, the fastest capable of crossing the 130 miles in three hours and five minutes, whereas the slower, local trains took six hours. (The same distance, the 130 miles between Luxor and Aswan, was traversed in seven hours by the fastest available train and nine hours by the local train, which departed at the ghastly hour of 3:45 A.M.)[87] Or consider how speed changed on the trip along the level plane between Cairo and Ismailia: Cairo–Behha, 40 mph, Benha–Zagazig, 36 mph, Zagazig–Ismailia, 33 mph.[88]

Indeed, since expediency could be bought for a price on the "European" lines, as long as regular passengers waited patiently in stations, railway delays were actually profitable. Egyptian second- and third-class passengers frequently waited hours for a train's arrival.[89] The habit of going to the station several hours early to catch a train came to be seen as a demonstration of the Egyptian peasant's time mindlessness and supported the conclusion that "punctuality, precision, haste—these are all matters beyond [the fellah]. Why should he set limits to the present or hustle it away?"[90]

Passengers' patience was secured by the monopoly of the railway over transportation of passengers and goods. Already in the 1860s, the camel—and by the early 1870s, also Nile transport—had received a major blow from the railway.[91] By the late 1910s, Cairo and Alexandria became almost exclusively dependent on the railway for food, so much so that the interruption of rail transportation during the 1919 Revolution created severe hunger in the capital, a problem that the temporary resurrection of these older forms of transportation could only mildly ameliorate.[92]

Coal-saving tactics such as matching trains with engines that could carry them only slowly and at great effort, as well as the fact that the locomotive fleet and the track were relatively old and poorly maintained,[93] meant that Egyptian trains were not only less punctual but also significantly slower than British trains. Slowness and unpunctuality cast light on one other, but they did not necessarily go together. For example, the eventual success of a major effort between 1900 and 1902 to improve punctuality was deemed to be "no great feat," considering that compared to English lines "the timing of the slow [Egyptian] trains on single track roads of 15 to 20 miles an hour gives plenty of time to make up for delays."[94]

The above examples suggest that comparison cast a long shadow on the experience of "time/space compression," the supposed removal of spatial barriers and restructuring of the experience of time that ostensibly characterized early modernity and then high- or postmodernity.[95] Consider 1915, the year that some historians consider to be the peak of "the first phase of time-space compression," usually located between the mid-nineteenth century and World War I.[96] During that year, the 130 miles between Alexandria and Cairo—a distance traversable in about two hours in Britain at that time—were still crossed in three and a half hours by the fastest Egyptian express train and in up to six hours by slower local trains.[97] Six hours (a little over 20 mph), it should be noted, was the duration of the same journey in an Egyptian express during the early 1860s,[98] at which point European trains could move at double that speed.[99] By the mid-1880s, local trains on the Cairo–Alexandria line already crossed this distance in six hours, while the express took only four and a half.[100] In short, limiting the comparison diachronically to the Egyptian context reveals a remarkable acceleration. The increase of train velocity between 1860 and 1915 was indeed a "time-space compression," and a thrilling one at that.

However, a synchronic perspective suggests that awareness of the dissimilar operation of trains in different places opened up temporal gaps and constructed spaces that were *comparatively* longer. Time-space compression, in other words, carried with it also a comparative time-space expansion. The railway, a key component of the infrastructure that allowed Egyptians to travel abroad and read about foreign places, brought these comparative horizons closer to home. Compared to Western standards, colonial standards of performance, speed, and punctuality made Egyptian trains simultaneously fast and slow, at once punctual and overdue.

If 1915 was the peak of an experiential time-space compression, it is not surprising to find that the kernel for theorizing this experience was planted at roughly the same time. In 1915 Émile Durkheim's *The Elementary Forms of the Religious Life,* which argued that time and space were social constructions, became available in English translation. David Harvey recognized the 1915 translation as one of the key sources of his notion of time-space compression.[101] Toward the end of 1915, Albert Einstein published his theory of general relativity, in which he defined time as conventional, as a synchronizing operation of clocks, dealing a devastating blow to Newton's early modern conception of natural time as a modification of the sensorium of God.[102]

We may take 1915 as a heuristic moment in which two notions of spatio-temporal relativity bifurcated. With Durkheim, the social sciences started confining themselves to a special domain of reality, human society.

Ontological time and space could be accessed in this "sociology of the social" only via epistemology, as time/space social conceptions.[103] Einstein's relativity, on the other hand, grappled with ontological spacetime directly and found it to be heterogeneous and dependent on the observer's frame of reference.[104] The difference between "time" and "time perception" was born.

Their differences notwithstanding, two of the most piercing minds of twentieth-century Europe, one observing trains in Bern[105] and the other studying a "primitive" society in Australia, came to the similar conclusion that time was relative. At the same time, Egyptians—placed as primitives onboard trains that combined technological acceleration and cultural difference, compression and comparison—were developing their own colonial theories of relativity. With what resources and constraints did the ESR furnish its workers and passengers in developing them?

THE HUMAN ELEMENT?

Whereas engineers like Knight translated technical difference into a cultural opposition, colonial officials often understood cultural difference in technical terms. What follows demonstrates that these gestures were two sides of the same coin. This was nowhere more evident than in the writings of Lord Cromer, Egypt's de facto ruler as British consul general from 1883 to 1907. Cromer resigned amid an outburst of political unrest, a financial crisis, and problems with his own poor health. His two-volume memoir, *Modern Egypt,* which he published in 1908–1909, was a manual for colonial officials to come as well as an attempt to do justice to three decades in the country's driver's seat.

As the work makes clear, Cromer understood colonial administration as a machine. His writing is full of mechanical metaphors: "The pressing questions were, What could be done at once to enable the machine of the state to work, however inefficiently?"[106] Or similarly, "For a few months, the new machine of government worked, although with great friction."[107] And again, "Is it probable that a Government composed of the rude elements described above . . . would have been able to control a complicated machine of this nature?"[108] Cromer's technical metaphors have been effectively harnessed by Timothy Mitchell to illustrate the mechanical nature of the power to colonize.[109] More important for the current discussion, and as the above examples indicate, was the fact that the colonial machine was not running very smoothly.

In a chapter titled "The Machinery of Government," Cromer crisply articulated this problem. He compared two steam engines. Within the first apparatus, which stands for civilized European administration, "the rate at which each wheel turns is regulated to a nicety[,] . . . the piston of the steam-engine cannot give a stroke by one's hair's breadth shorter or longer than that which it is intended to give[,] . . . the strength with which the hammer is made to descend is capable of the most perfect adjustment."[110] Within the engine that stands for Egyptian administration, by contrast, "the movement of each wheel is eccentric in the highest degree[,] . . . the piston is liable at any moment to stop working[,] . . . there is no adequate machinery for adjusting the strength of the stroke to be given by the hammer."[111] If political science was understood mechanically, what vision of mechanics animated it in the colonies?

As we have seen, Egypt and Europe could be incorporated into a hierarchical relationship only when they were made comparable, as universal techno-scientific yardsticks were applied in a way that disclosed Egypt's inferiority vis-à-vis what came to be its metropole. Yet techno-science came to the colonies with presuppositions about cultural difference. Though it replaced previous paradigms for addressing the "other," such as race and religion, in many respects techno-science absorbed and extended these earlier paradigms. We have already seen how assumptions about political, racial, religious, and cultural difference were welded into the equipment of the ESR. When Cromer used the machine as a metaphor for politics, he simply fleshed out the assumptions that were built into these machines.

A closer look at Cromer's two engines reveals how this came about. Notably, Cromer marshaled the technical processes that were carried out by people in the early days of steam technology. During the development of the steam engine, human workers were employed to mediate different parts and processes inside mechanical apparatuses. As nonhuman components gradually replaced these mediators, the process endowed machines with human properties. Apparatuses had to be able to *speak* to each other, *supervise* one another, and *inspect* each other. The engine was created and black-boxed by an infusion of human agency, just as God animated Adam from clay:

> It is hard for us to imagine how original the stratagems that generated automatons were. For instance, in the earlier Newcomen steam engine, the piston followed the condensing steam, pushed by atmospheric pressure, that was thus made to lend its strength to the pump that extracted the water, that

> flooded the coal mine, that made the pit useless. . . . [W]hen it reached the end of the cylinder, a new flow of steam had to be injected through a valve opened by a worker who then closed it again when the piston reached the top of its stroke. But why leave the opening and closing of the valve to a weary, underpaid and unreliable worker, when the piston moves up and down and could be *made to tell* the valve when to open and when to close? The mechanic who linked the piston with a cam to the valve transformed the piston into its own inspector—the story is that he was a tired lazy boy.[112]

The story of the lazy, playful boy ex machina was a staple of British popular scientific literature.[113] Adam Smith, a friend of James Watt, the inventor of the fire engine, deployed it in *The Wealth of Nations* to illustrate the principle of the division of labor.[114] Karl Marx in turn theorized the citational character of technological innovation, the fact that machines are often modeled after their human operators.[115] Cromer thus relied on a lively tradition of machines standing for the men that were once part of them,[116] a tradition that was especially fitting to address lazy, childlike, subject races. Indeed, according to Cromer, the typical Easterner was "devoid of energy and initiative, stagnant in mind, wanting in curiosity about matters which are new to him, careless of waste of time, and patient under suffering."[117] This and similar definitions of an Egyptian subjectivity shaped by indolence[118] were a perfect plug-in for machinery affording ample room for politics, race, and religion between its pistons and valves.

Whereas machines were humanized in a way that rationalized their different deployment in different settings, human workers were objectified in ways that rationalized controlling them as machines. In a speech on efficiency, Cromer claimed that the single most important characteristic for a good British administrator in the East, the one feature that distinguished him from Oriental subject races and even from continental Europeans, was the capacity to think and act creatively, in accordance with circumstances on the ground, a trait that made him the diametrical opposite of "an automaton."[119]

The figure of the automaton was repeatedly used in reference to colonized Egyptians and their relationship with their British masters. "There is one saving clause, which serves in some respects as a bond of union between the races. Once explain to an Egyptian what he is to do, and he will assimilate the idea rapidly. He is a good imitator, and will make a faithful, even sometimes a too servile copy of the work of his European teacher. . . . His movements will, it is true, be not unfrequently those of an automaton, but a skillfully constructed automaton may do a great deal of useful work."[120] This kind of personality, Cromer continues, obviates employing many Englishmen in Egypt. But it may also create risks, as the smallest amount of initiative given to Egyptians "may result in a relapse" when British supervision is withdrawn.[121] Though most Egyptians manifest similar habits of thought, starting with the "fellah" who "true to his national characteristics, is an admirable automaton,"[122] automation was a tendency most strongly evident in the Europeanized Egyptian of the bureaucratic class: "The Egyptian official was always predisposed to be an automaton. Once Europeanized . . . his automatic rigidity becomes more wooden than it was before."[123] Europeanized Egyptians, Cromer made clear, depended on strict and elaborate regulations. "Entrenched behind these codes, the Europeanized Egyptian is, to his joy, relieved in a great degree from the necessity of thinking for himself."[124]

Most of the examples of Egyptian automatons in *Modern Egypt* are taken from the ESR: an Egyptian stationmaster refusing to dispatch a fire engine to a burning town because regulations forbade connecting such vehicles to the available train; or a doctor sent to examine a stationmaster suspected to be insane and attacked by the madman while two Egyptian orderlies watched without interfering because they were not given the correct command.[125] Such examples reveal the automaton's importance to railway management in Egypt, as well as the significance of the ESR for the development of an objectifying conception of Egyptian subjectivity. We have seen how colonialism informed the rigidness and contours of the dividing lines between the human and nonhuman. We now move to examine some of the practical implications of such distinctions for timekeeping.

WORK TIME

During the first decades of the twentieth century, the ESR employed the largest permanent workforce in Egypt. Since the country had few factories to speak of, the railway was one of the key arenas for the process E. P. Thompson defined as the transition from "task-oriented time" to "clock time." Coal wedded time and money, yet it did so in a particular way: unlike labor conditions in England in this period, regular monthly salaries were not the rule in Egypt, not even in the ESR. Though time-is-money was the guiding principle in resource management, many ESR workers were employed as day laborers or paid per task as late as 1923.[126]

This anachronism was largely a result of the understanding of the Oriental makeup that informed the attitudes of British ESR officials toward Egyptian railway workers and passengers. Instances that captured for Cromer Egyptian inaptitude for self-rule were similarly interpreted by ESR administrators in the more limited framework of the railway service. For example, a British ESR official related an incident that purportedly revealed the Egyptian habit of taking orders literally. One time, he ordered a train to stop so that he could alight and engage in bird shooting near the track. As birds were plenty, he turned back toward the train only half an hour after the hunt commenced, finding it in the exact same place. The Egyptian drivers explained that they hadn't continued their journey because they were not ordered to do so. "It is no wonder," the lesson of the story is drawn, "that even the Egyptian Nationalist has no desire that the post of engine driver should be given to natives."[127]

This conclusion is particularly interesting because it was so patently untrue, speaking directly to the incommensurability between Egyptian demands and British employment policies. At any rate, "the Egyptian Nationalist" was by no means content with barring locals from coveted ESR positions. For example, Muṣṭafā Kāmil, the young leader of the Nationalist Party (and the son of an engineer), was vociferous in his calls for the replacement of British by Egyptian stationmasters and inspectors.[128] What is more, the ESR management itself used the nationality of railway functionaries as a bargaining chip in labor conflicts. When it announced, in 1908, a twelve-hour workday at busy stations and up to twenty-one hours (alternating with equal time off) at secondary stations, the management preempted strike action by announcing that Egyptians would now be eligible to apply for stationmaster and inspector positions.[129]

Tensions concerning the nationality of the railwaymen were not new. Viceroys Saʿīd and Ismāʿīl both strove to increase the number of Egyptians in the ESR, in the face of British reluctance, with some success.[130] Yet after the occupation, the railway workforce underwent a gradual Europeanization of several coveted positions, especially stationmasters and inspectors.[131] In 1896, 2,668 Egyptians were employed by the ESR, compared to 121 Europeans, who constituted 4.3 percent of the workforce. In 1906, the ESR employed 4,780 Egyptians and 424 Europeans, constituting 8.1 percent.[132] Put differently, during this decade the workforce doubled while the number of Europeans nearly quadrupled. Moreover, in certain jobs (and not only supervisory ones), Europeans held the most desirable positions. While in 1900 only 4 percent of the 1,251 engine drivers, firemen, and cleaners were Europeans, certain "high-profile" lines, such as the express train between Cairo and Alexandria, were manned solely by European drivers.[133] Addressing a similar disparity in office jobs in 1901, a report evoked the familiar conceptual language of the automaton, if not the word itself: "It is seldom that [Egyptians] will see the reason for what they have been told, or that they will use their own judgment or intuition; further, history shows how little they can, as a rule, be trusted in responsible positions. The better positions are therefore filled by Europeans, mostly English."[134]

As many Egyptians were well aware, this glass ceiling and the lack of fixed monthly salaries stood in sharp contrast to contemporary "best practices" in Europe. So too did the ESR's exclusive reliance on fines as a method of discipline. Nineteenth-century railway companies pioneered the development of new means of labor control,[135] including the "career." The word started to denote a steady movement through occupational stages only in the second half of the nineteenth century. Until then, it referred to unstable movement, as in the expression "horses careering out of control."[136] By providing incentives, careers effectively solicited self-discipline. From the 1860s onward, British railway companies gradually shifted from using fines as the primary tool for labor control to disciplining workers through promotion and demotion along these "ladders."[137] The problem with fining, an 1881 book on railway management in England stated, was its retrospective nature. Fining was to be replaced by means that cultivated "forethought" in the workforce.[138] These means (i.e., careers) led to a reduction of supervisory presence and costs and enabled British railway companies to offer considerably lower entry-level salaries, promoting efficiency and productivity.[139]

These principles also informed the contracts of the European workers of the ESR. From 1857 onward, foreign drivers received a fixed monthly salary and were incentivized by a system combining fines and bonuses: if a driver was reported in writing to the *mudīr* (supervisor), he was subject to salary deduction. The fines imposed on the European drivers were collected and divided among the most deserving drivers.[140]

But conceiving of Egyptians as automatons made the adoption of careers unthinkable for the indigenous workforce. Because the stability of the colonial project was predicated on the belief that "the smallest amount of initiative given to Egyptians may result in a relapse," careers—based on exactly such a delegation of agency—were out of the question. Well into the twentieth century, fining remained the key method of discipline in the Egyptian railway as well as in the tramway, and one of the main sources of worker unrest.[141] Worse still, the power to fine was exclusively vested in the hands of European supervisors. Instead of self-discipline, Egyptian workers were subjected to a discipline whose "otherness" was its main feature. Railwaymen had no way of internalizing and participating in the logic of their subjugation.[142] The stick of the retroactive fine, not the carrot of a prospective promotion, was at work in the ESR. Through fines and clocks, ESR workers were treated like a nonhuman resource, like coal. This was a particular configuration of time-is-money: not the forward-looking and agentive logic of subtle modern governmentality, but the objectifying, retroactive, and anachronistic logic of foreign coercion.

Egyptian workers did not have to look far to realize this. Their European colleagues, we have seen, enjoyed the "enlightened" version of time-is-money. Also, the emergence of organized labor militancy in the ESR during the late 1900s was connected to other labor struggles inside Egypt, such as tramway worker activism, as well as labor issues elsewhere in the Ottoman and British Empires that were covered regularly by the Egyptian press. A 1909 article in *Al-Niẓām,* for example, addressed matter-of-factly "the familiar reasons for labor strikes in England, i.e. low wages and long working hours."[143] During the previous year, 1908, indigenous workers of the Anatolian and Baghdad Railroad companies—both of which, like the ESR, paid fixed monthly salaries only to Europeans—launched a strike against employment of non-European workers by the hour and per task.[144]

Ilham Khuri-Makdisi has shown how such radical politics spread across the Levant in 1908 by means of intellectuals' and workers' networks.[145] Egyptian newspapers often contemplated possible railway connections between the ESR and other railways in the Ottoman Empire, a possibility that facilitated the connection of activists' groups and the circulation of ideas.[146] Visions of interfacing politics and interfacing transportation networks reinforced and extended one another. In the first decade of the twentieth century, the fact that railroad companies in Egypt, the Ottoman Empire, and India had different payment policies for Orientals and Europeans was impossible to overlook.[147] Such comparisons revealed a differential in payment standards similar to the double standards in speed and punctuality.

In 1909, just as Cromer's memoirs were published and the ESR workers formed a labor union "to reduce work hours and increase wages,"[148] an English ESR deputy chief mechanical engineer determined that a half day's wages might be withheld for five minutes' tardiness.[149] In Britain, similar policies of labor discipline had been criticized and effectively eliminated a century earlier. In *The Making of the English Working Class,* Thompson describes an 1818 London mechanic who bemoaned the withholding of a quarter day's wages for a few minutes' belatedness.[150] In the nineteenth century, English workers came to accept the temporal categories imposed on them by employers and learned to deploy the equation of time and money to shorten work hours and increase salaries.[151] That fines and similarly outdated techniques of labor regulation would be put to exclusive use in twentieth-century Egypt matched the outdated and belated transportation technologies Egyptian workers were operating.

In an anecdote mentioned in the introduction, we saw how railway workers fiercely resisted this policy and its various manifestations, such as the installation of toilet chronometers several months later. As their list of demands indicated, most of the workers' rage could be attributed to the intrusion on their bodily functions by foreign temporalities (like the new regulation, chronometers were put in place by the British deputy chief mechanical engineer). Indeed, fines gave a foreign character to this version of time-is-money. A worker's wages were determined by two main factors: the number of hours he worked minus the fines he accumulated. Workers associated fines with those who enforced them, and it was Europeans who held the supervisory positions.

The foreignness of the anachronistic manifestation of time-is-money implemented in the ESR did not stand in isolation. In the previous chapter, I showed how standards draw their power from appearing ahistorical, erasing the messy contingency of their origins and presenting themselves as preceding the circumstances of their own production. In Egypt, however, standard abstract clock time could not completely shake off its European historical origins. As a result, it could not be easily digested as empty, homogeneous, impersonal, natural, neutral, or apolitical—to name some of the masks it assumed elsewhere.

Though mechanical clock time was strongly entrenched in Egypt, it was often internalized not as "time" but rather as "European time." At least as early as 1870 and most likely before, time indices had to stipulate whether they were dealing with "Arabic" or "Frankish" time. The new train schedules, for example, indicated "Frankish" and "before-noon" or "afternoon" in every category of the timetable.[152] Initially, these were empty signifiers for most Egyptians. The "Arabic day" started at sunset, and the length of every hour varied seasonally (because the sun sets and rises at different times according to the season).[153] By contrast, the Frankish day occurred without seasonal variation and was divided into twelve even hours.[154]

As part of "Ottoman temporal culture,"[155] during the nineteenth century Egyptian officialdom and elites followed the *alla turca* timekeeping system, which kept equal hours (like "Frankish" time) but marked the beginning of the day at sunset (like "Arabic" time). However, the growing independence from Istanbul and the contrast with Frankish railway time resurrected Arabic fluctuating time as a foil or an object of nostalgia, a past missed (or despised) exactly because it didn't exist. Indeed, the very notion of "Arabic time" was a late nineteenth-century creation, conceivable only vis-à-vis "Turkish" and "Frankish" times. Schedules, calendars, and clocks, intended to homogenize and standardize time, thus came to have the opposite effect when introduced into Egypt, where they revealed the heterogeneity and multifarious political dimensions of timekeeping, side by side with temporal simultaneity and evenness.

BLOWING OFF STEAM

In Knight's model for explaining the development of timekeeping standards, railway passengers are a key factor in generating the pressure that gradually pushes a railway toward increased punctuality. In this model, one would assume that even a colonial railway, where standards of punctuality were more lax to begin with, might eventually attain a satisfactory timekeeping record if passengers duly clamored. Yet Knight's description of how the public gradually becomes more exacting hinged on several assumptions concerning the expression of public opinion and criticism, as well as the railway management's capacity to take notice of and correctly interpret and respond to such expression—assumptions that were untenable in a colony. Egyptian passengers and merchants were indeed clamoring for punctuality, but they were doing so under the radar of decision makers, for reasons to do both with how this radar was calibrated and how passengers articulated their grievances. Their failure to effect more prompt train performance reveals some of the reasons for Egyptian disillusionment with the pursuit of European standards of efficiency.

One explanation for this dialogue of the deaf was obviously a language barrier. When ʿAlī Mubārak launched his 1870 reforms, he partly attributed the chaos he found in the ESR to the fact that some of its employees did not speak any Arabic.[156] Yet after the 1882 occupation, the problem was seen as having more to do with the fact that "some of the native booking-clerks knew no foreign language," a situation remedied by the turn of the twentieth century, when it had been arranged that "all native clerks must speak either English or French."[157]

As this disagreement about the lingua franca of the ESR suggests, language use became a significant bone of contention in the first decades of the twentieth century. During this time, the use of Arabic, English, or French—in schools and post offices, as well as railway signs, schedules, and notices to the public—became a political matter.[158] For example, a 1905 article expressed popular frustration with the fact that the departure and arrival times of the Alexandria light railways were written only in French and English.[159] The language question flared periodically, and Cromer even commented on it in his 1906 report.[160] Yet advocates for Arabic, heatedly criticizing the use of English in the ESR,[161] made their case mostly in Arabic and mainly in the Arabic press. Their grievances were largely inaccessible to the English managers of the ESR, in the same way that foreign-language train schedules using "Frankish time" were initially inaccessible to many Egyptians. The languages of schedules and their critics were incommensurable. Rather than generating public pressure that improves punctuality and hence promotes a sense of participation, Egyptians were left with the dehumanizing and foreign aspects of clock time.

Though British ESR officials were deaf to Egyptian complaints, these committed professionals were certainly not blind to many of the ills of the system they managed, and they thus tended to attribute the seeming dearth of protest to Egyptians' passive and nonconfrontational character, as befit the automata they were thought to be. Already in the 1850s, it was suggested that "strangers might very naturally ask, how is it that, if the system pursued with the Egyptian railways is such as here described, complaints have not been duly formularized? Did any quantity of murmuring amount to complaint, many would be the complaints made; but . . . Eastern subjects are not forward either to entertain views of policy, or . . . to complain about the acts of their superiors."[162]

These views were persistent. In the ESR annual report for 1900, the locomotive superintendent claimed that "the drivers and firemen of Egyptian nationality are the most uncomplaining of men,"[163] echoing Lord Cromer's views that Egyptians are "patient under suffering."[164] Such understandings of

Egyptian character desensitized colonial officials, in the railway and elsewhere, to workers' and passengers' gripes. It seems that the British dismissed their own hearing impediment as a case of Egyptian muteness.

In addition, British authorities were proactive in muzzling criticism. By (re)imposing press censorship in 1909, for example, they prevented Egyptians from blowing off steam and kept themselves in the dark with regard to the accumulation of frustration about the railway and other technologies of rule. As we will see in chapter 6, much of the surprise vis-à-vis the sudden eruption of Egypt's 1919 anticolonial revolution around these infrastructures can be attributed to a self-inflicted deafness.

Press censorship was first imposed in Egypt in 1881, as a response to an anti-imperialist "Egypt for the Egyptians" press campaign.[165] An American observer, seeking to illustrate the castrated and apolitical nature of Alexandria's European-language press under censorship, used the "active correspondence on the unpunctuality of railway trains" to make his case. These "printed slips," he scoffed, "serve well enough to occupy a small portion of the twenty minutes' [light railway] journey from Alexandria to Ramleh, where most of the Europeans have their homes, and all real and serious news comes three times a week by the mail-boats from Europe."[166]

But from the mid-1880s, complaints about train schedules and delays began appearing in the Arabic press, carrying a particular political import.[167] Addressing issues of train schedules and other technical concerns offered the Arabic press an opportunity to broach (techno-)politics without directly deploying the language most associated with illicit "politics"—that of Egyptian nationalism. Timetables, train malfunctions, and the exposure of inefficiencies folded the instrumentalist colonial logic against itself, just as railway workers did with the language of time-is-money from the early 1900s.

The ESR occupied a high-profile position in the development of this kind of instrumentalist criticism, a fact that had much to do with the intimate connection between the Egyptian railway and press. Take *Al-Ahrām*, the first Egyptian private newspaper, founded in 1876. Already in that year, a comparison of a list of *Al-Ahrām*'s agents and a list of railway destinations reveals a striking overlap.[168] Inside Egypt, the newspaper covered and was distributed almost entirely in places connected to the railway. In other words, territorially speaking, the Egypt of the newspaper was that of the railway map. Newspapers, dependent from their inception on the railway and the telegraph network running parallel to it for information and distribution,[169] took the ESR as an emblem for Egypt and its ills.

The railway itself was a highly political space, partly due to this media exposure. Cairo Central Station was where arriving and departing prominent figures delivered their speeches (and where journalists recorded them), beginning with Aḥmad ʿUrābī's 1881 speech, which ignited the anticolonial uprising that triggered British occupation. It was where Eldon Gorst, Cromer's successor, feared an angry mob would congregate to violently send off the retiring consul general to England in 1907;[170] it was where feminist Hudā al-Shaʿarāwī publically removed her veil after returning from an international feminist meeting in Rome in 1923;[171] and as short stories like Muḥammad Taymūr's 1917 "Fī al-Qiṭār" (In the train) and numerous later ones reveal, second-class train carriages were a setting for heated political debates, many of which started with the mention of a news item.[172]

By the turn of the twentieth century, complaints about train belatedness and scheduling started including references to their own futility. A 1902 article complained that the ESR summer schedules (scaled back after the busier, and more punctual, winter tourist season had ended) prevented passengers from returning home on the same day, forcing them to spend the night in a hotel and wasting time and money.[173] The article opened with a comparison of Egypt with France, where the press was assumed to have the power to impact the schedules of trains, "a country where the people can have its voice heard and where newspapers that reflect public opinion have an effective say. We wish our own country were such a place."[174]

In 1906, editor and essayist Amīn Ḥaddād published an article titled "Ḥubb al-Surʿah" (The love of speed), where he celebrated the potential of mechanized speed. Alas, such potential was not realized in Egypt, Ḥaddād complained: "Even the railway trains, which in America and Europe can almost fly, do not operate in Egypt in their usual manner, even though they could cross the distance between Cairo and Alexandria in an hour and a few minutes if there existed the desire to do so." Among the explanations he provided for this slowness (including Egyptian laziness, the hot weather, and indigenous time mindlessness), Ḥaddād blamed Egypt's occupiers for deliberately embracing and exploiting the local lethargy. Why else, he asked, had they sat idly for twenty-four years, whereas if the Americans had occupied even the North Pole, "after twenty-four years you'd see hundreds of cities, fields, and farms on top of the ice."[175] Deploying several layers of comparison, Ḥaddād pointed out that the occupiers were clearly not living up to their own standards. And he astutely diagnosed the reason, directing attention to how the

British took advantage of the "Oriental tardiness" they claimed to be reforming.

Pessimism about the conditions of possibility for reform eventually led to a search for alternative ways of effecting change. As Aaron Jakes has shown, during the 1900s, and especially after 1906, anticolonial sentiments broke out of the iron cage of instrumentalism after realizing that "constructive critique" was unconstructive.[176] We have seen how a particularly colonial, substandard instrumentalism was forged and theorized in Egypt, and it is not surprising that this paradigm offered an unsatisfying and eventually unsustainable platform for anticolonial politics. Like the anachronistic and crude version of time-is-money employed in the ESR, the colonial substandard instrumentalism dished out by Cromer and others was not a logic Egyptians cared to internalize, certainly after trying to no avail for over a decade.

The shift to a nontechnocratic, postmaterialist discourse can be gleaned from the frantic discussions on how to restrain it, such as those taking place before the 1909 reimposition of press censorship. As Gorst put it in 1908, attacks now "opposed root and branch the Anglo-Egyptian Administration" that Egyptians had formerly tried to address in its own terms. A new kind of newspaper article was "calculated to arouse the passions of the mass of the people"[177] rather than cajole the intellect of the occupier. Failing to speak back to power in its own measured language, Egyptian nationalism, looking for its voice and consolidating its institutions during this half decade, started seeking new interlocutors and different registers.[178]

Instrumentalism, however, was never completely abandoned, at least not with a European audience. Take the criticism of the 1909 press law by Muḥammad Farīd, who replaced Muṣṭafā Kāmil as leader of the Nationalist Party after the latter's death in 1908. Lecturing in London, Farīd illustrated his critique with a story about the ease with which the minister of interior could telephone a newspaper editor who published certain criticisms of the railway, threatening him that if he did not publish a series of articles praising the ESR, his paper would be suspended.[179]

Further, the new inflammatory tone in the press should also be situated in the context of the rise of popular sensationalism, a new rhetorical posture emerging in the early 1900s out of the experiences of urban hyperstimulus and experiential intensification. This milieu included such shocks as tram accidents on the street and their commercialized form in the rollercoaster rides of amusement parks and, for that matter, the new hyperbolic press registers. It was also associated with a new, telegraphic Arabic language veering toward the colloquial. In other words, postinstrumentalism was "post" in the double sense of surpassing and extending (exactly as "postcolonialism" would be), and in many respects it carried with it traces of the paradigm it eschewed. One of these traces was the cultural difference animating materialism's colonial career.

FINAL STOP

As it was theorized by British engineers, railway scheduling was an ongoing process of fine-tuning whereby an increasingly fastidious passenger public exerts pressure that eventually pushes trains to keep to schedule, even when this goes against the railway's economic interests. (As we have seen, the desire to conserve fuel did promote having a schedule, but not necessarily strictly keeping to it.) During their first half century, and especially after the 1870 wave of reform and centralization, Egyptian trains indeed became increasingly fast and punctual, and passengers grew more exacting. Yet both the indigenous and foreign operators and the users of these trains viewed the march toward exactitude comparatively and with a growing awareness of its double standards. The uneven increase in speed and punctuality thus contributed, paradoxically but perhaps inevitably, to the accumulation of frustration with tardiness and underperformance.

Thwarted by the colonial conditions of legibility, machine operation, and labor control, this frustration could not be translated into the kind of pressure supposed to effect punctuality, and it could not be contained by the sphere of labor politics either. Nor could this frustration be effectively ventilated in the censored spheres of public opinion, thus attaining the politically necessary catharsis of blowing off steam within the system's safety valves. From around 1900, this critical energy was channeled toward noninstrumentalist avenues, animating an anticolonial nationalism that was not based on an "empty homogeneous time," as Benedict Anderson famously maintained. Rather it was predicated on rejecting and subverting it.

Rather than pure alternatives to empty mechanical time, the resulting countertempos fed off a standard they could not meet: colonial punctuality emerged against the background of its metropolitan horizon; Egyptian slowness was brought into relief by accounts of European speed; differential norms of compensation and punishment revealed to early twentieth-century Egyptians (and through them to us) that time-is-money had more than one face. These various sets of double standards could not always be neatly mapped onto one another. Yet as we saw in chapter 1 regarding the birth of standardization, the split nature of timekeeping in Egypt was its most salient feature. Standardization was itself standardized in this country as a double.

Yet Knight was correct that railways are shaped by feedback from their users and operators, even if he wrongly assumed that this process necessarily follows a generic path toward increasing exactitude. As far as the Egyptian railway was concerned, the inflected feedback of Egyptian passengers and the infusions of unacknowledged agency on the part of its dehumanized workers brought the ESR to life as an automaton, in the image and likeness of an indolent Egyptian. Colonialism's inability to handle the human agency of subject people—manifest in (mis)understandings of the role of the human element in accidents, in Cromer's mechanical metaphors, in ESR employment practices based on these metaphors, and in the outflow of public pressure—gave rise to an automaton that incorporated the temporal hierarchies and contradictions of Egyptian modernity into its operating procedures and equipment. As such, this railway was not unlike the "Turk," the eighteenth-century chess-playing automaton powered by clockwork but actually driven by a concealed human operator, famously evoked by Walter Benjamin to capture a political and philosophical project of infusing the empty homogeneous time of historicism with nonlinear messianic temporality. As we will see in the next chapter, however, in Egypt religious and traditional cyclical temporalities were not injected into but rather born out of this human-machine pregnancy. Such reversals of the roles of puppet and dwarf notwithstanding, my goal here is not simply to unmask or blow the whistle on the non-elite and even nonhuman agents rendered voiceless inside this apparatus but to examine and historicize the mechanisms that rendered them inaudible.

THREE

Effendi Hauntologies

Haunting is historical, to be sure, but it is not dated, it is never docilely given a date in the chain of presents, day after day, according to the instituted order of a calendar.

JACQUES DERRIDA, Specters of Marx

THE PIONEERING 1917 SHORT STORY "FĪ AL-QIṬĀR" (In the train), by playwright and essayist Muḥammad Taymūr, describes six passengers in the second-class carriage of a train traveling from Cairo toward the Delta. Onboard, a heated conversation breaks out over the proper ways to discipline the peasantry. When a Circassian asserts that the whip rather than schooling is what the peasants really require, everybody joins the debate and the carriage is split into two rival camps, conservatives versus reformists: an *ʿumdah* (village headman) and a sheikh join the Circassian to endorse physical violence, while a young student and a dandy effendi join the narrator in defense of education and governmentality. The peasants remain completely outside the train. They are understood as a resource to be managed, a problem, a backwardness antonymically constituting the train's modernity. From (and as) the outside, they bring together this radically diverse group of passengers, the old and new landed elites. Peasants are all these fellow travelers have in common as a second class in the class system of the train.[1]

The importance of the train in demarcating urban-rural divides and demonstrating the importance of education in negotiating them has become a central theme in Egyptian literature and drama.[2] But actual peasants regularly disrupted the conceptual boundaries sustaining effendi cohesion, by taking keenly to modern railway travel. And they were doing so, disturbingly, in pursuit of their own "backward" means and ends. Hundreds of thousands of peasants used the railway annually to travel to countryside *mawlids*—popular and often carnivalesque festivals celebrating the birth or death of a prominent religious figure—or to visit graves of holy men and enjoy the *baraka* (blessing) they extend from beyond the grave. Statistical data generated by the Egyptian State Railways (ESR) between 1880 and 1908

FIGURE 6. Interior of a third-class carriage in the late 1880s. From Charles Frederic Moberly Bell, *From Pharaoh to Fellah,* 1888. © The National Library of Israel.

makes obvious that third-class passengers, mostly peasants, constituted the largest source of income in the passenger section, steadily generating more than double the income accumulated from the first and second classes combined.[3] The number of third-class couches was likewise by far the highest.[4] In 1912 the first-class passengers carried in Egypt numbered 547,000, the second class 2,327,000, and the third class 26,000,000, a 3 percent increase from the previous year.[5] In the face of effendi selective blindness to the presence of peasants and their importance for train travel, peasants often physically passed through the second- and first-class coaches under the effendis' noses. In the early days of her singing career in the 1910s, peasant-girl-turned-diva Umm Kulthūm, chaperoned by her father, used to travel third-class to mawlid sites where she was commissioned to sing. Before reaching their destination, however, the couple would cross the train and alight from the first-class carriage to impress their hosts.[6] Evidently, peasants were present absentees.

Railway history in Egypt and later elsewhere in the Middle East, as well as the history of this device in other colonies, such as India or Indonesia, illuminates the connection between modern transportation technology and popular religion and culture in the colonial world.[7] Means of transportation and communication often act in the liberal imagination as agents of a modernity that is synonymous with enlightenment, rationality, and secularization.[8] The technological time of these devices, deemed "empty and homogeneous," is considered to be empty precisely of divinity and contrasted with the cyclicality of resurrections, second comings, and other eschatological and nonlinear incursions.[9] In the established social science traditions of Walter Benjamin and Max Weber, these transportation technologies were seen as vehicles of disenchantment.[10] Even critics of colonialism and its trains, such as the young Karl Marx, predicted that these vehicles would introduce linear, secular, temporal historicist progression to the colonial world.[11] While these were generally also the expectations of railway engineers, from the second half of the nineteenth century onward in many places outside of Western Europe and North America, colonial railways repeatedly astonished their Western designers and operators, and often also colonial middle classes, by being enthusiastically taken up by masses of lower-class religious pilgrims and grave visitors.[12]

In Western Europe, the industrialization of time and space (as Wolfgang Schivelbusch subtitled *The Railway Journey*) involved curtailing what came to be seen as popular, unproductive leisure time: market days, agricultural festivals, and most famously, Saint Monday, devoted to drinking and idleness.[13] In this context, disenchantment often meant curbing and regimenting the times during which "superstition" ran wild. In the nineteenth century, the Egyptian middle classes similarly developed a new interest in the leisure habits of peasants. Yet rather than limiting equivalent practices and especially religious festivals, the railway actually stimulated their unprecedented flourishing. Instead of being instrumental in imposing clock discipline, knowledge about popular religion was actually utilized by railway officials to benefit from the considerable revenue generated by millions of annual pilgrims, grave visitors, and mawlid goers.

How can the actual role of trains as driving forces of popular religion be reconciled with their steady image as agents of enlightened modern secularism? How can the train's linear time be reconciled with the cyclical and eschatological temporalities of its third-class present-absentee passengers? These questions continue to have implications for any project of political or cultural transformation through technology. The answers I propose in this chapter avoid two paths that, while not completely off track, are nonetheless insufficient. One is pointing out that in Egypt, technology intensified existing cultural practices, and thus "Egyptian modernity" cannot be neatly contrasted with "tradition."[14] The second is to point out the unintended consequences and contingency of the introduction of technology and its context-specific nature. Instead, I examine how the Egyptian railway indeed advanced along a unique historical course but also generated discursive mechanisms of binary simplification; how in tandem with and often as a result of temporal flux, railway travel also simplified and homogenized cyclical eschatological time, simultaneously derailing and resurrecting an effective distinction between modernity and tradition.

Such simplification was far from being itself simple or anxiety-free: the Egyptian version of modern, empty, technological time was haunted, constantly needing to exorcize the specters that threatened to undo it, specters it nevertheless kept summoning. For members of the effendiyya, or Egyptian middle class, disenchanting time from these specters, and from the jinn and *ʿafārīt* they started to deem superstitious, was an ongoing, laborious, scary, and only partially successful process, creating a "time out of joint," as Hamlet put his own ghostly encounter (which resonated powerfully in Arabic translation beginning in 1901).[15] To make sense of this spectral temporality, this chapter explores how it upheld and engaged with a conceptual domain Derrida called hauntology and our late nineteenth-century Egyptian protagonists termed *barzakh,* a limbo between "to be" and "not to be."[16]

MOTORIZED PILGRIMAGES

New technologies and modes of religious experience affected each other in ways too numerous to recount. Even the limited scope of the railway's impact on sacred time (and vice versa), which is the theme of what follows, can be sketched here only with broad strokes. The existence of such an impact is not difficult to illustrate. For example, a 1904 *fatwā* dealt with the fact that while

Islamic dogma stipulated specific distances that must not be crossed by travelers without the performance of prayer, trains traversed distances far exceeding the maximal space exempt from prayer in less time than what was required according to the regular prayer schedule. This generated the question of which protocol travelers should pray by: temporal, spatial, or both. In other words, trains put religious time and space in contradiction.[17]

In other instances, it was the train that succumbed to the logic of sacred time. One of Mehmet ʿAli's rationales for beginning construction of a railway between Cairo and Suez was to cater to pilgrims to Mecca.[18] A competing Ottoman line, the Ḥijāz railway, was deployed later to serve the same purpose. The path (and, as we will soon see, the schedule) of the Cairo–Alexandria line through the Delta town of Ṭanṭā, was likewise informed by religious considerations. ʿAbbās insisted on the construction of this line in the mid-1850s to facilitate transportation to the great festival of Sayyid Aḥmad al-Badawī, which he even attended on more than one occasion.[19]

Trains and steamers gradually replaced camel caravans and sailboats as the main means of transportation on the *ḥajj,* the annual pilgrimage to Mecca. Already in 1861, even the *maḥmal,* the litter carrying the *kiswa* (a set of ornamented curtains used for draping the *Kaʿba*), usually transported in a procession marking the beginning of the pilgrimage season, was hoisted into a special train carriage instead of being carried on camelback across Egypt.[20] From the early 1880s on, the state-sponsored ḥajj procession regularly avoided the desert route altogether, taking the train to Suez and then continuing by steamer to Jeddah.[21] Masses in Cairo, provincial towns, villages, and port cities started congregating in train stations to benefit from the *maḥmal*'s blessing as the convoy advanced along the railway from the capital to its port of departure.[22] The telegraph line running parallel to the railroad helped newspaper readers follow almost in real time the advancement of the *maḥmal,* its reception in train stations, and its protectors' encounters with bandits or the plague.[23] Telegraphy allowed readers to participate textually in the ḥajj.

Before the introduction of steamships and trains, the ḥajj was limited mainly to elite pilgrims (*ʿulamā,* state officials, merchants) and to a small stratum of beggars able to accompany the caravan on foot. The long and expensive sea passage, punctuated by the rhythm of the monsoon, and the similarly taxing desert passage limited the number of participants in the pilgrimage and functioned as a barrier to the spread of disease and even radical ideologies. During the second half of the nineteenth century, however, modern transportation made Mecca accessible to wider strata of the Muslim global population, along with their popular cultures, diseases, and political ideas. This new danger of "pauper pilgrims" and the "twin infection" of cholera and anticolonial radicalism caused growing alarm in the British Empire.[24]

But the technologies that created the problem offered some solutions. Though modern technologies brought the holy places in Arabia closer to Egypt, this was not always or universally the case. Submarine telegraphy helped coordinate and enforce quarantine arrangements, keeping pilgrims away from the holy places for extended durations. And when infectious diseases were reported to have spread in the Ḥijāz, as was regularly the case beginning in 1831,[25] pilgrims were prevented from returning home. After the outbreak of a cholera epidemic in 1865, spreading from India through the Ḥijāz and Suez to southern Europe, quarantine was enforced with growing rigor, especially in Suez and Alexandria, the main eastern gateways to the ports of Europe.

Railway and steamer lines likewise introduced new means of differentiation among pilgrims. In 1889 a new regulation prevented "poor people" from going on pilgrimage unless they could prove they had sufficient means to sustain themselves and pay for a return ticket.[26] If in the past some of the poor could beg their way to Mecca on foot and then stay in the Holy City, making beggars an inherent part of every Egyptian pilgrimage caravan (the sheikhs of the beggars' guild were a standard part of the *maḥmal* ceremonial departure from Cairo), this avenue was now formally closed.[27]

These transportation policies complemented a religious campaign against the outward manifestations of "popular Islam" in both Egypt and Arabia. The growing influence of the Wahhābīs in Arabia manifested in attempts to interfere with the Egyptian ḥajj caravan, which they deemed un-Islamic due to its carnivalesque nature.[28] Long-time observers of the procession's departure from Cairo noted that its character changed around the turn of the twentieth century, as the efforts of Egyptian reformers such as Muḥammad ʿAbduh stripped the *maḥmal* of its "unorthodox" features.[29] The ability to regulate access to the train facilitated this transformation. The poor were left to benefit from the *maḥmal*'s *baraka* at the stations but not to profit from it materially as part of the pilgrimage train. As we will see, the railway reconnected the ḥajj procession to a plethora of new mawlids inside Egypt. But in several important respects it also disconnected these rituals, promoting a distinction between the ḥajj, which was becoming increasingly "orthodox," and "folk religion," which was associated more and more with local mawlids.

Beyond the differential elongations and compressions of pilgrimage time, the movements of the *maḥmal* had other unexpected temporal effects. The occasion of congregating at stations to greet the convoy on its way to and from Arabia often produced new holy days whose dates were unstable. In 1891, two mawlid celebrations were canceled due to telegraphic reports about the spread of cholera in the Ḥijāz and fears that infection would be spread by returning pilgrims visiting a mawlid.[30] In 1905 the return of the convoy was again delayed, possibly due to a bandit attack.[31] Celebrations connected to the Islamic month of Ṣafar, popularly known as *Nazlat al-Ḥajj* because of the annual return of the *maḥmal,* had to be postponed and the convoy was expected to reach Egypt only during the following Islamic month of Rabīʿ al-Awwal.[32] The last year in which the Egyptian *maḥmal* was sent to Arabia was 1926; another deadly Bedouin attack and tensions with the Wahhābīs regarding music played by Egyptian pilgrims terminated this practice. This time, the convoy's Cairo homecoming occurred well ahead of schedule. Instead of exposing the convoy to attacks on the return, Cairo telegraphed the *Amīr al-Ḥajj* with orders to change route and sail back by steamer. The *maḥmal* arrived at the Egyptian capital during the second week of Muḥarram, the Islamic month preceding Ṣafar. The celebrations had to be rushed.[33]

Such temporal fluctuations set off wide-ranging chain reactions. The ḥajj occurs during the Hijrī month of Dhū al-Ḥijja and varies seasonally. The schedules and duration of tens of rural and urban mawlids, some of which were connected to the return of the *maḥmal,* were also closely interrelated, and a change in one event could trigger a series of subsequent changes. Different mawlids were scheduled according to different calendars, predominantly the Coptic and Hijrī ones, and their annual occurrence was also informed by ad hoc considerations of transportation, security, and public health, as well as by geographic proximity to each other and even by the historical relations among the dead saints.[34] From the end of the nineteenth century on, the inevitable indeterminacy of mawlid schedules became a source of concern and frustration for authorities attempting to harness the productive powers of the peasantry and seeking to benefit from the revenue they generated as train passengers. Mawlids thus increasingly became markers of peasant backwardness for members of the effendiyya. The backwardness of mawlids, however, was often an effect of the technologies sustaining them. Examining more closely the connection of mawlids and railways therefore elucidates the case of a modernity producing its own nemesis.

Though the ḥajj was key to the ESR from the beginning of its operation, between the mid-1850s and the early 1870s, during the pilgrimage and in times of mawlid, trains were often so crowded that pilgrims had to ride on the roof.[35] Prior to train schedules and centralized planning, this congestion came as a surprise. A European railway traveler recounted such a scene in 1868, just before reforms were implemented:

> On going from Cairo to Suez by train there was an unusual crowd of native travellers in consequence of some Moslem festival at Tanta. . . . Two stout fellows armed with sticks stood at the little turn gate leading from the railway office to the platform. They kept constantly belabouring the people who eagerly pressed to get through and fast and thick the blows fell on heads hands and shoulders. Neither age nor sex was spared. . . . Many of them had beds and large quantities of provisions and they were all delighted they had got through and had secured their places in the great rough boxes in the bottom of which they squatted themselves for there were no seats.[36]

Reports from the year 1870 still divulge significant disarray resulting from the masses who used the train, especially during the prominent al-Badawī mawlid in Ṭanṭā, the key railway hub in the Delta.[37]

Under ʿAlī Mubārak and with the growing attention to local traffic, the ESR began to recognize the financial potential that mawlids represented. Gradually realizing that many mawlids were large commercial events worthy of special preparations, often including agricultural fairs and, in the case of the Ṭanṭā festival, a famous cattle and horse fair, the ESR started scheduling special trains during these events. It also lowered third-class fares and improved the condition of the carriages.[38] In April 1895, for example, it announced a special readiness for Mawlid Ṭanṭā al-Ṣaghīr. In addition to regular trains, on April 12–18, ten special trains were dispatched daily from Cairo, five trains from Alexandria, five trains from Manṣūrah, five from Shibīn al-Kawm, five trains from Zagazig, three trains from Dhaftī, and two trains from Dasūq.[39] Three months later, 115,594 people traveled by railway to the larger, al-Badawī mawlid in Ṭanṭā.[40] Earlier in the summer, the ESR had allotted eleven special trains for the Imbaba mawlid (third-class tickets were sold at a special reduced price of ten *malim,* about one fourth of a first-class ticket).[41] Only one day later, the ESR announced four special trains between Zagazig and Inshāṣ for the Ustādh Abū Muslim mawlid.[42] During the 1901 mawlid of Aḥmad al-Badawī, 800,000 people visited Ṭanṭā. The same year also saw a congregation of 250,000 visitors at the mawlid of Sīdī Ibrāhīm al-Dasūqī.[43]

These figures indicate that the railway clearly contributed to the flourishing of "popular Islam." Indeed, alongside the mawlids, the railway also promoted grave visitation by Muslims, Christians, and Jews seeking the blessing of saints or *awliyā'*.[44] Though many of these manifestations of "folk religiosity" predated the railway, there can be little doubt that new technologies significantly increased the number of participants in these festivals and helped establish new commercial, personal, and religious connections among them. Trains and mawlids may appear to be opposed, but in fact they enhanced each other. The technological modernity of trains transformed what was previously a relatively local set of religious affairs of much smaller proportions into a mass religious phenomenon. As early as the turn of the century if not before, "backward" mawlids filled hundreds of thousands, if not millions, of train seats annually. Modern trains infused these festivals with masses that made them appear to middle-class observers as increasingly immoral, threatening, and archaic.

Muḥammad ʿUmar, an employee of the Egyptian Postal Authority who provided some of the aforementioned figures in a 1902 book, did so with an alarm that was characteristic of effendi aversion to the mawlids of the lower classes. The title of ʿUmar's book, *Ḥāḍir al-Miṣrīyīn Aw Sirr Ta'akhkhurihim* (The present of Egyptians or the secret of their delay), was an homage to Edmond Demolins's 1897 *A quoi tient la supériorité des Anglo-Saxons?*[45] This work by the influential French pedagogue was quickly translated into Arabic in 1898 by Aḥmad Fatḥī Zaghlūl, an Egyptian judge and legal reformer, and brother of the future nationalist leader Saʿd Zaghlūl. Aḥmad Zaghlūl, who also wrote the introduction to ʿUmar's text, slightly modified Demolins's title to *Sirr Taqaddum al-Inkilīz al-Saksūnīyīn* (The secret of the advancement of the Anglo-Saxons). The *supériorité* in the original was thus rendered by the temporal term *taqaddum* ("advancement" or "progress"), which ʿUmar subsequently inverted into *ta'akhkhur* ("delay").

The grounds for this inversion, and for ʿUmar's framing of the Egyptian quandary in temporal terms, had been prepared by Zaghlūl in other ways as well. In a preface situating his translation in the Egyptian context, Zaghlūl identified indolence as an explanation for a long list of shortcomings of Egyptian society.[46] *Indolence* had an important temporal sense, implying time mindlessness and time wastefulness.[47] Following Demolins, Zaghlūl and

ʿUmar saw education and a rigid structuring of the school and work day as the best remedies for indolence.[48] They considered the task of curtailing Egyptian delay and improper modes of time management to be the responsibility of the "middle class" *(al-ṭabaqah al-wusṭā)* in a train-like three-class system (including also an "upper class" and a "lower class").[49] Indeed, the centrality of this reformist agenda in the debate among the middle-class passengers in "Fī al-Qiṭār" was not coincidental, and neither was the fact that the argument was triggered by a newspaper item or conducted inside a train. The term *effendi* underwent significant change in this period. Once a rank in the Ottoman administration that distinguished military officialdom from the religious-scribal class, in early twentieth-century Egypt, *effendi* had come to denote an educated, urban, and nationalist male professional.[50] Throughout this evolution, however, "effendiness" was consistently associated with reading and writing, and increasingly with the two institutions par excellence that promoted these practices—the school and the newspaper, through their temporally structured day and the rational character they promoted.[51]

Attempting to provide an inventory of the annual mawlids in a subsection of *Ḥāḍir al-Miṣrīyīn* titled "Mawlids and the Poor," ʿUmar criticized the fact that many mawlids followed the "Arabic calendar" and could take place both in summer and winter. As a result, "only God knows" the actual number and dates of the mawlids celebrated in the countryside.[52] A similar apprehension of excess and indeterminacy characterizes the next section, "The Poor and Holidays." According to ʿUmar, sectarian and national holidays should generally be encouraged. However, in Egypt the great number of holidays and the fact that each religious sect has its own feasts, unfamiliar to members of other denominations, defeat the purpose of holidays, which is to enable visiting and bonding among different people. The poor, oblivious to this rationale, spend their holidays engaging in immorality and consuming intoxicants.[53] Other Egyptian writers of the period were even more critical of copying European holidays, which they considered un-Islamic and inauthentic.[54]

Much of ʿUmar's critique of the lower classes rehearsed older rebukes—focusing on mawlids and grave visitations—that stressed the immorality of folk religiosity and its deviation from orthodox Islam.[55] However, ʿUmar and others pushed this line of critique in several new directions. First, the indeterminacy of mawlids, symptomatic of the unstable appearance of the Islamic lunar calendar, could only emerge against an alternative timekeeping system, in this case the Gregorian calendar, as well as against the new need for planning and coordination characteristic of modern transportation and communication systems. (ʿUmar provides examples from his own experience in the postal authority pertaining to the flow of greeting cards around major holidays.)[56]

Second, ʿUmar's attacks on lower-class immorality and superstition were couched in a new language of timekeeping and productivity. Thus, the subsequent subsection, "The Nightlife of the Poor" *(Sahr al-Fuqarāʾ),* lamented new habits of passing entire nights in coffeehouses. According to ʿUmar, this change in lower-class nighttime and sleeping routines was especially detrimental to manual laborers, who could not sleep during the day, making them vulnerable to the fatigue induced by an overactive nightlife.[57] The emergence of time wastefulness as a new principle organizing effendi attitudes to the lower classes resonated with other effendi admonitions of the period.[58] Contemporary ethnographies of mawlids indicate that the stress of sleep deprivation and time-wastefulness had taken root.[59]

ʿUmar's attempt to map lower-class routines had a long lineage. *Ḥāḍir al-Miṣrīyīn* drew much of its material from ʿAlī Mubārak's *Al-Khiṭaṭ al-Tawfiqīyah al-Jadīdah.* This voluminous work, published between 1886 and 1889, carefully examined both rural and urban mawlids, attempting to plot them on the Islamic calendar.[60] Comparing the list of Egyptian mawlids included in the writings of the sixteenth-century mystic ʿAbd al-Wahhāb Ibn Aḥmad al-Shaʿrānī to those mentioned in Mubārak's more meticulous *Khiṭaṭ,* Michael Winter has found that Shaʿrānī does not mention many of the mawlids mentioned by Mubārak, even those named after some of Shaʿrānī's most revered sheikhs.[61] This suggests that, beyond its unprecedented, painstaking effort of documentation, Mubārak's *Khiṭaṭ* reflected a real increase in the actual number of mawlids, in tandem with the undisputed increase in mawlid participation.

In Mubārak, the director of the ESR and minister of schooling, railway management converged with ethnography, and gradually also with the emergence of ethnography's object—"culture." Identifying mawlids, estimating the numbers of their participants, and deciphering their times and places made it possible to assign the right number of trains at the right times to carry the masses that frequented these events. Simultaneously, awareness of the alarming proportions of this technologically enhanced phenomenon sustained the critical discourse that singled out mawlids as the clearest example of time wastefulness and peasant backwardness, and hence the need for schooling, rural development, and reform. For Mubārak the education minister during the morning, knowledge about popular beliefs and folklore could be used to promote literacy, rationality, and a structured day as antidotes to superstition and ignorance. For Mubārak the ESR director during the afternoon, the same knowledge could be used to coordinate traffic on the railway.[62] As with the ḥajj, technology aggravated the problem it was then applied to solve. This productive contradiction was workable as long as the presence and importance of peasants in trains remained unacknowledged.

In an earlier text, *ʿAlam al-Dīn* (The sign of religion), published in 1882, Mubārak addressed this seeming paradox. The book, meant as a pedagogical text for young readers, took the form of a series of informative dialogues among two or three characters. One was an English Orientalist, whom Mubārak modeled after E. W. Lane. The other two were Egyptians accompanying him to Europe: Shaykh ʿAlam al-Dīn, a religious scholar probably modeled on Rifāʿah Rāfiʿ al-Ṭahṭāwī, and the sheikh's son, arguably standing for Mubārak himself.[63] As the party's train passes through Ṭanṭā, the conversation turns to the subject of mawlids, and the Englishman asks the sheikh where he stands in the debate between sheikhs calling to abolish mawlids for their immorality and those more receptive to such practices.[64]

In response, ʿAlam al-Dīn claims that although immorality and infringements on the *sharīʿah* were undoubtedly rampant during the Badawī mawlid, "everyone can see that this mawlid benefits those renting out transport animals or boats, as well as the railway." In turn, he continues, "the railway facilitated and quickened getting to and from the mawlid in an unprecedented manner.... The railway has made the difficult easy and shortened what is distant." The sheikh also mentions favorably the economic activity taking place during the mawlid; he even claims that the respite it allows from grinding routines of labor helps people return to work refreshed and motivated, which is well worth the time they waste in the mawlid.[65] Mawlids have undeniable detrimental aspects. Yet they are also economically beneficial, especially to the railway, and this outweighs their disadvantages.

The implicit evocation of Lane in *ʿAlam al-Dīn* helps us retrace interest in the routines of Egyptian peasants and their temporal habits to its origins some five decades earlier. During the 1830s, Lane and Antoine Barthelemy Clot (Clot Bey), a French physician who was a key figure in the establishment of the modern Egyptian medical profession under Mehmet ʿAli, were the first to approach peasant time as an object of ethnographic inquiry. Lane's 1836 *Manners and Customs* and Clot's 1839 *Aperçu général sur l'Égypte* introduced a new research agenda that would later be taken up by indigenous effendi ethnographers.[66] Lane offers a participant observer's account of popular festivals during the Islamic year, along with the "superstitions" and supernatural entities associated with each of the different periods of the Hijrī calendar.[67] For this pioneer, as for the ethnographers who followed him, popular conceptions of time were a key object of inquiry not only in their own right but also because correctly deciphering them was a prerequisite for attending festivals and rituals, for being in the right place at the right time. (Lane recounts how he nearly missed the Cairo homecoming of the *maḥmal* because he had the wrong time.)[68]

Like Lane, Clot described the divisions of the week and year into good- and bad-omen days (depending on how prone people are to be attacked by evil spirits).[69] He depicted practices of divination[70] and risings from the grave[71] that collapsed the stable boundaries between past, present, and future. And he anchored the practice of mawlids in these temporal systems.[72] The data he collected was gleaned from official interaction with soldiers, peasants, and midwives. Yet, like Lane, Clot did not generate the kind of knowledge that the modern Egyptian state typically produced or required in this period. In Europe too, such "manners and customs" ethnography was usually classified as "entertaining knowledge" and contrasted with "useful knowledge."[73]

The connection of mawlids with the railway system in the second half of the century infused this interest with a new objective and value. Railway reforms in the 1870s corresponded with what Omnia El Shakry has called Egypt's "ethnographic moment" and the establishment of the Royal Geographic Society in 1875.[74] Lane's and Clot's projects were thus absorbed into a newly established European and later effendi ethnography. Reading this corpus genealogically reveals the changing attitudes of the Egyptian middle classes to their lower-class objects of study. For example, in the 1930s Aḥmad Amīn started composing *Qāmūs al-ʿĀdāt waʾl-Taqālīd waʾl-Taʿābīr al-Miṣrīyah* (The dictionary of Egyptian traditions, habits, and expressions). In familiar fashion, the dictionary mapped days of the week regarded as times of good or bad omens, inhabited by a variety of supernatural beings.[75] It even specified which spirits dominated each hour of the day, a fact determining whether the time was favorable or ill fated.[76] By this time, such studies in Egyptian folklore revealed the effendi admiration for the peasant, who was now imagined to be a living archive of pure Egyptian traits. The middle class had an increasingly paradoxical attitude to the peasants, whom they saw both as markers of authenticity and objects of reform.[77]

Even if we take Mubārak at his word in *ʿAlam al-Dīn* about consciously striking a balance between the harmful and superstitious dimensions of mawlids and their economic benefits, it still remains to be discovered exactly *how* such a difficult balancing act, embodied in Mubārak's split personality as educator and railway director, was handled. Examining this question reveals how members of the effendiyya negotiated their double roles as reformers and proprietors vis-à-vis the peasantry, the very tension we saw at once divide and unify the train passengers in "Fī al-Qiṭār." It also sheds light on several intimate protocols of middle-class subject formation and upkeep.

A time-tested point of departure for examining how technology underpinned the emergence of middle-class rationality is the notion of disenchantment, which Max Weber developed around the time that Muḥammad Taymūr wrote "Fī al-Qiṭār." In his famous 1918 essay, "Science as a Vocation," Weber claimed that "a savage" knows incomparably more about his tools than, for example, a modern streetcar passenger does about the technology that enables his movement. However, if he so desires (and unlike the primitive), the modern can come to understand the scientific basis of the conditions of his life. This ability to explain anything by resorting to techno-science creates the conditions of impossibility for metaphysical and spiritual theories of action, thereby disenchanting the modern world.[78]

Weber's presupposition that technical knowledge is equally accessible to all moderns is undermined by the history of differential access to education in Egypt, and the disenchantment thesis has also engendered other potent critiques.[79] But the automatic association of techno-science with disenchantment, secularism, and rationality withstood, and still resists, much evidence to the contrary. The technological determinism underlying the disenchantment thesis was itself a historical force. Like Weber, many Egyptians in the last decades of the nineteenth and first decades of the twentieth centuries were convinced that a rational scientific disposition could indeed dispel the supernatural. Therefore, rather than simply trying to decenter a Eurocentric history of technology, my interest here is in accounting for the resilience and afterlife of such explanations.

We may begin by rejoining ʿAlī Mubārak, an Egyptian who was certainly not deprived of technical education,[80] on his semifictional railway journey in *ʿAlam al-Dīn*. The text includes an emblematic moment of disenchantment, when a train passenger actually requests a technical explanation of the technology that carries him. This happens during ʿAlam al-Dīn's first railway journey. The experience initially causes him pangs of fear, but he relaxes when he realizes that the other passengers are unruffled. The Englishman acts on his ethnographer's impulses and asks the sheikh to describe his experience of this first ride. The sheikh complies:

> I am thinking about the steam engine that carries these carriages and reflecting on its extraordinary motion and on the amazing speed that made some deluded members of the lower classes say that it is moved by the power of a group of jinn and devils bound to [the train] by magic, invocations, and talismans, and that sort of stuff, a belief attributable to the strangeness of [locomotion] and to their ignorance. I know that [the train] moves with the force of fire whose sordid smoke I can see in the air. I also saw a man igniting it when we boarded . . . but I don't know exactly how it is used in this steam engine . . . and I wanted to ask you about it.[81]

In response, the Englishman provides a lengthy explanation of the principles of steam locomotion, demonstrating how disenchantment may offer an opportunity to rehearse colonialism's power/knowledge hierarchies. But I am more interested in the protocol employed by the novel in the sheikh's plea for a technical explanation. Mubārak's mouthpiece evokes and then dismisses a preexisting popular theory of action that explains locomotion with the agency of what would gradually become "supernatural." This modus operandi of calling the jinn to mind, associating them with the lower classes, and then scientifically conjuring them away, framed many subsequent effendi discursive rituals of disenchantment. Delving below this protocol of vociferously eschewing and unlearning preexisting metaphysics, I suggest that it entailed, ironically, the production of more discourse around the exorcized entities, retroactively enchanting them. It was a conjuring away that ended by conjuring up.

Beyond the train, various other modern technologies offered repeated opportunities for such effendi deus ex machina rituals. The following discussion relates several instances, often occurring in first encounters. It is noteworthy that such discursive protocols were most likely a response to Western anticipations of Oriental technophobia. For example, in 1880, Bell's emissary to Egypt contemplated how best to introduce the telephone into a country of pious Muslims who would surely regard the phone as a "device of the devil."[82] Technical explanation was directly geared toward dispelling superstitions, a protocol that members of the effendiyya later reproduced.[83]

On the first day of August 1896, people took to the streets to view the electric tram enter Cairo. Reports in the daily newspapers as well as later accounts of the streetcar's first test drive focused on an incident involving a group of children hanging on to the vehicle's back fender screaming, "The *ʿifrīt!* The *ʿifrīt!*"—an incident that could then be contrasted to how the tram "really" worked.[84] Shortly after the festivities, a new popular tramway engineering book framed its intervention as providing "all the information one needs to understand everything one sees and hears about the tram . . . in order to remove the pervasive misconceptions and delusions [*ḍalālāt,* or derailments from the righteous path]."[85]

Steam engines of hydraulic pumps in wells or agricultural machines were likewise potentially haunted apparatuses. According to Blackman's 1927 account:

> Within a year [of an engine's installment] three people were killed by the irrigation machinery belonging to the *ʿomdeh* of the village. . . . This *ʿomdeh* had made no sacrifice before using the engine, so a number of the villagers went to him and demanded that he should kill an ox on the spot. This he did . . . and some of the blood of the animal was sprinkled on the engine. Apparently this has appeased the *ʿafarit,* for I have heard of no accidents since the sacrifice was made![86]

Clocks were no exception. In another account from the late 1920s, an effendi lawyer described a simple-minded neighbor who accused him of causing the death of his child after he overheard the effendi complain that his watch was broken and its pieces scattered. The watch's "hands" (in Arabic, *ʿaqārib,* "scorpions") were understood by the neighbor to represent real scorpions that must have stung his son.[87] Finally, the inaugural lecture of the Egyptian broadcasting service in June 1934 was entitled, "The Radio as It Was Perceived by a Bedouin from the Desert." The lecture narrated at length the reaction of a bedouin sheikh to the radio. It described the sheikh's great fear of the device, which he perceived as a statue or wooden skull in which an *ʿifrīt* was imprisoned. This superstitious attitude afforded a foil for a rational middle-class explanation of the technological operation of the device.[88]

Even without a direct or unmediated way of gauging peasants' views of technology, we may probably assume that they indeed evoked jinn and *ʿafārīt,* as middle-class writers repeatedly insisted. But beyond whatever the masses may have thought about technology and its animating forces, for members of the effendiyya, modern devices offered a crucial opportunity to summon both the supernatural and the peasantry as foils for technical and middle-class theories of action. It was an overt disbelief in jinn and *ʿafārīt,* rather than agnosticism, that was the hallmark of the effendi. And thus, instead of doing away with unmodern vocabularies, effendis ended up proliferating them, just as trains did for mawlids.

For their part, jinn and *ʿafārīt* did not remain unscathed. Though effectively exorcizing them once and for all proved impossible, they were deontologized and could no longer be fully included in the inventory of being. They became "supernatural"—real (for peasants, and in many respects also for effendis), but not true.

POSTMORTEM

In January 1916 the disfigured body of a young Upper Egyptian peasant woman was found under the train on the Cairo–Luxor line. Investigators were puzzled to find her blindfolded, in circumstances suggesting that she herself had tied a red handkerchief over her eyes. It seemed that the girl did this while waiting between the tracks for the train that eventually ran over her.[89] The following paragraphs pick up the investigation where the perplexed Egyptian coroners left it. A first clue is provided in one of the first ethnographies of Upper Egypt, *The Fellahin of Upper Egypt* (1927):

> Sometimes if a woman has no children her friends will take her to the railway to make her lie down between the lines in order that the train may pass over her. One reason given me for this somewhat dangerous procedure is that the fear which the woman experiences assists conception, for it is said to cause the blood to circulate quickly through the body, making the womb expand, with the result that she will more easily conceive. Another explanation given me for this rite was that when the mother is thus frightened her *karineh [qarīnah]* comes to her with the soul of one of her dead children and causes it to re-enter its mother's body.[90]

Let us attend to how the *qarīnah,* the familiar or soul's twin in the parallel spirit world, operated vis-à-vis modern technology. First, an explanation of the relation of the *qarīnah* to fear is in order. In another section of the monograph, the author, Winifred Blackman, notes that the peasants believed that fear of *ʿafārīt* was sure to summon them.[91] In *Zaynab,* a pioneering 1913 novel, this understanding was even presented to the effendi protagonist as a rural belief: "As the saying goes—afarit appear to those who fear them."[92]

Indeed, in many cases, the agency of the *ʿafārīt* depended on the responsiveness of their human interlocutors, as was the case with "the 'calling spirit' who calls a man by his name. If he answers her call she takes him and throws him down an abandoned well."[93]

If the physiological and "superstitious" explanations for the efficacy of fear in conjuring *ʿafārīt* strike us as mutually exclusive, there are various indications that they actually worked in conjunction. Such cooperation was described by Sayyid Quṭb in his account of the death of his baby brother in the 1910s: "The newborn gasped for his last breath. Tetanus had overcome him due to the nonsterile knife used by the midwife on the umbilical cord. The tetanus microbe clung to it, infecting the wound. There it remained for the duration of its incubation period, which ranges between four to six days. With that, the *qarīnah* had accomplished her mission, venting her fury at the beautiful baby boy."[94]

This affinity between microbes and spirits, and more generally an analogy between agents of modern and traditional theories of action, resonated with the interpretations of two key Islamic modernizers of the time, exposing a common ground between lower-class "superstitions" and middle-class agendas of religious reform. Sayyid Quṭb was himself inspired by the attempts of religious scholar Muḥammad ʿAbduh (1849–1905) and Syro-Egyptian thinker Muḥammad Rashīd Riḍā (1865–1935) to harmonize Islamic orthodoxy and modern science.

In *Tafsīr al-Manār,* his famous interpretation of the Qurʾān, ʿAbduh attempted to curtail the supernatural by suggesting that the jinn mentioned in the holy book were what science labeled microbes.[95] Riḍā, ʿAbduh's disciple and interlocutor and the person to whom much of the *Tafsīr* should really be attributed, similarly combated superstition, just as the railway was paving new inroads for grave visitation and mawlids. The numerous *fatwās* he dedicated to this issue reveal its centrality as an object of popular concern, as well as Riḍā's deeply felt despair at the spread of superstition and its uncanny ability to feed off the very means deployed to exterminate it. This campaign was informed by the fact that Islamic orthodoxy and modern techno-science—the two intellectual spheres Riḍā strove to harmonize—both afforded ample room for the supernatural.

Riḍā's task seemed relatively unproblematic when addressing questions about supernatural entities that were not mentioned in the Qurʾān, particularly those concerning *awliyāʾ* (sing. *walī,* "friend of God" or "saint"). For example, in 1904 an effendi from Zagazig solicited Riḍā's opinion concerning reports in *Al-Liwāʾ*, a newspaper associated with the Nationalist Party, about a man visited in his sleep by a *walī*. In a dream, the *walī* asked the man to find his grave and relocate his corpse. When the dreamer awoke and visited the place, he found an intact body draped with clean garments. Even the beard of the deceased was still black.

Riḍā's response exemplified several typical analytical maneuvers. He began by drawing attention to the fact that visions and dreams were shaky foundations for knowledge. The belief in the survival of the body of *awliyāʾ* was likewise un-Islamic and unfounded. Even newspapers, "whose duty is to combat delusion, in Egypt have a misguiding effect on the people."[96] Riḍā then proceeded to demonstrate that reports of rising from the grave were always fraudulent. To make the point, he evoked and analyzed additional superstitious narratives, addressing the evocative power of fear, such as the case of a man smearing his face with a phosphorous substance to scare a group of unwelcome refugees away from his mosque. The refugees, whose minds "were full of *awliyāʾ* rising from their graves surrounded by light," fell for the trick and fled in terror. Then he mentioned another story, this one about an effendi walking past a cemetery and suddenly noticing a shiny-eyed figure emerging from one of the graves. Only when the terrifying figure neared the fear-stricken man did he realize that it was merely a dog.

The *fatwā* genre was predominantly predicated on analogy *(qiyās)*. Seeking to apply the existing rules to a new situation, the mufti examined other instances covered by the *sharīʿah* and inferred from them a general rule that could be applied to the new case. In the present situation, Riḍā sought to distill the basic procedure for producing a superstitious disposition so that it could then be applied to the *Al-Liwāʾ* story. The effendi approached by the dog was an example of a man whose "imagination was occupied by superstitions, and when he saw something extraordinary and shining rising from the ground, he did not doubt that it was a manifestation of the stories he had heard from the uninformed. The man's imagination took over his senses and he became one of the deluded."[97] Knowing the truth, Riḍā concludes despondently, will not prevent people from believing similar stories. People will change only when the fountain of superstitions has evaporated from their imaginations, and the grip of delusion is removed from their hearts: "Then the ignorant would be able to make the analogy *[yaqīs]* from what he doesn't know to what he knows, like the sentient man."[98]

The *fatwā* suggested that superstitions disrupted rational analogy, the very analytical principle *fatwās* themselves were predicated on (which is why *fatwās* seemed ineffectual against them). Superstition percolated through circuits of perception and seeped into the process of seeing. Rather than involving a correct perception that subsequently acquires a mistaken interpretation in the superstitious mind, according to Riḍā, superstition was a filter situated amid the senses, inflecting sensory perception itself. Input moves from the eye through the superstitious imagination, thus reaching the mind already deformed.

Riḍā's textual strategies for addressing superstition had an unintended effect. Trying to present sufficient evidence from which an analogy could be drawn for a particular case, Riḍā ended up increasing the number of superstitious narratives in circulation. Like ʿAlam al-Dīn, Riḍā based his analysis on summoning, then dismissing, competing theories of action, a conjuring away that involved conjuring up. Not unlike the newspapers he critiqued, Riḍā's mass-mediated *fatwās* played a role in reintroducing the supernatural into the public sphere.[99]

Riḍā's theory of superstition relied on an up-to-date understanding of perception. We saw in chapter 1 that during the nineteenth century, naïve realism was annihilated, as the eye was reconceived as part of the field of vision. European railway travelers in Egypt experienced this crisis as an impossibility of shaking off previously encountered images and narratives when viewing modern Egypt, leading to complaints about how "the imagination always prompts the eye." This modern understanding of vision also informed Riḍā's theories of superstitious perception.

Riḍā admired the popular scientific journal *Al-Muqtaṭaf*,[100] which showcased in Arabic contemporary European works on image retention. Another likely conduit for the percolation of this theory of vision into Riḍā's thinking was the work of Onofrio Abbate Pasha, a collection of whose writings over the previous half century had been published in Cairo in 1909.[101] An ophthalmologist and founding figure of Orientalist ethnography in Egypt, Abbate extended Lane's work on Egyptian superstition and divination, grounding it in the natural sciences. For example, after Lane failed to rationally decipher the "magic square" technique used to summon the dead, Abbate anchored Lane's description of the ritual in experimental research on hypnotism, nerve theory, and hallucinations. Divination and other superstitions could now be explained with the theory of retinal image retention and a new understanding of the persistence of old impressions that could be retriggered by certain colors or suggestive techniques. Abbate's attempt to ground the supernatural in science is echoed in Riḍā's similar endeavor, which explains his stress on considerations of visuality such as shape, color, and illumination. In the process, "superstition" acquired a new and solid ontological basis. As we have seen for jinn and *ʿafārīt,* superstition itself could be seen as "real," as having actual affects without being "true."

Yet another important source for Riḍā's attempt to address superstitions using the antidote of modern science was Muḥammad Farīd Wajdī's 1901 book, *Al-Madanīyah waʾl-Islām* (Civilization and Islam).[102] According to Wajdī, mental health is analogous to physical health in that both depend on avoiding pollutants: germs and microbes in the latter case, delusions *(awhām)* and superstitions *(khurāfāt)* in the former. Superstition leads to ailments of the soul, such as cowardice, which are equivalent to bodily diseases and are cured just as one rids oneself of microbes—by resorting to empirical science.[103]

But not everything metaphysical could be dismissed as superstition. Another *fatwā* by Riḍā, prompted by an inquiry about the existence of jinn and devils, in particular the *qarīnah,* is a case in point.[104] If in the above *fatwā* Riḍā disproved popular superstition, here he used a question about whether every human was born with a *qarīnah* to argue for the insufficiency of positivism: "If we rejected everything we cannot see or perceive with the senses, we wouldn't have been propelled to discover great mysteries such as electricity, whose effects we can sense and which has been attributed to the jinn."[105] Rather than promoting the vision of a world previously believed to be haunted by jinn and now understood scientifically, Riḍā makes clear that the discovery of forces such as electricity would not have been possible without exceeding the empirical or without receptivity and attunement to the supernatural. The natural and supernatural are mutually constitutive.

In yet another *fatwā* concerning the existence of the jinn, Riḍā claimed that "we regard as a type of jinn these tiny beings that cannot be seen without a microscope, and the expression '*janna*' [to hide, conceal] supports it. The *hadīth* according to which the plague is caused by the sting of the jinn offers further support."[106] As with electricity, venturing with a microscope beyond the immediately perceivable is what ties modern science to the world of jinn. And if receptiveness to what is beyond the empirical helped break new ground in the sciences, modern science in turn sustained the supernatural, helping to separate real jinn from spurious ones: "If we were told before the discovery of microbes that tuberculosis and the plague and other maladies are caused by small physical entities capable of quick reproduction inside the body, we would have regarded this claim as superstitious or imaginary."[107]

Of course, splitting legitimate from illegitimate metaphysics was a thorny project. If Riḍā used electricity to support the existence of a supernatural sphere previously attributed to the jinn, electricity also destabilized the boundary between life and death, the very border that Islamic reformers tried to prevent *awliyā'* from crossing. Indeed, temporal linearity itself—the stable sequence of past, present, and future—was on the line. Descriptions of the use of the electric chair in the United States appeared in Egyptian newspapers and contributed to an association of electricity with death.[108] But if an electric shock could end life, other experiments, which were also widely cited, suggested that it could also reverse aging and even revive the dead.[109] This was another junction where science bolstered religious ideas about resurrection, which was a primary concern for Riḍā and ʿAbduh, who frequently engaged in scientific interpretation of the Qur'anic notions of *ḥashr* and *qiyāmah* (resurrection).[110]

MACHINA EX DEUS

Popular periodicals other than Rashīd Riḍā's also regularly provided scientific evidence for the existence and efficacy of the supernatural, jinn, and magic. Such periodicals included *Al-Hayāt* (Life), edited by Wajdī and published between 1899 and 1914, and *Ṭawāliʿ al-Mulūk* (Horoscopes of kings), an "Astrological . . . , Spiritualist, Scientific . . . Journal"[111] printed between 1906 and 1914. *Ṭawāliʿ al-Mulūk* used the sciences of spiritualism and (electromagnetic) hypnotism *(tanwīm maghnaṭīsī)* to "publish news and current affairs before they take place," engage in dream interpretation, and design charts of bad-omen days, in addition to providing sober evaluations of the effect of electrical light on the respiratory system.[112] Spiritualism and hypnotism were so popular in Egypt of the first two decades of the twentieth century that the literary-scientific magazine *Al-Mufīd* correctly observed, in a series of articles titled "Spiritualism: The Natural and Supernatural": "One hardly flips through a periodical these days without coming across what is called in European languages 'Spiritism' or the science of spirits, or hypnotism, mind reading, and the study of the supernatural, as well as discussions of the effect of the living on each other, and that of the dead on the living, the truth of dreams, and the appearance of ghosts and imaginary beings which bring to mind the stories of old times and claims about seeing jinn and devils."[113]

The rather late emergence of spiritualism in Egypt was part of a global trend engulfing Victorian England and several of its colonies, which from the mid-nineteenth century developed a keen interest in things supernatural.[114] While spiritualism can be seen as a symptom of a dissatisfaction with nineteenth-century science and industry, it also intimately mirrored and mimicked its era's materialist language and modes of thought. Conjuring up this "machine in the ghost,"[115] Steven Connor demonstrated the entanglement of the séance with midcentury telegraphy and then telephony: communication with the dead was carried out first by a system of alphabetic knocks; spirits then began to communicate in Morse code, with a deceased telegraph operator facilitating the connection from the other side.[116]

Egyptian ghosts, at least the more conservative *awliyāʾ*, were less inclined to embrace technological innovations. In his 1903 critique of the *Zār,* the trance-inducing ritual of spirit possession, Muḥammad Ḥilmī Zayn al-Dīn claimed that practitioners had reported to him that the saints and *ʿafārīt* even felt slighted by the fact that some of their former clients sought the aid of modern doctors.[117] But despite their proclaimed technophobia, *awliyāʾ* and *ʿafārīt* too have been animated by modern technologies. Metropolitan spiritualism scientifically legitimized colonial categories of the "supernatural." And as with Victorian spiritualism, the proliferation of encounters with jinn, *ʿafārīt,* and *awliyāʾ* mirrored modern technology, while at the same time functioning as its traditional "other."

PATHOLOGICAL ANSWERS TO QUESTIONS OF LIFE AND DEATH

We have repeatedly seen how modern apparatuses and techniques that widened the gap between life and death, the natural and supernatural, orthodox and folk religion, linear temporality and eschatology, often also had the opposite effect of narrowing and blurring these divides. Another indication of the slippage between disenchantment and re-enchantment, or empty and spectral temporalities, can be provided by the modern science par excellence of determining death—that is, pathology, especially the practices of dissection and autopsy.

To be sure, in several important respects the gap between life and death seems to have widened during the nineteenth century and the boundaries between being and unbeing solidified. As Khaled Fahmy has shown, scientific notions such as the miasmic theory and related notions of hygiene and city planning led to relocating slaughterhouses and cemeteries to the outskirts of Egyptian urban centers.[118] In some cases, graves inside residential areas or houses were sealed with cement,[119] as were water sources feared to be polluted by grave soil.[120] Cadaver dissection, introduced into Egypt by Clot Bey as part of the creation of modern medicine, associated these processes with medical practice.[121] In a familiar narrative of modernity, death was exorcized from everyday life.

But dissections had another, more disturbing dimension that created the opposite effect. Performed on exhumed bodies to reveal the cause and time of death, these operations often disclosed that people had been buried alive and died while in the grave. In 1870, as the result of an increase in such mishaps, a decree was issued to the effect that interment required a waiting period of eight hours during the summer or ten hours during the winter and a death certificate signed by a doctor.[122] In the 1860s and 1870s, as a result of dissections, being buried alive was becoming one of people's major fears in Europe and the United States, inspiring a flurry of journalistic descriptions.[123] Communities that practiced early interment, including European Jews and the Irish, obsessed about being especially exposed to this risk.[124] In Egypt, similarly, the newly required waiting period contradicted the Islamic imperative to bury promptly.[125]

In 1910 Rashīd Riḍā was asked to comment on this tension.[126] He replied that the *shar'ī* requirement to expedite burial only applied when death had been ascertained *(ba'd taḥaqquq al-mawt)*. However, if there was doubt about the fact of death *(irtiyāb fī al-mawt)*, the *sharī'ah* required postponing the funeral. Medical examination, even when performed by a male doctor on a female corpse, was necessary "so that she doesn't lose consciousness, get buried, and come back to her senses only to die the most horrible death, as is often the case."[127] In other words, medical examination was the only way to remove doubts about the fact of death. Riḍā's position was that because the time or fact of death could only be determined in retrospect, every death was subject to doubt until examination. Ascertaining the exact time of death, through medical examination or autopsy, opened up a limbo, a waiting period in which death could not be declared.

This new pathological limbo could be mapped onto a preexisting interregnum, *al-barzakh,* the Islamic eschaton or intermediate state between life in this world and the hereafter.[128] Conceptually, the *barzakh* allowed allocating the dead into a different space-time continuum, thereby ensuring their hermetic separation from the world of the living.[129] During the two decades around the turn of the century, Egypt saw a resurrected interest in the *barzakh*. Al-Suyūṭī's famous medieval eschatological manual, abridged as *Kitāb al-Barzakh* (The book of the *barzakh*), was printed in Cairo in 1892, then reprinted in 1900, and again in 1911.[130] While in theory the *barzakh* was populated only by souls, al-Suyūṭī's text painted the picture of an active underground community of lively corpses. These dead men and women sometimes paid visits, in dreams and also in the flesh, to living people.[131] In the early twentieth century, this spectral itinerancy reached such proportions that Riḍā bitterly complained about Egyptian daily newspapers being full of such stories.[132]

The *barzakh* manual helps shed light on some eerie affinities between the techno-scientific and Islamic thanatologies, and how they informed Riḍā's *fatwā* supporting autopsies. Thus, the mention of a male doctor examining a female corpse would not only disturb the norms of the living but also have disconcerting ramifications in the context of the afterlife. Indeed, al-Suyūṭī recounts twenty-two narratives indicating that "the dead man knows who washes him and prepares him [for burial] and what is said of him during the funeral,"[133] which is why in the Islamic tradition corpses retained the right to conceal their private parts.[134] Riḍā's stress on the horrible death of those buried alive likewise resonated with the motif of the "torments of the grave" that sinners suffer in a narrow and dark hole in the ground, as opposed to believers, for whom the grave widens.[135] Even the manual's longer title, *The Explication* (literally, "opening and widening of chests") *on the Explanation* (literally, "dissection") *of the Issue of the Dead and Graves,* twice deploying the root *sha. ra. ha.* (to dissect, explain, operate on a body or cadaver), fused the operations of theological analysis and modern pathology.

Moreover, the new limbo probably lasted eight or ten hours only in theory. The introduction of cadaver dissection was part of the bureaucratization of death over the course of the nineteenth century, and state regulation made it quite complicated to die. In the early 1850s, news of death in the countryside required dispatching the local barber or midwife to conduct an external examination, which sometimes required another examination by the provincial doctor.[136] During the early 1860s if not earlier, harsh punishments were meted out to those rushing to bury.[137] A village barber explained to the prosecutor protagonist of *Yawmīyāt Nā'ib fī al-Aryāf* why he buried bodies without the required signature of a doctor on a postmortem exanimation certificate: "Sir, if we had to wait till we had examined every dead body, it would be time for us to die ourselves."[138] In the 1934 play *Al-Zammār,* Tawfīq al-Ḥakīm described the routines of a countryside infirmary packed with relatives of a deceased woman waiting endlessly for an absent doctor to release her corpse for burial. The hauntological phase seemed to drag on and on, not only in religious grave visitations but in quotidian deaths as well.

Rashīd Riḍā and Muḥammad ʿAbduh played leading roles in the *salafīyah,* a nineteenth-century Islamic reform movement influenced by the writings of the thirteenth-century Ḥanbalī scholar Taqī al-Dīn ibn Taymīyah, who reacted against saint worship and Sufism, which he saw as late and inauthentic additions to Islam, by trying to revive the pure Islam practiced by the Prophet and the early Muslims *(al-salaf).* If such a retrospective "fundamentalist" outlook seems at odds with a modern science understood to be progressive and forward looking, we have seen how, on the contrary, ʿAbduh and Riḍā's encounter with the science of their day served as a platform for legitimating and articulating their own revivalist project.

During the late nineteenth and early twentieth century, "foundamentalism," revival, renaissance, awakening, and resurrection *(salafīyah, nahḍah, baʿth,* and more recently the notion of *al-ṣaḥwah al-Islāmīyah)* formed a new political vocabulary based on nonlinear conceptions of time, with which anticolonialism and nationalism were negotiated. Modern medicine, pathology, hypnotism, and electromagnetic theory were key sources of inspiration for this lexicon, along with the new discipline of ethnography, devoted to locating living remnants of the past in the present.[139] Modern science was an indispensable context for the Egyptian modernity captured in the title of Muḥammad ʿUmar's *The Present of Egyptians or the Secret of their Delay,* wherein present and delay could be interchangeable markers, hinging on both sides of an *or.*

At the turn of the century, one of the most piercing critiques of the legal, political, and social institutions of the colonial state was launched by a fictive pasha who rose from the grave, summoned by the fear of a cemetery visitor. The ease with which the past could haunt the present in *Ḥadīth ʿĪsā Ibn Hishām (A Period of Time)*[140] was a modern phenomenon. Indeed, resurrection was dealt with simultaneously on the scientific, ethical, political, and historical levels. In the years before and immediately after the publication of *A Period of Time* (initially serialized in a newspaper, then published in book form in 1907), a spell of techno-political articles addressed issues such as "Indolence Is the Essence of Death"[141] or "Are We Alive or Dead?"[142] and raised concerns that

Egyptians were somnolent. An article on *tanwīm maghnaṭīsī* ("hypnotism," literally "magnetic sleep inducement") claimed that the West awoke from a magnetically induced trance and came to oppress Egypt. The writer wondered when Egypt would rise from its indolent slumber. Electromagnetic current accounted for the pull of metals to a magnet, the earth's attraction to other celestial bodies, interpersonal romantic attraction,[143] and the different flows inside the human body and mind.[144] And as the above articles suggest, it also informed political tensions in the colonial system.

TWILIGHT ZONES, TWILIGHT TIMES

I wish now to harness these insights to answer the question posed at the beginning of this chapter, about the connection between the temporal linearity of the train and its second-class passengers and the assumedly cyclical times of its present-absentee third-class travelers. To that end, I invoke *'Alam al-Dīn* once more, this time to frame the book itself as a disenchanting device. Thus far, I have situated the work as an early precursor to effendi ethnography. The emblematic dis/enchantment of specters in this pioneering textual railway journey may be further elucidated by pulling out a particular strand of the book's ethnographic subgenre, which we will call "evening entertainment literature."

Even before going to France in 1844, Mubārak presumably came across the 1817 book *Evening Entertainment; or, Delineations of the Manners and Customs of Various Nations* by the French scholar Georges Bernhard Depping, a work that was regularly assigned in the Egyptian school in Paris, and whose 1833 Arabic translation remained a staple textbook in Egyptian schools for the next century.[145] (The translator, Rifā'ah Rāfi' al-Ṭaḥṭāwī, was the inspiration for the character of Sheikh 'Alam al-Dīn.) Written as a series of conversations between a father and children, *Evening Entertainment* used ethnography to educate young readers about how the opposition of indolence and industry organizes instances of cultural difference. "I have often observed," Depping wrote in the preface, "that children . . . prefer travel to fairy tales. . . . I think we act inconsistently in confining the minds of children to barren and abstract sciences, while they are almost total strangers to what is passing around them."[146]

Compare how Mubārak introduced his own decision to construct *'Alam al-Dīn* as a series of paternal conversations punctuating a travel narrative:

"I have observed that the souls of people often prefer stories and anecdotes to pure arts and abstract sciences."[147] In both texts, the ethnographic account was meant to promote leisurely learning. Mubārak's book was even divided into 125 *musāmarāt* (friendly nocturnal conversations), providing further indication that it may be firmly situated in the "evening entertainment" genre meant to replace fairy tales with empirical ethnographic information (often about fairy tales turned into "folklore") in an easy format.

Such reading materials for the evening hours addressed exactly this fascination of the souls of people with stories. If the middle-class concern with popular leisure and afterhours, which we encountered in ʿUmar's 1902 *Ḥāḍir al-Miṣrīyīn,* mainly revolved around productivity and the fatigue-inducing effects of excessive nightlife on the peasantry, effendi anxieties about how they themselves spent the evening went well beyond nonproductivity. At the turn of the century, when the hours of the day were carefully regulated by school, work, and transportation schedules, and even the night began to be structured with sleep quotas and optimal bedtime schedules,[148] the in-between interval of the evening emerged as an ominous limbo. This liminality between wakefulness and sleep (known in Islamic terms as the "little death") was a quotidian *barzakh,* as it were.

As "Tadbīr al-Manzil" advice columns devoted to "rationalized home-making" reveal,[149] evening hours, "from sunset to darkness, when the light weakens and children are unable to study, but it is not dark enough to light the lanterns," were considered a time that mothers should spend with their children, instead of leaving them in the care of lower-class servants who fill their heads with nonsense about jinn and *ʿafārīt.*[150] It was assumed that children grow fearful in these twilight hours and require motherly guidance. The mother therefore has to tell her children that the dark has nothing in it to fear, specifying "that there are no monsters, no demons and nothing of that sort. And she has to firmly establish this in her children's minds and refute anything the servants might have said about these things. She has to repeat this point until it is firmly established in their minds." It was important to deliberately dispel jinn and *ʿafārīt* stories, the article explained, because of the danger that such stories, when implanted in the young mind and left unchecked, would weaken children's tenacity and transform them into delusional adults.[151] From the turn of the twentieth century onward, after-sundown hours—once the hours when jinn roamed the night (as the masses allegedly still believed)[152]—became times when jinn and *ʿafārīt* posed a new danger to effendi children, who were deemed vulnerable to a new kind of possession: the superstitious *fear* of the jinn they might contract from their servants and nannies.

Effendis seem to have been fully aware of the fact that by conjuring away they were also conjuring up. As Wajdī's analogies, Riḍā's *fatwās,* and these advice columns suggest, from fearing *ʿafārīt* they shifted to fearing fear itself. Some members of the effendiyya even deployed this fear of fear for productive ends. For example, confronting fear was one of the main rationales provided in 1899 by the so-called first Egyptian feminist,[153] Qāsim Amīn, for the education of women: "Is it not a mother's ignorance that compels her to bring up her child through fear of jinn and evil spirits? Is it not her ignorance that impels her to hang charms on her child for his protection, and to lead him around graves and shrines of *awliyāʾ?*"[154]

Until the beginning of the twentieth century, fear played an instrumental role in the Islamic tradition as a key device of moral betterment. "Eschatological fear"[155] of God, death, or the hereafter was deployed by Muslims as motivation for a pious life in this world. According to Smith and Haddad, modernist Islamic reformers and theologians downplayed, over the course of the twentieth century, the fear-inducing aspects of eschatology by naturalizing death, for example by comparing it to sleep and thereby domesticating it as part of life's natural cycle.[156] The success of this project is attested by the informants of anthropologist Charles Hirschkind, members of Egypt's Islamist piety movement (a trend appropriately called *al-saḥwah al-Islāmīyah,* the Islamic Awakening) who seek to renew this tradition in the twenty-first century. These preachers frame their endeavors as reintroducing fear into a modern society that has become immune to its ethical lessons.[157]

Yet if exorcizing eschatology and its insights, and banishing the hereafter and its frightening specters, were part of modernization, disenchantment, and secularization, the contours of the secular in Egypt retained a close affinity to the world it replaced. Rather than a generic modernist existential angst, early twentieth-century Egyptians deployed modern anxiety in a particular self-betterment project of their own. And like the belief that fear of *ʿafārīt* actually conjured up specters, the fear of fear was efficacious.[158]

Fear of things invisible was not simply displaced by instrumental reason, as a crude version of Weber's disenchantment thesis would have it,[159] but was replaced by fear of fear itself, a fear of jinn and *ʿafārīt* once removed, an anxiety closely modeled on the fear it sought to replace. Like its antecedent, the object of this new fear was irrational, nonlinear, and incalculable. Thus modern, mechanical temporality associated with middle-class rationality cannot be seen simply as empty, homogeneous time, but as time laboriously emptied and homogenized; it is not a stable state but a constant process of hollowing out and warding off the times that spell its undoing or reversal. This process was facilitated, but also perpetuated ad infinitum, by repeatedly associating superstition with the masses and their temporalities. Bracketing popular time as folklore or culture, and separating such "conceptions of time" from rational, secular, effendi temporality, animated the shifting attitudes to authentic "Egyptian time," ranging from admonition to admiration.

Our examination started with mawlids, understood by members of the effendiyya as representing an invasion of the unmodern into the space and time of modernity. Though analytically the division of modern and unmodern is destabilized when taking into account the role played by the railway in their proliferation, the "time out of time" of mawlids was in fact a key context for the imperative to reaffirm, resurrect, and police the porous boundary lines between modernity and tradition, between rational, linear, middle-class time and cyclical peasant time. Mawlids are an index of this liminality; they are still seen as themselves a *barzakh,* the shadow of a mawlid taking place in the next world, in which the dead saint, the Prophet, and a host of angels participate.[160] These popular festivals offered a unique focal point where the haunted times of *awliyāʾ,* the calendrical indeterminacy of the celebration of the saint's birth or death, the assumed time wastefulness of the carnivalesque gathering, and their connection to new concerns regarding sleep, productivity, resurrection, and dream encounters could be articulated. As such, mawlids were indispensable for effendis trying to establish simplified notions of punctuality, predictability, and productivity.

FOUR

Harmonization and Its Discords

> Once, in [Caliph] ʿUmar's time, when the Month of Fast came round, some people ran to the top of a hill, in order to have the luck of seeing the new moon; and one of them said, "Look, there is the new moon, O ʿUmar!" As ʿUmar did not see the moon in the sky, he said, "This moon has risen from thy imagination. Otherwise, since I am a better observer of the heavens than thou art, how do I not see the pure crescent? Wet thy hand and rub it on thine eyebrow, and then look for the new moon." When the man wetted his eyebrow, he could not see the moon. "O King," said he, "there is no moon; it has disappeared." "Yes," said ʿUmar, "the hair of thine eyebrow became a bow and shot at thee an arrow of false opinion."
>
> JALĀL AL-DĪN RŪMĪ, *"The Man Who Fancied He Saw the New Moon,"*

"THE MAN WHO FANCIED he Saw the New Moon," by the Sufi poet Jalāl al-Dīn al-Rūmī, offers an appropriate springboard for a discussion of the politics of fact setting and the relations between timekeeping and authority. ʿUmar, the caliph who established the Hijrī calendar, has the authority to command the observer to clean his eye, thereby revealing the absence of the moon (or the man's realization that he should be wiser than to claim to spot the moon before the most observant caliph). The opposite could not have been the case: had ʿUmar himself seen a hair rather than the moon, the hair would have become fact, launching the month of Ramadan, as none of his subordinates would have told *him* to clean his eyes. Fact setting, timekeeping included, involves hierarchies of power. When facts are contested, authority is what demarcates the objective world from the subjective one, distinguishing a moon in the sky from a hair in the eye of the beholder.

This chapter also examines a process of enforced correction, in which ʿUmar's lunar calendar was eclipsed by the Gregorian calendar in key spheres of Egyptian life, as the result of a series of shifts over a period of several decades beginning in the 1870s. A new division of labor between these temporal systems resulted in the transformation of the Hijrī calendar—once the primary timekeeping scheme in a comprehensive textual universe—into a mere "religious calendar," in a process that involved a reconfiguration of "religion" itself. Rather than offering a full explanation for this multicausal transformation, after sketching it in the following section, I examine one arena in which this "outdating" took place—the Arabic press—and one technology that helped bring it about: the telegraph.

The chosen sphere—the newly established Arabic press whose history begins in the 1870s after a few earlier stutters[1]—is especially revealing. In practically all preceding arenas of Arabic textual production, the Hijrī calendar was the undisputed organizing principle, ordering a text's internal structure, informing its diachronic position in a tradition or a canon, and defining its synchronic relations with contemporaneous works. The degree to which everyday life followed this lunar calendar was probably quite limited. Yet more practical calendars, such as the Coptic solar one (the main temporal scheme punctuating quotidian life in Egypt), made only unassuming incursions into texts. Like classical Arabic—nobody's mother tongue, yet the only proper medium for approaching written texts—the Hijrī calendar was the lingua franca of Arabic letters[2] until it was dislodged by the Frankish *(ifranjī)* Gregorian calendar. This new solar calendar, unlike the Coptic calendar it formally replaced in 1875, did not shy away from texts. On the contrary, it arrived with an entirely new form of (telegraphic) textuality, the newspaper, which was connected to a global economy and a global communications network that required meeting global synchronization standards. The replacement of the Coptic time of cotton agriculture with the Gregorian time of cotton finance and news had sweeping implications for the Hijrī calendar.[3]

This double-pronged focus on textual and calendric reform allows us to probe technology's role in shaping new "chronotopes"[4]—ways that newly introduced temporal conventions restructured communication and discourse, new modes whereby technology textualized time. Large-scale temporal schemes structure and are structured by quotidian temporalities. We have already seen how the rhythms of Egyptian modernity—experienced as moving swiftly ahead while always remaining one step behind—were associated with colonial standards of punctuality in train schedules. The astronomical time of months and years likewise informed the length of the hour and the point at which the day began.[5] What effects did the adoption of Gregorian time and the technologies that made it possible have on intimate temporal arrangements such as the rhythms of a written sentence? If the Hijrī calendar was the key system for organizing the premodern textual universe, how did this universe respond to the combined calendric and textual transformation brought about by telegraphy?

LUNAR ECLIPSES

The Hijrī calendar is a pure lunar calendar without intercalation, and is thus independent of the seasons. It is determined by observation of the evening sky and therefore unpredictable. Muslims have therefore always relied on solar and quasi-solar calendars for agriculture or taxation.[6] Al-Jabartī's chronicles of the French invasion (1798–1801) and police and court records throughout the nineteenth century contain multiple dating systems side by side.[7] Labor migration from Southern Europe and increasing interference from Western Europe were among the factors making this multiplicity increasingly common and also increasingly contested during the nineteenth century, eventually recasting cultural difference and multiplicity as cultural opposition and dichotomy. In this context, 1870 marks a heuristic beginning for the shift in how these systems were harmonized and the subsequent decline of the Hijrī calendar.

We may begin with the first printed calendar to be widely distributed for private use, printed in the year 1870 by *Maṭbaʿat Wādī al-Nīl,* one of the first semiprivate Arabic printing houses in Cairo. The appearance of the calendar was tied to developments in printing technology in the last third of the nineteenth century, particularly to new possibilities for fitting more words in a line and more lines in a page, which made printed products significantly cheaper and affordable for mass consumption.[8] Printing presses facilitated the concentration of data in legible formats that gradually replaced hand copying.[9]

The first Arabic printing press to be brought into Egypt was carried by Napoleon's army of occupation in 1798. The Orientalists accompanying the troops used it to print pamphlets about the compatibility of the French Revolution and Islam. These printouts revealed, however, the incommensurability of the timekeeping systems used by occupiers and occupied: for instance, the first pamphlet was printed on either the thirteenth[10] or the fifteenth[11] day of the revolutionary month of Messidor, the sixth year of the republic, which al-Jabartī thought occurred "toward the end of the month of Muḥarram [1213 A.H.]"—about ten days off the mark.

The subsequent adoption of the printing press by Egypt's rulers, from Mehmet 'Ali on, offered a prêt-à-porter technological connection between the ideals of the French Revolution and the *Nahḍah*—the literary "awakening" of the second half of the nineteenth century, often understood as a response to European influence. Indeed, throughout the century, the governmental Būlāq Press, founded in 1820, printed hundreds of Arabic translations from European languages, including several almanacs harmonizing the Coptic year with the Hijrī one.[12] Even as far as the press's efficiency and professional standards were concerned, European printing houses were used as the yardstick for quality and speed.[13]

Yet we saw in previous chapters that every technology is always anchored in a particular setting, from which it derives much of its meaning. In its early decades, Arabic print was closely tied to the calligraphic culture it later replaced. *Wādī al-Nīl*'s calendar is a good example of a product tailored for a particular readership and a market dominated by hand-copied texts, such as *Dalāʾil al-Khayrāt,* a popular almanac stipulating prayer times—a best seller of the eighteenth and nineteenth centuries.[14] Indeed, before the middle of the nineteenth century, almanacs including the Hijrī and Coptic calendars seem to have been the most popular paper products after the Qurʾān, circulating in high-quality calligraphy among elites and in low-quality commercial copies among commoners.[15]

Another example of the tension between technology's intended design and its eventual local use is provided by newspapers: in 1867 *Maṭbaʿat Wādī al-Nīl* started printing the pioneering semiprivate, biweekly newspaper *Wādī al-Nīl* (The Nile Valley). The newspaper was subsidized by the Khedive Ismāʿīl, for whom the absence of a private press was a lacuna in Egypt's modernization. It was modeled after European newspapers that proliferated in Alexandria (such as its namesake, *Le Nil,*) which were *Wādī al-Nīl's* main sources of inspiration and news. Like contemporary European periodicals, *Wādī al-Nīl* was serialized and its readers were encouraged to leather-bind the sections together. Such hybridizations helped familiarize the newspaper form to a reading public accustomed to less ephemeral texts.

Yet European influence was again only one part of the story. Just as important was the fact that the biweekly issues of *Wādī al-Nīl* regularly reproduced portions of such landmark Arabic works as Ibn Baṭūṭah's fourteenth-century travel narrative, serialized in 1870 (later that year, *Wādī al-Nīl* sold a printed compilation of the entire book).[16] Whereas in Victorian Britain, Germany, and the United States, serialization was a format for science, politics, and new, often avant-garde literature of varying quality, in Egypt serialization was also used for the "classics." And while this misnomer incorrectly assumes that such books have not been constantly read by modern readers, even though hand-copied versions of texts by Ibn Khaldūn and Ibn Baṭūṭah were never out of vogue, it is possible that printing and serialization themselves transformed these texts into classics.[17]

In 1870 *Wādī al-Nīl* offered a readymade platform for advertising the press's newly printed calendars. As the first ad put it, "*Wādī al-Nīl* printing house launches a meticulous and systematic rendition of calendar time as is the practice in the European countries. It is a presentation of the year 1287 A.H., including a juxtaposition of the correct lunar Arabic months with the Coptic, Frankish, and Roman *[rumi]* months." After indicating the novelty of this temporal device in Egypt, the ad further suggested how to use the calendar (to glue it on two sides of a piece of cardboard or hang it on a wall), and who might benefit from it (bankers and employees of the Egyptian administration). As the ad makes clear, several temporal systems coexisted in Egypt. The Coptic solar year regulated agriculture and taxation, the "Frankish" Gregorian calendar was used in banking and cotton exchange, and the Hijrī calendar was used by the administration and the educated public. Finally, the "*rumi* months" probably referred to the Seleucid calendar or possibly the Julian calendar. Both the Julian and Seleucid calendars served Christian communities in Egypt and the Ottoman lands, while the Julian calendar also had an Ottoman administrative purpose. The new printed calendar promised to help navigate this multiplicity.

However, the calendric harmonization unraveled already in its festive inception. The first ad was published on "Friday, 21 Muḥarram 1287, corresponding *[al-muwāfiq]* to April 19, 1875, the fourth year of the newspaper." Yet if *Wādī al-Nīl* started printing in 1866–1867, the fourth year should be 1870–1871, the year corresponding to 1287 A.H. A computerized date converter indeed reveals that 21 Muḥarram 1287 corresponds to April 22, 1870, rather than to April 19, 1875. Such mismatches appeared frequently on the header of the front page of the newspaper. Notably, it was always the case that an incorrect Gregorian date was coupled with the correct Hijrī one. For example, the calendar was advertised again on a Hijrī date "corresponding to April 45."[18]

Such mismatches in calendar dates reveal the synchronization efforts of a system that was anything but natural. These breakdowns expose the fragility of an ostensibly seamless temporal grid. They stand in sharp contrast to

Johannes Fabian's seminal claim in *Time and the Other* that cultural difference is coeval, or simultaneous.[19] Rather than a natural state of coevalness that in turn gets denied, or the plurality of a multicultural world at the end of a liberal horizon,[20] we see a radical alterity made commensurable only with difficulty and very partial success.

Admittedly, 1287 A.H. was a confusing year for calendar conversion. Consider the Ottoman financial calendar: the *Maliyye* year was a scheme based on the Julian calendar that attempted to keep the counting of tax years in line with the years of the *Hijrah* by omitting one year for every thirty-three. In 1287 the system broke down when the omission scheduled for that year was not implemented for some reason, creating a discrepancy between the *Maliyye* and Hijrī years.[21]

Whereas Egyptian almanacs referenced the Ottoman *Maliyye* year until the First World War,[22] up to 1875 Egypt conducted its financial affairs according to the Coptic calendar. Yet the pressures of debt repayment for European creditors and state bankruptcy after the bursting of a cotton bubble inflated in the 1860s forced the Egyptian government to adopt the Gregorian calendar, severing the time of cash from that of cash cropping and agriculture, which continued to follow the Coptic calendar: "Whereas the ministries' engagements with Europeans are mostly conducted according to the Frankish months while budgets and calculations follow the Coptic months, and even though in both systems the annual number of days is the same, to prevent date disagreement we decree that the government will conduct its financial affairs according to the Frankish months."[23]

In 1876, *Al-Ahrām,* a private Egyptian paper founded by two Syrian-Christian brothers, adopted a dating procedure that employed a Gregorian date as the standard. The Gregorian date appeared on the right side of the page, with the Hijrī date corresponding *(muwāfiq)* to it on the left. (Since Arabic is read from right to left, placing the Gregorian date on the right gives it primacy.) In the mid-1870s, similar shifts in standards also took place in other texts. Consider the autobiography of the champion of timetables, ʿAlī Mubārak, included in *Al-Khiṭaṭ*. Mubārak's narration of his childhood and early government service deployed the Hijrī calendar. Yet when Egypt's debt is first mentioned, in 1876, he suddenly adopts the Gregorian calendar, which he then uses throughout the text.[24] In such shifts, debt provided the particular context for the introduction of the equation of time and money into Egypt. The Gregorian calendar (and the monetized quotidian temporalities associated with it) indexed, and was tainted by, the beginning of an epoch of imperial debt collection and management. Because it was calendrically synchronized with the global economy, Egypt was already behind—on its payments, among other things. Commensurability revealed itself again to be a protocol of differentiation.

What I call "the time of money" has a particular history: according to Jacques Le Goff, the rise of commercial capitalism in medieval Europe involved a transformation in the telling of the hour, from the unequal hours of the monastic day to the precision of the clock, a shift from "church time" to "merchant time."[25] The Hijrī calendar, by contrast, was connected to a different system of quotidian timekeeping. Because the Hijrī month begins with a moon sighting in the evening sky, the "Arabic day" starts at sunset, as opposed to the "Frankish day," which was believed to start at high noon.[26] Thus, for Egyptians the twelve-hour day was divided into "evening" and "morning" rather than A.M. and P.M., as was the case in train schedules, also introduced in 1870 and printed in *Wādī al-Nīl*.[27] Because the sun sets and rises at different times according to the season, the length of every hour during the "Arabic day" varied seasonally. Watches and clocks had to be reset daily.[28] By contrast, the "Frankish day" occurred without variation and was divided into twelve even hours.[29]

Such differences in timekeeping systems were repeatedly discussed in new scientific journals that were published from the mid-1870s, such as *Al-Muqtaṭaf* (1876) and *Al-Hilāl* (appearing in 1892). Not infrequently, the readers raising the issue in question-and-answer columns were employees of the Egyptian administration or the ESR.[30] The logics of train schedules and debt management required a stable time-to-money conversion rate and seemed to favor the Frankish day and Gregorian year.

The Gregorian calendar was gradually yet firmly established in Egypt, and dating errors in the press slowly became more common in Hijrī dates and less so for Gregorian ones. Disagreements over the determination of the lunar month acquired a new visibility. The journal *Al-Siḥāfah,* for example, apologized on January 6, 1905: "Whereas the previous edition carried the date Friday, the first day of Dhu al-Qaʿdah, it was in fact 30 Shawwāl, even though some astronomers say the former date is correct." The periodical requested readers to stop alerting its editors about such mishaps—a request suggesting that more than a few of these complaints had been filed.

By 1916, young ʿAbd al-Razzāq al-Sanhūrī, the future Egyptian legal reformer, wondered just before leaving to study in France why he should remember the Islamic date of his birthday. In a diary entry from August 14, he writes about the day before yesterday, his twenty-second birthday: "I don't know why I do not know my birthday according to the Arabic calendar. Why does it matter to me if I knew I was born in Rajab or Shawwāl or Dhu al-Hijjah as long as I know I was born on August 12, 1895 A.D. *(Mīlādī)*. . . . Why should I want my birthday to be Arabic? I want to strengthen my will power; will I succeed?"[31]

Al-Sanhūrī belonged to a generation of effendis born in the 1880s and 1890s (after the mid-1870s calendar shift), whose fathers were the first to document the birth dates of their children according to the Gregorian calendar or with both the Gregorian and Hijrī calendars.[32] Al-Sanhūrī was not questioning the importance of having "a birthday" per se, or of knowing the exact moment of his birth. The celebration of the birthday, a personal nativity scene, became popular in Egypt during the first decades of the twentieth century.[33] Premodern Islamic scholars sometimes also recorded their birth year, and less frequently also the month and day, but they did so in Hijrī time and for reasons to do with the need to situate a *ḥadīth* transmitter in time and place. For members of the effendiyya, knowing one's exact age distinguished oneself from the lower classes and provided an apt response to British assumptions about Egyptian attitudes to time. "Few uneducated Egyptians," wrote Cromer, "know their own age. The usual reply of an Egyptian, if asked the age of some old man, is that he is a hundred years old."[34] Birth dates were class markers wedded to colonial renditions of the trope of Oriental time mindlessness.

The practice of recording births started in parish churches, which registered candidates for baptism, thereby signifying "the appearance of Christian souls in new corporeal forms." In the nineteenth century, compulsory registration of births became the practice by which an infant was included in citizenship in many places in Western Europe.[35] The secular registration of births was distinctly post-Christian. Indeed, the Gregorian calendar became post-Christian in a context whose significance outshines the mere fact that this calendar bore the name of Pope Gregory XIII: its eventual adoption even by Protestants forged an interconfessional unity predicated on separating social harmony from religion. The calendar united European Christendom while simultaneously secularizing it. In Egypt this calendar had a similar secularizing effect, splitting "the social," which it now organized, from "the religious," which was relegated to the Hijrī calendar.

The calendric shifts in Egyptian newspapers and in the writings of figures such as Mubārak and al-Sanhūrī offer scattered signposts of a standard shift whose telos is familiar: the hegemony of Arabic dates as points of reference was undermined and eventually overridden. As Abdelfattah Kilito sardonically put it, "Arabic literature is subject to a double chronology. At first, and for a long time, it was tied to the Islamic calendar, then one day, without warning, it moved to the Christian calendar! One day, after seven centuries of recumbency, it leaped up suddenly and gracefully over six centuries, and found itself in the middle of the nineteenth century."[36]

Like Kilito, I am concerned here less with trying to date this outdating—an incomplete and messy process that happened differently in different spheres—than with tracing some of its mechanisms, implications, and contexts. According to Talal Asad, the emergence of secularism in Egypt involved relegating a new object—"religion"—to the private sphere.[37] Asad's analysis of family law reform during the last third of the nineteenth century may be complemented by stressing the colonial origins of the notion that Islam, like European Christianity, had two dimensions: a benign "religion" and a "social system" in serious need of reform.[38] This may be a key context for (and one of the outcomes of) a new division of labor between the Gregorian and Hijrī systems, wherein the latter's role shrank to regulating religious festivals and holidays.

Along these lines, even in the limited sphere of "religion," the Hijrī calendar did not remain intact. Consider the practices of Ramadan moon sighting with which this chapter opened. In 1903, Rashīd Riḍā issued two *fatwās* that indicate how these protocols had changed. The first came in response to a question about varying moon sightings before Ramadan and the resulting differences in the start of fasting. The inquirer asked whether, to avoid such discrepancies, it was permissible to replace actual sightings with printed calendars. Riḍā replied that temporal incongruity among communities located in relative proximity can only be explained by false sightings. But printed lunar calendars cannot solve the problem because they disagree on the beginning of the lunar months. Riḍā's solution was to adopt the time dictated by the authorities in the capital.[39]

What needed no mention in this early twentieth-century *fatwā*, though it vitally conditioned it, was that since the early 1870s, in tandem with the new train schedules, Cairo time had been disseminated telegraphically to the Egyptian provinces. This allowed Riḍā to assume in 1903 that a moon sighting in the capital could instantly initiate the month of Ramadan even in the remotest corner of Egypt. This was by and large a safe assumption. But already in 1873, a belated telegram from Cairo about the sighting of the

Ramadan crescent caused the Muslims of Port Said to miss the first day of the fast.[40] Beyond the suboptimal performance of the telegraph, such mishaps reveal how much people relied on this device as a new timekeeping technology.

In the second *fatwā,* Riḍā makes clear that the start of Ramadan stipulated in Egyptian newspapers applied only inside Egypt and should not be followed by readers in other countries, where direct sighting of the moon should remain the yardstick. Riḍā explained that it was important for all Egyptian Muslims to begin and conclude the fast together, as collectivity and concord *(al-ijtimā' wa'l-ittifāq)* in performing religious rituals are essentials of the Sharīʿah, but that different countries must adopt their own procedures.[41] What needed no mention was the fact that Egyptian newspapers circulated onboard trains and steamers quickly enough to raise the question (posed to Riḍā) of whether their calendric information should be followed abroad.

We have already seen how disagreements about moon sightings could be a political concern. Indeed, in both *fatwās,* Riḍā gave a political solution, one that accepted the centralizing logic of his day. Rather than resolving disagreement locally, Riḍā succumbed to the authority of the central government of the nation-state, thus ensuring temporal harmony.[42] If, in Benedict Anderson's *Imagined Communities,* it is temporal simultaneity that provides the conditions of possibility for the nation-state, for Riḍā, the nation-state guarantees religious simultaneity. Finally, we see that simultaneity inside the community hinges on the community's temporal difference from other communities. The national homogeneity of time is always in comparison, constantly supported by temporal heterogeneity.

Importantly, Riḍā did not renounce the need to physically sight the moon. Though he implicitly relied on the telegraphic transmission of central Ramadan time to the provinces, the moon still had to be properly spotted in the capital. Along with his teacher Muḥammad ʿAbduh, Riḍā is known as a key turn-of-the-century synthesizer of Islam and modern technoscience. Though usually this project serves to make Islam compatible with technologics, converting new technologies to Islam and understanding them in religious terms was just as important. For the telegraph, this task was carried out in the first two decades of the twentieth century by Shaykh Muḥammad Bakhīt al-Muṭīʿī (d. 1354/1935), the Qāḍī of Alexandria and later the grand mufti of Egypt.

In his 1911 *Kitāb Irshād ahl al-Millah ilā Ithbāt al-Ahillah* (The book on guiding the religious community to the verification of the crescents), al-Muṭīʿī made an analogy between telegraphic transmission of moon-sighting news *(akhbār)* and the transmission of the *ḥadīth* (accounts of the life and actions of the Prophet Muḥammad, also called *akhbār*). Placing the telegraph in the framework of *ḥadīth* transmission was crucial to allowing the technology to be used for the dissemination of Cairo time: according to the *sharīʿah,* for a sighting of the Ramadan crescent to count, it has to be reported by an upright *(ʿadl)* Muslim. But what about the mediation of telegraph operators who might be unjust or non-Muslim? Should it matter how many telegraphers are involved in transmitting a sighting report? Should the procedures of court testimony, requiring two witnesses, be applied to telegraphy? Such questions were addressed to al-Muṭīʿī, and to Riḍā before him.[43]

Al-Muṭīʿī's solution was to regard telegraphers as passive "mediators" (sing. *wasīṭah*) rather than as "transmitters" of a telegraphic *khabar.* Bracketing operators made telegraphing a moon sighting comparable not to testifying in court but to narrating a *ḥadīth,* requiring only one transmitter. Further, if several telegrams were received, even through the same telegraph line, they should be regarded as *akhbār mutawātirah*—a category of *ḥadīth* analysis denoting independent reports that corroborate one another.[44] Unlike Riḍā, who did not question the need for an initial physical moon sighting in Cairo, al-Muṭīʿī followed the opinion of the Shāfiʿī jurist Taqī al-Dīn al-Subkī (1284–1355 A.D.),[45] according to which testimonies of crescent sighting should be rejected if they contradicted astronomical calculations.

Indeed, the credibility of deriving time from observable natural phenomena was beginning to erode. In 1913 Samuel Marinus Zwemer, an American missionary in Egypt, recorded a suggestion by a certain "al-Zarqāwī,"[46] printed in the nationalist newspaper *Al-Shaʿb,* to introduce a "solar Hijrī year." Using the Gregorian calendar, al-Zarqāwī determined that the *Hijrah* took place on September 22, 622 A.D. He suggested adopting this date as the beginning of the Muslim calendar for everything but religious festivals, which would be determined by moon sighting.[47]

By 1357/1939 the moon was definitely waning. That year, the Supreme Sharīʿah Court in Egypt determined that the month of Dhu al-Hijjah began on Saturday, January 20. ʿĪd al-Aḍḥā (the Festival of Sacrifice) was hence celebrated in Egypt ten days later, on Monday, January 30. But Egyptian readers of *Al-Muqaṭṭam* knew that the Saudi Arabian government had decided that the first of the month was not Saturday but Sunday, January 21, and the *ʿĪd* was thus celebrated in the Arabian peninsula on Tuesday, January 31. And readers of *Al-Balāgh* discovered that the Muslims of Bombay celebrated the festival on Wednesday as a result of the establishment of the beginning of Dhu al-Hijjah on Monday, January 22.[48] According to jurist Aḥmad Shākir, a member of Riḍā and al-Muṭīʿī's milieu, such discrepancies were not the exception but the rule: "In some Muslim countries crescent sightings result in some people sighting it while others are unable to do so. As a consequence the religious festivals differ from one Muslim country to another: some countries fast while others do not, some celebrate the Festival of Sacrifice, while on that very day others observe a fast."[49] Given that the moon sets progressively later than the sun as one goes west, western Muslims were likely to observe a new moon earlier than their eastern coreligionists, as this instance indicates. But in the age of telegraphy and steam navigation, Muslims in Cairo, Mecca, and Bombay experienced the tensions of a new connectivity. The telegraph was not only disseminating the homogeneous time of the capital; through the newspaper, it also spread the word about temporal heterogeneity, thereby bolstering national togetherness at the expense of a larger religious concord.

Shākir's solution to these discrepancies was to abandon the principle of sighting in favor of a single calendar based on scientific computation. This was the explicitly logical conclusion of the telegraphic dissemination of Ramadan time and the successful attempts to give temporal homogeneity official Islamic sanction. To make his case that in its current form the Hijrī calendar was unruly, Shākir resorted to the standard of Gregorian dates.

Shākir's view remains a minority opinion on the commencement of Ramadan. Yet if the resilience of physical moon sighting is taken as an indication of the autonomy of the Islamic calendar, this resilience should also be seen as reinforcing its limited scope as a religious calendar only. Dissenting views like Shākir's reveal that if Europe shifted in the Middle Ages from church to merchant time, in modern Egypt even the religious establishment faced significant pressures to adopt monetized time. Other domains were even less resilient.

TELEGRAPHIC TIME, SPACE, AND TEXT

Clearly the telegraph was a key culprit in the rearrangement of calendric timekeeping in Egypt. Shifting from calendars to the newspapers that advertised and followed them, we can now examine the implications of the telegraphic reshuffling of temporal systems. How did telegraphy affect the textualization of time?

We must now return to *Wādi al-Nīl.* The newspaper was launched in June 1867, during a khedival visit to France and England.[50] The highlight of the royal trip was the signing of two treaties to sink submarine telegraph cables between Alexandria and the Italian shore, and to connect the Malta–Alexandria–Cairo telegraph to a new London–Bombay network.[51] As we saw in chapter 1, this second attempt at intercontinental telegraphy (after the first underwater cable succumbed to sea termites) was partly financed by news agencies operating in key nodes of this grid, including since 1865 the Reuters office in Alexandria.[52] Khedive Ismāʿīl actively participated in this process: several months after signing the aforementioned treaties and establishing *Wādī al-Nīl,* he started subsidizing Reuters.[53] The genesis of the private press embedded Egypt in these new communication networks. In 1870, *Wādī al-Nīl* subscribed to Reuters' telegram service.

It seems likely that ʿAbd Allāh Abu al-Suʿūd, the head of the translation school and the person appointed as *Wādī al-Nīl*'s editor-in-chief, was part of the large entourage accompanying the khedive in Europe in 1867. Translation was undoubtedly integral to an Egyptian press telegraphically connected to the wider world, as demonstrated by the many translations from European newspapers and books published in *Wādī al-Nīl.* Translators were central not only in rendering news items into Arabic but also in producing them: since the late 1850s, graduates of the Egyptian translation school had been manning the telegraph service.[54]

In the closing months of 1870, telegraphic Reuters' news started appearing in *Wādī al-Nīl*'s Foreign News section, bearing Gregorian dates. Domestic Egyptian news kept their Hijrī dates. The newspaper thus revealed a temporal schism whereby foreign and local news occurred in different temporal (and not only spatial) domains. The Gregorian dates of foreign news were often accompanied by the corresponding Arabic date in parentheses. The telegraph thus promoted a standard shift whereby Arabic dates were for the first time bracketed, exorcized to a parallel realm that required agreement. This "outdating" happened just as a correspondence was established between these two incommensurable time systems.

Before the paper subscribed to Reuters, foreign news—translated from the European-language newspapers proliferating in Alexandria—hardly ever occupied more than half a page in *Wādī al-Nīl*'s three to four pages. But the subscription to the agency's service quickly transformed the Egyptian newspaper into one mostly devoted to foreign news. Such shifts demonstrate how telegraphy reshaped the conditions of knowledge acquisition and dissemination even before the British occupation. In pretelegraphic Egypt, proximity roughly translated to familiarity: one knew more about one's immediate surroundings than about faraway places. With the advent of telegraphy, an excess of foreign news and a "thick description" of the alien quickly overclouded local knowledge. *Wādī al-Nīl* thus became one of the technologies that formed the worldview of the colonial subject, characterized by an out-of-focus world picture that was sharp around the edges and fuzzy in the center.

The imbalance of local and foreign news produced an imbalance of dates: a larger portion of the news was happening in Gregorian time, which required translation into Hijrī, and not the other way around. This protocol, wherein Gregorian dates were the source or yardstick and Hijrī dates were derivative, quickly became the rule.

Wādī al-Nīl's editors attempted to deal with the excess of telegraphic information by creating foreign news summaries. They approached the matter with unease:

> In the previous editions of *Wādi al-Nīl* we have so far made an effort to translate the telegraphic news accumulating until July 8 (9 Jumādā al-Ūlā) and we have transmitted them in their original texts, quoting and presenting them one by one, despite their excess, so that the reader could have the choice and select the news he deems sound *[akhbār mustaḥsanah]* from which he can get a true understanding of current affairs. However, the volume of the telegraphic news amassed on July 9, 10, and 11 (10, 11, and 12 Jumādā al-Ūlā) [forces us] to render them in a summary.[55]

This editorial comment captures some of the concerns regarding telegraphy's ability to collapse a multiplicity of voices into a single flattened narrative.

The necessity of devising new tactics for handling information excess generated other changes in important procedures of textual production. One striking development was that foreign news became shorter with the telegraph, because the newspaper omitted the news items' chain of transmitters. Pretelegraphic foreign news included an internal history detailing the circumstances of its own production, a preface modeled on the *isnād* (the chain of transmitters of a *ḥadīth*). Thus a translated news item about violence in Mecca from May 9, 1870, opened as follows: "Translated from the journal *L'Égypte [mā tarjamatuhu]:* the following text appeared in a journal titled *Alimbrsial Dosmir* distributed on April 27 (26 Muḥarram): several newspapers *[ba'ḍ al-ghazetāt]* discussed oral reports *[mā yuqāl]* about what happened in Mecca."[56] This introductory paragraph situates *Wādī al-Nīl* at the end of an elaborate sequence of sources, following *L'Égypte, Alimbrsial Dosmir,* anonymous newspapers, and unspecified oral sources. Beyond the fractured and intricate process of news transmission, this paragraph exposes the many temporal delays involved in news circulation. With the telegraph, such introductions disappeared, making room for actual news stories that now stood as independent pieces of information.

Traces of *ḥadīth*-like textual conventions and terminology in early newspapers (*isnād, tarjamah,* or *akhbār mustaḥsanah,* "sound reports"—a term taken from the field of *ḥadīth* criticism) help us appreciate how their textual extinction interfaced with calendric reform. The Hijrī calendar was connected to a particular paradigm of textuality and knowledge transmission revolving around the *ḥadīth.* The science of *ḥadīth* and the imperative to ascertain whether a reported prophetic tradition was sound or spurious were a main driving force in the development of Islamic geography, biography, and historiography. These auxiliary disciplines provided information about *ḥadīth* transmitters, their reliability, and the probability that they could occupy the same time and space to pass information from one to another. Reviewed by *ḥadīth* critics in retrospect, this textual universe was diachronically indexed by the Hijrī calendar in a perfectly reliable and legible manner.

Newspapers, by contrast, were media of synchronic information transfer. While the same word, *akhbār,* denoted journalistic as well as prophetic pieces of information, synchronic and diachronic times were for the first time competing over the domination of textual information exchange. By effacing chains of transmission and compressing news into summarized narratives, the telegraph severed the connection between message and messenger, transmitter and text. Readers could no longer actively choose sound reports. Such a critical reading—involving constant evaluation of the genealogies of texts that lay bare the devices of their making—was replaced by a passive intake of "news" without circumstances of production, mechanically produced and reproduced, immaculately conceived like the event that launched the calendar which organized them.

NEWSPAPERS MADE OF COTTON

A late 1870 *Wādī al-Nīl* ad described the recently opened building of the Cairo Cotton Bourse in al-Azbakīyah. Alongside services such as a mailbox and a postal clerk, the bourse offered a café and a newspaper reading room where local and foreign periodicals were at the public's disposal. More importantly, daily telegraphic news from Britain and Alexandria were hung on the bourse walls, which also featured governmental publications, foreign consular announcements, and public announcements by the various branches of the administration.[57]

Thus while the credit for being the first private daily newspaper in Egypt usually goes to *Al-Ahrām,* which started printing across the street from the Alexandria Cotton Bourse in 1876, the first Egyptian daily newspaper was actually a posting (or wallpaper) inside the building. This shift in perspective casts light on the oft-ignored role of cotton and telegraphy in the annals of Egyptian journalism.

Reuters, whose telegrams hung on the walls of Egyptian bourses in the 1870s, established itself as a news agency in the early 1850s by providing bourse closing prices and commodity prices (including cotton prices from Alexandria) to Lancaster newspapers. Though repeatedly rejected by the *Times* and other leading London dailies during most of this decade, newspapers in Manchester—the world's center of cotton manufacture—and Liverpool, its cotton port, were first to print Julius Reuter's "telegraphic summaries of foreign intelligence" and his commercial information.[58] The convergence of global telegraphy and agricultural industry helped commodify up-to-date information and gave rise to institutions such as the cotton bourse and the daily press.

The crucial role of cotton in the history of the Arabic press has mostly been ignored. This omission can be explained by the fact that historians largely reproduced the anthropocentric biases of journalists, editors, and publishers who presented their newspapers as building blocks of a cultural and later nationalist "Nahḍawī" renaissance. Cotton, which usually belongs to an economic or agricultural history, does not mix with the cultural history of newspapers. (One person who was aware of the affinity of these seemingly different "fields"—the actual agricultural field and the metaphoric journalistic one—was ʿAbd Allāh al-Nadīm.)[59]

In contrast to the *Nahḍawī* narrative, price fixing, the fluctuation of the Nile level, imports and exports, and the exploits of one of the most important media protagonists in the 1870s, the cotton weevil, were key objects of concern for newspapers like *Al-Ahrām.* The newspaper depended on the bourse for readership and information, and the telegraph was a key mediator in this dependence. When applying for a governmental permit in 1292/1875, Salīm

Taqlā, a cofounder of *Al-Ahrām,* claimed, "The newspaper for which a license is requested, to be printed in Alexandria, will contain telegrams, and commercial, scientific, and local matters."[60] Other newspapers were also becoming dependent on the telegraph. The *Egyptian Gazette,* for example, was contractually obliged in 1882 to pay Reuters 25 percent of the proceeds of all sales of the paper.[61]

LANGUAGE AND/AS RIVER

If cotton was a central concern for the early Egyptian press, newspapers were immediately influenced by material conditions informing cotton agriculture in the Nile Valley. Again, the telegraph was an important mediator in the process. Disconnecting language and information from their circumstances of production, the telegraph may create the impression that language exists in an independent realm. Yet the very history of telegraphy disproves this assumption.

In chapter 1 we encountered the complexity and contingency of sinking submarine telegraph cables. The structure and route of the telegraph and consequently the price of the words communicated through it was affected by marine borers, imperial politics, the yield of cotton crops, syntactical structures, and the weather. Despite this multiplicity of actors, humanists and social scientists typically follow certain paths of language production and ignore others. For example, it is conventionally assumed that modern Arabic prose was a result of the emergence of the Arabic novel from chapters serialized in private newspapers. Yet the connections between communication technologies and the world in which they operated ignored disciplinary divides. Close attention to these connections may open up new paths of inquiry, such as a marine biology of the Arabic novel, an electrical engineering of neoclassical poetry, or an agricultural science of Arabic semantic fields. What follows is an attempt to flesh out some of these connections.

Electrical telegraphy was predicated on making and breaking an electrical contact that resulted in a perceptible signal transcribed by an operator at the other end of the cable. After the infrastructure was in place, what telegraph companies sold was usage time of their equipment and personnel. Letters, words, and sentences were converted into money based on the wire time they occupied. This generic description seems to apply for every telegraph system everywhere, revealing why the logic of time-is-money seems so applicable to telegraphy. It offers an attractive model for understanding the emergence of a new telegraphic Arabic: translated by the telegraph into money, "the great equalizer," language was subjected to "the logic of capitalism," which may well be the equation of time and money.

Yet the platforms of money, language, time, workers, and equipment converged differently in different settings. First, other hierarchies could trump money in telegraphic prioritization, as a mid-1850s agreement for telegraph operation in Egypt demonstrates:

> Art. 8. The official dispatches of the Egyptian Government and of every other Government shall have a priority over all others, and according to the priority of receipt of the telegraph office, those which arrive simultaneously will be forwarded alternately.
>
> Art. 9. Private dispatches shall be transmitted according to their priority of receipt at the telegraph office.
>
> Art. 10. The Egyptian Government shall pay for its dispatches one-half the rate charged for commercial messages.[62]

Second, the route of the line, the physical terrain across which it stretched, the priorities of users, and their financial circumstances all informed how telegraphy could be used. Consider the effects of the Nile: in Egypt, the "Gift of the Nile," the river determined the pulse of agricultural life, travel conditions, and accessibility of parts of the country that, during the annual flood, were disconnected for weeks or even months.[63] Significant sections of the Egyptian railway and telegraph systems ran parallel to the river that provided water for steam production and boiler cooling, and connected most population centers.

Prior to 1881, it was customary for the various provincial authorities to send telegrams to Cairo about the level and condition of the Nile.[64] From there, daily telegraphic reports about the level of the river went out to all provincial engineering departments, who prepared for the inundation[65] and prevented the water from reaching the railway.[66] This arrangement was financed by a designated budget in the Ministry of Public Works that retroactively underwrote the bills periodically submitted by the Egyptian State Railways and Telegraphs Authority.[67] However, if the Nile flood occurred at the end of the fiscal year (when the budget had already been spent), such telegrams came under the financial responsibility of the ESR.[68]

The 1880s were years of dire financial insolvency. To a great extent, it was telegraphic connectivity and instantly available global commodity prices that allowed Egypt to quickly take advantage of the U.S. Civil War (1861–1865). With the temporary dwindling of American cotton production and trade, European markets shifted to Nile basin cotton, creating an Egyptian cotton boom during the 1860s and early 1870s. Yet the same wired, global cotton market shifted back to American cotton after the war. Large Egyptian investments in infrastructure, financed by heavy borrowing, dragged the country into escalating indebtedness. Egypt's debt to foreign creditors became an engine of European imperialism, first in the veiled form of the Caisse de la Dette, the agency set up in 1876 by European governments to oversee Egyptian debt repayment, and in 1882 in the form of direct British occupation.

The 1880 Law of Liquidation stipulated that the Caisse was to direct all net revenue from the railways, telegraph, and ports to debt repayment. Accordingly, from 1880, use of the telegraph was limited to time-sensitive matters.[69] From 1881 on, the budget allocated to Nile-related telegraphs decreased significantly.[70] The same year also saw special decrees to make sure that only the most important Nile reports, written in the most cost-effective style, would be wired.[71] According to other decrees, telegrams contained superfluous words and long expressions that delayed their telegraphic transmission and resulted in high costs to the government. Senders were instructed to use abbreviations and dense expressions that fit the medium of telegraphy.[72]

Language was responding to these changes in the political climate at the same time as it responded to the river level. As the Nile overflowed, telegraphic language had to become more abbreviated and condensed. During years of exceptionally high flooding, such as 1300/1883, the rising river doubled the telegrams that flowed from the provinces to Cairo,[73] straining the capital's drained coffers and provoking a flurry of calls for terse language and economy of style. Indeed, in times like this, the excessive number of telegrams also caused delays in the various telegraph offices—a problem seen as further cause for stylistic abbreviation.[74]

In 1884, the Ministry of Finance discovered the magnitude of the sum spent by the provinces on Nile-level telegrams during the inundation of 1883. It dispatched a decree forbidding long telegrams. The decree also limited the number of telegrams each province was allowed to send, stipulating, "It is necessary to use abbreviation and make sure the content is condense and clear, limiting the number of words as much as possible so that the coffers will not be burdened with further fees."[75]

The flood had various related effects on telegraphy. The inundation caused telegraph cutoffs and delays.[76] In addition, the rising water unfastened telegraph poles from the ground; peasants took advantage of the situation and repositioned them away from their fields.[77] This caused further disruptions and communication delays, generating new administrative measures to impede this phenomenon and increase the security of telegraph poles in the countryside.[78] Apparently, the telegraph was never a stable and passive line through which time, money, and language could be exchanged and economized, but always a contingent result of constant negotiation among peasants, engineers, the river, village headmen, provincial authorities, and Cairo ministries.

The intricacies of river telegraphy led to the development of new accounting protocols.[79] They also necessitated the policing of poles and wires[80] and led to tighter collaboration between the Railways and Telegraph Authority, the Ministry of Finance (both using the Gregorian calendar), provincial authorities, and the Ministries of Public Works and Interior (using Hijrī time). Such collaboration made it necessary to rely on new temporal conversion protocols, as reflected in the prolific correspondence among these administrative branches, which addressed damage to equipment, protection of infrastructure, and the division of responsibility among enforcement agencies.[81]

The telegraph's ability to outrun the river, when effectively utilized, allowed locations downriver to prepare for the flood. Canals and trenches could be dug, the railway and the parallel telegraph could be protected from the rising water, and fields could be better irrigated. Thus, while the river affected protocols of telegraphy, language formation, accounting, timekeeping, and policing, these new practices in turn affected the river. Streamlining flows of information, money, time, and people entailed streamlining the river and vice versa.

Other conflicting logics, beyond time-is-money or even Nile inundation, also animated telegraphy. For most practical purposes, electricity facilitated instantaneous communication. Telegraphic messages could be transmitted as fast as they could be written, wired, and interpreted, making writing and encoding, instead of delivery, the new bottlenecks of communication. This speed should be taken into account among the changing conditions of language production. The telegraphic signal could move faster than any other medium: it outran the river (when the river permitted), the fastest animal, and the train. Written language for the first time could move at great speed, giving rise to new types of rapid writing.

The new technology was used, for example, by policemen who wanted to alert Cairo to a breakthrough in an 1890 murder investigation, superseding

FIGURE 7. Remains of the Cairo-Alexandria railway embankment after an overflow of the Nile. *Illustrated London News,* November 21, 1863. © Illustrated London News Ltd/Mary Evans.

a less flattering report sent earlier by mail.[82] In this case, as in many others, telegraphic time/space compression was selectively used in tandem with existing media and their temporalities. With the telegraph, space was at once compressed and slack, traversable at multiple speeds.

Likewise, the telegraph's capacity to outrun was put to use in 1895 for apprehending a hashish smuggler: a telegram from a village headman bought time for a successful police ambush.[83] And there were various other malignant actors to outrun. In 1891, the telegraph was a key device in a campaign against a locust infestation. Because telegrams flew faster than the insects, they allowed provincial authorities to organize peasants to combat the pest. This meant quickly allocating new budgets in a number of government ministries in Cairo to pay one *qirsh* for every *uqqah* of locust that was collected and destroyed, drafting emergency regulations that equated the locust crisis with the Nile flood, allowing extraordinary punitive measures against peasants who delayed in joining the campaign, and disseminating knowledge about the life cycle of the bug and its vulnerabilities.[84]

In sum, the telegraph's potential instantaneity and the monetized logic of its operation were selectively (and sometimes randomly) activated, and they were constantly informed by other logics and circumstances. Though the device could compress space and time, the often haphazard nature of this compression rendered different places both far and near from each other, making space simultaneously condense and slacken.

NEWS TIME

Before the telegraph, newspapers such as *Wādī al-Nīl* mostly printed official announcements, translations of agricultural manuals, or translations from the foreign newspapers in Alexandria. Reporting current events in real time posed a significant challenge. Even a seemingly basic matter like the movements of officials was hard to cover with any degree of certainty. For example, on 10 Muḥarram 1287, *Wādī al-Nīl* acknowledged that a report in the previous issue on a voyage to Europe of Nūbār Pasha (the second most important political figure after the khedive) was based on a rumor *(ishāʿah).* As it turned out, the Pasha never left Cairo, where he was engaged in high-profile meetings.

With time, the interfaces of the press with the railway and telegraph made such mistakes less likely. Yet this happened very unevenly. Consider *Al-Ahrām:* during 1876, the newspaper's distribution, carried out by the mail, followed a geographical logic whereby proximity to the head office in Alexandria meant a cheaper subscription. *Al-Ahrām* was cheapest in the port city. Subscribing from Cairo and Syria (including Lebanon and Palestine) was more expensive than an Alexandria subscription, yet cheaper than a subscription from Europe or India.[85] Moreover, inside Egypt, the newspaper covered and was distributed almost only in places connected to the railway. Territorially speaking, the Egypt of *Al-Ahrām* was that of the railway map.

However, the direct telegraphic connection linking Cairo, Alexandria, and Europe via Malta provided urban readers with fresh daily foreign news. By contrast, reports that were sent by mail inside Egypt sometimes took several days to find their way into the newspaper, and news from neighboring countries without a railway connection with Egypt took even longer. For example, on October 7, 1876, *Al-Ahrām* printed a letter sent on September 29 by its Beirut agent: "We do not have anything new to inform you of: all matters are peacefully following their usual course, civic serenity prevails, and everybody is happy. . . . Rumor has it that His Holiness the Roman Catholic Patriarch is expected to arrive at Beirut from Damascus in the beginning of

Tishrīn al-Awwal and will continue by sea onboard the Austrian [steamer] toward you, arriving at Alexandria on Monday, October 9."

This typical item is revealing in several respects. First, it is a report of a nonevent, an account of an undisturbed routine. Second, it reveals two temporal systems, the lunisolar month of Tishrīn al-Awwal (the Levantine month corresponding to October), at which time the "Patriarch" is expected to arrive at Beirut, and the Gregorian October, when he is to arrive at Alexandria. Finally, the item reveals several degrees of specificity: the patriarch is expected at Beirut during the vague "beginning" of Tishrīn al-Awwal, but exactly on Monday, October 9, at Alexandria. Clearly, the schedules of Austrian steamers were more exact than those of patriarchs.

Though the correspondence of the agents retained its personal nature (the patriarch was sailing "toward *you*" in the above item), telegrams adopted the monetized, compact, and impersonal language of the medium: "Security exists. Attention is paid to the crops," reads a terse Ministry of Interior report from al-Daqhalīyah;[86] "Security in place and health is fine," reads another from Banī Suwayf.[87] Information from the Egyptian countryside came to newspapers either by mail or by telegraph. Mailed reports often stressed nonevents and were written in a personal and unhurried style. Telegrams, especially governmental ones, exemplified the new logic of importance: they were terse, specific, and fresh. However, not all telegraphic connections ensured promptness. Alongside its connection to Europe via the Malta submarine telegraph cable, Egypt was also connected to Istanbul via the Ottoman land line. This connection was so fraught with cutoffs and delays that in 1897 the Baedeker tourist guide to Egypt explicitly warned against sending telegrams by this "provokingly dilatory route."[88] This configuration of news reportage positioned Egyptian urbanized newspaper readers in an uneven and uneasy relationship vis-à-vis the seemingly action-packed and "close" European centers and their slow, stagnant, uneventful, and "remote" immediate surroundings.

AUTHENTIC WIRED PROSE

Telegraphy reconfigured basic communication procedures, including the syntax, grammar, and lexicon of the Arabic language. The decrees from the early 1880s, calling to refrain from superfluous words and long expressions, reveal the new need for compact modes of expression that would fit new mediums. But the penetration of the logics of time-is-money and electrical speed into language did not push it toward abstract simplification. Rather, telegraphic Arabic was understood using ready-made templates for the compression, simplification, and acceleration found in colloquial Egyptian Arabic (the *ʿāmmīyah*) and other, older idioms.[89] Indeed, the *fuṣḥā*/*ʿāmmīyah* dichotomy and the opposition between present-day verboseness and the concise speech of old have become key frameworks for thematizing telegraphic Arabic, and thus for quieting the telegraph's contribution to the conversation.

Ṭāhā Ḥusayn, who followed the renewal of the Arabic language with a keen ear, diagnosed movement toward the colloquial dialect in the field of Arabic prose,[90] "in accordance with the demands of this new age of speed."[91] The association of the *ʿāmmīyah* with speedy, commercialized communication dates back to the last third of the nineteenth century, precisely when telegraphy's impact on print was first felt. In 1870, a new commercial biweekly journal, *Al-Munbih al-Tijārī al-Miṣrī,* started printing in Alexandria. The journal, written in Italian and colloquial Arabic, gained the support of the editors of *Wādī al-Nīl.* Foreseeing possible reservations about the use of the colloquial, an editorial in *Wādī al-Nīl* claimed that for merchants in need of *speedy* updates of price fluctuations, the rules of classical Arabic are totally insignificant.[92] Between 1877 and 1930, at least 168 new periodicals written partly or entirely in colloquial Arabic appeared in Egypt.[93] Likewise, linguist Niloofar Heari has identified shifts toward the colloquial lexicon in *Al-Ahrām* from the 1880s on. She explains these shifts with the fact that the press put classical Arabic to use in new spheres of action, forcing it to adapt.[94]

This analysis can be complemented by paying attention not only to the emergence of new spheres of content but also to new media and new rhythms of communication. What may have prevented scholars from considering the telegraph, usually a prime suspect in the emergence of modern compressed and monetized forms of writing, is the fact that the heated debate about language reform in Egypt was waged with different terms, and even when telegraphy was mentioned, it was seen as a conduit to other agendas.

The connections of telegraphy with the emergence of new written registers, the political implications of such connections, and the camouflage of the telegraph's traces are all revealed in the life and work of ʿAbd Allāh al-Nadīm. Al-Nadīm is generally considered the progenitor of the Arabic short story and a pioneer of the new modes of expression that gave rise to the Arabic novel.[95] Though al-Nadīm's career as a telegrapher is mentioned in several biographies, its impact on his writing has not attracted scholarly attention. Al-Nadīm's very arrival upon the Cairo cultural scene owes much to the telegraph.[96] In the 1850s, he befriended a Cairene railway supervisor in Alexandria who managed to convince him, in 1861, to leave the port city and enter the telegraph school in Cairo. This institution accepted literate Egyptians, mostly graduates of the religious educational institutions, like al-Nadīm himself. After graduating as a telegraph operator, al-Nadīm was appointed as a telegrapher in the Banhā train station and then transferred to the Cairo palace of Princess Khushyār, Khedive Ismāʿīl's mother.

His Cairo days were the period of al-Nadīm's artistic growth. They ended in 1875, when he was dismissed from the telegraph service after criticizing the khedive. Al-Nadīm's political activism culminated in the early 1880s with the publication of *Al-Tankīt waʾl-Tabkīt* (Humor and criticism), which later became the official mouthpiece of the ʿUrabist movement. This struggle against a creeping European colonialism, and the ensuing anticolonial revolt, culminated in the British occupation of Egypt in 1882.

Al-Nadīm expressed his politics not only in the contents of *Al-Tankīt,* but also in its form, in a new language that he introduced in a June 1881 editorial:

> I am urged by a sense of duty and patriotism and by love and care for you, O speaker of the Arab tongue, to introduce this simple journal. It is a literary and reformative magazine, which introduces wisdom, literary anecdotes, proverbs, jokes and other entertaining and useful items to you in clear and simple language; which does not earn the derision of the learned, nor compel the simple man to seek help in order to comprehend it. . . . It shuns verbal embellishments, avoids figurative adornments, and refrains from attracting attention to the eloquence of its editor, for it relies on everyday language and familiar concerns.[97]

The endeavor to create a simple language devoid of verbal embellishments, the refusal to use language as a (classed) emblem of expertise, the shunning of an idiom that draws attention to itself rather than to its object—all bear the mark of telegraphy. As we have already seen, 1881 was also the year in which decrees stipulating telegraphic abbreviated writing began circulating in the various branches of Egyptian administration.

While this aesthetic valuation of brevity was a sharp departure from preexisting styles and linguists have demonstrated that such reforms pushed written Arabic closer to the colloquial, al-Nadīm (who explicitly used the

ʿāmmīyah in writing) was ideologically uneasy about resorting to such a "lower" register.[98] Furthermore, as a staunch critic of European technology and opponent of the wholesale adoption of Western notions of civilization, al-Nadīm did not theorize the telegraph as a driving force of linguistic change either. Like other writers and poets of his day, he preferred to regard his language reforms as a return to the pure Arabic of what stabilized at the end of the nineteenth century as the ʿAbbasid "golden age," a pure idiom devoid of "artificial" embellishment. Whatever the real origins and inspiration of brevity and concision in writing—telegraphic, colloquial, or ʿAbbasid—these conventions were gradually sneaking back into formal elite writing manuals, which retrospectively reshaped "classical Arabic." Comparing *Inshāʾ* (composition) manuals from the 1830s to such works written in the late 1870s and early 1880s reveals that succinctness was becoming fashionable.[99]

Al-Nadīm's reservations about the register he himself used (strategically, in an attempt to be understood by a wider readership) emanated from a strong belief in the inherent, even organic connection between language and consciousness. Over the course of time, he claimed, Egyptians had muddled pure Arabic with other languages, patching it into a dialect whose origins were undetectable. Surrendering to the physical and spiritual impressions of this crossbred language, they had lost their distinctness.[100] Such linguistic as well as moral corruption was exacerbated by colonialism. Al-Nadīm explored this predicament in such short stories as *ʿArabī Tafarnaja* (A Frankified Arab), which introduced Zaʿīṭ, an Egyptian who forgets his Arabic after returning from an educational mission in France. The story's heart is a farcical dialogue between Zaʿīṭ and his mother, who attempts to retrieve an Arabic word the boy has on the tip of his tongue, the name of an ingredient he now dislikes in her cooking, "that which makes the eyes water and is called *oignon*." Zaʿīṭ, a peasant's son, has been eating onions all his life. When it finally dawns on her, the mother cries, "Oh dear, Zaʿīṭ, my son, you forgot the *baṣal* and *baṣal* was all you ate," delivering al-Nadīm's point that one is not only what one eats but also what one speaks.[101] If the telegraph pushed writers like al-Nadīm to use concise monetized language, it did so by prompting them to anchor this idiom in preexisting templates and explicitly shun Western influence, thus promoting a retrospective recourse to authenticity and a celebration of cultural distinctness vis-à-vis generic notions of progress.

Even intellectuals willing to own and even boast their "telegraphic" style were harnessing telegraphic Arabic to promote (competing strands of) authenticity. This was the agenda of writer and translator Salāmah Mūsā (1887–1958), a Copt who became a Fabian as a student in England during the early 1900s. Mūsā credited the scientific journal *Al-Muqtaṭaf,* established in 1876 by Syrian Christians, for inspiring his "telegraphic style" and enabling him to look beyond "those frozen patterns of eloquence and rhetoric that we had learned by heart":

> To *Al-Muqtaṭaf,* then, I am certainly indebted for the scientific inclination that remained with me all my life; and I am equally indebted to it for the "telegraphic style" that I use in my writings, and which many readers believe to be invented by myself. Dr. Ya'aqub Sarruf was adverse to the use of ornaments of style. In general he did not like at all eloquently arranged sentences, subtly chosen words, or brilliantly figured expressions, and most of all he scorned the puerile trivialities that were, until shortly before the first great war, so exclusively cultivated by our authors.[102]

Mūsā complemented his telegraphic style with avid promotion of the use of *ʿāmmīyah* in writing. In his eyes, the movement of Egyptian written Arabic toward the vernacular was crucial to the cultivation of territorial nationalism. Thus, when calling on Egyptians to adopt the *ʿāmmīyah* as a written language, Mūsā claimed that "[classical Arabic] confuses our Egyptian nation and makes it partner to Arab nationalism."[103]

In the early twentieth century, spoken colloquial Arabic was associated with the countryside and the authenticity of the fellah, thus becoming a natural medium for Egyptian nationalism. Mūsā added another dimension to this rationale, one which competed with al-Nadīm's conception of authenticity predicated on classical Arabic. We have seen how telegraphic religious time confined simultaneity within the borders of the nation-state, contrasting it with a heterogeneous outside. Inflecting the classical Arabic of "the Arab world" by infusing spoken registers into writing, telegraphy could have a similar effect on language, contrasting the "inside" of emergent national communities with an "outside." By revealing or creating a temporal and linguistic discrepancy within extensive imagined communities such as the *ummah* or the Arab World, technological connectivity reorganized their fragments in adherence to the geography of a system of nation-states. Between al-Nadīm and Mūsā's incommensurable horizons, over the course of the century the telegraphic language of the Arabic press and other printed correspondence was mainly seen as the former—a transregional idiom, a "classical Arabic" in contradistinction to everyday speech. If the telegraph contributed to propagating this register far and wide, it did so in ways that masked its own crucial contribution.

IMPERIAL BREAKDOWNS

Not less than their speed, the new delays and breakdowns in modern communication systems—and the potential for taking advantage of them—defined the politics that emerged around these systems. Consider telegraph cutoffs. At the end of 1891, to cite just one example that would prove significant in what follows, the connection between Egyptian and Ottoman telegraphs was cut off between December 30, 1891, and January 4, 1892.[104] Telegraph cutoffs were a common matter, and procedures existed for alerting the public of them. Cutoffs were usually announced in daily newspapers (such as *Al-Nīl,* which had just become a daily when the telegraph went down),[105] adding another layer of interdependence between these media, and on yellow slips of paper posted in telegraph offices. Notably, however, Ottoman telegraph cutoffs were not part of this notification scheme. Probably due to the regularity of interruptions on this line, backup paper copies of telegrams from Istanbul and other parts of the Ottoman Empire were regularly sent to Egypt by steamer from Syria.[106]

Less than a week after the telegraphic connection between Cairo and Istanbul resumed, on January 7, the Egyptian khedive, Muḥammad Tawfīq I, died after a short illness. The treatment of the khedive's death by Egyptian and Ottoman officials, as well as by the Egyptian and European press, further illustrates but also complicates the telegraph's impact on Egyptian politics. On Saturday, January 9, *Al-Nīl* printed the breaking news, "His Majesty, only yesterday our beneficent ruler, our compassionate great Khedive, Muḥammad Tawfīq I, is today the Deceased Khedive, is today the Great Departed, is today the Late Resident of Heaven."[107] The dramatic rhetorical opposition between yesterday and today poorly covered a journalistic blunder: the newly self-proclaimed daily was two days late in reporting the most important news item of the year. The editor, who felt compelled to provide an explanation, justified the belatedness by the fact that he had attended the khedive's funeral (!).[108] Ironically, Egyptians could have sooner read about the death of their khedive in the *London Times,* which was alerted telegraphically of the news on Thursday night and printed it on Friday. Also on Friday, Reuters's summary of the foreign-press coverage of the khedival death was available in Egypt. *Al-Nīl* quoted it on Saturday.

Whereas Egyptian newspapers demonstrate the distorted temporal configuration whereby even key domestic news was first printed as foreign news, Egyptian and Ottoman politicians were much quicker.[109] The khedive breathed his last breath at 7:15 P.M. on Thursday. He had lost consciousness already at 10 A.M., but this was kept secret. His close aids telegraphed the foreign consuls that morning to the effect that the khedive's health was good and he was only suffering from slight fatigue. The prime minister was telegraphically alerted to the seriousness of the condition only at 2 P.M., after the royal doctor returned from the Ḥilwān Palace to Cairo. By 3 P.M. the crown prince was telegraphed in Vienna about his father's condition. That night, the Egyptian government telegraphed Istanbul with the sad news. The sultan immediately convened a Friday morning urgent government meeting where it was decided to appoint the oldest son of the late khedive, ʿAbbās Ḥilmī, as the new ruler.

The Ottomans had to move quickly: the heir's young age and his distance from Egypt opened the door to European meddling with the appointment. On the same day, the sublime Porte sent an official Ottoman-language appointment telegram in lieu of a *firmān.* (Official telegrams moved much faster than private ones.) The telegram was translated into Arabic and published in the official newspaper *(Al-Waqāʾiʿ al-Miṣrīyah)* as well as in the private press on Saturday. In the meantime, before departing from Vienna, the new khedive telegraphed the Egyptian prime minister, notifying him of his imminent return to Egypt. Taking the reins of government, he instructed the prime minister to keep matters calm and not make any changes until his arrival. Telegrams continued to fly back and forth between Istanbul, Cairo, and various places in Europe during the following days. In a January 11 editorial, *Al-Nīl* analyzed this speedy postmortem communication, concluding, "It was the speed with which our Lord the Khalīfah [the sultan] arranged the appointment of Our Sovereign Khedive ʿAbbās Ḥilmī II that prevented foreign intervention."[110]

In 1892, a whole decade after occupying Egypt, Britain had established in the country only an "informal empire." The fragile official connection between Egypt and the Ottoman Empire was kept alive for another two decades, with the aid of technologies such as the telegraph, which enabled the Ottomans to circumvent the British physical presence in the country. Telegraphs did not lend themselves to a particular party. In fact, Ismāʿīl, the late khedive's predecessor and the greatest promoter of telegraphy in Egypt, was himself telegraphically overthrown by the sultan, following British pressure a decade earlier.[111] Taken together, these examples demonstrate how the telegraph kept the Ottomans in the picture, forcing but also enabling them to take part in decision making from a spatially remote and politically disadvantaged position. The telegraph made colonialism possible, but it also made it incomplete by sustaining the powers that resisted it—be they the sultan and his attempts at remote control or local actors such as al-Nadīm and his anticolonial journal. It functioned as machinery of government, but at the same time its technical reproduction of language helped rekindle the aura of ʿAbbasid authenticity, promote new spoken registers, and sustain counterhegemonic religious and aesthetic agendas.

Egypt's "semicolonial" condition was to a large extent a product of this aporetic connectivity. International telegraph networks "westernized" Egypt to an extent, but they simultaneously tightened its links to the Ottoman Empire, while also demonstrating the insurmountable gap between action-packed Europe and the sluggish Egyptian countryside; telegraphy introduced monetized time into the country in newly intimate ways, but clothed in authentic garb.

As a familiar narrative of modernity would have it, the telegraph indeed introduced new forms of textuality and temporality into Egypt, decommissioning older ones, such as the Hijrī calendar and the quotidian temporalities associated with it, the Arabic day and the uneven "temporal hour." It contributed to the formation of a new modern standard Arabic and had a prophylactic effect on linguistic ornamentalism and embellishment. And yet, in a manner similar to the way telegraphic language changed in response to the physical terrain through which it passed—reacting, for example, to the inundation of the Nile and to the cotton fields along its banks—the telegraph interacted with preexisting semantic and cultural fields that likewise diverted it from its supposedly generic course. The telegraph charged ʿAbbasid language and the *ʿāmmīyah* with new energies while depleting the practical import of other traditional spheres, such as the Hijrī calendar. But even as far as this calendar was concerned, the telegraphic metamorphosis from an objective scheme (a clear moon in the night sky) into a matter of faith (a subjective eyelash) transformed it into a free-floating, powerful cultural symbol, one whose very impracticality made it a suitable vessel for new ideological substance.

FIVE

The Urban Politics of Slowness

> We declare that the splendor of the world has been enriched by a new beauty: the beauty of speed. A racing automobile with its bonnet adorned with great tubes like serpents with explosive breath . . . a roaring motor car which seems to run on machine-gun fire, is more beautiful than the Victory of Samothrace.
>
> F. T. MARINETTI, *"The Futurist Manifesto,"* 1909

> Every day I return home unharmed I pray twice
> Thankful that I didn't lose my legs or my arms
> Our Automobiles consider every street a racing track
> . . . And the tram, may God derail it from existence
> Darts out of station like a bullet
> Making those standing hop like apes on top of those sitting
> And those riding on the sides fall left and right.
>
> BAYRAM AL-TŪNISĪ, *"Speed,"* 1910s

DURING THE FIRST FEW DECADES of the twentieth century, Egyptians began to mark out their era as *ʿaṣr al-surʿah,* "the age of speed." The new epochal characterization, part of a larger trend in the English- and French-speaking worlds,[1] was not attached to a particular historical period or a specific event. It was wedded, nonetheless, to technological developments and particularly to the introduction of modern means of transportation: trains, trams, automobiles, and later airplanes, and to the social changes these devices brought about.[2] "Everything dashes in this age, everything hastens," reads the opening line of *Al-ʿĀlam Yajrī* (The world dashes), a 1933 article by the future Islamist ideologue Sayyid Quṭb that echoes the prevalent sense of epochal rupture understood as quickening, jumping to warp speed.

While Egypt was dashing along with the rest of the world and modernity was experienced everywhere as rapid overstimulation,[3] in Egypt the new swiftness was particularly fraught. The difference, heuristically illustrated above in the disparity between the triumphalist, futurist manifesto and the cautious Egyptian popular poem, eventually gave rise to what can be called a politics of slowness. If, for the Italian futurists, the lethal beauty of speed was individualized (its emblem was the private automobile) and its future was fascist, the popular poet and songwriter Bayram al-Tūnisī used very similar metaphors to convey trepidation and point toward an anticolonial nationalist horizon of a collectivist politics in a streetcar.

During this period of rapid change, standards of mechanical speed were volatile and in need of constant updating and redefinition as the plane outran the train and the wireless radio surpassed the electric telegraph. One day's dazzling rapidity became the next day's frustrating sluggishness.[4] Making sense of this fickle velocity in Egypt often required situating the country within a larger geopolitical context. The speed of transportation and communication in places such as Cairo and Alexandria was regularly compared and contrasted both to the Egyptian countryside and to European and American cities. As we have already seen, "time/space compression" went along with "time/space comparison." In colonial Egypt, questions of speed, where time and space converged, indexed both yearning for and unease with technological modernity.

Discussions of speed in Egyptian religious journals, automotive magazines, novels, poems, or *fatwās* differed on whether rapidity was good or bad per se, on whether Egypt should follow Western Europe and North America in the race toward increasing swiftness, and if so, how. But they also shared several important characteristics. Such texts tended to assume, for instance, that acceleration, like the wheeled vehicles responsible for it, originated in the West. This did not necessarily imply a simplistic theory of technology transfer across an unambiguous West/East divide. On the contrary, various early twentieth-century Egyptian writings reveal a keen awareness of intricate distinctions on both sides of this heuristic divide, between Egyptian urban centers and the countryside and within cities themselves, as well as inside the "West." Thus many texts pointed toward a different horizon than the old imperial metropole: the United States, not England, was considered the swiftest nation, a technological cutting edge where the transportation system is the most expeditious, "telegrams are sent at unimaginable speed," and people devotedly live by the principle of time-is-money and make haste in their personal affairs.[5] This was especially the case in urban transportation, where Cairo's electric tramway system preceded the first fully operational electric tram services in the Greater London area by about half a decade.

It was also commonly assumed that in Egypt, as in Western Europe and North America, the desire to accelerate was not confined to the street and its new modes of conveyance but percolated from there to personal spheres. Indeed, as it entered private life, speed was said to stir "infatuation" *(ḥubb al-surʿah),* "intoxication" *(nashwat al-surʿah),* or "fever" *(dāʾ al-surʿah),* thereby restructuring one's personal and family life. As an Egyptian railway worker put it, "Our job has taught us to be quick in everything we do. To read quickly, to quickly coordinate the movement of the trains, and to quickly exchange signals. It also gave us speed in jumping between the tracks. This habit has taken over us in our private lives. We started eating quickly and doing everything with speed. Even during our stroll we can no longer walk leisurely and unhurriedly, and our families clamor behind because of the frightening swiftness of this speed."[6] The aggression only barely contained in the above paragraph becomes a full-fledged threat when the author elaborates: "Food must be on the table within one or two minutes from the moment a quick command is issued, and pity the wife who does not respect speed."[7] At this point it becomes obvious that talking about speed is a way (for the writer as well as for us) to talk about power.

This assumed trajectory of speed from West to East, and from the street to the home and then to the self, as well as its thinly masked association with coercion, helps retrace the origins of a prevalent aversion to speed, a dislike characterizing much of the writing on the subject in colonial Egypt and elsewhere in the colonized world. Rather than depicting such attitudes as a shared set of primeval and unchanging personal traits directed outward, writings on speed suggest that we must reverse this causality: encounters with new technological rhythms and velocities on the street, in the workplace, and eventually at home should be seen as the basic context within which attitudes to new speeds took shape.

A major impediment to seriously considering this possibility has been the fact that many Egyptians embraced culturalist explanations for what seemed like an unwavering aversion to quickness and a proclivity for slowness. Owning sluggishness as a characteristically Egyptian cultural trait involved retroactively anchoring it in the Islamic tradition by evoking, for example, the famous statement by the Prophet Muḥammad, "Al-ʿAjalah min al-shayṭān waʾl-taʾānī min al-Raḥmān" (Haste is from the devil and composure is from the Merciful).[8] But a *ḥadīth* from the seventh century might be inflected by modern urban experiences in a colonial setting.

FIGURE 8. "Speed is from the Devil." Husband (in the station): "It's your fault—you delayed in the restroom for an entire hour, powdering your face white and red, and now we missed the train!" Wife: "It's your fault—you rushed me to leave the restroom before the time of the next train." *Kull Shay' wa'l-Ālam,* January 2, 1928.

Modernity often generates and fuels tradition rather than always following suit, bringing old devils up to speed.

The developing thought of the archetypical Islamist, Sayyid Quṭb, is a good case in point. Consider *Al-Ālam Yajrī,* which he published in 1933, when he was a recent graduate of Cairo's teachers' college, Dār al-ʿUlūm, before his turn to Islamism. After recounting how modern technologies are responsible for life's acceleration, Sayyid Quṭb went on to analyze mechanical speed as a psychological phenomenon. He located the origins of this disposition in the West, warning that Egyptians were blindly imitating powers that are themselves oblivious of their destination. Speed has blinded man to his surroundings: "He doesn't see anything except for what's in front of him, never heeding his right or left. Even when he hits something, he doesn't stop to check or try to rectify the damage he has caused. Instead, he goes on dashing ahead, so that clash follows clash and the man is followed by total destruction."[9]

As this quotation suggests, the central metaphor for social leadership or the avant-garde was that of the driver: "A driver who knows how to drive but doesn't know how to stop, or knows to accelerate but not to slow down, is an ignorant driver."[10] But as Sayyid Quṭb makes clear, speed should not be rejected entirely. Instead, he introduces a distinction between "activity" *(nashāṭ)* and "haste" *(ʿajalah),* the former defined as an aspect of speed that may be beneficial to the individual and society, whereas the latter is categorically detrimental. If this distinction between "activity" and "haste" was itself new, both terms fed off a long lineage. "Activity" came in response to a longstanding critique of Egyptian torpor, passivity, and indolence, attributed by Europeans and Egyptians alike to anything from the country's hot climate to the "Egyptian character."[11] "Haste," on the other hand, was shunned as devilish already in the aforementioned *ḥadīth* and then in its early twentieth-century appropriations. As Sayyid Quṭb suggested, though they need to retain "activity," Egyptians, and Easterners in general, must do away with the infatuation with haste if they are to retain their unique consciousness and profundity.

Sayyid Quṭb's connection of haste with mechanical speed was likewise unoriginal. It drew on an intimate semantic affinity in Arabic between *ʿajalah* (haste) and *ʿajal* (wheel), as well as on the centuries-long preference for riding animals rather than wheeled vehicles in what we now call the Middle East.[12] This connection might also account for the evocation of the metaphor of the speeding driver in *Al-ʿĀlam Yajrī,* even if such metaphors also echo accounts of drivers of the electric tram, a vehicle whose inability to swing sideways from its metal track was seen as both an indication of laudable focus and the cause of numerous lethal accidents.[13] Other writers were even more explicit about the connection between haste and wheels. During the 1910s, Bayram al-Tūnisī devoted several poems to the question of speed (in the requisite context of discussing modern means of transportation), punning in one of them: "We will go back and forth with haste *(ʿajal)* / And he who dies under the wheel *(ʿajal)* / Shall not die without reason *(ʿajal)* / And death is not a big deal."[14]

Compared to time and space, two categories that have received ample attention from historians,[15] speed remains unhistoricized, and thus, for better or worse, at the mercy of art and architectural critics.[16] Yet once we set out to write a history of speed, we cannot confine ourselves to looking at the development of a specific discourse shaped by the interaction of texts and writers. Valuable as it may be, such a framework might leave unexamined velocity itself, actual accelerations and decelerations (and hence also key dimensions of the textual corpus archiving them). If we accept that social, political, or cultural realities are inherently shaped by vectors of movement, we must begin developing a historically specific grasp of the speeds that render phenomena into experience. Discursive and tangible experiences of speed shaped each other, defining speed's entry into politics and its emergence as an emblem for the colonial condition. In turn, political and cultural constructions informed the ways in which actual speeds were experienced in the street.

What follows examines the relation between the apprehension of speed and the history of one of the devices most associated with the age of speed in colonial Egypt—the electric tram. While trains, automobiles, and airplanes were all seen as important driving forces in discussions of the "age of speed," the tramway occupied a prominent place in discussions of mechanical speed and its social implications. This might come as a surprise. Appearing in Cairo in 1896 and a year later in Alexandria, the new system of mass transportation did not feature the fastest vehicles ever introduced into Egypt. In the first decade of their operation, the average velocity of streetcars in Egypt was 15–20 kilometers per hour (9–12 mph). By comparison, automobiles, introduced in 1903, were legally limited to 15 kph inside the city during the first decade of the century. Agricultural trains averaged 30 kph, and express trains reached more than double that speed.

Yet the language of average speed does not take us very far in understanding how the speed of streetcars accelerating through busy urban settings was experienced. It cannot explain, for example, complaints made by Egyptians during the first decade of the century, according to which trams and automobiles—the slowest vehicles in the above list—moved so fast that people couldn't make out their (very short) license plates.[17] Such abstract language, used by the Belgian tram company and British colonial officials, obfuscates more than it reveals.

The tram's perceived speediness was clearly related to the fact that it was moving along teeming streets. Beyond redrawing the parameters of cities such as Cairo and Alexandria, tramways redefined urbanity itself by introducing into the urban experience new tensions and contradictions, and by forcing Egyptians to confront the colonial aspects of their modern urbanity. As a newspaper article devoted to the introduction of this technology framed the paradox, "On the one hand, the electrical carriages that have been introduced into the capital of Egypt demonstrate that we have entered into the circuits of civilization *[ḥaḍārah]*, broken through the doors of urbanity *[madanīyah]*, and perfectly imitated our peers among the civilized *[al-mutamaddinīn]*.... On the other hand, this indicates the degree of our humiliation . . . and our reliance on foreigners in everything we do. The operation of tramway coaches in Egypt by a foreign company is a sign of shame."[18]

The language of urbanity, progress, and civilization was essential in descriptions and discussions of the tramway and key to exploring how the vehicle's speed was experienced. High-speed road accidents were becoming a bone of colonial contention in the 1900s. In July 1905, right after the particularly grisly fatal crash of a streetcar and a carriage, the weekly journal *Al-Ṣiḥāfah* launched a series of articles on the benefits and dangers of the tram, revolving around the question: "Do the Benefits of *Tamaddun* Entail Killing Humanness?"[19] *Tamaddun,* meaning "urbanity" or "civilization," was a term usually wedded to the space of the city *(madīnah),* which was indeed undergoing rapid change around the turn of the nineteenth century.

Yet the articles make clear that spatially the tramway was seen as a purely beneficial technology. The writers even stressed that criticism should not be taken as a call to discontinue the tram service, whose benefits included shortening great distances, increasing the price of real estate in the suburbs, and reducing inner-city crowdedness.[20] Rather than targeting spatial compression, the texts attacked the velocity that made it possible while causing road accidents along the way. For the anonymous writers of these articles, the dark side of *tamaddun* was first and foremost characterized by "dizzying speed," an attitude echoed also in the later work of Sayyid Quṭb on Western civilization: "This civilization, based on science, industry, and materialism, operates with crazed speed and is without heart or consciousness. Driven by invention and material advancement, it sets forth to destroy all that humanity has produced."[21]

The electric tram was introduced into Cairo in August 1896, with much pomp. On the first of the month, a party of dignitaries was taken on a test ride from Būlāq to the Citadel via ʿAtabah al-Khaḍrāʾ Square, moving through tens of thousands of people who took to the streets to behold the spectacle. The moving vehicle was chased by a large group of children shouting, "Al-ʿifrīt, al-ʿifrīt" (The jinni, the jinni).[22] According to an *Al-Muqaṭṭam* reporter who covered the event with the fleeting insight of a first encounter, the tram "sped so that it raced the wind when the road was clear, suddenly slowing down or abruptly halting as children or pedestrians blocked its way. In such instances, the driver would stand up with his hand on the lever that drives and stops [the tram]."[23] Though such oscillations also characterized the movement of trams in subsequent years, they tend to disappear when described in the language of average speed, the common denominator reducing speed to a nexus of abstract space and time. This was true for all vehicles, but more so with regard to streetcars: though the speed of trains and automobiles was legally limited by a formal maximum, the only limitations on the acceleration of trams were their technological capacity and their schedule. Different governmental concessions laid down, between the 1890s and the 1920s, a plethora of contradictory speed limits for trams. But as noted by colonial officials, "In practice the Company's time-tables result in a considerable excess of concessional speeds—this has been tacitly acquiesced in."[24] Drivers therefore tended to compensate for slower sections by accelerating dangerously when the road was clear.

The seemingly random irregularity of an Egyptian tram's speed was often informed by the social class, ethnicity, and gender of the people blocking its path, and of those driving and riding it. One's risk of being run over by, or falling out of, a moving tram depended on one's social standing. Consequently, these oscillations archive yet untapped insights into the lived experience of urban speed and the trajectories of its entry into politics and culture. The impact of accidents resulting from such oscillations was in turn intensified by the fact that accidents were accessible mainly through the magnifying glass casting them as instances of colonial violence.

METRO POLITICS

In 1893 the Egyptian government authorized the establishment of tramways in Cairo and, depending on their success, also in Alexandria, stirring the interest of several European and American engineering companies.[25] After granting, in 1894, a fifty-year concession to a tramway company registered in Brussels, the Egyptian government began confiscating land for the project in 1895.[26] Between the following year and 1898, a system of overhead wires divided into eight tram lines spread from ʿAtabah al-Khaḍrāʾ Square, the central tramway hub in the capital, out toward the Citadel, Būlāq, and al-Nāṣirah via Bāb al-Lūq, al-ʿAbbāsīyah, Old Cairo, al-Rawḍah through the mouth of the Khalīj and from there to Giza, and finally a line running parallel to the Ismāʿīlīyah Canal from Qaṣr al-Nīl Square to Qanṭarat al-Līmūn (see map 2). In subsequent years, the system sent tentacles beyond the city proper, bringing new areas, especially in the north and northeast, into the ambit of the quickly expanding capital. Between 1896 and 1917, Cairo tripled its size without any change in the travel time from the remotest point to the center—about an hour between the central tram station in ʿAtabah and the outskirts of the city, and fifteen to twenty minutes to go to most points within the built-up zone.[27] By the end of this period, hundreds of streetcars, dispatched at average intervals of three to six minutes, were moving along thirty tramway lines,[28] carrying 75 million passengers a year.[29]

The Cairo Tramway Company (henceforth CTC) was part of the Empain Group, led by the Belgian industrialist, engineer, and eventually baron, Édouard Empain.[30] It implemented in Egypt lessons learned from the diversification of the group's international business, from local railways in Belgium and France in the early 1880s to horse-drawn trams and later to their electrification in the 1890s, and subsequently into electrical light and power.[31] Thus the coal-based power station that provided electricity for the new tram network (situated where the Ismāʿīlīyah Canal met the Nile) was used in 1896 by another Belgian company associated with the group to begin providing Cairenes with domestic electrical lighting, followed by electric streetlights in 1898.[32] In 1902, 1,180 households were connected to the electric grid in the capital, and the following year the number of users climbed to 1,409.[33] Along similar lines, electric light also followed the introduction of the tram in Alexandria from 1897 onward.[34] As it did elsewhere, electric illumination in Egypt provided a nighttime market for the infrastructures of the daytime transportation sector and vice versa.

The tram's appearance in Egypt during the 1890s was the culmination of a larger urban transformation that started several decades earlier. The nineteenth-century "Haussmannization" of Cairo and Alexandria entailed the creation of a landscape of straight and broad streets newly paved with a hard and durable surface built over a modern network of drainage and water supply pipes, and which were regularly maintained and cleaned. Before a piped domestic water supply was combined with excrement removal in the age of toilet flushing, these once separate functions were carried out by means of carts, beasts of burden, and—in the case of water distribution—also on human backs. The installation of pipes, sewer, and drainage networks under the newly paved streets gradually pushed many animal owners, cart drivers, and water carriers to find alternative means of livelihood. One new source of occupations that attracted many laborers who found their skills superseded was the rapidly expanding urban transportation sector.[35] The sewage drainage technologies, in tandem with novel health policies and new notions of hygiene, significantly reduced urban death rates. A steep population expansion beginning roughly during the last decade of the nineteenth century resulted from a combination of natural growth and migration from the villages to newly opened territories made available by the new transportation networks.[36] In turn, the modern networks were now sustained by these villagers-turned-passengers. The emergence of ostensibly traditional donkey-drawn carts was a new, nineteenth- and early twentieth-century phenomenon, which was supported by cutting-edge underground technologies.

Modern streets fit for wheeled means of transportation did not necessarily promote animal-drawn vehicles, and sometimes barred them entirely. In 1897–1898, the old Cairo Canal, the Khalīj, an open sewer annually flushed by the inundation of the Nile, was filled in and a new tram line between Sayyidah Zaynab and Ghamra was stretched along its course.[37] In 1901, to reduce traffic congestion, the government banned cabbies and others from driving along the Khalīj, one of the few major arteries cutting through the old city, granting the tram company sole access.[38] The transformation of the Khalij from a sewage line into a tram line was made possible by, and in turn further promoted, the gradual introduction of modern drainage, influencing the lives of water- and refuse-carriers-turned-cabbies. This transformation captures the convergence of the flows of water, sewage, electricity, and urban traffic, and the entanglement of what was underground with what was above ground. It also illustrates how distinctions between the "modernity" of the tram and the "tradition" of the coach required not only discursive rearrangements but also far-reaching spatial and material ones.

Along similar lines, as shown by both Janet Abu-Lughod and André Raymond, the two major historians of Cairo, the streetcar system was overlaid onto Khedive Ismāʿīl's planned modern city. This was made possible by metropolitan renovations carried out in the 1860s and 1870s under ʿAlī Mubārak, who introduced straight boulevards and wide squares to ventilate bad smells and "thick airs," which were considered unsanitary.[39] The absence of such thoroughfares from the "medieval" part of Cairo explains why it was never fully incorporated in the evolving transportation network.[40] Repeated complaints by the residents of the old quarters that were left behind, requesting connection to the tramway so that they too might save time and money,[41] reveal the evolution of the new transportation system to be uneven and selective: while the new speed and connectivity were making the western part of

Cairo "modern," they were simultaneously making such circumvented areas as Islamic Cairo "medieval."[42]

The convergence of running water, modern sewage, electricity, financial capitalism, modern modes of conveyance, and new trends in public opinion was perhaps best demonstrated in the construction of Heliopolis, one of the new suburbs that sprouted outside of Cairo. Built by the aforementioned Belgian transportation moguls, Heliopolis represented the entry of European capital into Egyptian urban real estate. In 1905, combining expertise in banking and transportation and drawing on a network of political connections, Baron Empain was able to buy six thousand acres of desert land northeast of Cairo at the ridiculous price of one pound per acre. (The lucrative deal with the Egyptian government was facilitated by Boghos Nūbār, son of former prime minister Nūbār Pasha). Property values skyrocketed two years later when this recently built "New Cairo," which enjoyed running water, modern sewage, and electrical illumination, was connected to the city center with two tram lines, a regular tramway, and a fast line called "the Metro," which covered the distance in fifteen minutes. In 1911, to promote this fast and glamorous new way of life, Empain's Heliopolis Oases Company even built a neon-lit Luna Park, which featured an electric rollercoaster as one of its main attractions. Accounts of people using this and other electric amusement facilities suggest that Egyptians were beginning to consume high speed and the rush of risk for cathartic purposes and as a means of getting a taste of what they assumed was the West.[43]

Spatially as well as administratively, Heliopolis was at once inside and outside Cairo proper.[44] The emergence of such new neighborhoods helps introduce an important caveat into the notion of the "annihilation of space with time" accompanied by the spatialization of time, both so prominent in the historiography of modern means of transportation. While in several important respects trains and trams, with their standard schedules, certainly helped spatialize time by promoting a linear temporality—the notion of time as a straight line[45]—their speed also did much to decouple space and time. After all, the residents of the newly built suburbs moved there because these suburbs were at once (temporally) near and (spatially) far from the busy, congested, unhealthy center. As a character in Ṭāhā Ḥusayn's 1935 novel *Adīb* (A man of letters) quite typically put it: "I must admit that I feel much gratification when I enter the city in the daytime, descending upon it from these heights as though invading it. . . . [Yet in the evening] I feel as though I am slipping out of the town, discarding its burden, casting its sins behind me, and purifying my body and soul from its filth and dirt."[46]

URBAN MODERNITY AND ITS DISCONTENTS

While Egypt's urban renewal was a long time in the making, the deployment of streetcar networks accelerated these transformations tremendously, to the extent that they appeared to constitute a watershed. It was this acceleration-experienced-as-rupture and the tram system's entanglement with running water, modern sewage, and the new dawn of electric light that made streetcars into one of the most powerful symbols of modern urbanity, along with its great promise and, for many urban dwellers, even greater disappointments.

Unsurprisingly, one of the first arenas where such tensions became apparent was the development of new suburbs. As areas connected via streetcar became closer, in temporal terms, to each other and to the city center, the value of their real estate soared. In both Cairo and Alexandria, property values near the new tram lines sometimes quadrupled within a few years.[47] And in both cities, the boom was accompanied by hostile responses to real-estate and price speculation. In addition, from the moment of its appearance, the streetcar was criticized on various grounds, technological, occupational, moral, nationalist, and economic. It was claimed that for a city like Cairo a tram system operated by horses would be more appropriate; that the tram hurt the livelihood of cabbies; that it contributed to an immoral mixture of the sexes; and that it was simply dangerous. These different objects and modes of critique poured into each other, intensified one another, were conflated and inflected.

The Empain Group, controlling both the Cairo and Alexandria tram companies, was a key player in various other imperial and colonial projects around the globe. The group's work in Egypt was part of an international enterprise engulfing transportation, banking, and electrification in China, Russia, France, South America, and Central Africa. The CTC's involvement in these affairs and its connections to large metropolitan banking and holding companies[48] infamous for their exploitative profit seeking was an object of much critique in the Egyptian nationalist press.[49] If at the turn of the century nationalist criticism of the tram company was phrased in the abstract, directed against the generic foreignness of the company, the more Egyptians learned about the actual economic and political forces that powered their trams, the more the tram itself became a symbol of the colonial condition. In 1919, the tram trolleys and stations were the first infrastructures attacked by protesters in a large-scale anticolonial uprising.

The insult of large-scale yet distant imperialism was added to local moral injuries and actual physical ones. The tram operated between 6 A.M. and 1 A.M. Together with gas and then electric lighting, a new urban nightlife was developing, especially in new entertainment centers such as Azbakīyah Gardens and Heliopolis. This brought mounting conservative criticism of what was seen by many as the corruption of public morals. The Azbakīyah Gardens adjoining the central tram terminal—in the beginning of the nineteenth century a locus of snake charming and fervent performances of Sufi mawlid and *dhikr* rituals, and later Khedive Ismāʿīl's pleasure gardens—were transformed by the tram into one of the main modern entertainment quarters in Cairo, with bars, brothels, and backstreet peepshows. Streetcars and tram stations also attracted pickpockets, beggars, and other criminals.[50] It seems that even the new standards of punctuality and promptness that the streetcar helped establish were undermined by the technology's more sinister social impact. Thus, much of the time and money saved by trams was wasted in new bars and coffeehouses spawned by the tramway.[51] Indeed, much of the criticism of these institutions stressed the time wastefulness and indolence associated with them.[52] This dark and slothful side of modernity owed its existence to the new time consciousness and to technological temporal compressions, but it was often understood as a tradition standing on its own feet and not on modernity's shoulders.

Beyond reshuffling the city's neighborhoods (while extending and reconfiguring preexisting transportation networks),[53] streetcars themselves afforded a new social space in which matters of hierarchy, difference, and conviviality were worked out. And clearly, the new neighborhoods, stations, and the tram cars were sites where existing social norms and time-tested moral codes were constantly challenged. As one motor car could carry two trail cars, a maximum of 120 passengers could ride the tram. In practice, the ratio of 180 motor cars for 60 trail cars in 1901 Egypt (there were 128 motor cars to 79 trailers in 1903 Cairo and 55 to 45 in Alexandria that year) indicates that most motor cars were unaccompanied by a trailer or accompanied by only one.[54] Depending on their routes, trams were divided into either two or three classes, fitted with seats that faced each other, in addition to a women's compartment sheltered by blinds. First class and the women's compartment were located in the front of the motor car near the driver, while the second

الفكاهة
العدد ٦
١٠ مليمات
الاربعاء
٥ يناير سنة ١٩٢٧
الكمساري : ليه الزنقه دي كلها ؟... كلكم كوم وهي لوحدها كوم...!

FIGURE 9. Woman in tram. Conductor: "Why all this crowding? All of you on one bench and her on a separate bench all to herself!" *Al-Fukāhah*, January 5, 1927.

and third classes were located toward the back or on the roof in a double decker.

By the 1920s, the Egyptian press claimed that the streetcar had become the preferred mode of urban travel for the modern Egyptian woman, even when she could call a cab or drive an automobile. Writers analyzing women's transportation proclivities often complained about their tendency to look for a seat in first class in the company of men, avoiding the special women's compartment. Writer Maḥmūd Khayrat recounted the story of a male acquaintance who climbed onboard a packed streetcar where first class was full of women. When he tried to sit in the women's section, which was completely empty, the conductor asked him to leave.[55] Such practices went along with a general relaxing of the rules of gender separation at the beginning of the century.[56] Moreover, new spaces such as the women's compartment in trams as well as trains, which brought together female strangers, fostered conversations about issues such as feminism and unveiling, making them pioneering sites of experimentation and reform.[57] Sharp criticism of these sites as being responsible for corruption and depravity soon followed.[58]

At the same time, ostensibly "fast" women in streetcars and tram stations were becoming objects of rampant sexual harassment. In 1898, *Al-Muqaṭṭam* described a new phenomenon of young men prowling tram stations and riding the tram in search of women unaccompanied by a man.[59] The tram stop near the Sunīyah girls' school had to be moved to prevent boys from harassing the students.[60] Female passengers of all ages, especially students, were subjected to sexual harassment even in the women's compartment, at least according to realistic stories such as Iḥsān ʿAbd al-Quddūs's *Anā Ḥurrah* (*I Am Free,* whose female protagonist is a student in Sunīyah, as it happens), which recounts how older women often pinched and felt young girls' bodies to check if they were good matches for their sons.[61] It is not hard to see why the modernity of the tram reeked of promiscuity and duress.

A STREETCAR NAMED DISASTER

The boom in inner-city traffic during the last third of the nineteenth century was contradictory and conflict ridden. The constant influx of new cabs and passengers made it almost impossible to establish an acceptable, stable fare for the ride. In a volatile place like early 1880s Alexandria, price disputes between passengers and drivers of different ethnic groups sometimes developed into large-scale conflicts. The onset of two of the most significant political events of this period, the ʿUrābī revolt and the British invasion of Alexandria, involved such price disputes.[62]

The newly paved streets were chaotic and dangerous places, sites of clashes and accidents. This appears to be especially the case in Alexandria, where the ratio of vehicles per inhabitant was significantly higher than in Cairo and where streets were paved with slippery granite offering dangerous footing for horses.[63] The spread of the tramway had various and sometimes contradictory effects on these frantic streets. On the one hand, the public quickly became dependent on the regularity, frequency, and punctuality of the new transportation technology, which, like the train, did not require rest, and whose profit was predicated on continuous motion. In 1898, less than a year after the tram was introduced into Alexandria, the public was accustomed to a streetcar every five minutes, and the municipality granted the local tram company tax benefits that enabled extensive track deployment within two years.[64]

However, less than ten days after the news of the tram company's plans reached the newspapers, Alexandria coach drivers gathered in front of city hall to protest the approval of the new plan, which, they claimed, would deal a fatal blow to their livelihood.[65] Though in the long term the tramway did not hinder, and even promoted, other modes of conveyance, the tram and carriage were time and again seen as rivals. Tram poles at street corners and intersections often made it hard for coaches to make the turn. The deployment of these poles therefore quickly became a bone of contention occupying municipal authorities, which had to approve the erection of each and every pole.[66] At the turn of the century, urban authorities were constantly disentangling the growing network of tram poles and overhead wires from the network of telegraph poles and wires.[67] Within less than a decade, various plans were being considered to reduce the risk of electrocution[68] and solve the congestion that trams and their infrastructure brought to Egyptian streets by moving them underground.[69]

As a nexus of real-estate and financial speculation, immorality, and competition with other means of transportation, the tramway provided an intersection and focal point for various kinds of discontent with capitalist urban modernity in a colonial setting. The most widespread critique of the streetcar, the one that had the most popular appeal and therefore became a conduit combining other critiques, was related to the vehicles' role in road accidents. Coaches and trams changed the character of city streets from relatively static social interaction into swift and dangerous movement. Tram accidents began to occur within a week of the system's inauguration—when a toddler's body was torn in two between the metal wheels and track[70]—and they never stopped. The language of such news items, as well as of poems[71] and visual representations of tram accidents, veered toward the grisly. Such accounts mark the emergence of a new popular sensationalism that the Egyptian press shared with counterparts in Europe and the United States, where in these very years newspapers also started printing items about mangled bodies shoveled from under streetcars.[72] *Al-Muqaṭṭam* tells of a special publication, *Al-Nashrah al-Kahrabāʾīyah* (The electrical bulletin), which was devoted to recording these accidents beginning in 1896. In subsequent years, road accidents became a constant part of new "Police News" columns *(Akhbār al-Būlīs)* in various newspapers.[73]

If during the tram's dry run the vehicle was followed by children shouting "Al-ʿifrīt al-ʿifrīt," a new image of ʿAzrāʾīl (the Islamic Angel of Death) following the tram to collect the souls of its victims quickly became so compelling that lawyers began formulaically opening lawsuits against the company by referring to it.[74] We have seen in chapter 3 how evoking such specters was a common middle-class strategy of domesticating new technologies. If, according to the *ḥadīth,* "speed is from the devil," the devil followed the streetcar. Cairo and Alexandria were by no means unique in summoning the Grim Reaper with an electric tram. British and American popular newspapers were also filled with skeletal figures in the tram's driving seat.[75] But whereas turn-of-the-century newspapers in many advanced urban centers around the world summoned their respective cultural imageries of sudden death, in Egypt this protocol evoked the difference between an Islamic tradition and the dystopias of the modern Belgian tram. When speed could be made to speak with a foreign accent, its antithesis could assume a domestic tone.

At first glance it is not easy to reconcile the mounting public alarm regarding the new danger of road accidents with the sparse and unreliable statistics concerning this matter, which indicated that during the early twentieth century Egypt did not experience an exceptional accident rate. For example, a 1905 report composed by the Englishman heading the Egyptian Public Works Ministry stated that in Cairo, "nine fatal, five serious, and ninety-one slight accidents occurred in the tramways in 1904, *not a large number if the number of people travelling by these lines be taken into account.*"[76] Indeed, during the previous year (1903), five hundred persons were killed in Britain by horseless vehicles.[77]

It is unclear if this data, when compared to the newspaper hype, reflects underreporting on the part of the tram company or an exaggeration in the press, or both. But one thing seems plausible: a rate of two accidents per week, seen as tolerable by foreign officials, was unacceptable to the effendis forming public opinion. As stated above, the urban renewal involving the tram significantly reduced the rate of mortality related to health in Egypt's cities. But as fewer and fewer urbanites were dying of disease and poor hygiene—taken by God in the privacy of their homes—more people were taken by ʿAzrāʾīl, dying a ghastly public death in the street, spread on newspaper sheets. It was this new visibility of death, and the new possibilities for assigning blame and contextualizing them, that helped politicize road accidents. Whereas in a place like New York it was "the violence, suddenness and randomness (and, in a sense, the humiliating publicity) of accidental death in the metropolis" that made road accidents categorically different,[78] in Cairo all of the above were intensified and inflected by the fact that, rather than being vehicles of randomness, streetcars seemed to target certain victims and spare others.

Indeed, road accidents were frequently presented in Egyptian newspapers as instances of a foreign company risking the lives of local Egyptians:

> Not a week goes by without us hearing tragic news about the accidents involving the electric tram in Egypt, running over this person and hitting that other person.... And we do not see anybody complaining to the company. Our respectable government seems either oblivious about these tragic accidents, or incapable of punishing the company because it is foreign, leaving things as they are, as it gave the company free reign with its vehicles and drivers to roam the capital's streets with no regard to the blind, children and old in its way.[79]

If the framework for explaining accidents in the above article was nationalist, another stance, critiquing the commodification of human life, was almost as common. As another article from 1896 put it, "The price of human life has greatly cheapened and the tramway carts have opened the door to buying and selling it."[80] These modes of critique were often woven together, as in the case of the typical claim that the lives of Egyptians were cheap in the eyes of the foreign management of the tram company, as revealed by their use of malfunctioning equipment and barbaric drivers.[81] In short, tram accidents offered an avenue for the development and intersection of pointed anticolonial and anticapitalistic critiques.

Criticisms of the commodification of time and risk not only overlapped with anticolonial understandings of accidents; they often also converged in the street. On June 27, 1899, when a passenger coach carrying an English gentleman started to turn near the police station of the Laban district in Alexandria, one of the horses lost its footing on the slippery granite and fell on the ground exactly on top of or very close to the tramway. The coachman hurried to alert the driver of an approaching tram, calling on him to stop. However, the latter refused and ended up hitting the horses. The story might have ended with the arrest of the tram driver, but minutes later another tram approached the crowded street. When people at the scene asked the driver to stop and wait until the crowd could disperse, he refused. Several people then climbed onto the tram and started beating the driver. When a policeman tried to interfere, they attacked him, too.

The Alexandria reporter covering the story for the Cairo-based *Al-Tilighrāfāt al-Jadīdah* (The new telegrams) provides a revealing explanation for the reckless behavior of the tram drivers: "All these accidents are the outcome of a new regulation issued by the tram company according to which drivers may stop their trams under no circumstances, and may only alert of their coming [by using their horns]. A driver not complying with this regulation is subject to a salary deduction."[82]

This was an astute observation. Unlike private carriages, which picked up their passengers wherever they could find them and stopped whenever requested, during this time tram companies in Egypt and other places started enforcing exacting schedules. To accustom people to waiting at the station, they forbade drivers to stop anywhere other than at designated stops. While (in Egypt, foreign) inspectors were meant to put these new regulations into effect, the best method proved to be self-regulation by the drivers themselves. Tying these reforms of time and space to the drivers' salaries led to road accidents in places as distant as Alexandria and Rhode Island, where exactly a year after the aforementioned clash a similar collision occurred, leading to the worst mass transportation accident in the state's history, which was attributed to "the desire of all motor-men to make time" and to new schedules introduced by a hard-hearted management.[83]

Such incidents might resonate with a familiar narrative concerning the inherent internal contradictions of modern urbanity, recorded anywhere from Rhode Island to Berlin. But the *Al-Tilighrāfāt al-Jadīdah* reporter stressed the European origins of the new temporal arrangements, thereby contextualizing the predicament of the (Egyptian) tram drivers.[84] Later analyses of accidents often featured a similar distribution of fault and tended to stress that deadly speed originated in directives issued by the European management of the tram company. Indeed, this is the key context for understanding Bayram al-Tūnisī's poetic rendition of the instructions of the European tram's director:

> We shall go back and forth with speed
> And he who dies under the wheels
> Shall not die without reason
> And death is not a big deal.[85]

In Egypt, the critique of the capitalist arrangements that made such accidents likely intensified the anticolonial stance according to which a *foreign* tram company was making profits at the expense of *Egyptian* passengers and pedestrians. Cairo and Alexandria, of course, were far from being the only cities undergoing significant adjustments in the age of the tram trolley and automobile: early trams wreaked havoc in Western Europe and North America not very long before (and more often after) doing so in Egypt. Yet in Egypt, road accidents were identified as surface outbursts of the deep-seated violence of colonial modernity.

The Alexandria regulation cited above depicts almost literally the new time-is-money logic that was gaining ground in Egypt and elsewhere: a tram driver who does not stick to the schedule is fined. In this respect the accident captures a paradox. On the one hand, as demonstrated above, the public had already become dependent on the punctuality, speed, connectivity, and regularity of trams, as well as on the competitive fixed fares that such a network of swift and efficient mass transportation could offer.[86] This was especially true for scores of urban dwellers who moved to suburbs such as Ramleh near Alexandria or Heliopolis near Cairo and for the business owners in Azbakīyah, all of whom became dependent on the tram's annihilation of space for their daily commute.[87] By 1902, a daily average of 46,373 passengers (8 percent of the population) rode the tram in Cairo, and this number climbed to 52,673 in the subsequent year (this was about double the number of daily tram passengers in Alexandria).[88] The new swiftness and punctuality of the tram was eventually even commodified to advertise Tramway Watches "chosen by the ESR and the Electric Tram Company."[89] On the other hand, neither the public nor the physical infrastructure was ready for the implications of introducing abstract clock time into Egyptian urban space, as the crowd articulated violently and clearly.

Despite the oblique predictions of their owners, horse-drawn vehicles did not disappear with the advent of the tram. The opposite was the case: coaches extended tram lines and benefited from the trend toward more passengers, better roads, and rapidly growing cities that offered more space to cover and more hours of activity to do so.[90] Yet despite (and probably because of) the mutual dependence of animal-powered and electric vehicles, newspapers plotted them as emblems of tradition and modernity respectively. In a rhymed open letter written on behalf of an anthropomorphized tram car to an omnibus coach in 1904, the former addressed the latter (in the feminine) as "old" *(ʿAjūz)* and "ancient" *(ʿAtīqah).* By contrast, the tram described itself in the letter as an upholder of order and respectability, as opposed to its competitor, on whose benches thigh brushes against thigh and morals are jeopardized. What is more, the tram complained that it runs over pedestrians simply because it has to share the road and stations with the coach, making the streets hopelessly congested. The tram eventually gives the coach an ultimatum and refuses to wait for a reply even one minute. If the coach should fail to comply by clearing the street, the tram would crush it along with its driver![91]

Rather than trying to disguise its violence, the tram in this piece boasts of its brutality, tooting its own horn about its strict orders, unencumbered speed, and unbending trajectories. And indeed, what was labeled "tradition" and "modernity" and symptomatized by coaches and trams respectively, came to be attached to two modes of violence akin to those depicted by Foucault as premodern and modern. In the former, the body is the theater of physical violence applied nonuniformly and haphazardly. In the latter, discipline is evenly and economically distributed in a controlled manner.[92] At least in Egypt (and probably also in Foucault's nineteenth-century France), these different manifestations of power coexisted, though labeled in a way that temporalized them as belonging to two distinct epochs. For example, whereas coaches were characterized by constant interpersonal disputes about the fare of the ride, the fixed price of the tram ticket dislocated this violence from the interpersonal realm, making it seem inhuman, a carrier of "the violence of abstraction."

The difference and coexistence of these modes of violence are both demonstrated in the following case. In January 1916, a young boy boarded a Cairo tram with a shirt so soaked in blood that his fellow passengers first thought he was a butcher boy, until the wind blew open his shirt and revealed a gory wound in his shoulder. Despite the boy's obvious distress, the tram conductor ordered him to step off the vehicle for not purchasing a ticket. Fellow passengers quickly paid the fare on behalf of the injured youth so that he could be rushed to get treatment. When they inquired about the circumstances of his wounding, the boy told them that he was accidentally stabbed during a fare dispute between a cabby and another passenger.[93] Little further commentary is required: if the coach generated such blatant physical violence between cabbies and passengers, the tram's violence was abstract, the malignant banality of proper conduct and regulations followed by the book.

IMPROPER CONDUCT

The abstract violence of the tram was easily identifiable as violence in a place like colonial Egypt because of its asymmetrical manifestation. While local and lower-class Egyptians confronted trams characterized by unbending abstraction, this was not always the case for more privileged citizens. Thus the writer Aḥmad Amīn recounted the story of a Cairo pasha who, during the 1900s, used to park his carriage on the tramway in front of his house. "It stopped the tram traffic and the vehicles stood in a long train until the pasha's children came downstairs and took the carriage to their schools."[94] Indeed, delinking hierarchies of waiting and social status could happen only in theory. Amīn's story ends aptly: when the great pasha's luck turned and he lost all his fortune, he was reduced to the humiliation of standing at the tram station, waiting for a ride like a regular citizen.[95]

The differential manifestation of the violence of the tram was perhaps most evident in the uneven distribution of the ill effects of its speed. Whereas "accidental" outbursts of violence often revealed underlying structures of domination, there were also many instances in which stable social hierarchies and structures of subjugation were momentarily undermined. Examining how violence between locals and foreigners was dealt with in Alexandria's court system, Will Henley claims that local and often lower-class drivers controlled heavy and fast machines, giving them unprecedented power vis-à-vis more privileged classes and ethnic groups. Lower-class locals working as conductors and ticket salesmen in trams and trains had a new power, which was unrelated to their class or status, in disciplining higher-class (and often foreign) passengers and enforcing order.[96]

Whereas drivers commanded (and were commanded by) the power of fast, heavy machines, with the choice to stop or not stop, tram and train conductors held (and were held by) a different kind of power. Foreigners (Greeks and Italians) controlled the high-ranking and supervisory positions in the Cairo and Alexandria tram companies; much of the workforce, amounting to over two thousand men in Cairo alone in the first decade of the twentieth century, was Arab. Local conductors and drivers were paid low wages and subjected to frequent payment deductions, as is evident from the account of the tram and coach encounter in Alexandria.

Employees responded to salary deductions in various ways, from striving to comply with the discipline imposed on them to inventing sophisticated ways of cheating the company.[97] One of the most common strategies involved selling the same ticket several times. If the ticket (like the cab's meter) was meant to enforce a stable cipher for translating travel time into money,[98] ticket reselling destabilized this index, subverting the possibility of performing such a translation. On top of this, tram tickets were printed in Europe, which led to occasional shortages or delays in supply, and hence to the confusing usage of surplus tickets from empty lines on busier ones.[99]

For about a decade, passengers tended to be complacent and even cooperative with such methods as ticket reselling, allowing these acts to be legitimized in the press as a common nationalist resistance strategy. *Egypt and the English,* which aimed to capture British public opinion on Egypt in 1908, reveals that this practice was well known to Europeans, who saw it as one of the unique features of Egyptian trams:

> The employees on the tramways excuse themselves for cheating over the tickets because they say that though the service pays so well it pays them so badly. It is a common thing for an Egyptian to tell the tram conductor not to give him a ticket which means that the conductor can keep the fare for himself. "You get so little," he says "and the company so much. They can go to hell." A friend of mine was asked right out by the tram conductor, "Do you want a ticket?" "Yes," said my friend, "I want my ticket and here is another small piastre (penny farthing) to teach you to be honest." I have myself been asked by a tram conductor—and often by Egyptians in the tram—for my tram tickets, which were, of course, going to be used in defrauding the company. This is done with added zest because the company belongs to Belgians—presumably Christians.[100]

This practice was so pervasive (also in the Egyptian State Railways, where it became a target of British rebuke)[101] that the press seriously entertained a proposal to use tram tickets also as free lottery tickets, to dissuade people from giving their tickets to conductors who would resell them.[102] Because the tram was seen as one of the key driving forces for the emergence of gambling, and particularly of the lottery in the middle of the first decade of the twentieth century,[103] this proposal nicely fit the image of the tram as an immoral device. Passenger cooperation with conductors' "corruption," which justified the appointment of European supervisors and led to lower revenues, lower wages, reduced levels of maintenance, and the use of older and deficient streetcars, as well as increased accidents, provides yet another example of how technologies operate differently in different historical and political settings.

Beyond the political aspect of riding a foreign-controlled tram run by Egyptian conductors and drivers, there were more mundane reasons for the constant subversion of the tram ticket. There was, for one, the matter of change. Though paper notes were of five or ten malīm (*millième,* or half piaster), before World War I the price for the second-class car was set at four malīm and six malīm for first class, and conductors regularly lacked change.[104] During the war itself, British soldiers enjoyed a special fare of two malīm, yet repeatedly complained that the actual cost was often three malīm because conductors pretended never to have ample change.[105]

Yet exactly when ticket reselling and similar modes of subversion were at their peak, such practices began to lose their public legitimacy. Using the power of the company against itself for advancing the interests of local conductors could work at the individual level only. And by the end of the first decade of the twentieth century, such improper conduct was gradually falling out of favor. This transition overlapped with a general disillusionment with folding colonial instrumentalism against itself and disenchantment with working the system from within, thus participating in the colonial dialogue equipped only with the faulty and limiting terminology of substandard materialism. A 1908 newspaper article described an instance in which a cheating conductor got away with his dishonesty, whereas another's salary was unrightfully deducted by an inspector who did not believe the conductor was innocent. The combination of unjust deductions and improper conduct, the writer predicted, would eventually push honest conductors to supplement their deducted income by reselling used tickets. The writer also pointed out that while the tram company was indeed foreign, many of its shareholders were Egyptian. Passenger cooperation with cheating conductors therefore meant cheating other Egyptians.[106] A resistance strategy legitimated as nationalist several years previously was now seen as harming the "Egyptian collective."[107]

That individual modes of resistance fell out of public favor may be explained by the fact that new collective modes of resistance were being explored and developed at this very time. The perspective stressing Egyptian ownership of the tram was further developed throughout the decade leading to the 1919 revolution by such writers as the preeminent Egyptian economist and industrialist and later founder of Bank Miṣr, Muhammad Ṭalʿat Ḥarb. The sophisticated economist criticized the Belgian-dominated management of the CTC for gouging working-class passengers to enrich foreign shareholders, especially the holders of the founders' shares. Ḥarb also attributed the company's huge profits to the low wages it paid its Egyptian workforce. As Robert Tignor has pointed out, these writings demonstrated Ḥarb's unmatched talent for simplifying and popularizing economic issues by casting them as national concerns.[108] Moreover, in 1908 the Egyptian government reviewed and renegotiated the fifty-year concession it had granted to the Empain Group in 1894.[109] The new charter granted 5 percent of the company's monthly profits to the government.[110] Also in 1908, Egyptian tram workers began a decade-long irregular strike campaign leading to the 1919 revolution. These processes overlapped with the unionization of railway workers and the emergence of the equation of time and money as a central arena of labor struggle in Egypt.

Yet, though the legitimacy of "improper conduct" eroded in the press with the ascent of collective modes of agitation, in practice these individual tactics never disappeared, even after the revolution. For example, a 1921 report by the Cairo police about the work of plain-clothes policemen in fighting the problem of free riders indicates that in 1920 the police handled 3,081 such contraventions.[111] These numbers surely represented only a small fraction of a widespread phenomenon that could not have taken place without the active support of tram conductors.

The most elaborate and sensitive account of improper conduct from the 1910s was authored not by a police officer or a nationalist journalist but by the British novelist E. M. Forster. While serving in Alexandria during World War I, Forster fell in love with Muḥammad al-ʿAdl, a young Arab tram conductor.[112] After first setting eyes on the handsome al-ʿAdl, the only conductor who moved among the passengers without treading on their feet, Forster would occasionally catch the Bacos line tram, hoping to spot the young conductor onboard. One evening in January 1917, Forster sat where al-ʿAdl kept his coat and al-ʿAdl asked him to rise. "You speak English," remarked Forster as he complied. "Practice make perfect," replied al-ʿAdl with an implicit invitation to talk. Thereafter, if they happened to see one another at the Ramleh terminus, al-ʿAdl would offer a half salute. During their next meeting, as Forster offered his fare, al-ʿAdl stated, "You shall never pay," reminding the Englishman of his courtesy in the coat incident. By sharing a transgression with Forster, al-ʿAdl transformed the novelist into a co-conspirator against the tram company. Al-ʿAdl might not have known about Forster's desire "to part with respectability"[113] (not an uncommon fantasy for European men in the Orient), but dropping his conductor's cloak eventually made this possible.[114]

Ultimately, Forster abandoned the pretense of accidental meeting. He also no longer attempted to pay the fare, and the two spent many joyful rides together, until an inspector caught Forster on the tram without a ticket and confronted al-ʿAdl, who found himself under threat of being fired. Forster then intervened on his friend's behalf with the stationmaster and, in their next encounter, asked al-ʿAdl if they could meet. The grateful young man answered, "Any time any place any hour." The ticket affair pushed the two men—finally as two men—into one another's arms. Years later, Forster still carried with him al-ʿAdl's picture affixed to a tram ticket.

The improper conduct animating Forster and al-ʿAdl's relationship took place at a time when such practices were publicly frowned upon and no longer considered to be legitimate action. For sure, the intimate relationship between the Englishman and Egyptian crossed the very boundaries that permitted national togetherness to occur in the first place. Yet this incident nonetheless sheds light on the structures of desire and the libidinal economies associated with acts of improper conduct on board Egyptian streetcars. Ignoring clear class and even ethnic alliances, conductors were cooperating with passengers in reselling the resources of the tram company under the nose of foreign supervisors. Conductors and passengers shared a transgression based on a mutual assumption that underneath their uniforms or clothes, they shared important commonalities. Commonality and affinity, however, were not preexisting features. Rather, they were products of acts of symbolic striptease nurtured by improper conduct, like the love of Forster and al-ʿAdl.

THE BIRTH OF DROMOPOLITICS

If ticket reselling was the conductor's preferred way of surviving and subverting the oppressive time-is-money logic underpinning the tram system, how did a typical tram driver respond to the bundling together of his salary, speed, and schedule under the watchful eye of foreign supervisors who secured this linkage? As we have seen, the tramway unevenly compressed urban space and time. The speed that facilitated this compression became a central object of criticism in the Egyptian press.[115] The abstract categories of risk available to us cast the speed of modern means of transportation as class-, gender- and colorblind. But it was clear to readers of Egyptian newspapers that the unfortunate effects of the tram's speed were unevenly distributed.

The dangerous speed of the tram was often linked in the press to tram drivers' obligation to keep to schedule and heavy workload.[116] This was indeed an accurate observation: by 1900 there were no clear speed limits for trams. Tram drivers were instructed by law to adjust their speed according to their schedules.[117] The schedule was simultaneously the driver's objective and the means of supervising him; it was keeping its keepers. Yet it was always clear that the schedule, an ostensibly abstract standard or yardstick that seemed to precede the circumstances of its production, was imposed from outside, indexing a colonial power hierarchy. Even the schedule's language let this fact slip: a 1905 *Al-Kawkab* article cited complaints by "many local Egyptians" about the fact that the departure and arrival times of Alexandria streetcars were written only in French or English and followed the "Frankish" timekeeping system. "What should an Egyptian who does not know these languages do? Should he go to the translators' school?"[118]

The danger of unrestricted speed manifested itself mainly in two ways. First, speed resulted in road collisions with other vehicles and pedestrians. Streetcars driving at full speed through Cairo and Alexandria's crowded streets without being able to change course violently introduced new braking distances, modes of attentiveness, and hazard zones. Cabbies and cart drivers halting twenty meters or more in front of a moving tram often discovered, sometimes with fatal consequences, that this did not allow the tram sufficient time to stop.[119] Tram drivers in turn resorted to unconventional methods for clearing a crowded street, including—beyond frequent use of their horn—shouting, spitting, and in some (probably extreme) cases, throwing stones.[120] Because the horn and bell pedals were operated by foot,[121] tram drivers were left with free hands for steering and stoning pedestrians. In one instance in 1905, a driver threw a heavy block with such force that he himself fell out of the vehicle, which then collided head-on with another tram.[122]

Second, to keep to schedule, tram drivers regularly refused to stop at stations to allow passengers to get on and off, pretending not to notice people waiting in stations or to hear requests to alight coming from within the tram.

They kept moving unless the request came from a foreigner or a woman, in which case drivers were more inclined to stop.[123] In the 1910s, Bayram al-Tūnisī tried to capture, in a colloquial carnivalesque poem titled "Al-Trām," the vehicle's hierarchies as it ignored a local woman waiting at the station with her young children; refused to stop and let an old man afraid of breaking his neck get off at al-ʿAtabah and instead took him all the way to Giza; separated a beautiful young woman from her father and exposed her, unguarded, to men in the street, and so on.[124]

What is more, when trams did stop and even when they only decelerated, conductors would hasten passengers on and off the vehicle, risking their own lives and the lives of passengers. The latter not infrequently fell off the high steps, while conductors were exposed to the anger of passengers. For instance, Muḥammad al-ʿAdl, Forster's lover, told the novelist how, when he once asked an officer "either to get on the tram or off it," the officer hit him with his cane.[125] In other instances, passengers had to jump on and off the moving streetcar, often resulting in injury.[126] Finally, *Al-Ṣiḥāfah* and other Egyptian newspapers argued that the tram company regularly compensated accident victims if they were foreigners but refused to compensate Egyptian victims.[127]

At least in the way these realities were transformed into cultural representations in newspapers—the media that made them available for experience—most victims of the tram's speed were local Egyptians, and accidents were more frequent in popular neighborhoods. A 1904 colloquial poem published in *Majallat al-Dunyā al-Jadīdah* (The new world magazine) even beseeched the tram to balance out its killing sheet by directing its lethal energies toward al-Ẓāhir (a neighborhood populated mostly by foreigners at the time) instead of al-Fajjālah (a popular quarter).[128]

Paradoxically, policies and protocols that were derived from the logic of time-is-money often translated into the opposite logic of "haste makes waste," adding fuel to the fire of haste aversion. Conductors reselling tickets, rushed drivers refusing to allow passengers onboard, and avoidable road accidents that damaged equipment and forced the company to pay compensation all made little economic sense. One could certainly claim that haste was from the devil without appearing unmodern or irrational. We may evoke "colonialism" to explain this puzzle: in this context, colonialism entailed labor practices that favored fining and punishment over incentivizing, as we have seen to be the case in the Egyptian State Railways. Colonialism also accounted for the fact that, at least according to critiques in the press and even in popular poetry, members of the managing elites seldom used the tram and showed little interest in understanding it as a social space.[129] As workers repeatedly complained, the CTC in Egypt had only an assistant manager who reported to the head office in Brussels, a circumstance leading to frustrating delays in addressing complaints.[130]

Questions of speed and risk gained a new urgency with the appearance of automobiles in Egypt's streets in 1903. The 1904 "Automobile Law" stipulated that car drivers were required to "slow their vehicles to the average speed of a human walking on foot when approaching narrow or crowded streets, and they are obliged to fix their speed to a velocity that would ensure preventing any danger to the public, never exceeding fifteen kilometers per hour inside the city."[131] Yet laws often reveal the persistence of the norms they aim to alter. A 1908 article titled "Death under the Wheels" reveals something of how pedestrians experienced the speed of trams and cars.

> A pedestrian walking in public streets nowadays cannot guard his life from the dangers waiting on the road. You always see him cautious around tramways and in the vicinity of cars, and he is always afraid, looking right and left, up and down. Car drivers move at such speed as if racing the wind, and they have nothing with which to alert pedestrians except for the horn, which they use when approaching pedestrians, who in turn have little chance to escape from death under the wheels ... but the warnings of newspapers and their calls for reinforcement of legislation that would prevent cars from going at such speed fall on deaf ears. The reason is that the officials in charge are not among those pedestrians who fear the automobile. On the contrary, those officials move by means of coach or car and therefore do not pay heed to those who earn very little.... Cars move at such a speed that even if one wanted to know their registration numbers [this is impossible] as they fly past his gaze.[132]

In what may best be understood as a political analysis of unrestricted speed, exactly when a new collective consciousness about the need to oppose its harms was in the making, the writer connected acceleration to the tendency of Egyptian government officials to blindly imitate foreigners. The only remedy, he concluded, would be for those officials to step out of their offices and walk the streets on foot, in which case they would realize how dangerous things had become. Government officials were probably less oblivious to road accidents than the writer assumed; actually, they were discussing the dangers of both trams and automobiles at the time.[133] But the main points of the article are valuable nonetheless: things look different from inside a fast-moving vehicle than they do when trying to dodge such vehicles as a pedestrian, and Egyptian politics tended to favor the former perspective at the expense of the latter.

The insights of Egyptian newspapers critiquing the tram reveal—not despite but because of their anticolonial biases—that speed, like time and space, was becoming a political category. Though the violence of trams was supposedly class-, gender-, and colorblind, its risks were in fact unevenly distributed, justifying claims in the press that Egyptian life was cheaper in the eyes of the foreign tram company. Lower-class Arabs were more likely to be among the pedestrians exposed to this danger, and as passengers they were more prone to being injured as a result of jumping on and off a moving tram than were foreigners, for whom drivers tended to stop. Moreover, the former received inferior medical treatment when injured and were less likely to receive compensation from a company that was more prone to compensate foreigners, who could resort to Egypt's Consular and Mixed Courts, which were inaccessible to locals. If risk is a "systematic way of dealing with hazards and insecurities induced and introduced by modernization," as Ulrich Beck puts it,[134] the Egyptian colonial "risk society" was organized in response to the risks of mechanized speed in ways that revealed its dominant power hierarchies. As a focal point for all these tensions, supposedly empty mechanized speed gradually came to be perceived by many Egyptians as fraught with new ways of experiencing, critiquing, and analyzing their pervasive conundrums. Against this background, slowing down could emerge as a form of anticolonial critique.

SIX

Counterclockwise Revolution

Marx said revolutions are the locomotives of world history. But perhaps it is quite different. Perhaps revolutions are the grab for the emergency brakes by the generations of humanity travelling in this train.

WALTER BENJAMIN, *"Preparatory Notes to the 'Theses on the Philosophy of History'"*

THE GROWING DEPENDENCE OF THE colonial project in Egypt on technologies of rule such as railways, tramways, and telegraphs—its "networked" nature—made it pervasive and effective. Yet it also opened up unforeseen avenues of anticolonial contestation for the Egyptian operators and users of these technologies. As a result, the technological aspects of colonialism in Egypt helped demarcate the spectrum of possibilities for anticolonial action and informed the shapes and foci of anticolonial modes of affinity, first and foremost nationalism.

It has become commonplace to assume that by connecting distant places and peoples and creating a shared temporality, technological networks promoted community building. Previous chapters demonstrated that in Egypt this might indeed have been the case, but not so much by homogenizing space and time as by solidifying a set of constitutive differences (temporal and otherwise). The current chapter explores what happens when such technologies suddenly stop working—what the exception may reveal about the norm. The case in point, Egypt's so-called 1919 revolution, involved a cutoff of almost all the country's transportation and communication lines and consequently an abrupt suspension of the temporal and political orders that these lines held together.

We begin by examining patterns of industrial conflict in the preceding decade. Beyond preparing the ground chronologically for the eruption of the revolt, these experiences reveal that technical infrastructures taught their operators lasting lessons in activism and provided opportunities for the rehearsal and development of militancy. During the 1910s, Egyptian railway and tramway workers turned the tables on their foreign supervisors and bosses, demanding shorter workdays and increased wages, thereby claiming the benefits of membership in the same monetized temporality that governed their labor. Workers participated in the 1919 revolt mainly by organizing large-scale strikes—a tactic they had fully acquired and perfected during the previous decade.

Yet the time-is-money equation that workers tried to put into egalitarian effect through work stoppage was only one of the temporalities punctuating the revolt. Middle- and upper-class nationalists focused their struggle on the pressing need for immediate political independence. Faced with the protracted deferrals of British diplomats, who tried to postpone addressing the question of Egyptian autonomy, they struggled for a prompt resolution. Their medium of choice was the telegraph, which they transformed into a political technology that helped make their grievances heard instantaneously and widely. Finally, for Egyptian peasants attacking rail lines and telegraph and telephone poles in 1919, the uprising was characterized by wholesale rejection of the monetized notion of time and the resurrection of long-suppressed millenarian utopias and cyclical temporalities.

These various notions of time corresponded to clashing understandings of independence and different horizons of freedom and well-being. Eventually, the revolution promoted only one of these agendas, bringing about political emancipation from the formal bonds of colonialism while stifling competing visions. As Marx put it, "The limits of political emancipation appear at once in the fact that the state can liberate itself from constraint without man himself being really liberated; that a state may be a free state without man himself being a free man."[1] Marx suggested that the individual liberal freedom from interference may create a barrier to attaining real human emancipation based on the community and nonalienated labor.[2] The former kind of liberty was the one that Egyptian nationalists aspired to and eventually attained. Retracing the vexed genealogy of Egypt's nominal emancipation from colonialism and its realization of the anemic effendi notion of freedom, the chapter examines some of the connections between temporality and political possibility, including the ways in which anticolonial nationalism not only involved heterogeneous temporalities but also managed to bring them together, reluctantly and unevenly.

MECHANICAL TIME, WORK DISCIPLINE, AND INDUSTRIAL COLONIALISM

Despite earlier struggles, organized, direct labor activism in Egypt did not start until 1908, roughly when conceptions of "workers" and "the working class" began to surface in the effendi imagination.[3] As Zachary Lockman shows, the Egyptian tram and rail workers who pioneered this wave of militancy were not passive receptacles for their image in the effendi imagination. Instead, they discovered their collective agency also through other sources, such as Greek and Italian workers who had been exposed to unionization and syndication in their countries of origin or European discourses of class.[4] Ilham Khuri-Makdisi similarly traces the development of new patterns of contestation, particularly the strike, through networks of workers, labor migrants and intellectuals all over the eastern Mediterranean.[5] The 1908 strikes in Egypt, she shows, were part of a larger Ottoman wave of strikes in the aftermath of the Young Turk Revolution.[6]

To these human role models, an important source of inspiration and pedagogy may be added: the technological networks these workers activated. The operation of the tram and rail systems was predicated on synchronization and cooperation, which the techniques of collective labor struggle replicated. Interfaces within and between systems eventually increased the degree of collaboration among their operators, swelled their numbers, and enriched their repertoires of contention. Distinct from other arenas of work stoppage, technologies of transportation and communication could be physically stopped. Unlike tangible commodities, movement and information could not be adequately supplanted by other means or stored as spares in warehouses. And they were literally what made all other economic sectors move. For these reasons, the Egyptian transportation sector led the way in frequency and intensity of strikes, beginning with European train drivers in the 1860s;[7] coal heavers in Port Said and Alexandria during the 1860s, 1880s, and 1890s;[8] Alexandria and Ramleh tramwaymen in 1900;[9] and Cairo cabbies in 1907,[10] paving the road for the tram strike of 1908.

Labor unrest was catalyzed by an economic crisis in 1907 and inflation rates that spelled a drop in real wages.[11] The October 1908 strike, the first tramway stoppage in Cairo, reveals how the industrial logic of time-is-money that characterized the tramway system seeped also into the discourse and political horizons of its human elements. Thus better pay and reduced working hours were the top items on the strikers' list of demands, along with an end to fines by foreign supervisors.[12] In this light, we may paraphrase E. P. Thompson's famous statement about the relation between industrial capitalism and clock discipline[13] in a way that broadens the picture to include more than employers and employees. While workers equated time and money so as to fight their employers, the human antagonists inherited and internalized the mechanical rhythms of their devices.[14]

Forcefully suppressed by the police within less than a week, the 1908 strike nevertheless sent widely felt shockwaves throughout the capital. The supportive nationalist newspaper *Al-Liwāʾ* described, with an evident degree of happy dismay, how Cairo's populace seemed to have suddenly swelled, "filling the streets and sidewalks, where a passerby bumps into this person and knocks down that person as a result of the congestion of people coming from all directions."[15] This newly emergent multitude captured the attention and imagination of the nationalist press. The budding awareness on the part of middle-class nationalists that Egypt's transportation workers held the keys to more than their own fates would be nurtured in the following years.

Workers too gained a valuable lesson about the power given them by their machines. As Beinin and Lockman indicate, as in other cases, the emergence of a formal labor organization followed, rather than preceded, a major strike—in this case with the establishment of the Cairo tramway drivers and conductors union in March 1909.[16] This alliance of the workers situated inside the streetcar would mushroom over the next decade to include the entire tramway workforce.

Khuri-Makdisi directs our attention to the "contagious" nature of labor unrest and its tendency to spill over from one arena to another, attributing this phenomenon to the circulation of radical discourses and tactics.[17] That such turbulence was uncontainable may also be seen as an indication of the connected and interfacing nature of infrastructures that build off each other physically or institutionally. Indeed, the next few years saw a rapid increase in connectivity among labor struggles in interfacing networks. Between 1910 and 1911, tramway workers gradually escalated their demands and increased their cooperation, gaining experience with the power of collaboration inside the workplace as well as establishing alliances with the general public. In early November 1910, less than two weeks after the violent suppression of a railway repair workers' strike, workers in the tramway repair shops struck for a ten-hour day, already achieved by the traction workers, and for higher wages.

Several months later, in 1911, they joined forces with the drivers and conductors, fighting for an even more radical arrangement of time and money.[18] This time they not only stopped working and blocked the tracks but also attacked trams operated by strikebreakers. Tram workers also implemented some of the railwaymen's tactics in blocking the tracks.[19] Later that year, a general strike of the entire tramway workforce was coordinated by bicycle messengers, leaving the public "astonished at the appearance of complete unity among the tramway workers despite their different nationalities and their large numbers."[20] These struggles were eventually crushed by the police.[21] However, the new unity was not missed by members of the effendiyya, nor by the workers themselves. After the strike, an article in *Al-Liwāʾ*, quick to appropriate and recast the new techno-political forms of togetherness in middle-class terms, co-opted the workers' struggle: "Your cause is the cause not only of the tramway workers, but of all the workers of Egypt. Your strike, coming after that of the *ʿAnābir* [railway workshop] workers, is proof that a new power is emerging in Egypt, which cannot be ignored."[22]

In 1911, striking Cairo tramwaymen were joined by workers of the gas, water, and electric companies, the railway workers at Bāb al-Ḥadīd and Būlāq, and a month later the tram workers of Alexandria.[23] Any account of this collaboration has to consider the technical interfaces among these work environments[24] and the managerial overlap of their directors and owners. Technical connectivity also facilitated long-distance politics: during the summer of 1911, the residents of Būlāq could circumvent the summer migration of the Egyptian administration from Cairo to Alexandria by telegraphing the khedival *qāʾimmaqām* in the port city, thus supporting the striking Cairo tram workers.[25]

For the rest of the decade, tram workers developed elaborate means of struggle that did not amount to a full-fledged strike but managed to severely reduce work pace and employers' profits. Gradually, resistance became more and more coordinated and machinelike. Drivers sabotaged vehicles and the track, while maintenance and workshop workers dawdled over repairs. Lawyers representing the workers then used the poor condition of the streetcars and network to damage the tram company's reputation in the press, and exploited the explicit power hierarchy between Egyptians and foreigners—evident to every passenger—to argue that the foreign company didn't care for the lives of locals and was willfully using defective equipment so that it could distribute bigger dividends.[26] Dissent, it appears, was assembled on the same line that fused the material parts of the tramway.

Though this new workers' coordination cannot be reduced to its technological dimensions alone, it is likely that the leadership role assumed by tram and rail workers in the Egyptian labor struggle should be associated with the synchronized systems they operated: "Near machines we act like machines."[27] In the words of an Egyptian railway worker describing several years later how the railway punctuated his life, "During my studies I did not care for months and years, but in my job I have learned to calculate minutes and seconds, and on my way to the station I have learned how to direct my steps along the shortest line in the street, avoiding encounters that would make me slow my pace, while growing angry with pedestrians who walk in a crooked line that forces me to slow suddenly so that I can calculate how to avoid running into them. But I have also learned how to compensate for these delays."[28]

The company of trains had made this worker into a human motor steadily driving itself along the street. The linearity, speed, and punctuality that permeated the body also informed its capacity for intersubjectivity and communality: as the text continues, it becomes clear that auto-mechanizing and surrendering oneself to "unnatural" industrial tempos allow for a new kind of collective synchronization down the ranks, "from our distinguished director to the smallest in our midst. Our director is woken by the *Nāqūs* [a wooden or metal gong] for every unusual event. He gets out of bed without paying heed to the orders of nature. The inspector and the engineer, the doctor and the station supervisor, the locomotive driver and the technician, do exactly the same. Is this not one of the noble aspects of the moral link binding the members of the railway family?"[29] Becoming automatons empowered workers to organize and promote a collective political agenda. But drawing such power from machines also meant securing workers' allegiance to these artifacts, better joining human and nonhuman elements and barring any political horizon that excluded such devices.

WARTIME

In tandem with mounting labor unrest, which was growing in sophistication and zeal, as the First World War started, the vulnerability of transportation and communication systems to stoppage and the political potential of this tactic were repeatedly demonstrated across Egypt. During the war, the British, who could finally declare Egypt a formal protectorate and subject it to more direct governance, were extremely protective of their transportation and communications networks, imposing severe restrictions on rail travel and increasing the guard around train stations and telegraph offices.[30] Consider the following examples, which illustrate this edginess and the public lessons it provided. In the evening of the last day of 1915, the British garrison guarding the army telegraph in Alexandria violently attacked a cabby lingering suspiciously in front of the telegraph office. The beating continued until British officers observing from the upper-floor windows shouted orders to stop. The title of the article recounting this attack was "For What Reason? *[Mā Huwa al-Sabab?]*."[31] A day later, the Mīnā al-Baṣal police branch in the port city reported a shot fired at a freight train on its way to Alexandria, wounding one of its drivers. It was later discovered that there had been no gunshot: the malfunctioning door of a train moving in the opposite direction had slammed open just as the freight train passed on a parallel track.[32] Two days later, British military authorities disallowed civilian use of telephone lines connecting Cairo and Alexandria to Port Said, Suez, and Ismāʿīlīyah.[33] Such reports were a daily matter throughout the war. They suggest that evidence of British anxieties regarding wartime inland security of communication and transportation was accumulating in the Egyptian press, disclosing the political potential of attacking these systems. By the end of the war, the naiveté of questions like "For What Reason?" was forever gone.

Beyond these anecdotes, one issue in particular drew attention to the pervasiveness of Egypt's reliance on modern networks: a severe wartime coal crisis. If the transportation strikes of the preceding decade exposed the extent to which urban life depended on these infrastructures, coal scarcity revealed the intricate connections between city and countryside. World War I significantly destabilized the hegemony of coal as the prime global energy source, along with the industrial, labor, and political arrangements it fueled. As the war began, western front coal fields quickly became military targets in repeated attempts to capture needed energy sources and prevent rivals from doing the same. By the end of the decade, mines all across Europe were severely damaged. An entire generation of European miners was sent to the trenches, where their tunneling expertise was in great demand. Tens of thousands of British, French, and German miners died or were wounded. The war also promoted increased production of oil-burning vehicles: destroyers, tanks, and airplanes, and led to an increase in efforts to access and secure oil supplies.[34] After the war ended, especially between 1919 and 1921, a global wave of labor unrest swept through the coal-mining industry. Britain witnessed the most disruptive strikes, but labor-management conflicts occurred also in France, Germany, Belgium, and the United States.[35]

Egypt, on the receiving end of the coal industry and dependent not only on foreign mines but also on coal-burning freight steamers to import coal, experienced this turbulence with particular intensity. In 1920, the wave of English coal strikes led Britain to cede its control over the Egyptian market to the United States.[36] But the impact of these tectonic changes was felt already during the war. Consider the coverage of the wartime fuel shortage during the typical month of January 1916 in the Alexandrian newspaper *Wādī al-Nīl.* On the first of the month, the Egyptian State Railways had moved from almost complete dependency on English coal, whose price radically increased as its availability plummeted, to cheaper South African coal.[37] A day later, the Al-Ramal Tramway Company in Alexandria announced that it was cutting its lines in half as a result of the increase in coal and coal gas prices. (Gas was being sold in police stations to prevent racketeering.)[38] The company's diesel engines consumed gas imported from the United States, which was no longer available as a result of a steamer shortage.[39] The following week, the Cairo Tramway Company, whose generators burned coal, announced that it had sufficient supplies for three more months, after which it would have to stop all its lines.[40] During the first half of 1916, Egypt imported 369,683 metric tons of coal. The total imports during 1915 amounted to 1,700,074 tons, compared to 1,435,882 tons in 1914 and 1,721,415 in 1913.[41] At such reduced rates, it was only a matter of time before the country's entire coal-based infrastructure would come to a halt.

An article titled "Ghalā' al-Ghāz" (The inflation of gas) was devoted in January 1916 to the argument that the price of coal gas was not only the concern of its direct users but a general problem manifest in the prices of all basic commodities.[42] The following week, another article, titled "Is It True?" challenged the pervasiveness of the networked nature of Egyptian society, debunking the widespread claim that "the high price of coal depletes agricultural crops."[43] Attempting to influence discussions of this issue in the Khedival Agricultural Society, the article claimed that while the high coal prices hurt farmers watering their land with steam pumps, there was no indication that other farmers were being affected.

Yet compelling evidence to the contrary accumulated in the following days, from reports on the rise in rail fares and its impact on agricultural transportation[44] to data connecting the shortage of coal with the high price of flour.[45] The gradual expansion of modern systems of transportation and communication and their interconnectivity might have gone unnoticed when these systems were working smoothly. When these technologies faltered, however, their prominence became evident to all. At the very end of January, *Wādī al-Nīl* analyzed the connection between a fuel shortage and a new darkness that was suddenly palpable in Cairo as streetlights stopped working and people could not illuminate their homes, a situation leading to a sharp increase in crime rates.[46] As is often the case when a technical process is made invisible by its own success, such blackouts were precisely what brought technical complexities and fragilities to light.[47]

Even creative solutions to these problems ended up teasing out the previously veiled dependence on coal in ostensibly unrelated sectors. For example, during the war it was found that burning cottonseed-oil cake was cheaper than coal. Before the war Egypt annually produced about 85,000 tons of oil cake in excess of its domestic needs. Yet with no steamers for importing coal or exporting oil cake, in 1918 oil cake replaced coal in several industries.[48] This exchange was also facilitated by the fact that the government, artificially fixing cotton prices well below market price at the end of the war, kept the price of cottonseed-oil cake very low ($15 per ton in 1918—less than half the price two years earlier). Moreover, cake ash was a useful fertilizer, relieving the wartime shortage in nitrate fertilizers.[49] Such exchanges brought to light the intricate affinities between industry and agriculture in Egypt and their mutual dependence on similar energy sources.

ON THE SPOT

On January 8, 1918, President Woodrow Wilson delivered his famous "Fourteen Points Speech" to a joint session of the U.S. Congress, where he outlined the U.S. postwar vision, championing the right of colonial peoples to self-determination. A few weeks later, he delivered another speech, "The Four Points Address," where he again referred to his vision for the colonies.[50] Much has been written about the new Wilsonian lexicon, especially "self-determination," including its impact in the colonial world.[51] Less attention has been given to the novel style of "talking in points" developed by the wartime American president, even if this novelty was not lost on his contemporaries. "Tho Mr. Wilson has been accused of 'note-writing,'" wrote *The Literary Digest* about the Fourteen Points speech, "nobody has a keener sense of the value of the spoken word, as was shown when he amazed Congress by addressing it instead of sending it a voluminous message."[52]

The development of this telegraphic rhetoric should be understood in relation to the mechanisms put together to disseminate it internationally. Drawing on advertising techniques and new media technologies, a new U.S. propaganda machine[53] effectively utilized wireless telegraphy that reduced reliance on the British-controlled submarine cables, as well as regular cables and news agencies.[54] The Fourteen Points Speech, for example, was transmitted to Europe from the New Brunswick Marconi wireless telegraph station. Walter Lippmann, then a young journalist and the presidential aide who drafted the speech for Wilson, claimed in 1921 that "without cable, radio, telegraph and daily press the experiment of the Fourteen Points would have been impossible. It was an attempt to exploit the modern machinery of communication to start the return to a common consciousness throughout the world."[55] Part of the power of Wilson's message was found in its media. Wilson was talking over the heads of the old imperial powers, directly to the reading classes in places such as Egypt, Korea, India, and China. His call for popular democracy was practiced, not only preached. Indeed, in Egypt many attempted to reciprocate by opening up direct lines of communication with the U.S. president via the telegraph.[56]

In the postwar, interconnected world, the autonomy and stature of "men on the spot," the independent de facto British rulers who had run the empire for centuries, were coming under considerable pressure. During the late nineteenth and early twentieth centuries, many predicted that telegraphy would turn diplomats into automatons.[57] Not unlike rail and tram workers, who were at once constrained and empowered by their technologies, diplomats in a wired international arena enjoyed new kinds of leverage and agency even though they were closely supervised. But there could be no denying that things had changed. Advocates of British imperialism looked on with anxiety as public opinion and party politics at home encroached on colonial questions, and with sheer panic as colonized elites started telegraphing the Parliament and press.[58] As many contemporaries agreed, Lord Cromer's Egypt was one of the only enclaves where the "man on the spot" doctrine was still practiced. As one of them put it in 1905, "For once in the history of the Empire a really free hand has been given to the man on the spot. The four great bogies which have damped the ardour and tied the hands of some of our greatest pro-Consuls—the Home Government, Parliament, the Press and Public Opinion—have in their mercy left Egypt severely alone. In this instance they have obeyed the behest 'not to speak to the man at the wheel,' with the result that the ship has been brought to the haven by a plain straightforward course."[59]

Only a year later, public opinion penetrated even this relative bastion of autonomy. In June 1906, a small group of British officers on a pigeon-hunting expedition shot at domestic birds belonging to the villagers of Dinshaway in Lower Egypt. In self-defense, the peasants attacked the soldiers. The British overreacted, sentencing four of the villagers to death after a farcical trial. The subsequent public outcry in Egypt rumbled all the way to London, shaking the foundations of the "man on the spot" doctrine itself. British MPs addressing the issue refused to accept "the old plea that they must leave the matter in the hands of the man on the spot. He knew no more absurd line of action than that the man on the spot was to be trusted because he was the man on the spot."[60] The no fewer than five consuls general who tried to fill Cromer's boots on the ground between his 1907 resignation and 1919 were far more constrained.[61]

One of the most anachronistic aspects of this old-style mode of colonial governance, which was tailored for a fragmented empire, had to do with its temporal conventions. In sharp contrast to American rhetoric, with its bullet points, industrial metaphors, and relentless present tense, British gentlemen on the spot relied on the strict hierarchies and convoluted temporalities of the civilizing mission. They spoke in the future tense, advocated patience, and exploited the insurmountable gap between favorable dispositions in theory—say, toward Egyptian independence—and the deferral ad infinitum of their practical implementation. When Saʿd Zaghlūl (1858–1927), a former education and justice minister, requested in October 1918 that the Egyptian Legislative Assembly be reconvened, the British high commissioner, Reginald Wingate, replied: "*'Allāh ma es Sabirin izza Sabiru,'* or God helps those who are patient."[62] At a November meeting, when Zaghlūl and two colleagues demanded Egyptian independence on the basis of the standards of the civilizing mission itself, Wingate again advised patience and accused his irritated guests of lacking foresight.[63]

Afraid of losing the postwar momentum and letting the proclamation of the British protectorate over Egypt become a fait accompli, after the declaration of the armistice in November 1918 several members of the political elite sought permission to sail to London to meet directly with British decision makers and negotiate major concessions. They were Zaghlūl, Muḥammad Maḥmūd, and the two defense lawyers of the Dinshaway trial, Aḥmad Luṭfī al-Sayyid and ʿAbd al-ʿAzīz Fahmī. Wingate, aware of the nationalistic clamor across the country, was of the opinion that they should be allowed to travel, but his views were dismissed.[64] After a long delay, the Foreign Office telegraphed its refusal. The telegram stated that His Majesty's government was inclined to increase Egypt's autonomy, but the time for such freedom had not yet arrived. Also, though it would not negotiate with Zaghlūl, the government invited Prime Minister Rushdī to London at some unspecified future date but suggested that he defer this visit. In the meantime, nationalists were welcome to submit their complaints to the Residency.[65]

While awaiting their passports, Zaghlūl's supporters learned that even Wingate did not recognize them as the representatives of the Egyptian people. In response, they decided to formally establish "the Egyptian Delegation" *(al-Wafd al-Miṣrī).* They also charted a course of action that would demonstrate their representative powers not only to the British but also to the Egyptian monarchy, rival Egyptian politicians, and the Egyptian people.[66] Under martial law, nationalists were unable to call for elections. They were also restricted from holding public assemblies and subjected to strict press censorship. Under these conditions, the Wafdists were pushed to develop a new political technology of representation in the form of *tawkīlāt,* power of representation or proxy authorizations. Printed in thousands of copies and manually or telegraphically circulated in urban centers and the provinces, the certificates asked people to sign a short statement delegating to the *Wafd* full powers of representation.[67] The *tawkīlāt* were hastily drafted without a clearly articulated political program (when asked for one, Zaghlūl urged people to "sign without reading").[68]

Using *tawkīlāt* was a common legal practice in Egypt, and not a surprising choice given that Zaghlūl and his associates were all trained as lawyers. The power of a concerted media and petitions campaign relying on telegraphy, typewriters, and carbon copies was demonstrated already during the Dinshaway incident, which for several key Wafdists was their first experience in national politics.[69] But this was the first time *tawkīlāt* had been used for such political ends.[70] On November 21, faced with a barrage of signature-bearing telegrams, the British attempted to prevent people from signing the *tawkīlāt* and started confiscating them on the grounds that they violated martial law.[71] The Wafd responded by sending a series of telegrams to Woodrow Wilson and to British prime minister Lloyd George.[72]

Within a narrow window of ten days (November 13–23), the Wafd managed to gather approximately a hundred thousand signatures, representing about 10 percent of the male population. Sent by Wafdists from Cairo to their fellow members of the Legislative Assembly, the *tawkīlāt* quickly spread in the provincial constituencies of these politicians, reaching the rural masses to be signed and telegraphed or mailed back to Cairo.[73] The success of the campaign revealed an impressive political machine that relied on commitment, personal connections, and funds, as well as effective utilization of print and communication technologies. At once galvanizing and demonstrating the Wafd's popular backing, the telegraph and printing press fused the constitutive and the performative, forging a national community that nobody could ignore. Such overflowing enthusiasm was hard to curtail. Though the British forbade the campaign in November 1918, signature-bearing forms were telegraphed to the Egyptian "sultan" until the outbreak of the revolution in March 1919.

It should be noted that the title *sultan* for an Egyptian ruler was a recent innovation, meant to secure the consent of the first person to bear this title, Prince Ḥusayn Kāmil, to the deposition of his nephew, Khedive ʿAbbās Ḥilmī, who had aligned himself with the Central Powers at the end of 1914.[74] As the new ruler and his British puppeteers conceived it, the Islamic-sounding title was meant to appease the Egyptian people by conveying a degree of autonomy, lubricating the transition of Egypt from Ottoman to British suzerainty. Neither the British nor the sultan had any illusions that this would mean "anything but increase of British control."[75]

Yet immediately after the war, Sultan Fuʾād, ascending the throne in 1917, found the title to be a liability exposing him to a wave of Ottoman-style petitions.[76] In the Ottoman palace, petitioners would run through the grounds holding a burning mat above their heads, to alert the sultan with smoke to the injustice they endured. Such performances were part of an ideology of the just prince, wherein injustice was necessarily the result of the ruler's ignorance.[77] Using such Ottoman symbolic semiotics, Egyptian nationalists cleverly raised themes of justice and independence, just as Egypt's connection to the Ottoman Empire became untenable, giving way to a new ideology of territorial nationalism.[78] At the beginning of March 1919, the sultan was bombarded by telegrams and petitions boldly pressing on him the fact "that every single one of your subjects demands independence." These daring documents and their viral circulation left the sultan "shaken." Though it had been determined that they would not give cause for prosecution, neither could these texts be ignored, and they made ruling the country increasingly difficult.[79]

Indeed, though they were prevented from leaving Egypt, Wafdists were not completely stranded. Nationalists used telegraphy also to internationalize their grievances. As London was out of the question, they now sought to be heard in Paris, which for the first time hosted a sitting American president. There are records of dozens, if not hundreds, of telegrams sent to Wilson from Egypt, written by students and nationalist leaders alike, representing probably only a small fraction of the actual volume of this campaign.[80] On January 3, 1919, Zaghlūl himself telegraphically complained to Wilson that his two previous telegrams were unanswered. Ten days later, he wired again, and then again a month later. The last cable was intercepted by British intelligence.[81] Indeed, even though most of these appeals went unanswered, they were far from ineffectual. Dispatching them was the symbolic equivalent of running with a burning mat in the sultanic divan. And because the British were closely monitoring all communications, these gestures often found an audience, if not always their original addressees.

On March 6, 1919, General Watson, the commander of the British forces in Egypt, summoned Zaghlūl along with three other Wafdists and demanded that they stop their campaign against the British presence in the country. As was often the case after such meetings, both parties turned to the telegraph: the Egyptians, signaling that they knew who was pulling the strings, sent a defiant telegram to Lloyd George,[82] whereas the British sought the approval of the Foreign Office to arrest and deport the insolent Zaghlūl.[83]

On March 8, Zaghlūl and three other prominent Wafdists were arrested and put on the first steamer out of Egypt. News of the arrest sparked a wave of demonstrations in Cairo and Alexandria, and across the countryside. Egyptians of various classes, religions, and genders targeted communication and transportation lines, bringing the entire country to a halt. Realizing that the situation was getting out of hand, the British dispatched to Egypt Field Marshal Edmond H. Allenby, the most celebrated British war hero, and announced the release of the exiled Wafdists as a sign of good faith. Moreover, Allenby granted the Wafdists permission to sail to France.

Incidentally, Zaghlūl and his associates had been deported to Malta, exactly the meeting point of the submarine telegraph cables connecting the streets of Cairo to the halls of Versailles. Using this connection, Allenby attempted to remotely control the international diplomatic arena to quell the revolt at home. Within days of his late March arrival in Egypt, he started pressing for American recognition of the protectorate, trying to dissuade the Wafdists from challenging a decision supported by their hero, President

Wilson.[84] Frantic telegrams about "the grave situation" in Egypt were sent to the U.S. president from his own consul general in Cairo. On April 19, just as Zaghlāl landed in Marseilles, Wilson recognized the protectorate.[85] For the stunned Egyptian delegates, this was a "bolt of lightning"[86] or "a thunderbolt from the clear sky"[87]—statements applying to the message as well as to the medium.

Two weeks later, Allenby urgently telegraphed the British delegation in Paris his assessment that "the nature of [the Wafdists'] reception in Europe will have considerable effect on situation here," trying to arrange for them to meet with "responsible Allied statesmen" who would support the British presence in Egypt.[88] The field marshal was attempting to orchestrate the movements and interlocutions of the delegates, shaping the kinds of opportunities available to them in Europe. Such strategies assumed that the Egyptian delegates would maintain some long-distance control over what happened at home. The British knew this to be the case, as they kept close watch over the telegraphic communication among nationalists and journalists in Egypt and Europe.[89] The occupation authorities attempted to control the flow of information in and out of Egypt also to limit what the British Parliament and other forums of public opinion knew about the revolt and the measures used to suppress it, especially with regard to the harsh collective punishments being meted out. Allenby's men made sure, for example, that "any communiqués from Egypt dealing with the burning of villages etc., should be carefully censored before publication, otherwise questions in Parliament are almost certain to arise."[90]

Yet the telegraph was a double-edged sword. Circumventing press censorship, many Egyptians, particularly the members of dozens of student organizations, used this medium to directly contact people in Europe and the United States to inform them of unreported atrocities carried out by British soldiers across the country.[91] Materials were also sent to the Egyptian delegates to be used for propaganda in Paris. The Egyptian delegation stayed in Europe for almost a year, trying to bring their cause to the attention of the delegates and journalists at the conference. They sought, for example, to expose British brutality by arranging to document and photograph marks on the bodies of flogged villagers in the Delta. Such evidence was widely circulated, forcing the British to conduct a thorough investigation.[92] Moreover, Egyptian leaders telegraphing home from Paris seemed to be able, to some extent, to fan the flames at home insofar as developments in the diplomatic arena required.[93] Nationalists and colonialists alike took advantage of telegraphic instantaneity for mobilization, long-distance politics, and contestation in different courts of public opinion. But for the nationalists, technological immediacy also became a political principle in its own right, an ideal to which they aspired. The telegraph was the emblem of a new nationalist politics of here and now.

REVOLUTIONARY TIME

In early 1919, a few months before Zaghlūl's arrest, two labor struggles were brewing in Egypt. The Cairo tramway workers petitioned at the beginning of the year for a shorter workday and increased wages. In February, railway repair workers demanded doubled wages, termination of arbitrary fines, time off for the Friday noon prayer, and a leave of absence for the ḥajj.[94] A day after the March 8 arrest of the Wafdists, students took to the streets.[95] They called for a general strike on March 10 and gathered for a large "peaceful" demonstration in which they attacked trams and broke windows of foreign businesses.[96] On March 11, tram and cab drivers joined the strike, and transportation in Cairo stopped completely.[97]

Tramwaymen were playing a complicated game. Three days after Zaghlūl's detention, their representatives telegraphed the British authorities claiming that, because months of repeated demands to reduce working hours and increase wages had been ignored, they were now resorted to striking.[98] The telegram was sent exactly at the moment the British forbade political meetings, and it is therefore impossible to say whether workers were jumping on the strike wagon to promote their own interests or whether they were couching their strike in "apolitical" language, using the time-is-money discourse in place of the illicit language of nationalism. The distinction itself might be false: as we have already seen, the violence of the time-is-money logic and that of the colonial differentiating logic often converged in the transportation sector.

March 12 saw an unprecedented disruption of rail, telegraph, and telephone communication between Cairo and the rest of the country, and subsequently among other Egyptian towns.[99] Masses attacking the Ṭanṭā train station were met by British forces, leaving sixteen people dead.[100] Rather than apologize, the military authorities formally announced on March 13 that "any person who destroys, damages, or tampers in any way with railway, telegraph, or telephone communication, or who attempts to commit any of these said acts, is liable under martial law to be shot."[101] They also threatened to burn to the ground the nearest village to the scene of such destruction.[102] In the following weeks, both threats were put into effect on several occasions.[103] On March 15, the four thousand railway workers of al-ʿAnābir joined the strike, cutting rail communication to Upper Egypt and the Delta. Everywhere along the railroad, the stations, track, and trains were under attack.[104]

On March 16, the CTC managed to operate a small number of streetcars under military guard. But these trams were almost empty, because the public boycotted them.[105] Instead of trams and trains, March saw the renaissance of horse-driven carts. Vegetable carts still loaded with merchandise transported effendis who "sat side by side with the regular passengers of such carts, exchanging stories and news about the revolution."[106] Unlike trains and trams, carts did not separate passengers into classes, thus allowing for new kinds of exchange. With communications cut off and strict press censorship in force, discredited modes of information interchange such as rumor and word of mouth were revived on board these vehicles.[107]

Writer Tharwat Abāẓah later captured the feeling of invigorated solidarity on board the carts, describing such a ride as a consciousness-transforming experience. His effendi protagonist is surprised to find the cart more pleasant than the tram, and he is moved by the genial conversation on board to make a hefty contribution to the cause.[108] Another "traditional" mode of transportation, Nile sailboats, became the main intercity means of transportation for passengers and food.[109] On board these outmoded vehicles, Egypt seemed to be traveling back in time to a pretechnological period of slowness and togetherness. Moments like this, when concord resulted from the suspension of modern technological unifiers, reveal that trains and trams—to paraphrase Guy Debord—united the separated, but only in their separateness.[110]

The disruption of regular temporal orders was registered everywhere. In a semiautobiographical novel, Tawfīq al-Ḥakīm described the moment when the news of the revolution spread through his school: "The school bell rang, but no one paid any attention to it. It was an amazing moment in the history of the schools. The pupils rallied in this fashion and on all their faces was the same awesome expression. . . . It was as if the Day of Resurrection *[Yawm al-Qiyāmah]* had come."[111] The Day of Resurrection was evoked not only by the temporal suspension of the linear time of the school bell, but also by the sudden creation of a human multitude — another one of the signs of the eschaton. It was simultaneously a communal and temporal transformation. With a wave of strikes and communication cutoffs, Egyptians of various classes began understanding the revolution as doomsday. Reinhart Koselleck has shown that the linearity and homogeneity of modern abstract time became conceivable only when Europeans stopped believing in doomsday and its cyclical, eschatological temporality.[112] It seems that in colonial Egypt this was a reversible process: when the support systems of linear abstract time faltered, suppressed temporalities reared their eschatological heads.

The technologies that gathered and regulated students in schools, moved workers to and from work, prevented dangerous congestion in the street, and produced and transported food were all inoperative. As the revolt spread, provincial towns were cut off, sometimes declaring themselves autonomous, rekindling supposedly lost local solidarities. Even streetlights, which made possible artificially controlling the duration of active hours and demonstrating the city's difference from the village, were broken by demonstrators.[113] On March 16, the Light Company workers joined the strikes, darkening the capital completely. After that, demonstrators marching at night carried torches.[114] This was more than an aesthetic transformation: Fikrī Abāẓah, Tharwat Abāẓah's uncle and the person who wrote the 1919 revolution's anthem, then a young lawyer in Asyūṭ, described in an autobiographical text how the fire of the revolution, accompanied by looting and a collapse of public order, started spreading just as the town's electrical generator faltered and Asyūṭ was thrown into bloodcurdling darkness.[115] During the coming months, artificial illumination became highly politicized. In Cairo, lanterns were a constant target of attacks, and even the poles used to light the gas streetlights had to be protected in police stations.[116]

Gradually, the military managed to quell the riots by imposing blockades and curfews. Such measures further interrupted the regular flow of time. As Naguib Mahfouz put it in a semiautobiographical early novel, "Until that time, [Yasin] had never experienced such a long period of enforced idleness, deprived of all forms of activity and amusement for hour after hour. . . . [H]e felt depressed and humiliated, forcibly and tyrannically separated from the flow of time which was plunging ahead outside the house."[117] Especially when contrasted to the frantic activity of the previous days, the lassitude of curfew proved unbearable to young revolutionaries like Mahfouz's protagonist. By contrast, the British in the streets were evidently busy, and their time seemed to accelerate. As Fikrī Abāẓah described the situation in Asyūṭ, after an initial shock and regrouping came the phase of expedited justice. "Investigations would be conducted with the speed of lightning. Arrest warrants were issued like the bullets of a machine gun, hitting the innocent or guilty, young or old. . . . The Q&A was accompanied by [real] British gunshots, hitting people whose figure the soldiers disliked . . . or whose cloths they found messy . . . as if these were not even worthy of arrest, or investigation, or trial—why waste time and ink and paper?!"[118]

Struggling to regain control, the British themselves dreaded a temporal reversal—what Cromer had once called the potential for "relapse" to the precolonial past. The removal of British influence and technology, a report claimed, would result in "the same terrible state of affairs you had in Egypt during the seventeenth and eighteenth centuries, when things were more or less left to themselves."[119] Another report, addressing the cutting of railways and telegraph lines, stated: "Within a few hours we saw the Egypt of 1882 again before us."[120] The sentiment was echoed in the views of Egyptians, for whom it was martial law and not the feelings it tried to stifle that was anachronistic. The heavy-handed quelling of the riots, involving collective punishment and the imposition of curfews, was seen as nothing less than a return to the Middle Ages:

What do the Middle Ages have to do with the year 1919?
What does it have to do with Asyūṭ?
Ask the British, Australian, and Indian soldiers marching on Asyūṭ.
Ask the British public prosecution established in Asyūṭ.
Ask the martial courts set up in Asyūṭ.
Ask the victims and the bloodshed in this poor humiliated town.
The fire of the revolution was extinguished in the capital of the Ṣaʿīd.
And the fires of governance began burning.[121]

In other instances, when time was not described as moving backward, it seemed to stretch and become more elastic. In a rendition into neoclassical poetry, Ḥāfiẓ Ibrāhīm captured the waxing of revolutionary time in a *qaṣīdah:* "The hours of struggle seemed so long / that embryos might have become gray-haired."[122]

NILE TIME

In 1919 Cairo regularly received most of its food supply by rail. But as repairs to the railroads lingered for months,[123] food supply to the capital, Alexandria, and the canal towns was debilitated to such an extent that officials considered directing farmers to grow grain and vegetables instead of cotton that year.[124] This would have the effect of reverting from cash crops to subsistence-based agriculture, turning the clock in the countryside back to the early nineteenth century. The foregoing sections sought to unpack the uprising by following some key technologies that helped orchestrate and drive it and the temporalities they introduced into revolutionary politics. To understand the role of the Egyptian peasantry in the revolt, let us follow the Nile, the single most important infrastructure of agrarian economic, social, and political life.

Egypt's growing independence from the Ottoman Empire in the nineteenth century pushed it to develop new agrarian techniques and novel labor practices, eventually transforming the semi-independent Egyptian farmers into "the Pasha's peasants."[125] Ambitious irrigation and agricultural projects were accompanied by the introduction of long-staple cotton in 1821 and the intensification of cash-cropping, as well as a gradual transition from basin to perennial irrigation. The industrialization and streamlining of Egyptian agriculture, and the emergence of a modern centralized state, entailed a record reliance on forced labor (known as the corvée, *al-ʿawwna,* or *al-sukhrah*).

In the 1880s, another shift in rural labor practices was in the making, involving a growing reliance on wage labor and eschewal of the corvée. Forced labor created the conditions of its own obsolescence. The nineteenth-century agrarian reforms initially targeted a communal subject: villages were regarded as fiscal-administrative units, responsible for allocating ever-growing masses of workers and work animals for the corvée. The shift to centralized taxation likewise relied on various schemes of tax solidarity, for example redistributing the tax for land left dry by the flood onto more fertile land.[126] And these measures were also resisted collectively, as peasants led by millenarian leaders protested them en masse, intensively during the 1820s,[127] then more and more sporadically until the early 1880s.[128]

Yet over the course of the century, these governmental measures ended up having an individuating effect. They eventually led to a reduction of village autonomy and the emergence of a large landless class. As more and more peasants were unable to enjoy the fruits of their own labor and legal reforms made it easier to alienate land, property was reallocated to those who could pay land taxes. By the end of the century, the vast majority of the country's peasants could not, and they had to seek their livelihood in sharecropping or wage labor.[129]

By the time the British arrived, the conditions for adopting more efficient means of controlling agricultural labor were thus already in place. British military occupation in 1882 was the culmination of a debt-management enterprise meant to ensure returns on foreign loans. Similar tactics were brought to the fore in the management of the country's rural workforce. Money and time—"the great equalizers"—and the sanctity of the contract replaced the unquantifiable pain of the whip and the forceful deprival of freedom.[130] During the next decade, various institutions and agencies were created to put into effect the 1877 Anglo-Egyptian Anti-Slavery Convention and curtail the slave trade in Egypt, and by 1890, abolition was effectively in place.[131] In 1885, the use of the corvée for irrigation works was formally abolished.[132] Over the following years, reliance on this form of labor recruitment was on the decline, and by the 1910s it had practically disappeared. Egyptian peasants were thus freed from the compulsion of the whip at their backs and abandoned to "the birds of their stomach," as the Egyptian colloquial rendition of the voice of hunger would have it.

The contractual and individual freedom of wage labor derived its dignity and authority from these acts of abolition and from wage labor's antonymic relation with physical compulsion: "Amongst the many achievements which England has accomplished in the cause of suffering humanity, not the least praiseworthy is this act, that in the teeth of strong opposition, the Anglo-Saxon race insisted that the Egyptian labourer should be paid for his work, and that he should not be flogged if he did not wish to work."[133] Members of the effendiyya, however, often saw through these schemes. During the early 1890s, newspaper columnists ridiculed the British obsession with abolition, claiming that for millions of Egyptians who were treated like slaves, the only freedom under the current legal and economic conditions was the freedom to be poor and bankrupt.[134]

Indeed, as cash crops replaced food production, money lending and debt management became important means of control in a system where one could not eat what one harvested and was hence completely subject to the mercy of the market. As theorists and historians of slavery have shown, emancipation often entailed a transition to forms of coercion that were more subtle and less explicit but not necessarily less cruel.[135] These features of the new labor regime informed the possible modes of resistance and participation. As these measures became more exacting, collective resistance and its utopian horizons declined along with village autonomy, giving way to more fragmented and individual kinds of resistance: small-scale banditry, slacking off, and damaging equipment.

Attacking the railways was one of the favored tactics in the peasants' new arsenal. We have already seen how sabotaging rail tracks and stoning passing trains became, starting in the early 1880s, ways of taking revenge for the death of farm animals hit by trains. From 1882 to 1952, between thirty and sixty acts of vandalism against the railroad were reported yearly.[136] Sometimes these acts served as indirect attacks on the reputation of local officials, who would be seen as unable to maintain public order.[137] At other times, they were ways of avenging the killing or reclamation of farm animals, and on still other occasions attacks were deliberately perpetrated by camel or donkey owners to sabotage competing modes of transportation.[138]

Attacks against the railroad flesh out an important difference between the forms of militancy developed by peasants and those of transportation workers. Unlike rail and tram workers, who adopted the temporalities of their employers and networks, Egyptian peasants, though clearly unable to defend their traditional tempos and utopias, were nonetheless uninterested in or incapable of replacing them with capitalist ones.[139]

The fact that such an ethos of time-is-money did not develop in the Egyptian countryside had much to do with the fact that rural life could not be lived "without paying heed to the orders of nature," as our railway worker characterized his work environment. Like urban workers, peasants were tied to the temporalities of their infrastructures. The time of agriculture was connected to the changing seasons and seed cycles, to sunrise and sunset, and perhaps most importantly, to the inundation of the Nile. Though several generations of engineers had gradually changed the timing of the river's flow with dams and barrages, with the goal of perennial irrigation, in the 1910s much of agricultural life in Egypt was still organized around the annual flood.

Summer rains over the Ethiopian highlands gradually swelled the Nile, first in Upper Egypt and then in Cairo, where the flood reached its peak around late August. The river then steadily fell, reaching half its flood level by mid-November and its minimum by May.[140] During the flood, a large portion of Egypt's arable land was underwater for several months, except for the villages, which were situated on hills. Many villages were completely cut off during the inundation or accessible only by small boats. Sayyid Quṭb reminisced about how the flood affected the temporal order during his childhood in the village of Mūshā in Upper Egypt during the 1910s:

> The land of the village was covered by water for two months every year in preparation for the year's planting. . . . For most of the year [students coming to the village school from outside] would mount their donkeys at the

> appropriate time and arrive just before the school bell rang. . . . During the time of the flood, however, they would take skiffs and sailboats. They did not keep to any schedule and usually did not arrive until almost ten o'clock, so that they would miss the first two classes. And on some beautiful Saturdays they might not arrive until noon.[141]

Even for the increasing numbers of day laborers (by 1919 over a third of Egypt's peasants),[142] translating fieldwork into quantifiable labor time and then into money was already a difficult process before the war. The opening scene of the 1913 pioneering novel *Zaynab* depicts the ordeals of the peasants as they try to get paid for their work, only to be repeatedly rejected, cheated, and abused. "A group of workers surrounded the desk, the waterer holding their work slips in his hand, while some tried to ask the number of days they had worked. At the window a number of younger workers, boys and girls, began to mutter between their teeth, showing their dissatisfaction with the clerk who was making them wait for their pay. But after keeping them waiting for another hour, he announced that he would pay them in the market the following day."[143]

The saga stretches over several days and three pages. Peasants receive the payment due them only after several bureaucrats have made them wait deferentially, thereby performing the social power hierarchy. Any account of capitalist advance in the countryside has to be qualified by such inflections of the commodification of labor, in which real social relations never completely give way to abstract exchange relations and human labor cannot be neatly translated into work hours, even when the laborers themselves try to monetize their work. Such noncapitalist relations of production were not relics of an ancient past but newly introduced practices connected to land alienation, central taxation, and the development of a modern bureaucracy charged with managing and supervising rural work. This account, one of the first Egyptian experiments in literary realism, described the peaceful days of 1913. Only a year later, the war prevented Britain from providing Egypt with the gold used to purchase cotton in the countryside, greatly aggravating matters.[144]

The war created a new state of affairs that gave peasants, for the first time in about a century, both the motivation and the long withheld power for effective collective resistance, revitalizing dormant modi operandi in their arsenal of contention. At the outbreak of hostilities, Britain prohibited cotton exports to its enemies, which constituted nearly one quarter of Egypt's prewar cotton exports, thus causing demand and prices to decline sharply. To meet both Egyptian domestic and British military needs, already at the end of 1914 the Egyptian government severely restricted the cultivation of cotton (limiting it to one-quarter, then to one-third of a landowner's property, and sometimes barring it completely), to ensure that basic grains would be grown.[145] The war dealt other blows to cotton production. Transportation problems in 1917–1918 prevented the transfer of cotton from interior to port. In 1918, when global cotton prices rose, the British Treasury purchased the country's entire yearly crop at slightly over half the world market price[146] without taking into account the sharp inflation during that year, thus bringing about a wave of protests.[147]

If the return to food production seemed like travel back in time, other wartime policies only reinforced this sentiment. High rates of inflation induced by the war eroded the value of money and with it the willingness of peasants to serve the agricultural war machine as wage laborers. As a result, the British reimposed the corvée. Between half a million and a million and a half peasants were conscripted this way. Even by British estimates, the magnitude of wartime forced labor reached and perhaps even surpassed the nineteenth-century corvée at its apex.[148]

Further, by the end of the war, a coal shortage took hold across the countryside and especially in Upper Egypt, where thousands of steam pumps were concentrated. Irrigation problems were aggravated by the requisition of farm animals necessary to operate traditional irrigation apparatuses. The Khedival Agricultural Society concerned itself during the war with the effects of the rising price of coal on the quantity of foodstuffs and similar problems, such as a shortage in artificial fertilizers. The society, founded in 1898 to promote scientific agriculture, introduced nitrogen fertilizer into Egypt in 1902 to complement the first Aswan Dam, also inaugurated during that year. Increasing the area of cultivable land, the dam disrupted the depositing of silt and nutrients during the annual inundation of the Nile, forcing farmers to resort to imported fertilizers.[149] Steam pumps, dams, and nitrate-based fertilizers were part of a compound system that enabled Egypt's gradual transition from basin to perennial irrigation, a process completed only with the construction of the High Dam in Aswan.[150] Yet in 1918, a memorandum from Prince Kamāl al-Dīn, president of the society, warned that the following year's wheat crop would fall significantly short if fertilizers—in short supply as a result of the military demand for nitrates for explosives—were not replenished.[151]

Various other basic foodstuffs, such as onions and beans, as well as livestock, were requisitioned by the government and the large British army stationed in the Egypt-Palestine theater.[152] As Ellis Goldberg maintains, by the end of the year, available food in the countryside decreased to the point that peasants refused to exchange food for money.[153] The deportation of Zaghlūl and its frenzied aftermath coincided with the harvest of the second major wheat yield of the agricultural year, the so-called summer crop *(al-ṣayfī)*. The wheat was still in the fields or in rural train stations, used as countryside storehouses, about to be transported to urban centers. Attacking these stations was an intensification of the familiar attacks on the railway, but in a more bold and collective manner reminiscent of nineteenth-century attacks on grain storehouses.

Different and sometimes conflicting rationales animated violence in various parts of the countryside. Yet for many peasants, attacking railways was a way of disconnecting the countryside from markets that had little to offer in return. Attacks on train stations were meant to recover requisitioned grains, probably for eating: as Allenby himself observed, "To the fellaheen who sacked the stations, the sight of the grain which had been collected for the Army was often the sole inducement necessary to incite them to pillage."[154] As the list of damaged facilities reveals, attackers specifically targeted storehouses, scales, and weighing machines.[155]

Peasants selected transportation infrastructures and avoided other machinery, such as steam pumps. But attacking the railway had unforeseen consequences not only for the transport of crops but also for cultivation. For instance, because many pumping engines burned, aside from coal, either Mazoot or Kerosene, which were normally transported by rail, the disruptions in transportation and communications affected the availability of these fuels across Upper Egypt and the Delta.[156] This had an impact on irrigation in the Delta even before the summer. The water shortage was, in turn, used for anti-British propaganda among the peasants.[157] The flows of fuel, water, food, and political awareness again poured into one another.

The war partially reversed decades-long and at that point only partially successful efforts to subject Egyptian agriculture to monetized clock time. As steam pumps faltered, so did the perception of water as the flow of cubic meters per minute.[158] When wage labor was left uncompensated and the corvée reimposed, the liberal veneer was torn away from British policy in rural Egypt. As Reinhard Schulze argues, capitalist penetration into the countryside had a significant impact on millenarian traditions of resistance in the communal village. Yet the war and its aftermath, and the reintroduction of eschewed forms of governance, aroused dormant modes of social protest, particularly the belief in Mahdism. The new millenarianism had absorbed urban political terminology (which was seeped in the discourse of resurrection).[159] The national movement could be portrayed in the countryside as representing a new form of Mahdism.[160] ʿAbbās Ḥilmī, the deposed khedive, was seen as the long awaited *mahdī,* the just ruler and precursor of the Day of Resurrection, *Yawm al-Qiyāmah.*[161] Just as it did in Cairo, the suspension of linear time and the resurrection of anachronistic forms of community, subsistence, and governance promoted an understanding of the revolution as a return to cyclical time, a counterclockwise revolution.

CONNECTING THE DOTS

The sweeping impact of the uprising owed much to the interconnectedness of its chosen targets, which seemed to turn against their creators. During the first student demonstrations, protesters armed themselves with pavement blocks torn from the street to stone trams and streetlights.[162] Until telephone poles were brought down, local notables in the countryside[163] and nationalist elite women in urban centers organized demonstrations over the phone.[164] Telegrams could inflame riots from Paris[165] and furnish Wafdists abroad with fresh propaganda materials. Inside cities and across the countryside, train stations, railways, and telegraphs were under attack. Tram workers even forged weapons in the company's workshops.[166]

Different segments of the Egyptian public had different reasons to launch these attacks. Indeed, Egyptians experienced the turmoil as spontaneous and unplanned. The Wafdists deported to Malta even suspected that initial reports about the riots were fabricated to prolong their detention.[167] The British were similarly surprised, partly due to the means they themselves imposed to stifle expression of discontent.[168] Their initial shock was soon followed by conspiracy theories, which went so far as to compare the disruption of communication and transportation to the carefully orchestrated German staff plan from 1914.[169]

Colonial authorities, used to observing developments from the bird's-eye view produced by the railway and telegraph networks (and the airplanes they used for military intelligence and riot control),[170] were convinced that the riots were premeditated and synchronized.[171] Following this logic, British analysts read intention and premeditation into the chaotic beginning of the uprising. The more removed the observers were from the scene, the more certain they were that the violence was organized and premeditated. The deportation of the Wafdists, the Foreign Office assumed, "was followed by a carefully planned and systematic destruction of the railway in Upper Egypt, in the mechanical details of which the technical officials seem themselves to have been largely implicated." Even the March 18 death of seven British soldiers cornered by a rampaging crowd on board a train in Upper Egypt was deemed "an organized incident in this systematic destruction."[172] In hysterical reproaches telegraphed to Egypt, policy makers demanded explanations for the "totally insufficient and misleading information as to the true nature and character of the Nationalist political movement, as to the strength of support which it enjoyed, and as to the organization which it had prepared for outbreaks in every part of the country."[173]

The railway, tramway, and telegraph lines connected dots of revolutionary action, outbursts connected by uneasy and unstable relations, into a seemingly unified broader picture whose sum was larger than its parts. These systems offered the only legible syntax for a master narrative of the Revolution with a capital *R*. Nationalists were seen as masterminding what was actually a result of conflicting interests and colliding agendas, a clash of different attitudes to technology, time, money, and politics. What brought this (mis) representation into existence was the attention directed, by the interconnected targets of the revolt, to the points where these agendas were mutually reinforcing and away from where they were mutually exclusive.

A fact-finding mission headed by Lord Milner came to Egypt at the end of 1919 to investigate the causes of Egyptian discontent. It concluded that the underlying problem was Britain's "abnormal" status in Egypt since 1882, its ambiguity vis-à-vis the question of Egyptian independence, and the anachronistic style of repeated yet constantly deferred pledges of evacuation.[174] Indeed, Milner accepted the nationalist perspective lock, stock, and barrel and identified the temporality of the civilizing mission as the key to the Egyptian predicament. Britain acted accordingly. After three years of protracted negotiations with the Wafd, it unilaterally ended the protectorate, leading to the establishment of a nominally independent Egyptian parliamentary monarchy in 1922. This political transformation did not translate into a social one, nor did it improve the welfare of the peasants and workers who made it possible. Nevertheless, it established the framework within which "the Revolution" would emerge as a historical event in the following years.

Revolting peasants and transportation workers struggled in 1919 to gain access to the fruits of their labor. The former fought to secure the crops they planted and harvested. The latter, whose production was measured by the revenue they generated as well as in saved travel time, framed their demands for a share of this economy in the language it made available and strove to gain more money and less work time. Similarly, both segments of the working class promoted a collectivist vision. For workers it was the community of the synchronized; for peasants it was the unity of the village. Yet both visions were absorbed into the ostensibly larger but in many respects more limited nationalist vision of togetherness, which unified people in their separateness.

As "Egyptians," members of the effendiyya, urban workers, and peasants were progressing together through empty homogeneous *cyclical* time. Indeed, this configuration of a community of strangers excluded other communal possibilities not by rejecting but rather by co-opting and depoliticizing their nonlinear temporalities and modes of synchronization. Effendis conjured up peasant temporality only to conjure it away. The uneasy synthesis of the three revolutionary temporalities infused into the time of Egyptian nationalism the cyclical chronotope of return, resurrection, *nahḍah,*[175] but in an impoverished way. Eschatological time was internalized as aesthetics emptied of its political import. As Salāmah Mūsā framed the revolution, "In 1882 the British condemned us to a political death. . . . We remained dead until 1919, when we were resurrected and returned to history."[176] It was exactly this return to history that attacks on the railway tried to derail.

Let me illustrate this hollowing out with a famous example. While in Paris in 1919–1920, Egyptian delegates met a brilliant young Egyptian sculptor, Maḥmūd Mukhtār, whose work *Nahḍat Miṣr* had just won an important international competition.[177] Inspired by the events of 1919, *The Awakening of Egypt* depicted a peasant woman near a sphinx rising up on its forelegs. This encounter and Mukhtār's international acclaim helped him to successfully propose constructing a monumental version of *Nahḍat Miṣr* in front of Cairo's central train station. For nationalists this was a way of carving in stone their unilateral union with peasants, evoking a pharaonic past to which the latter had no way of relating.

In 1920, a well-publicized fundraising campaign for the construction of the statue collected large and small donations from bankers, railway workers, and peasants.[178] "The Genius's Clock," a 1921 caricature in the satirical journal *Al-Kashkūl,* depicted Mukhtār riding on the sphinx, holding alarm clocks in both hands. "Did the alarm clock awake you to behold the Awakening statue?" asks a voice in the picture. "It gave me a headache," answers another. "All I see in the Awakening is noise, commotion, and discord."[179] Egypt was indeed riding toward the dawn of parliamentary politics, where the only legible temporal, and by extension social, discord would be found in the bourgeois, impoverished public sphere.

The withdrawal of the effendiyya from the radical politics unleashed in 1919 may be further illustrated by their changing attitudes to eschatological time. While in March of that year the language of the Day of Resurrection and a utopian revolutionary horizon could be shared by urbanites and peasants, there were already several important fault lines. Because peasants withheld their crops, by late April the lower-class residents of Cairo and Alexandria were starving.[180] Middle-class students too could lose more than their shackles from an open-ended revolt; as the uprising went on, students and their parents expressed fears that the demonstrations would cost them the academic year.[181] Eschatology was gradually deflated. In a June 1922 article titled "The Day of Reckoning" *(Yawm al-Ḥisāb),* Fikrī Abāẓah, who earlier experienced the revolution as a return to the Middle Ages, captured the shift as he sarcastically addressed the student demonstrators,

> You've gone on strike, you've boycotted, you've shouted so many "Down withs" and "Long lives," you've demonstrated and you've protested. But now the day of reckoning has arrived. Yes, June is here and it's time for the year-end exams. For the first time all year we see you walking down the street in twos and threes, whispering together, instead of parading in bands and shouting. We hear you talking about "geography" and "geometry" instead of "politics" and "freedom." And, finally the flag of "peace and quiet" flutters where "independence" had you jumping up and down.[182]

As it happens, that year's exam in English composition focused on the history of English coal. Even though the typical Egyptian student had never encountered a coal worker or a coal mine, so Abāẓah complained, he was now asked to recount their institutional life and history, when all he knew about coal was that "it was bought at the highest prices by the Egyptian State Railways during the war, a fact leading to the rise in fares, the breakdown of locomotives, and an ill effect on the general public." Schooling officials who want to avoid another Day of Reckoning, Abāẓah concluded, would do better to keep away from such political choices.[183] The historiography of 1919, both scholarly and popular, seems to have heeded the warning, cautiously avoiding the political history of coal, railways, and the revolutionary impulses they generated. It thus excised from the collective memory of the revolt the lower-class utopian horizons, including the alternative visions of community and freedom toward which this usable past might have pointed.

SEVEN

On Hold

> Desire only exists when assembled or machined. You cannot grasp or conceive of a desire outside a determinate assemblage, on a plane which is not pre-existent but which must itself be constructed. . . . In retrospect every assemblage expresses and creates a desire by constructing the plane which makes it possible and, by making it possible, brings it about.
>
> GILLES DELEUZE, Dialogues

THE BELL TELEPHONE WAS INTRODUCED into Egypt in August 1881. The not insignificant diplomatic efforts of Edwin De Leon, Bell's emissary to Egypt, in gaining government permission, were dwarfed by technical complications. In particular, a resolute minister of public works, ʿAlī Mubārak, insisted on creating a network without telephone poles.[1] Poles—first for telegraphs, then for telephones, and later for trams—repeatedly became bones of contention in Egyptian urban and rural reconstruction schemes.[2] They interfered with urban traffic,[3] raised land taxation issues and even questions of *waqf* (an inalienable religious land endowment),[4] and were seen as aesthetically displeasing.[5] Moreover, poles were extremely expensive in Egypt, a country completely reliant on imported wood, and they quickly rotted and became useless in the hot, dry climate. In the nineteenth century, a pole imported from Sweden proved to be the most enduring, but even these seldom lasted more than four years, and they were eventually replaced with white cedar poles from the United States.[6] In the early 1880s, therefore, telephone poles were used in Cairo and Alexandria only where there were no alternatives, as in connecting the old and new cities across Cairo's Azbakīyah Gardens.[7]

The first line in Cairo stretched between the khedival palaces in ʿAbdīn, about a mile apart, and it was rumored that Tawfiq spent hours on end conversing with his wife on the telephone, to the detriment of public affairs.[8] This telling allegation about the interference of private feminine chatter with public masculine business over the prototypical stately telephone is emblematic of the sociotechnical environment in which Egyptian telephony would come into its own, and it introduces the central concern of this chapter, the gendering of delay.

ʿAli Mubārak's aversion to poles was instrumental in the centrality of a gendered perspective in the history of the country's telephony. Consider Alexandria, where the palace was connected with the offices of the governor and the chief of police, as well as with the public schools at the other end of town. This trajectory of the chief trunk line secured official aid when residents refused to allow the company workmen access to their rooftops. It was necessary to enter the flat-roofed houses to deploy the telephone lines. As a result of the anti-pole policy, wires had to be stretched between roofs, where they were supported by iron fixtures.[9] De Leon mentions two key concerns regularly raised by residents who refused to allow workers into their houses (often succumbing eventually to official pressure). The first was the "uncanny" character of the instrument and its diabolic attributes. The second was the violation of the sanctity of the women's quarters by the entry of foreign men:

> One old sheik—a pious pilgrim from Mecca—whose house unfortunately for him stood on the line of the Khedive's communication with the governor, on being peremptorily ordered by the palace officials to permit my workmen to pass up his stairway, which led past his harem apartments, tore his gray beard, spat on the ground to show his loathing, and, throwing wide open all the doors of his house, declared he would never close them again, but invite the whole public of Alexandria freely to make use of it, since he never was to enjoy privacy any more.[10]

The telephone indeed opened wide the door between the feminine, private sphere of the home and the masculine, public sphere of politics, allowing the outside in but also the inside out. It is this last dimension that mostly interests us here. Telephones informed effendi togetherness in complex and contradictory ways. They connected and delinked the spheres of labor and domesticity, home and office, in various new ways. The telephone allowed middle- and upper-class wives to enforce from home the clear temporal boundaries of the workday of their husbands, while at the same time opening new spaces for manipulation by husbands. For instance, a cartoon shows a husband answering the phone with his sexy secretary sitting on his lap. When he tells his wife that he can't return home because he has more work to do, she knowingly suggests he bring his "work" home.[11] In another cartoon, a wife calls to remind her husband to return home early for a prescheduled social event. The reluctant man eats so much garlic that the wife is forced to cancel.[12]

FIGURE 10. Unexpected benefits of telephony. *Kull Shay'*, December 7, 1925.

These episodes seem to reveal a particular telephonic uncanniness that is different from Freud's notion of uncanny—the *Unhiemlich,* literally "unhomelike," an affect triggered by a sense of unfamiliarity in the midst of the apparently familiar. Instead, they reveal a somewhat different effect triggered by the injection of a measure of homeliness into the public sphere, charging politics with desires and violence one usually keeps tucked inside.

Though the telephone may very well have been encroaching on the home, violating women but also empowering them in this sphere, its introduction also facilitated female labor outside the house. And while elite wives policed the boundaries between leisure and labor time from their salons, middle-class, unmarried, female telephone operators were held responsible for much of the frustration emanating from time lost on the phone. These young women occupied a central junction of male connectivity. Is it possible that by upsetting the simultaneity of the masculine "public sphere," women invigorated men and charged phones with the kinds of desire that held the nation together not because of, but *in the face of,* practically unattainable instantaneity?

Posing such questions allows us to reconsider several assumptions regarding what is regularly seen as the instantaneous connectivity essential to telephony, thus complicating the conventional wisdom concerning the political arrangements the telephone supposedly sustains generically. Perhaps more than any other technology, the telephone "annihilates space with time." (Though we problematized this notion in previous chapters, in the context of the current consideration of its gendered dimensions, it is worth mentioning that it was Alexander Pope who coined this expression, a century and a half before Marx: "Ye Gods! Annihilate but space and time, / and make two lovers happy." In other words, "time-space compression" has always been a libidinal utopia.)[13] The potential instantaneity of voices crossing vast spaces at the speed of electricity seems to lend itself seamlessly to theories of togetherness based on empty, homogenous time and their imaginaries. Indeed, phone networks in Egypt participated in the connectivity attained by the circulation of print, radio signals, and other modern systems of mass transportation and communication, such as railways, tramways, and telegraphs.

Yet while notions like simultaneity may be valuable heuristic devices, it should already be clear that they are insufficient in technical, cultural, and analytical respects. As I demonstrated for trains, trams, newspapers, and telegraphs, telephonic simultaneity was not always expected, easily attained, or necessarily desired. It adhered to multiple standards and created unforeseen social arrangements. Nevertheless, even though (and probably because) it was unattainable in practice, such simultaneity gradually became a horizon of expectation for many Egyptians. What follows examines the tension between a potential instantaneity and its volatile and partial materializations from a gendered perspective.

This gap between potential and realization, which we call delay, is the key object of this chapter; the telephone is the main but not the only conduit through which we speak to it. What follows tries to historicize delay and retrace its politics, first by describing the development of a telephone infrastructure in which—with the growing expectation of speed and synchronicity—setbacks could begin to appear. We then examine such setbacks in accounts of male telephone users kept on hold by female telephone operators. Finally, we will situate the phone within a broader media ecology, particularly alongside the radio, 78-rpm records, and the cinema—media that also grappled with suspensions that were gendered feminine. Like the telephone, these technologies redrew existing boundaries between public and private. They brought women, with and sometimes without their bodies and voices, outside, and they transmitted this outside into the domestic sphere, thereby reconfiguring both the home and the street.

Before beginning, it is important to make clear what the following lines do not attempt to do. Though dealing with women and voices, what follows does not directly address questions of female agency. This is despite the fact that Egyptian women seem to have been invisible yet voiced actors in the early days of telephony. For example, several significant moments in the 1919 Revolution were telephonically orchestrated by women. Though accounts of the revolt tend to locate politics only in the public sphere of the street, key public events, such as the famous "Women's Demonstration" of March 16, 1919, at the beginning of the revolution, or a 1922 women's boycott of British goods immediately following it, were telephonically coordinated from home by elite women, through the mediation of middle-class female phone operators.[14]

However, because the writers, sketchers, and directors of the materials sustaining the argument below were men, these sources cannot support yet another attempt at retrieving silenced "women's voices" in the metaphorical sense that has become so commonplace. Moreover, such "voices" usually need to be forcefully squeezed out of reluctant documents "read against the grain" or otherwise "interrogated," using methods critiqued by Saba Mahmood as revealing our liberal and secularist presuppositions concerning power and resistance.[15] These attempts to read resistance to and resignification of male hegemony in every female action often get in the way of taking both male and female actors seriously—taking them at their own words.

Rather than looking for women's agency and empowerment, then, what follows is an account of bourgeois men's anxieties of disempowerment, already revealed by De Leon's violated sheikh.[16] In the perceptions of these effendis, the telephone might very well have been a conduit of female initiative and enterprise, a mouthpiece for women who—unlike the (often true) cliché about their Western counterparts[17]—did not sit passively by the phone waiting for a suitor's call. In the Egyptian setting, waiting was a role often reserved for men,[18] even if there was nothing passive about how men waited. It was, I will argue, an agentive waiting.

Exploring this frustrating but also arousing position, I examine how members of the effendiyya heard actual female voices. I seek to trace how the metapolitics of empire and nation were lived every day, structuring gender relations and sustained by material networks. Female voices, the chapter suggests, provided a suitable soundtrack for awaiting the promised independence at the end of the civilizing mission's rainbow.

LONGING, SHORTENING, AND OTHER ARCHITECTURES OF DELAY

After deploying local telephone networks in Egypt's two key urban centers at the beginning of the decade, in 1889 the Egyptian government expanded the concession to Port Said, Suez, and Ismāʿīlīyah[19] and in 1895 granted a ten-year franchise to an Austrian company for telephone lines in al-Fayūm and Ṭanṭā.[20] In 1902, the Alexandria–Cairo telephone line, first established in 1881, was refurbished with better cables.[21] During the following decade and a half, the network expanded rapidly. Al-Minyā and Banī Suwayf were connected in 1909, and a new infrastructure was laid in Ismāʿīlīyah in 1912 and in Damanhūr in 1913.[22]

A 1917 Egyptian telephone guide, published one year before the state took over the telephone companies to form the Egyptian Telephone Administration,[23] reveals that by this time most government branches were connected to the telephone network. So were many private train and steamer companies, all Egyptian State Railways stations, and most police stations, newspapers, and post offices. Between 1920 and 1930, the annual profits of the telephone company soared from £E 220,000 to £E 700,000, and its investment in infrastructure climbed from £E 780,000 to £E 2 million.[24] By 1925, at least 101 cities and towns were connected to the telephone.[25]

This new connectivity was differentiated by gender, social class, geography, and profession.[26] For example, the telephone guide indicated that almost all lawyers certified to appear before the Mixed Courts had phones, but most lawyers appearing in the Sharʿī Courts did not.[27] The network reinforced preexisting hierarchies, even as it introduced new ones. Bringing some places, institutions, and people closer to the center, it left others behind. Though the phone compressed space and time, this happened gradually and unevenly: as is often the case, the shortening of distance coincided with new experiences of longing.

Further, the success of a new technology often depended on creating new needs, expectations, and desires. In the 1880s the usefulness of a novel device "allowing subscribers to exchange vocal statements while remaining in their places"[28] had to be demonstrated to a limited and skeptical potential clientele.[29] By the 1920s, however, consumer demand far exceeded the capacity of the network to provide adequate service. In various places in Egypt, waiting lists were quickly growing for those who wanted to join the slowly expanding pool of available numbers and lines.[30] Complaints about delays in getting connected to the phone network and the amount of time it took to get a line were sometimes understood as a typically Eastern tendency to automatically engage in finger-pointing, even if simple technical realities were the cause.[31] Whatever the reason, yesterday's wonder was today's cause of frustration. Technology's success constantly revealed its shortcomings, and its remarkable speed quickly became banal, leaving room only for apparent sluggishness.

Inside cities and eventually between them, telephones allowed users to converse in real time, but they created new kinds of delay and frustration even for those fortunate enough to get a line, a frustration exacerbated by potential instantaneity that materialized differentially and unpredictably. Until the mid-1920s, callers relied on the services of manual switchboard operators. Getting a line was a slow affair that entailed protracted waiting, sometimes for hours. A 1928 magazine article entitled "The Telephone, Its Order and Progress in Egypt" situated a detailed account of the device's history and current development vis-à-vis an inescapable paradox, the elephant in the room: "The subscriber reading these lines [recounting the quick spread of telephony in the country] might say: 'If all this development is indeed true, why do subscribers face such torments in getting a line?'"[32] The better and more sophisticated the infrastructure, the slower and more difficult communication appeared.

There were several reasons for delays, the article explained. One was the fact that unlike other countries, Egypt had a unique price structure wherein subscribers paid a yearly fee for unlimited usage of the phone. This resulted in unnecessary and long phone conversations, redundant pressure on the centrals, and preventable annoyance to callers trying to reach people engaged in a long conversation. The time-space compression of the phone was also informed by the language of comparison: "Comparison is perhaps the best means of revealing the difference between bulk price and price per call. In London, a city famous for its intensive and diverse business scene, the number of daily average phone calls per user does not exceed twelve. Cairo's average, by contrast, is twenty—that is, almost double that of London. The government should therefore consider introducing a new fare structure that becomes the spirit of the age and the nature of civilized progress."[33]

Another reason for telephone delays mentioned in the article was accumulated dust or humidity on the line, which caused a busy signal to be transmitted to the central even when the line was not in use. This happened also when users didn't put back their handset properly. Because operators were working under pressure, handling seventy to eighty callers simultaneously, these frequent technical glitches created a paradoxical situation: the more efficient an operator was, the more quickly she responded by saying, "The line is busy," and moving on to the next caller. The caller would repeatedly try the out-of-order number. These attempts created further pressure on the system, yielding the same brisk and frustrating response, a reply that seemed less plausible with every attempt. Eventually, subscribers would complain about the operator to her supervisor.[34] Evidently, operators were positioned at the bottleneck of a system in which efficiency and delay could not be easily separated.

In 1926, automatic exchanges were introduced in Cairo to expedite communication and extend service to more users.[35] In 1932, Cairo and Alexandria were connected by an underground cable that reduced delays to no more than five minutes.[36] The same year also saw Cairo connected to London and hence to about 90 percent of the telephonic world.[37] In 1935 automatic switchboards arrived in Alexandria, around the time that new automatic switchboards were being installed in the Cairo suburbs of Heliopolis and Zaytūn. Yet automation was not easy to come to terms with. In particular, it was expected that many users "would be saddened by being deprived of the voice of the maidens previously at their service." The public found consolation in an important advantage of the new system: it allowed for an intimate, private conversation to which only the two users would be privy.[38]

This gradual replacement of maidens with dials and automatic switchboards required much learning and unlearning. First, users were urged to consult a current phonebook to make sure they had the right number.[39] As a result of user and publisher inexperience with gridlike forms of textual arrangement, attempting to figure out where a number was classified often proved at best humorous and at worst frustrating and time consuming.[40] Second, callers were repeatedly instructed to wait patiently without turning the dial until they heard an elongated dial tone that indicated a line was available. At this moment, only a careful and very slow turn of the dial registered the number in the switchboard. Finally, many users forgot to return the phone to its hook after concluding the call, which often kept lines busy until the situation was rectified, sometimes only after a physical house call by company inspectors.[41]

In short, without human operators, the user interface was significantly reconfigured, with blame for failed calls reallocated ("Every user can now only blame himself when getting a wrong number").[42] New styles of decorum, literacy, patience, intimacy, attention, and vigilance in handling the equipment were necessary to successfully make a call, as well as to ensure the smooth operation of the entire interdependent system. These new modes of human-machine interaction are part and parcel of telephony and its history. During the interwar period, phones were gradually sealed off as the "black boxes" we are familiar with today.[43] Directing critical attention to these processes in this formative moment reveals how such changes were archived in phones and the ways they were used.

PHONE SEX

During the 1920s and 1930s, as automatic equipment replaced the old manual switchboards, amortized apparatuses were transferred to small towns and to the countryside,[44] demonstrating again that progress could take the form of delay. A paragraph from Tawfīq al-Ḥakīm's 1937 *Yawmīyāt Nāʾib fī al-Aryāf* (Diary of a county prosecutor), a semiautobiographical novel based on the author's experience a decade earlier, suggests that this exchange, like various other phases in the expansion of Egypt's phone network, involved gendering the telephone as feminine:

> I beheld a spectacle I could not understand at first. There was the head of the *ghafir* and his deputy, and some others, carrying an object in their hands. Around them were crowds of men, women, and boys, reciting prayers and verses, while the women ululated as they do at joyful celebrations and beat on tambourines. I looked closely to find out what they were carrying and the pathologist followed my gaze in stupefaction. We saw that it was an official telephone! The doctor exclaimed in astonishment, "The telephone's got a procession like a bride!"[45]

The protagonist later discovers that the phone was moved after the government dismissed the *ʿumdah* (village headman) and appointed another man in his place. The telephone would reconfigure village hierarchy based on the differential proximity to power and enable the head of the rival family to benefit from direct connection to Cairo. Beyond the importance attributed to the telephone, the description also reveals the gender of the device. The notion that objects have gender runs in the face of conventional feminist critiques of the "objectification of women," inherent to which is the assumption that inanimate things lack agency.[46] Keeping open the question of agency for the time being, let us turn to how the phone became a "she," and how this process was linked to existing and new understandings of vocality and temporality.

Telephone labor was gradually feminized in Egypt, as was the case elsewhere.[47] In 1927, for example, the new al-Madīnah central in Cairo replaced the Azbakīyah central, "and the merchants of al-Muskī could sigh with relief

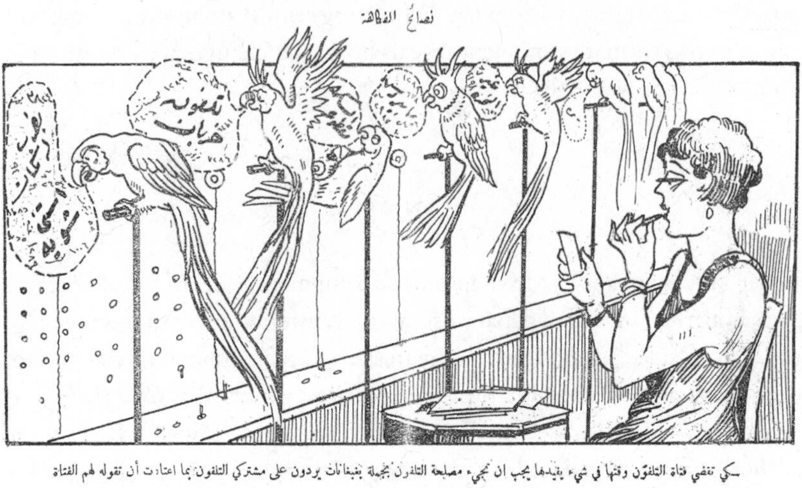

FIGURE 11. Inside the phone central. *Al-Fukāhah,* June 6, 1928.

with the passing of its incredible annoyances . . . finding the new central and the lovely voices of its girls a far better alternative to the crude boys of al-Azbakīyah."[48] Already in 1900 the phone was regularly referenced using the feminine pronoun *she* (e.g., "The telephone deceives with *her* voice, making man often fall into the trap"),[49] gradually coming to incarnate the disembodied feminine voice. The femininity of the phone, which stemmed from its auditory, seductive, and capricious nature, was regularly contrasted in Egyptian newspapers with the masculine nature of the telegraph, based on textuality and vision.[50] Central to this gendering process was the invisible female operator, an absentee present in the effendi imagination. The operator appeared in numerous cartoons depicting the phone central, archiving a masculine desire to penetrate this alluring feminine space reminiscent (in theme if not in style) of orientalist harem paintings.[51]

Phone operators were usually unmarried middle-class women whose manners and parlance allowed for polite conversation, whose voice was pleasant, and whose other physical features (such as arms long enough to reach the top of the switchboard) were fit for the job. Being unmarried was such a central requirement that in 1905 several leading Egyptian newspapers seriously discussed, in a proposal to introduce automated switchboards in France, establishing a Canadian company to find Canadian husbands for the thousands of young Frenchwomen who would lose their jobs in the transition.[52] The effendi culture of emotionalism was animated by provocative asynchronies: male bachelors

FIGURE 12. Phone in the shape of a woman. *Al-Mar'ah al-Miṣrīyah,* May 1, 1923.

were defined by their time wastefulness in cafes, and maidens by their enticing procrastination. Ideally, these asynchronies ended at wedlock, which formed a well-ordered, harmonious household in which wives helped husbands keep to prompt and productive schedules and raised time-conscious offspring.[53] As al-Ḥakīm described, male callers seemed to have indeed approached the phone like prospective grooms, at once irked and aroused by its delays.

In 1925, one year before the introduction of automatic switchboards in Egypt, there were 1,675 Egyptian telephone workers, most of them operators (mostly but not entirely women), who worked six-hour shifts day and night.[54] One year after the introduction of automatic switchboards, in 1927, there were nine hundred female phone operators, both foreign and local.[55] According to a *Rūz al-Yūsuf* article about women's labor, the telephone company regularly published calls for educated young Egyptian women to join its workforce, claiming that "the telephone is the maidens' job" *(al-tilifūn mihnat al-ānisāt).*[56]

Female operators were at once the heart of the telephone system and a hindrance to smooth masculine communication. It was even humorously suggested that phones should be in the shape of women operators, so that frustrated men could vent their rage against them. Because a key feature of the phone was its disembodied female voice, such a scheme would allow men to visualize the operator and even slam her to the ground if she distressed them.[57] This plan was actually not farfetched: in 1923, several years before it was conceived, a new phone in the shape of a woman's hat had been introduced in Egypt.[58]

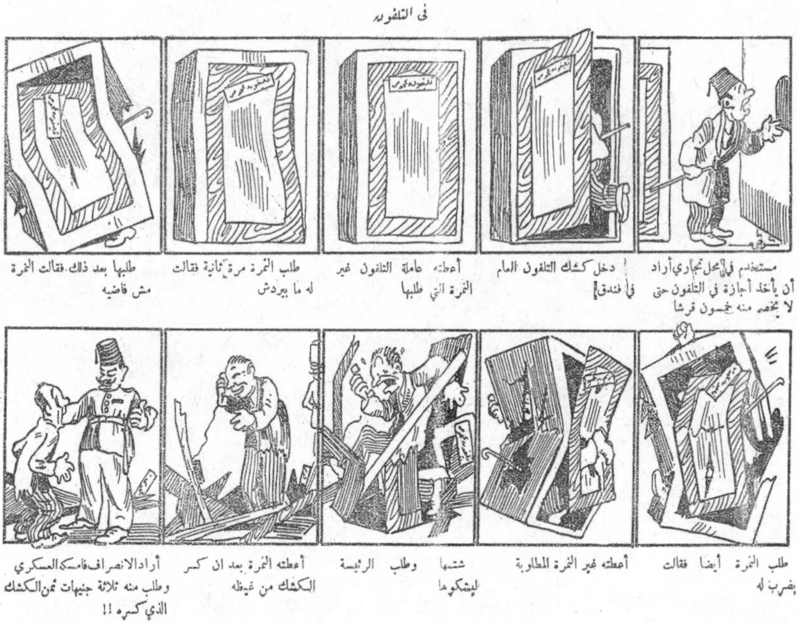

FIGURE 13. Rage against the machine. *Al-Fukāhah,* June 20, 1928.

Caricatures of frustrated men demolishing public phone booths (of which there were 180 in 1925)[59] and home or office devices (numbering 50,000 in 1928)[60] suggest the sublimated place of physical aggression in seemingly benign processes of social synchronization and the precarious nature of time-space compression. While telephones potentially enabled instantaneous communication across great distances, they also hierarchized and extended the experience of delay involved in holding the line by gendering it and making it socially and politically fraught.

Cartoons and humorous inventions helped to vent (but also proliferate and legitimate) violence, which is also recorded in printed descriptions of phone conversations. A revealing example involves an alleged phone conversation between Fikrī Abāẓah, our sarcastic acquaintance from the previous chapter, and an *Ānisah* phoning in to protest his claim that women should be relabeled "the scary sex" (*al-jins al-mukhīf* instead of the rhyming *al-jins al-laṭīf,* "the tender sex"). Abāẓah explained to her that women deserved this label because of an inherent double standard in their conduct: "They are scary because they claim tenderness *[luṭf]* while actually being the cruelest of the sexes . . . controlling men's lives." His protracted, misogynistic phone monologue culminated in abruptly hanging up the phone, leaving his interlocutor with a piercing disconnect sound that neatly extended Abāẓah's line of argumentation and led the caller to angrily throw the phone to the ground.[61]

The double feminine standard that threatened men like Abāẓah may be seen as a manifestation of the contradictory role of women embedded in effendi circuits, sustaining masculine routines while being labeled as their other. To meet other men as colleagues, business partners, litigants, nationalists, state officials, or friends, effendi men depended on their womenfolk and at the same time on their absence.[62] Telephony, which provided a labor setting in which middle-class women could retain their invisibility and respectability, was emblematic of this paradox.[63]

Such female labor interfered with men's work. In a typical cartoon, an effendi on hold hurries the young woman, saying, "We have work to do here!"[64] Women's infiltration of masculine work environments (seen also in the above examples where the telephone "presences" wives in husbands' offices) informs effendi rage against machines. If objectifying or dehumanizing women made possible certain kinds of violence, the feminization of objects rerouted aggression to new avenues, facilitating the handling and focusing of contradictions of the kind young professionals like the lawyer Abāẓah and his ilk grappled with daily.

TELEPHONE MADNESS

Effendi writers provided explanations other than misogyny for their rage against telephones, linking these frenzies to the maddening devices or, in other accounts, to machines that were themselves mad. Such "telephone madness" was often attributed to being kept on hold by female operators. A 1928 skit, again by Fikrī Abāẓah, titled "Tilifūnī al-majnūn" (My mad telephone), reveals the temporal foundations of this challenge to mental stability. Abāẓah attributed telephone madness to the fact that every day around noon it took him two hours to get a connection, no matter how many times he cranked the handle. After two hours, the central responded calmly, and when Abāẓah cried out, "Ya mademoiselle, my phone is out of order for two hours!" she responded serenely, "No, ya effendi, the phone is fine."[65] In what follows, examining the meaning of "madness" *(junūn)* in this historical context discloses the particular meanings and frameworks of a unique lived experience of delay.

Before delving into this particular madness, it is important to point out that male anger with telephone delays and female labor was certainly not unique to Egypt. Frustration with the telephone, manifested in cursing, seeking the aid of the complaints department, and violently cranking the handle, was also described during this period in places as diverse as colonial Cameroon[66] and Walter Benjamin's Berlin. Describing the introduction of the telephone to his home, Benjamin recounts:

> Disagreements with the switchboard operators were the rule, to say nothing of the threats and curses uttered by my father when he had the complaints department on the line. But his real orgies were reserved for cranking the handle, to which he gave himself up for minutes at a time, nearly forgetting himself in the process. His hand on these occasions was *a dervish overcome by frenzy*. My heart would pound; I was certain that the employee on the other end was in danger of a stroke, as punishment for her negligence.[67]

As in Cairo, civilized middle-class telephone users were losing their tempers everywhere, seeming to slip into the same fanatical irrationality. Yet rather than collapsing these reactions as a response to some essential aspect of early telephony, it is important to point out that in Cameroon delays were understood to be related to the native operators' racial deficiencies. And unlike the case with Benjamin senior, for effendis the dervish and his frenzy were more than exotic metaphors; as we saw in chapter 3, they were imminent threats looming close by, perhaps inside the self. What, then, were the particular kinds of madness generated by the effendi phone?

Various notions of madness, divergence from the right path, and decline into irrationality and sin—which corresponded to competing or overlapping theories of selfhood—circulated in colonial Egypt, and many seemed to converge in the telephone. As in Europe and the United States, telephony was sometimes understood in terms of haunting and spirit possession.[68] In this respect, the response to telephony was one example of a more general attitude to other modern devices and particularly to technologies of audition. For example, the inaugural broadcast lecture for the opening of the Egyptian broadcasting service in June 1934, "The Radio as It Was Perceived by a Bedouin from the Desert," which narrated the reaction of a Bedouin sheikh to the radio,[69] described the sheikh's great fear of the device, which he perceived as a wooden skull in which an *ʿifrīt* was incarcerated.

While such attitudes were attributed to superstition and conjured up only to be contrasted with scientific explanations, it was clear that it was their acoustic dimensions that made them potent. Thus, in 1934, *Al-Ahrām* printed a series of stories on *mulūk al-jinn*—"the Kings of the Jinn"—that addressed various manifestations of "the problem of superstitions," especially women or blind men who used ventriloquism to imitate supernatural voices.[70] Egyptian readers of the early 1930s would recognize the Genie Kings as conventional targets of fictional incantation in works such as *A Thousand and One Nights,* where they are summoned to aid in an act of aural therapy performed by a woman on a mad king.

Phones resonated also with a long-standing Islamic ambivalence regarding the female voice. In the first decades of the twentieth century, such discussions were conducted in modern venues such as Rashīd Riḍā's magazine *Al-Manār*[71] and in singers' manuals,[72] as well as in reprints of classical works like Ibn al-Jawzī's twelfth-century *Talbīs Iblīs* (The insinuations of Iblis), reprinted in Cairo in 1922 and still a standard reference on Islamic attitudes to audition.[73] Commentators argued that women's voices induced excessive desire *(ʿishq),* which might lead auditors to sin.[74] The telephone, with its intimate proximity of orifice to orifice, mouth to ear, exacerbated the problem of the female voice and its association with desire.[75]

The problem of *ʿishq* was mental as much as ethical: if unconsummated, *ʿishq* was seen as a possible cause for madness or as itself a form of madness.[76] The problem of the female voice manifested in content, form, and linguistic register. Though female singing had been used in the past as therapy for the insane,[77] conservative commentators claimed that modern songs, particularly *anāshīd* and *taqātiq,* which were sung in colloquial Egyptian Arabic, had become as dangerous and maddening as addictive drugs (deemed to cause insanity),[78] leading to "inflammation of the senses and desires, and the steering of the soul toward degradation."[79] The female voice caused an autoimmune reaction: it simultaneously cured and caused madness.[80]

This slippage between desire and madness was demonstrated in two of the most famous Arabic epics—the story of *Majnūn and Laylā* and the *Thousand and One Nights.* Numerous late nineteenth- and early twentieth-century adaptations of these classics exemplify the acoustic characteristics of maddening desire. They also reveal how romantic notions of incorporeal, platonic love retroactively sprang authentic Arabic roots, positioning them vis-à-vis modern, Western, sexual love. The best-known adaptation of *Majnūn and Laylā* is the 1933 version written by Aḥmad Shawqī (1868–1932), the "Prince of Poets," whose lyrics were sung by prominent singers such as Muḥammad ʿAbd al-Wahhāb[81] and Umm Kulthūm,[82] reaching wide audiences of listeners and readers. Shawqī's version mixed the tropes of a longing-induced derangement resulting from jinn and devil possession. But in contrast to pre-Islamic approaches to time,[83] lovers Qays and Laylā experience desire temporally as a modern effendi couple would: for Laylā, an hour's reunion with Qays equaled an entire lifetime, while impatient Qays endlessly awaited his beloved.[84]

On October 11, 1933, most likely after the publication of Shawqī's text, the magazine *Kull Shay'* devoted a special issue to "The Death of Love" *(Fanā' al-Ḥubb).* One of the articles cited *Majnūn and Laylā* as emblematic of the kind of pure virginal love that was now going extinct. In the old days, when people believed in apparitions *(awhām),* we are told, they also endorsed a nonphysical love—so much so that when Laylā came to meet mad Qays in the desert, he didn't recognize her, claiming that his real beloved was a purely abstract idea that had nothing to do with the corruptible bodily manifestation in front of him. However, according to the article, his belief in the imaginary realm soon gave way to sexual desire.[85] The modern undermining of belief in the supernatural also changed notions of love.

In 1934, Tawfīq al-Ḥakīm published *Shahrazad,* a pioneering play based on the *Arabian Nights.* It begins where the classic tale ends, after 1,001 nights of narrative therapy whispered from a mouth that the play equates to a cup of pearls.[86] This prolonged aural deferral of climax left King Shariyar cured of his lethal misogyny yet suffering from a new and "real insanity," a "mental disturbance" opposed to the madness induced by his love for Shahrazad.[87] In al-Ḥakīm's version, Shariyar has moved beyond sexual desire and is afflicted with an abstract yearning to get to the bottom of the philosophical mysteries of existence. Talking about Shahrazad, women in general, and even nature herself, Shariyar provides an explanation for the puzzle at the root of his madness:

> She is the prisoner in her boudoir all her life, yet she knows everything on earth as though she were the earth. She has never left her bosk, yet she knows Egypt, India, and China. She is a virgin, yet she knows men like a woman who lived among men a thousand years. . . . Who could that one be who had lived fewer than twenty years which she spent like her contemporaries in a room with the curtains drawn? What is her secret? Is she twenty years old? Or is she ageless? Was she confined to one place or did she exist every place? My mind boils over wanting to know.[88]

The figure of Shahrazad was repeatedly recast in subsequent years, frequently haunting the boundary between corporality and spirituality, tenderness and cruelty, that was inherent to femininity as Abāẓah, Shawqī, and al-Hakīm understood it.

Bayram al-Tūnisī, the famous popular poet and songwriter, addressed phone madness in his poems, linking the matter to the problem of wrong numbers and the accidental connection of total strangers. In a long piece from around 1930 devoted to the telephone, "Al-Maqāmah al-Tilifūnīyah,"[89] he demonstrates the seductions lurking in the lines for the uninitiated. The protagonist, using the phone for the first time, recounts how he goes to a pharmacy and with the owner's aid dials the number of a friend. But something unexpected happens: "Then I heard a voice like the chirping of birds or the harmony of hymns, and it said, in a harmonic tone, 'hallo.'"

It takes him several moments to understand he has a wrong number and to realize that the beautiful voice—which at first he addressed in the masculine and as disconnected from an actual speaker—belongs to a young woman, someone's niece, Iḥsān. As soon as this dawns on him, he blesses "the Creator of women with a device that gives us the pleasantest voice." Al-Tūnisī's protagonist completely forgets what he was calling for and immerses himself in the tête-à-tête. As the flirtation progresses, Iḥsān asks the protagonist to recite a *sūrah* (a Qurʾanic chapter). He clears his throat and utters a *taʿwīdh,* the formula preceding the recitation of the Qurʾān to prevent the devil from intervening in the recitation of the holy text: "Aʿūdhu biʾllāh min al-shayṭān al-rajīm" (I take refuge with God from the accursed Satan). But when he starts reciting, the pharmacist grabs him from behind and kicks him out, shouting that the phone cannot be used for such purposes.

Bayram's *taʿwīdh* should be understood in the context of the auditory character of temptation. Indeed, in another formula of *taʿwīdh,* Muslims are instructed to seek refuge from Satan, "the whispering tempter who whispers in the chests of men" *(al-waswās al-khannās alladhī yuwaswisu fī ṣudūr al-nās).* Like the supernatural entities we are already acquainted with, which are summoned by human intentionality, fear, and recognition, the devil is assumed to lack the capacity to enter a man's heart until he desires to sin, and thus works through aural suggestion, or *waswasah*—a word translated as both "whispering" and "temptation."[90] In a cartoon depicting a similar invocation of this protective formula, a man gradually loses his composure when the "mademoiselle" telephone operator keeps him on hold for over half an hour, giving him wrong number after wrong number. Neither curses nor pleading to the Complaints Department helps. One frame before he physically attacks the telephone, the effendi protagonist says, in colloquial Egyptian Arabic, "I seek God's refuge from this [telephone] department"

FIGURE 14. Telephone madness. *Al-Fukāhah,* October 31, 1928.

(*Aʿūdhu biʾ llāh min dī maṣlaḥah*), a vulgarization of the formulaic *taʿwīdh*. Its evocation at the threshold of madness, after the protagonist loses his spectacles, his tarboosh, and finally his nerves—that is, everything that makes him an effendi—marks a descent into language that borders the superstitious, thus resembling the feminine or lower-class "other" whose abjection constitutes effendiness.

Existing notions of mental health were also challenged by newly introduced epistemes, such as Freudian terminology or the new mechanistic view of the human body. The notion of *waswasah* is a case in point. Whereas, according to traditional Islamic ontology, whispering temptation emanates from real, external, devilish sources, in the twentieth century *waswasah* and *al-waswās al-qahrī* came to acquire a Freudian meaning of obsessive-compulsive, internal, oral imperatives. Egyptian practitioners of psychoanalysis still struggle to reconcile a theory of selfhood that considers such voices as emanating from within the self with the beliefs of patients and sometimes of analysts that these voices may have a real external source.[91]

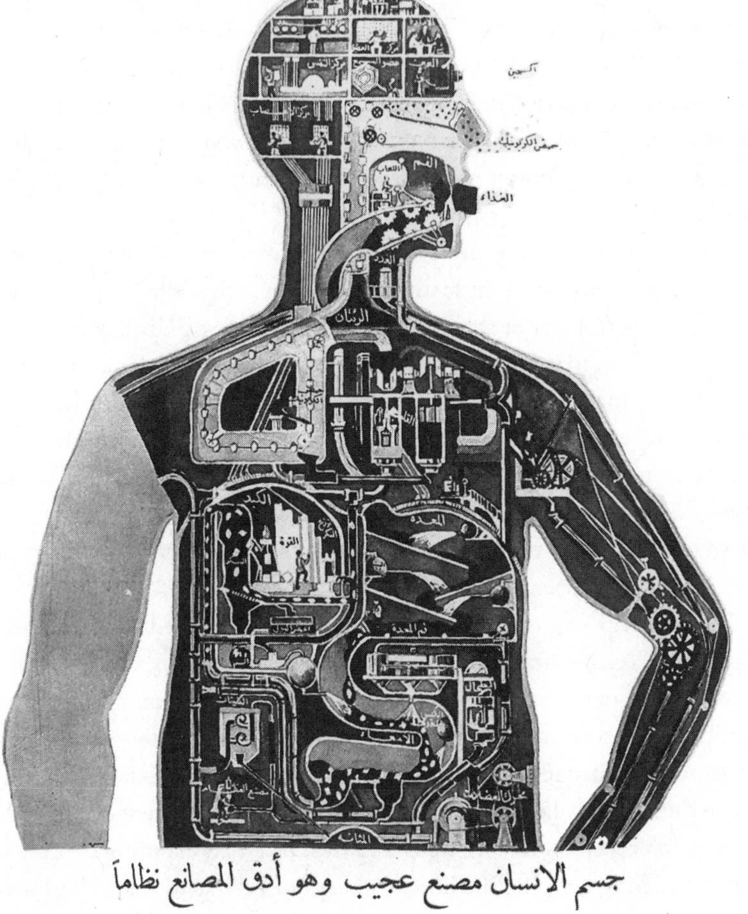
جسم الانسان مصنع عجيب وهو أدق المصانع نظاماً

FIGURE 15. The human body—the wonderful and most organized factory. *Kull Shay' wa'l-'Ālam*, June 25, 1928.

The internalization of love, temptation, and madness was always partial and fraught.

Another modern scientific paradigm that informed telephony, and modern subjectivity more broadly, concerned electricity (a force that fused religious and scientific epistemologies). Because the electricity that allowed transmission of information in communication systems also animated the human nervous system, these communication systems gradually became models for bodily and emotional communication (and vice versa: telephone and telegraph networks were seen as national or global nerve systems).[92] Thus, in 1928 the magazine *Kull Shay' wa'l-Ālam* published a diagram of the human body under the title "The Human Body—The Wonderful and Most Organized Factory."[93] Body parts are portrayed as mechanical instruments and systems—refineries, furnaces, wheels in motion. In the back of the skull, a small area is labeled "the Nervous Center" *(al-markaz al-ʿaṣabī).*[94] It is a room from which communication lines stretch in and out of a telephone switchboard, manned by two phone operators.

The image was a reproduction of the iconic 1926 *Der Mensch als Industtrieplast* (Man as industrial palace) by Fritz Khan, a prominent European popularizer of the man-as-machine analogy.[95] Today many readers would recognize it from the cover of Deleuze and Guattari's *Anti-Oedipus,* an analysis of the relations of desire and capitalism, wherein the body is seen as a desiring machine and its object as another machine connected to it.[96] Such an interpretation was becoming thinkable in early twentieth-century Egypt too. If nerves were controlled by internal switchboard operators, their mental effects could now be understood using these scientific vocabularies.

The transcript of an imagined phone conversation printed in *Al-Muṣawwar* as part of a "Telephone Entertainment" *(Fukāhat al-Tilifūn)* series[97] connects the discussion of the telephone operator to middle-class terms of endearment. In the imagined conversation, the switchboard operator sabotages what she diagnoses as a failed relationship between a gentleman and his fanciful fiancée. When the fiancée calls, the operator delays the connection, first by pretending she couldn't get the correct number and then by falsely claiming that the line is busy ("Telling herself: 'The line isn't busy but I'd like to teach this hurried woman the meaning of patience.'"). When the tête-à-tête becomes a lovers' quarrel, she sabotages attempts to place a makeup call and instead talks to the young man directly, telling him that his fiancée is not the right woman for him because she does not truly love him. "There has to exist in nature an electrical current transmitted from heart to heart, even via great distance," she informs him, regarding the true meaning of modern love. Eventually the operator and caller fall into each other's arms.[98] Love becomes electricity, a current generated by feminine control and amplified by deferrals.

While such modern notions of the networked body were rapidly becoming universal, it is important to consider how Egyptian readers understood them at the beginning of the twentieth century. The notion of the body as machine emerged in Europe around questions of fatigue and energy conservation.[99] In Egypt, issues of energy, lethargy, and indolence were at the center of British admonitions about indigenous time mindlessness and thus central to anticolonial projects of reform, education, and the reorganization of gender relations. The manipulative deferrals of the operator, intended to teach callers "the meaning of patience" *(maʿnā al-ṣabr),* brought into collision two conflicting values—patience and expediency. Preexisting understandings of *ṣabr,* "which is from the benefactor"—as the proverbial rendition of a *ḥadīth* goes—contrasted it with haste, "which is from the devil." Positive new valuations of swiftness and the gendered aspects of temporal reform often put these notions on a collision course, triggering the autoimmune reaction wherein women possess a power that is both curing and maddening.

Old and new understandings of madness, though sometimes diametrically opposed ontologically, stressed its aural nature and the problem of hearing voices, either real or hallucinated. The acoustics of delay likewise could not be contained in the telephone grid alone. A comprehensive examination of this experience must pursue delay's resonances and spillovers also in other media used for broadcasting and listening to maddening female voices.

COLONIAL ACOUSTICS: THE AESTHETICS AND POLITICS OF WAITING

We may begin by returning to madness and *ʿishq,* and their rhythms. One of the most elaborate texts to address the affinity of folly, Egyptian nationalism, and effendi terms of endearment is Tawfīq al-Ḥakīm's *ʿAwdat al-Rūḥ* (Return of the spirit), a 1933 semiautobiographical novel about the days leading to the 1919 anticolonial revolution. As the novel's title indicates, the prerevolutionary period is seen as a time of maddening spiritual absence directly connected to romantic longing. Indeed, the revolutionary crescendo in the political sphere overlaps a series of courtships in which representatives of the effendiyya—a student intellectual, an engineer, a civil servant, and an industrialist—compete for the heart of the feminine protagonist, the fair Sanīyah. The revolution coincides with the sobering conclusion to these maddening courtships. And, as in a series of earlier nationalist novels in which woman and nation stand for each other,[100] Sanīyah symbolizes Egypt. When she finally falls for Muṣṭafā, Sanīyah's seduction tactics exemplify the role of timekeeping in the relation between male and female representatives of effendi culture. The paragraph below is taken from a balcony scene, one of several courtship encounters characterized by similar chronotopes, wherein delay generates desire:

> [Sanīyah] looked at the sky and after that at her small alarm clock on the bedside table to see how much time was left before nightfall. The moon came out full that night. The clock struck ten. The members of the household had gone to sleep. All was still. . . . [Sanīyah] went to the window and opened it. . . . Muṣṭafā gazed at her, leaning his arm on the balcony railing, as though his heart were suddenly overflowing. He looked up at her and said with a tone of censure softened by a quavering tremor of love, "You were half an hour late tonight." She replied with a smile, "Right!" "Why?" She looked at him mischievously. Then, laughing again, she said, "Why? . . . Do you want me to interrupt your tête-à-tête with the moon?"[101]

In this scene and others,[102] time is of the essence: missed and belated appointments are conversation starters, such that schedules not only frame and enable the relationship from the outside but—like the weather in a Jane Austen novel—constitute its actual stuff, the discursive conduit for expressing anything from censure to tremors of love. Moreover, Sanīyah's carefully orchestrated belated window appearance illuminates the relation between delay and punctuality. Not only does the clock categorically structure delay as delay, but it sometimes coordinates it. Sanīyah's coaxing delays are not the result of time mindlessness but exactly the opposite—she requires all her willpower to keep from rushing to meet Muṣṭafā at the appointed time. As the couple's nocturnal rendezvous continue, Sanīyah makes Muṣṭafā wait for increasingly longer periods (which she measures carefully while he experiences them as eternities).[103] In these encounters, Sanīyah uses well-planned deferrals, always mindful of the clock time she disregards.[104]

The same temporal relation that binds the effendi couple in romantic love—the procrastination that arouses the male desire—appears also in the wedding ritual that formalizes this bond. Consider another scene from *Return of the Spirit,* describing the performance of a wedding band: "An hour passed while the artists did nothing more than tune the instruments, smoke cigarettes, drink coffee, sip fruit punch, chatter and criticize. Perhaps their most important accomplishment was to vex the audience and exhaust their patience. In actuality, this is a portion of the art of the people and of that profession. Indeed, it is perhaps the sole art which the artists of Egypt do to perfection: the art of vexation and keeping the audience waiting."[105]

The members of this women's troupe explicitly acknowledge that calculated "delay and procrastination" are the essential tactics of their profession. Al-Ḥakīm's account of the long-awaited climax of the wedding, two pages of artistic deferrals later, mixes the sexual and the national, invigorating politics with the clichés of romanticism: "The audience of enthusiastic guests surrounded the troupe *like the crescent moon around the star on the Egyptian flag.* They listened as though they were all a single individual. . . . [T]heir faces all had the same expression: one of boisterous happiness. . . . [T]he music had that effect on them."[106]

This ecstatic togetherness is finally achieved in a climax produced and preconditioned by delay. Awaiting culmination (be it political independence or consummation of romantic desire) befits a colonial condition that repeatedly promises and then defers ad infinitum its own conclusion. Clearly, al-Ḥakīm's rendition of artistic and romantic delay as a driving force of national desire was meant to serve the novel's didactic nationalistic chronotope, paving the way for the revolutionary return of the Egyptian spirit (and the convergence of plot lines whereby the quotidian and historical reflect and reinforce each other). However, other sources suggest that this nexus of delay and desire was not merely or not always didactic.

The musical performance of delay was based on true events. In 1902, the musician and theorist Muḥammad Kāmil al-Khulaʿī disapprovingly concluded a section titled "The Way Singing Is Performed in Egypt Today" with a description of singers who only begin singing in the middle of the night. "It is much better," he claimed, "for people running festivities to accustom singers to start singing early so that listeners have ample time to return to their homes bodily and mentally relaxed."[107] Yet if the actual conditions of live performance didn't adhere to the didactic stipulations of the pundits, by the 1930s such frowned-upon procrastination was coming under a new kind of attack. Several Egyptian periodicals discussed the impact of new recording and broadcasting technologies on Arabic music. The issue was especially urgent for *Al-Rādiyō*—a new magazine published because the daily newspapers initially refused to print the broadcast schedule of a medium they perceived as a competitor. The radio, phonograph, gramophone, and cinema were criticized for forcing music into fixed temporal frames that flattened singers' ability to improvise spontaneously, to grow and shrink the melody as a way of interacting with audiences.

In 1933, the same year *Return of the Spirit* was published, pioneering Egyptian director Muḥammad Karīm released his first musical, *Al-Wardah al-Bayḍāʾ* (The white rose), with music by the renowned composer and singer Muḥammad ʿAbd al-Wahhāb. The novel on which it was based tells the story of the making of a great musician, involving a dramatic love story and an evil stepmother manipulatively sabotaging it (telephonically and otherwise). *The*

White Rose was the first film to confront the problem of compressing long classical Arabic songs (which lasted at least fifteen to twenty minutes) into six-minute sequences.[108]

An Egyptian film producer working on another film that year told *Al-Ahrām* about his efforts to explain the difference between cinematic time and the time of live performance to musicians who had been hired to record the soundtrack. The reluctant musicians were instructed to compose and play melodies that would not exceed 1.5 minutes. They had to be convinced that this interval, which they regarded as very short, was actually long and respectable in films. Moreover, each of these short melodies had to be divisible into five parts lasting eighteen seconds each so that the music would correspond to the camera angle, long shot, or close-up, and the recording would reflect acoustically the changing distances of the camera from the objects.[109]

Cinematic compressions were facilitated by and in turn reinforced shortenings caused by commercial recording and the radio. In the 1930s, this cycle of shortening forged the *ughnīyah* (pl. *ughnīyāt,* translated as "song"), which became the most popular form of Arabic music from 1950 on.[110] Yet such processes of temporal compression did not go uncontested.[111] For instance, music critics commented on the impact that scheduling changes had on the quality of live radio performance. In the last week of 1936, the Egyptian Radio shortened the time allotted to each live performance from half an hour to twenty minutes. A reviewer of one such radio concert, by the famous singer Nādirah Amīn, argued that the performer was obviously singing "without feeling" (*min ghayr nafs*, literally "without spirit"), a fact he attributed to the temporal constraint that prevented her from slowly developing the melody.[112] This was not the first time new media excerpted Nādirah's songs; the singer's complex relationship with the radio was explored in the film *Anshūdat al-Rādiyō* ("Radio anthem," starring Nādirah), which started screening in the beginning of the year.[113]

Some performers negotiated the new temporal constraints better than others. Perhaps the best example of a singer who managed to retain and develop a traditional style in these new media was Umm Kulthūm, a diva "more powerful than thousands of telephone lines in connecting the Arab world."[114] Just as radios deprived audiences of live performers, affecting their routines and listening habits in various ways, they also deprived singers of live audiences, thereby changing traditional performing practices where the audience actively participated in the creation of a musical piece.

Initially ambivalent toward media that required performing without an audience,[115] Umm Kulthūm gradually carved a place for traditional singing in this new mediascape. Her strategies are illuminating: though she sang *ughnīyāt* in films, Umm Kulthūm elaborated on these short compositions during concert-hall improvisatory performances, where she used to wait five to seven minutes before even stepping on stage in order to vex her audience.[116] These were broadcast live on the radio, on the last Thursday of every month. Such venues allowed Umm Kulthūm (unlike the short-breathed Nādirah) to demonstrate her vocal strength by singing hours on end.

Critical of a weak *(ḍaʿīf)* voice, listeners appreciated such vocal prowess and the ability to sing a long phrase: "In the ideal performance the singer would vary one or more lines upon encouragement from the audience and thus extend a five-minute song to twenty or thirty minutes or more."[117] Such protocols of longing were anchored in a long tradition of spoken transmission of *ḥadīth,* poetry, and Qurʾān recitation, in which oral transmission and agentive audition were the glue of sociability.[118] This was a tradition in which listeners, like readers, were not passive receivers of the divine word but active evaluators of its transmission and plausibility.

The singing style that developed within this tradition and which Umm Kulthūm mastered generated a mystical elation, *ṭarab,* produced by elaborate maneuvers, including the ability to keep to tempo without strict adherence to the metric pattern, unexpected shifts from one *maqām* to another, and the effective delay of a *qaflah* or cadence.[119] I highlight these features because they share a common theme of subverting the musical frameworks in which they take place.

To be considered truly artistic, such subversions had to exemplify premeditation and intentionality.[120] Like Sanīyah's delays in *Return of the Spirit,* they showed careful orchestration. Umm Kulthūm's growing sophistication in this art was received with delight by her male listeners. For instance, in 1926 a member of the audience pointed out how the singer, who started as a simple girl, had become flirtatious, witty, and equipped with "female wickedness which fills the soul with bewilderment and surprise."[121]

The role of such delays in teasing masculine (artistic, political, or romantic) desire calls for rethinking the relations between desire and transgression. Conventionally, the law (e.g., the standard set by the clock, schedule, or meter) is seen as curbing illicit desire, as in Kant's example from *Critique of Practical Reason:* "Suppose that someone says his lust is irresistible when the desired object and opportunity are present. Ask him whether he would not control his passions if, in front of the house where he has this opportunity, a gallows were erected on which he would be hanged immediately after gratifying his lust. We do not have to guess very long what his answer may be."[122]

However, as Slavoj Žižek presents Jacques Lacan's counterargument, "What if we encounter a subject (as we do regularly in psychoanalysis), who can only fully enjoy a night of passion if some form of 'gallows' is threatening him, i.e., if, by doing it, he is violating some prohibition?"[123] The temporality punctuating effendi conjugation, radio and concert-hall audition, and telephone delays opens up a similar possibility. Masculine desire is aroused when its object is itself transgressive, when the woman (and nation) marks her otherness, her resistance to the masculine/Western standard he himself represents. When transgression is coded as a term of endearment, women can become at once objects and subjects of (temporal and other) discipline.

Compartmentalizing music (and Qurʾān recitations) into fixed short periods was essential to the creation of regular radio programming in the mid-1930s. Beginning in this decade, radio devices quickly replaced live performers—singers, storytellers, Qurʾān reciters—in coffeehouses, where bachelors spent their free time.[124] Radio programming appeared to structure this free time, providing the conditions of possibility for a new simultaneity among audiences across Egypt, who could now consider themselves to be members of a single "imagined community" of listeners.[125]

Yet highlighting only the effects of an ostensibly generic simultaneity leaves out of Egyptian nationalism the fact that these rearrangements of the temporal into a seemingly synchronized horizon often invigorated existing and new temporalities predicated on delay and procrastination. Thus, alongside a fixed broadcast schedule and its politics, the radio spread aesthetic styles based on resignifying and disrupting this accord.

Critiques of musical compression emerged in semicolonial Egypt at around the time that Theodor Adorno published his controversial 1936 essay, "On Jazz," one of several critical analyses of contemporary popular music, most famously jazz, and the technologies of its dissemination, most notably the radio. For Adorno, the repetitive structure of jazz, particularly the standardized deviations, reveals the operations of a cultural industry that saps all spontaneity from music, thus making art participate in reaffirming and harmonizing the existing social order. Adorno saw jazz as extending to aesthetics the technologies of domination of industrial modernity, a castrating genre demonstrating the force of the collective over the individual.[126]

The similarity of this analysis to Egyptian lamentations of lost spontaneity indicates the generality of the workings of media technologies, industrial rhythms, and culture industries. Yet, while Adorno's reading focused on class politics, in Egypt musical deferrals effaced by the radio, gramophone, and cinema were also linked to colonial and then anticolonial orders, and thus animated a very different politics.

CLIMAX?

What was the place of the phone within this media ecology and the experiences of waiting it popularized? May we conflate telephony, the gramophone, cinema, and the radio—different media with completely different logics and histories? May we mix quotidian suspensions with grand political ones to characterize some kind of "Waiting" with a capital *W* and, what is more, associate it with an "Egyptian time"?

To begin answering these questions with a qualified affirmative, it might first be stated that the Arabic word for telephone, *hātif,* coined in the 1920s, brings together the semantic fields of madness and mystical audition. Unlike the English word *telephone,* which highlights the *distance* crossed by the voice, *hātif* refers to the source of a disembodied voice, a voice heard but not seen. For example, in Aḥmad Shawqī's neoclassical 1933 rendition of *Majnūn and Laylā,* when Qays kisses the threshold of his beloved's tent while moaning "Laylā," a question comes from inside: "Who is the *hātif?*"[127] Muḥammad ʿAbd al-Wahhāb (the composer of the music for *The White Rose* and the inspiration for its narrative) brilliantly chose this sentence to open his musical rendition of Shawqī's *Majnūn,* fusing the disembodiment inherent in modern recording and broadcast media with the disembodiment of spiritual craving and romantic love. As Toshihiko Isutzu suggests, the word *hātif* resonates with a long Sufi tradition of audition and desire for God, the ultimate source of such unseen voices,[128] and it has been affirmed that the *ṭarab* singing tradition mastered by Umm Kulthūm should be seen as an offshoot of this Sufi genealogy.[129]

Further, Fikrī Abāẓah, Aḥmad Shawqī, and Bayram al-Tūnisī, three writers responsible for elaborating notions of delay-induced "phone madness," were also the main songwriters for performers like Umm Kulthūm and ʿAbd al-Wahhāb, shaping the cultural attitudes that informed the telephonic, gramophonic, and radiophonic soundscapes both in print and aurally. We have encountered these writers also in previous chapters, rendering into rhyme and rhythm the politics of slowness that emerged in response to the mechanical speed of the tram and the counterclockwise revolution of time in 1919. The kinds of longing kindled by *ṭarab* resonated musically in their lyrics, stressing the wait for a lover or beloved who sometimes stood for the nation-state. Other performers reinforced the connection of the telephone to wider mediascapes in other ways. For example, Egyptian films are rife with singers who use the telephone as a microphone.[130]

Finally, alongside the telephone service, during the roaring twenties the Egyptian recording industry and cinema offered perhaps the only, and undoubtedly the most prominent, work environments open to middle-class women, and even more so women seeking to climb into the middle class. Female work was also a central theme in the songs of this period.[131] Together, the telephone, radio, and cinema offered visible targets of masculine anxiety and frustration concerning women's labor, as well as the main avenues for venting, focusing, and working out these tensions.

It appears that as telephone operators were eliminated, thereby shortening on-hold time, the gendered waiting that characterized the age of manual exchange metamorphosed into aesthetic codes animating other media. Though the dynamic that contributed to the feminization of the telephone at the beginning of the century was disappearing by the mid-1930s, some gendered aspects of waiting shaped by phones were sustained by other support systems. In the media ecology of urban, middle-class Egypt, different media cited each other: cinematic and radiophonic shortening and compression were compensated by live elongations in the concert hall or over the phone. The other side of the coin was that the staccato notes of modern life resonated with a deeper, slower stratum that anchored technical compression in the elaborations of a lived and shared experience.

The political life of Egyptian telephony kept evolving in the following decades. In the 1940s, one of the most conspicuous symbols associated with the hedonistic corruption of King Farouk, Egypt's last monarch (who ascended the throne in 1936), was a battery of six green telephones by the side of each royal bed in each of the king's palaces. Farouk even passed a special law forbidding anyone else in the country from having a green telephone.[132]

According to one version, the officers who took over these palaces and deposed the king in 1952 conspired telephonically from Café Groppi. Unlike the revolution of 1919, which ended in only nominal independence, the Free Officers Revolution of 1952 seemed like the long-awaited climax of political independence come true—the grand finale that would end the colonial civilizing mission, the dynastic monarchy that existed in its shadow, and all the social injustices that ensued. The rise to power of one of these officers, Gamal ʿAbd al-Nasser, the nationalization of the Suez Canal, resistance to foreign powers, land reform, and the expansion of public education were understood by many Egyptians as the belated and hence superpotent realization of the promise of "Egypt for the Egyptians" made seven decades ago.

Yet this bliss was short-lived, ending with a six-day war in June 1967. Three years after the humiliating defeat to Israel, Nasser died of heart failure. Anwar al-Sadat's Corrective Revolution of the early 1970s, intended to eliminate the Nasserist police state, targeted the phone surveillance complex Nasser had established soon after taking power.[133] Appropriately, Sadat's new era was symbolized by the public burning of tapes from over 22,000 telephone taps,[134] ushering in free-market capitalism and a shift in Cold War alliances called *Infitāḥ*—"open door"—through which mainly Western investment and intervention poured back into Egypt.

Like the enmeshed public and private spheres through which we entered this chapter, the agendas of the political and the tempos of the aesthetic were hard to disentangle. In 1969, Umm Kulthūm premiered one of her most famous songs, "Alf Laylā wa-Laylā" (A Thousand and One Nights). Based on a rich twentieth-century tradition of adapting the epic to theater, radio, and cinema,[135] the lyrics of her love song employed the trope of the waiting woman, while the live performance was a culmination of the aesthetics of deferral. In the same year, Naguib Mahfouz published a short story that likewise played with the classics. Its protagonist, a journalist and writer, receives phone calls from an anonymous woman who seduces him into listening to installations of her life story. The caller is in complete control of the timing and duration of the calls, and the story's title, "Shahrazād," which is also the pseudonym given to the woman, reveals that procrastination is deliberately and strategically deployed by caller and novelist alike as a means for advancing the plot, generating suspense, stirring up desire, and moving toward the climax. But the nocturnal strategies of sleepless Arabian nights, sustained by the orality and invisibility of the caller, come to an abrupt conclusion as the two finally meet. Clapping eyes on the caller breaks her hold on the journalist, who is free to terminate the affair.[136]

Mahfouz's depiction of the Shahrazadlike powers of the caller, an account of the uneven distribution of female agency along the sensorium, was

FIGURE 16. Sleepless. Movie poster of *Lā Anām*.

influenced by the cinematic tradition of depicting telephones in film. Consider, for example, the 1957 film *Lā Anām* (Sleepless), based on a story by Iḥsān ʿAbd al-Qaddūs, the editor of *Rūz al-Yūsuf* and a confidant of the revolutionary officers. *Sleepless,* one of the first Egyptian color films, was described by its director, Ṣalāḥ Abū Sayf, as anchored in the tradition of "White Telephone" Italian cinema. It was one of several Abū Sayf adaptations of texts by ʿAbd al-Qāddūs dealing with female liberation.[137] Specifically, *Sleepless* should be seen in the closely related context of films such as the 1949 *Ghazal al-Banāt* (Candy floss, or the flirtation of the girls) or the 1953 *Bint al-Akābir* (Daughter of nobility), in which the telephone played a central role in connecting men and women of different classes in bonds of love and freeing secluded women who were trapped at home or by tradition. In *Sleepless,* Nadia, the young protagonist, begins making telephonic advances toward an older man she sees in a club. Nadia has the upper hand as long as the relationship is mediated by the telephone: she is the one initiating the prolonged calls and controlling their duration. This changes once the long-awaited meeting finally takes place: her interlocutor sees Nadia for what she is—an inexperienced young woman whom he can easily manipulate.

Actual experiences over the phone, depictions of this device in various media and genres, and understandings of how female voices are conveyed by different technologies were mutually reinforcing, especially when waiting was involved. Like early telephony, which was rife with static noise, with overlapping lines and unexpected crossovers, these processes spilled over and into each other, together shaping the acoustics of waiting in Egypt. Even when the political and technical conditions that propelled the aestheticization of deferral were no longer in place, procrastination retained its importance as a protocol for conveying emotion and hierarchy.

CONCLUSION

Countertemporality

I have a metal watch so rusted and gunky
It ticks as fast as the heart of a junkie
The hands and hour are never conflated
If it stops, I don't care If it leaps, I'm not elated
If it's late, I don't worry If it speeds, I don't whine
I only keep it as a mask of time.

AL-MAJALLAH AL-MIṢRĪYAH, December 15, 1900

CLOCKS HAVE BEEN THE PRESENT absentee in the preceding chapters. While examining time in Egypt, I have avoided the technology of timekeeping, thereby trying to evade the conventional bias according to which, as Lewis Mumford famously put it, "the clock is not merely a means of keeping track of the hours, but of synchronizing the actions of men. The clock, not the steam-engine, is the key machine of the modern industrial age."[1] As this book has shown, "society" or "social synchronization" cannot be so easily disentangled from "technology," and clocks sometimes follow (and not always set the pace) for the actions of men. By not privileging clocks over other technologies—in fact shunning them altogether—we have been able to keep open the question of timekeeping.

On Time tried to get at timekeeping circuitously, exploring the temporal effects of technologies designed for other purposes. Each of these examinations ended with the technology receding into the background, thus clearing the foreground for the emergence of "culture" as the relevant terrain. Electric trams promoting the idea that slowness is from the Merciful, phones and telegraphs recalling modes of Sufi audition or ʿAbbasid textuality, and trains haunted by the forces of popular religion introduced paradigms that camouflaged their own roles and agency. Thus "writing themselves under erasure," they slyly removed their traces from the story.

Against this background, it is appropriate to conclude the book in similar fashion and briefly examine the mechanical clock, a technology whose abstract time supposedly came to override the rhythms of all other devices of the modern industrial age. Exploring the nexus of clocks and newer technologies affords a bird's-eye view of the ways these technologies worked together and the unique kind of (dis)harmony they shared and propagated. Moreover, during the eighteenth and most of the nineteenth centuries, timepieces in Egypt were successfully integrated with preexisting Ottoman harmonization schemes and artifacts.[2] Sketching how they were affected by the newly introduced technologies of transportation and communication helps retrace the historical trajectory of Egyptian time vis-à-vis both European and Ottoman time.

Rather than providing a history of clocks, this conclusion breaks with the pattern of examining the convergence of a single technology and temporality yielding a specific countertempo, and aims to achieve a broader perspective on a comprehensive "countertemporality." Indeed, clocks not only provide a canvas wide enough for delineating the longue durée of timekeeping, due to their extensive career in Ottoman and then colonial Egypt; they also provide an opportunity to examine the emergence of a historically specific counterhegemonic notion of "duration."[3]

This kind of account builds on what we already know about the emergence of such countertemporality as a historical construct comprising all the countertempos recounted in the preceding chapters. Each chapter anchored in its technical platform of emergence a particular countertempo—colonial substandards of punctuality (chapter 2), middle-class spectral, outdated, cyclical time (chapters 3, 4, and 6), politicized slowness (chapter 5), and eroticized delay (chapter 7). In following these countertempos, the opening chapters retraced the development of colonial protocols of differentiation and their inversion at the hands of their original targets, the members of the burgeoning Egyptian middle class. Members of the effendiyya redeployed and reproduced colonial modi operandi to handle their own others: women, peasants, and workers. As the closing chapters of the book demonstrated, this multidimensional plane of interaction structured an anticolonial milieu wherein effendi repertoires of contention were enriched by lower-class and feminine forms of resignification of, resistance to, and engagement with the infrastructures that held together the world of these actors and made it tick.

The operation of interfacing technological networks in a colonial setting thus forged an affinity among unpunctuality, slowness, delay, and outdated religious calendrical schemes predicated on the same moon that shines on waiting lovers. The result was a largely coherent countertemporality that masked its intimate connection to mechanical time by resorting to the novel spheres of "culture," "tradition," "religion," and "nation." What follows complements this historical account by seeking not only to retrace the cumulative effects of these diverse inflections of standard mechanical time but also to capture their common denominator.

FROM "READING CLOCKS" TO "TELLING TIME"

Between the early 1830s and the late 1930s, Egypt became a very different place, and timekeeping in this transformed realm came to be associated with novel theories and practices—with new local, regional, and global projects and social groups, and with different, arguably much higher stakes. As Avner Wishnitzer puts it regarding the Ottoman Empire generally, from the beginning of this period through most of the long nineteenth century, mechanical clocks were successfully integrated with other temporal schemes, creating a system of "reading clocks *alla turca.*" In this system, people set their watches to twelve upon hearing the call for sunset prayer radiate from the minaret of the local mosque. They did so once a day, regardless of the accuracy of their timepieces, to account for seasonal variation in the setting of the sun.[4] Clocks closely reflected local natural observable conditions and were seen as prosthetic devices used to better align their bearers with natural phenomena.

As we saw in chapter 1, at the beginning of the nineteenth century, semi-literate Egyptian army scribes ignorantly copied numbers from the face of silver watches. It was not their illiteracy that prevented them from accessing metaphysical "time" but the absence of such a socially operative abstraction. As Daniel Stolz has shown, even sophisticated Azharite elite astronomers, who had used clocks at least since the opening decades of the eighteenth century, were trying to divine with these devices not "the time of prayer" but "the positions of the clock's hands" corresponding to the positions of the sun at which prayer is stipulated.[5] Assuming an established conceptual sphere of *single abstract* "time" before well into the nineteenth century would be—how to put it?—anachronistic.

The gradual emergence and spread of the abstraction "time" was embroiled in the spread of new technological, institutional, economical, and political infrastructures. The shift from "reading clocks" to "telling time" involved the emergence of a centralized state equipped with modern legal, military, educational, commercial, administrative, and material technologies. The process entailed a gradual separation of the Egyptian state from the Ottoman Empire in tandem with the country's synchronization with and incorporation into the global market of cotton, finance, news, transport, and increasingly direct yet never full-fledged forms of European imperialism.

The transition also involved formation of a modernizing professional class, whose members were groomed in and in turn operated the legal, commercial, cultural, and educational institutions that translated time into money, thus promoting new valuations of "time." Eventually, even the literary output of these effendis began circulating in periodical form (indeed, periodicals had to be routinized—"periodicalized"—into dailies, weeklies, and monthlies). A few years before or after 1910 (depending on how one dates "the first Egyptian novel"—a debate that is itself indicative of the teleologization of "literature"), texts appearing in periodicals were sometimes serialized in the form of novels, a literary form that further promoted abstract simultaneity. Finally, the emergence of "telling time" required developing new notions of abstract space. This was a result of global, rural, and urban spatial renovations, which created new sites for time reckoning, such as public clocks in train stations and other centrally located settings, which competed with preexisting loci.

These (re)routinizing effects have been at the heart of scholarly interest in Egypt over the last two and a half decades.[6] The existing literature oscillates between a focus on the violence of abstraction, and attempts, especially by social historians, to salvage nuance, retrieve the agency of local actors, and examine how abstractions "on the ground" dissolved upon contact with the acid bath of the everyday.[7] Left out of the false choice between abstraction and nuance was the crucial fact that not all abstractions are created equal. As this book has demonstrated, abstraction itself may be generated in historically specific settings, yielding variations on a standard and hence the system where standards found their meaning. I have attended to the multiple and often opposing ways in which historical actors organized the nuances and flux of their lives into simplified abstractions they could grasp and operate, examining how they deployed their own abstractions vis-à-vis competing constructs, claiming universality or specificity.

In the force field generated by newly introduced technologies of transport and media, the abstraction of "time" took a path that was intimately dependent on, yet inherently distinct from, Western time. This articulation was not a free-floating discursive formation or (mis)representation of the real, nor did it give rise to something ephemeral that can be dispelled or analyzed away. Like Western time, Egyptian time was historically constructed and made durable by railways, telegraph lines, and various other artifacts, big and small; confusingly, both times were constructed as essential, ahistorical phenomena concealing the circumstances of their making, albeit in different ways. *On Time* has offered an account of how these essentialisms complemented and reinforced one another. If, like other places in its vicinity and far beyond,[8] Egypt over the course of the long nineteenth century underwent a transition from reading clocks to telling time, the time Egyptians told was at once generic and unique. It was an abstract time they could call their own.

EVEN A BROKEN CLOCK

If it is indeed the case that time was uniquely modulated by Egyptian trains, trams, telegraphs, and telephones, we might expect to see these rearrangements indexed by the clocks embedded in these sociotechnical infrastructures, informing how they were read, understood, and used, and framing how the time told by such clocks was inscribed on the body, how it became gendered, classed, and politicized, and how it became abstracted. The poem opening this chapter is a case in point, as it depicts the emergence of both the abstraction "time" and its particularly Egyptian articulation. Indeed, in the year of its publication, 1900, instead of the earlier interest in "the position of the clock's hands," there was now a watch whose "hands and hour are never conflated," indicating the existence of "time" (or "the hour") independent of the devices of its keeping and measurement. The pendulum in fact had moved to the other extreme: such devices were now used not to adhere to time but to masquerade as time, and to mock it. By contextualizing this poem, the paragraphs that follow seek to explicate this odd disposition.

The most immediate context for the broken clock's subversive posture was Egypt's transition to the universal day, which represented a new phase in its globalization. The poem's mid-December publication followed Egypt's September adoption of Greenwich mean time and the country's further incorporation into a system where time signals from the master clock in the Greenwich observatory were transmitted along the Malta–Alexandria submarine telegraph cable to the subordinated Egyptian slave clocks.[9] Appropriately for the first year of a new century, a year inaugurated with fanfare,[10] 1900 indeed constituted a watershed in the sphere of timekeeping, a culmination of processes that had started several decades earlier, in which abstract time was severed from nature and from observable local phenomena and started taking its cue from the metropole. And as the language of "master and slave" makes apparent, beyond the initial confusion that such transition surely created, its political overtones were unavoidable. Within a global network thus synchronized, a broken slave clock exposed commensurability as a scheme of subjection and offered a means of resisting it. As we saw in the introduction and chapter 2, the decade following the poem's publication was marked by a gradual dispelling of instrumentalism's veil of impartiality, by disillusionment with the hope of reform guided from above, and by disenchantment with technological modernity and its mechanized time.

Abstract clock time could no longer be avoided, of course: the disenchantment of the first decade of the twentieth century corresponded not only with Egypt's incorporation in the temporal schemes of Greenwich but also with a marked increase in the local circulation of clocks and watches, as revealed by the growing number of clock repairers and watchmakers counted in official censuses and the growing number of press references and advertisements for watches, now regularly found in the announcement section of almost every daily newspaper. In 1907 there were 926 clock- and watchmakers in Egypt. In 1917, there were 1,317.[11]

But the rapid introduction of abstract clock time came with reservations. Misgivings could be discerned in literary representations of the pocket watch or wristwatch, whose popularity was likewise rapidly growing. Wearing a watch and being able to tell time marked a class distinction, usually setting the effendi man apart from his subordinates—women, servants, peasants—who in turn were represented as a constant hindrance to proper orderly timekeeping, even if their domestic, agricultural, and (in the case of phone girls) technical labor was what made the neat effendi world tick.[12] And yet, despite or perhaps because of this trend, already several years before the turn of the century, "a watch and chain" was regularly counted among the superficial trappings of modernity, which did not amount to genuine refinement.[13] Members of the effendiyya lived with a temporality that in many respects reproduced colonial double standards of punctuality, directing them toward their own inferiors. Whereas effendis considered themselves "Westernized," the time they allotted to peasants, workers, or women became "Egyptian," and it was loathed and later also admired as such.

As the decade progressed, and increasingly after the Dinshaway incident of 1906, the 1908 Young Turk Revolution, and its regional aftershocks, Egyptians began exploring other approaches to timekeeping. Over the following decade, middle-class nationalists discovered new horizons when they looked admiringly at the country's organized labor movement, which perfected the use of work stoppages and delays—replicating the deferrals so readily deployed by the colonial authorities—against the powers that be and their technologies of rule. Especially after Dinshaway, the time-mindless fellah (the emblem of the effendiyya's rural origins) was likewise extolled as a marker of authenticity and defiance, and commended for a gallant (if impractical and slightly ludicrous) negligence of clock and calendar time. In a 1906 novel relating the court interrogation of an Egyptian eyewitness to the violence in Dinshaway, the chief justice asks the witness, "What were you doing on the 13th of June?" To which the simple man replies, "Which thirteenth? Which June, Effendi?"[14] New uses, valuations, and representations of slowness and procrastination did not simply cut across class, gender, or geographical divides. Rather, they indexed these divides and fed off their potency.

Egyptian clocks likewise did not parody time by ignoring it. Rather, as we saw in chapter 7 with Umm Kulthūm's live performances or Tawfīq al-Ḥakīm's Sanīyah, who carefully timed her belated balcony appearances with an alarm clock, they did so by explicitly acknowledging the power of abstract time. As a British statement pointed out, "The Egyptians are the most observant people when it comes to setting their clocks . . . but the most time-wasteful people when it comes to their professional lives."[15] What this detractor missed was the fact that his observation did not necessarily reveal a contradiction: on some occasions unpunctuality was politically, artistically, or romantically potent. To realize unpunctuality's potential, an accurate clock was indispensable.

Comparing this trajectory to that of the rest of the Ottoman Empire throws Egypt's semicolonial features into sharp relief. At the beginning of the twentieth century, Istanbul embraced committedly mechanical clock time *alla franka,* under the guidance of middle-class reformers who hoped this would expedite the Ottoman Empire's march toward modernity. In Egypt, by contrast, technological modernity and imperialism could not be so easily disentangled. The interface of these projects was most acutely felt in the fact that imperialism represented its exploitative technologies as civilizing and beneficent artifacts. This ploy sensitized Egyptians to the masked political aspects of British technopolitics and placed trains, telegraphs, trams, and telephones—along with their disruptive social effects, alienating temporal regimes, substandard operation, and vulnerability to disruption—at the center of anticolonial contestation.

And thus, the 1908 Young Turk Revolution that prompted in Istanbul the replacement of *alla turca* with *alla franka* time was celebrated in Egypt with a neoclassical poem titled *Taḥīyat al-ʿĀm al-Hijrī* (Long live the Hijrī year). (The word *taḥīyah* comes from the root *Ḥ-Y-Y,* "to revive, resurrect").[16] This 1909 poem by Ḥāfiẓ Ibrāhīm reclaimed for Hijrī time important developments during what modern historians recognize as the tumultuous year of 1908: constitutionalism in Turkey, civil unrest and struggle for political rights in Iran, anticolonialism in Afghanistan, and scientific progress in India. Situating Egypt in this continuum, the poet applauded the new spirit animating the nation and proclaimed that the days of slumber were gone. As we saw in chapter 4, by discrediting the derivation of Hijrī time from moon sighting and situating the Hijrī calendar in the sphere of religion, technological infrastructures had liberated this timekeeping system from the burden of practical constraints, allowing it to become a powerful free-floating cultural symbol.

If the Gregorian calendar and the universal day linked Egypt to a world system under European hegemony, the same technologies of synchronization embroiled the Egyptian nation-state also in another milieu, that of the *ummah* and a late nineteenth-century pan-Islam transformed into a mass movement by steamer, telegraph, and railway lines. This Islamic world was reconfigured as a new horizon of internationalism whose organizing principle was Hijrī time. Egyptian nationalism developed in the contact zone of these interfacing internationalisms.

The new geographies of colonialism and pan-Islamism, Egypt's unique semicolonial position amid the Ottoman and British Empires, and the middleness of the Middle East were all connected at the navel to the countertempos recounted in this book. As philosophers from Bergson to Koselleck have claimed, what made linear modern time empty and homogeneous was its rendition into spatial terms. Along these lines, Egyptian time was animated by a unique technopolitical articulation of abstract space. As colonial Egypt started moving swiftly and simultaneously with the metropole, always staying one step behind it to await the satisfaction of the conditions for civilization and political independence, the "time" that emerged was a slightly delayed version of modern mechanical temporality, yielding a modernity that was slightly behind.

Like the technological space that informed it, this temporality was external neither to the abstract time of clocks nor to the modernity punctuated by clocks. The delays of Egyptian time, its substandard colonial punctuality and sometimes deliberate slowness, were the very stuff out of which Egyptian modernity was forged vis-à-vis modernity at large. This was not an alternative modernity outside the abstract logic of historicism, and thus free from notions of progress or linear chronology. Rather, Egyptian time should be taken as an indication of how multifarious and contradictory technical, political, and cultural processes taking place across the globe could be hierarchically rearranged into and represented as a unidirectional course labeled "modernity," which ostensibly originated in Western Europe and spread to the colonies. This book's account of the technological history of Egyptian time along chronological historicist lines, in a manner that might be read as reinstating the order its object disrupted, conveys a commitment to the emancipatory potential of this countertemporality *within* the contours of a single hierarchical modernity.

In this, I follow Fredric Jameson's critique that the fashionable embrace of "alternate" or "multiple" modernities, especially from subaltern and postcolonial positions, leaves the globalizing powers of capitalism untroubled.[17] Slavoj Žižek has added that such recourse to multiplicity disavows the antagonism inherent in the universal notion of modernity: "The Universal is not the encompassing container of the particular content, the peaceful medium or background for the conflict of particularities; the Universal 'as such' is the site of an unbearable antagonism or self-contradiction, and (the multitude of) its particular species are ultimately nothing but the many attempts to obfuscate/reconcile/master this antagonism."[18]

This book adds a caveat to this critique: carving out counterhegemonic modernities that indigenous people could domesticate is not simply a theoretical impulse, nor did it begin today. This misrepresentation of (the temporal aspects of) modernity was a reality-forming procedure, inherent to and constitutive of modernity as such. In the face of the universalizing impetus of empty mechanical time, carefully attending to some of the multiple inflections that made this universality possible helps point to new horizons of being in the world and especially to different ways of being in it together.

I have tried to show not only that we cannot think of universal homogeneous time apart from the inflections and reverberations it generated as it traveled "in translation" around the globe, but also that these inflections were themselves constitutive of this universality. Egyptian time, which this book presented as at once generic and unique, was not simply a variation on a standard that came from elsewhere, an example of colonial or subaltern temporality. Its explicit particularity and substandard standing were conditions of possibility for the universalization of its antithesis—empty mechanical time—and in this respect Egyptian time preceded mechanical time. As we saw in chapter 1, though, standardization often depended on misrepresenting the relations between standard and examples, type and variation, presenting the former as always preceding the latter. To restate this puzzling assertion as an answer to the question "What is uniquely 'Egyptian' about this story?" we may say that the flagrant particularity or "Egyptianness" of Egyptian time, its antagonistic character, and the fact that the assimilation of mechanical time into Egypt hinged on stressing a-similarity made mechanical time generalizable, and thus made such questions possible to begin with. The question, in other words, is part of the answer.

Finally, like "Long Live the Hijrī Year," the broken clock poem was part of a new aesthetics emerging between the last third of the nineteenth century and the first decades of the twentieth. During this period, so-called Arabic neoclassical poetry was developed by poets like Maḥmūd Sāmī Al-Barūdī (1838–1904) and credited with reviving the simplicity of ʿAbbasid poetry, which had been corrupted by linguistic superfluity and verbal artificiality.[19] Al-Barūdī shared this aesthetic sensibility with his interlocutor, ʿAbd Allāh al-Nadīm, an avowed enemy of artificiality in prose. Like other literary-minded ʿUrabists, both writers sought to resist foreign encroachment in the aesthetic sphere by identifying indigenous sources of authenticity.

As with al-Nadīm's telegraphic prose, modern technology provided a key impetus for the emergence of this poetry, and later for the defense of its anachronistic formulas. One is struck by the abundance of references to clocks, telegraphs, zeppelins, trains, trams, the telescope, the telephone, and later airplanes, the radio, and a host of other new devices in this genre. As Sasson Somekh points out, "New technologies and devices [were] felt by these poets to provide the 'modern' ingredient necessary to balance their dependence on medieval poetic modes, and thus to fulfill the implied formula of 'new wine in old vessels.'"[20] *Al-Majallah al-Miṣrīyah,* one of the main platforms for the propagation of this poetics and the magazine that printed our broken-clock poem, published several months earlier a clear ideological expression to that effect.[21]

Paradoxically, modern technology sustained neoclassicism. For example, prominent writers such as Maʿrūf al-Ruṣāfī, al-Barūdī, Ḥāfiẓ Ibrāhīm, and even al-Nadīm, as well as anonymous and less famous authors who published in *Al-Majallah al-Miṣrīyah* and elsewhere, rendered the experience of the railway journey using the conventions of the *qaṣīdah,* the pre-Islamic ode perfected by the ʿAbbasids. These poets frequently replaced deserted encampments with train stations and formulaic descriptions of camels with those of locomotives. As one poet put it, "If a steam engine carries my friends on sea or land, why should I complain to the camels?"[22]

At the turn of the twentieth century, using such modern topoi, as well as adopting the telegraphic vogue of linguistic simplicity clothed in ʿAbbasid garb, helped poets preserve and develop the system of classical meters, the ʿArūḍ, which around this time were newly theorized as an echo of the measured stride of the camel.[23] It also helped defend them against an intensifying instrumentalist critique of linguistic sluggishness and archaism, as well as the claim that Arabic neoclassicism stood in the way of introducing European technoscience in the Arab world.[24] As camels ceased to be a poetic theme, they reemerged as a temporal trace, a spectral rhythmic structure. Modern devices provided the fresh wine poured into anachronistic, convoluted meters and intricate rhythms, serving as the new engines keeping these old vessels afloat.

The contents of the clock poem should be appreciated in light of the neoclassical meter and rhyme complementing the subversion of modern abstract mechanical time by injecting echoes of the camel's spasmodic stride into the poem's pace. Burdened with harmonizing content and form, culture and technoscience, modernity and tradition, slave and master clocks, Gregorian and Hijrī times, the ʿAbbasid past and the colonial present, only a broken clock could point to the right time.

AFTERIMAGES

As these exercises in neoclassicism reveal and every historian knows, revisiting the past is never simply an act of retrieval. Can the experiences related in this book somehow illuminate the postrevolutionary, open-ended Egyptian present? I again answer this question by resorting first to a poem, one written by the person most associated with the promotion of neoclassical poetry in the twentieth century, Aḥmad Shawqī. The theory of time of "the Prince of Poets" is encapsulated in an undated rhymed and metered neoclassical couplet:

> Man's heartbeats tell him:
> "Life is minutes and seconds"
>
> After you die recall their memory in your soul
> For *dhikr* is a person's second life.[25]

Clock time seems at first to be the be-all and end-all, reducing the multiplicity and heterogeneity of life to unvarying, inflexible minutes and seconds. Abstract time is inscribed on the body; it structures the heartbeat. But as the second stanza reveals (and as the meter reinforces), empty homogeneous time cannot fully contain life: life spills over, is doubled, resurrected, and connected to other monotonies, like the *dhikr,* remembrance or Sufi rhythmic recitation. Evoking Islamic thanatology in the second line, the poem's opening is reincarnated as an indication of the fleeting nature of life, and hence as an implicit invocation to pious conduct and a revaluation of time. Clock time thus sets the beat for a haunted subjectivity based on a multidirectional temporality, punctuating the community of the living and the dead, a collective whose togetherness refuses and re-fuses the divide between people and objects.

ʿAbd al-Fattāḥ Abū Ghuddah, the Syrian thinker and a member of the Muslim Brotherhood, suggested that Shawqī's poem neatly captures the concept of time endorsed by the brotherhood's founder, Ḥasan al-Bannā (1906–1949), a provincial effendi schoolteacher who traveled in Rashīd Riḍā's Salafī circles, and who also owned a store where he repaired watches and gramophones, as his father did before him.[26] The Society of the Muslim Brothers, which al-Bannā founded in 1928 as an anticolonial Islamic opposition, was predicated on forging a view of solidarity that drew on authentic Islamic roots. Al-Bannā famously stated, "He who knows the true nature of time knows the true nature of life, for time is life."[27]

The Muslim Brothers relied on modern organizational methods, new institutions, and mass media to promote the "struggle for the revival of forgotten Islamic customs," calling for the adoption of pure Islamic "greetings, language, the calendar, dress, household furnishing, times of work and rest, food and drink, arriving and departing."[28] Such an agenda would be unthinkable apart from the history of the transformation of the Hijrī calendar into a "religious," authentic one, the new possibility of "Islamic times" of work, rest, arrival, and departure, and the notions of classics and authenticity, engulfing language, manners, and customs.

In the name of such authenticity, the Brotherhood boldly circumvented the conventional progression protocols of Islamic tradition and the genealogies promoted by institutions such as Cairo's thousand-year-old center for Islamic learning, al-Azhar. Like other traditions, what is seen in Islam as the basic scriptures (the Qurʾan and *ḥadīth*) is mediated and stabilized by a substantive corpus of later interpretive texts designating the versions to be considered canonical and informing the range of readings and meanings that one can base on these scriptures. Al-Bannā chose to go directly to "the source," breaking with the cumulative episteme of Islamic tradition.

The genealogies of Islamic tradition were not the only thing the Muslim Brotherhood turned on its head. The group subverted modernity's professed pedigrees, anchoring its origins in different places and times, historically as well as conceptually and qualitatively. For example, Islamizing new practices of timekeeping often meant rhetorically decoupling time from money. In a letter to a Muslim student in the West at the end of the 1920s, al-Bannā wrote: "I have looked into the saying, 'time is golden,' and I do not approve of it. Time is far more precious than gold, for time is life. Is it not true that your life is nothing but a few hours and you never know when they will end? Dearest brother, be strict with your time and do not spend it except on that which is significant, and acquire pleasure in that which is lawful."[29]

Al-Bannā returned to the subject of Islam and time during the 1940s, in one of his famous weekly "Tuesday Speeches," meticulously providing Qur'anic citations that promoted punctuality. He concluded the lecture by claiming that "it is unfortunate that we have grown accustomed to underestimate the value of time *[qīmat al-waqt]* in our lives; we do not value it appropriately. We waste [time] on things that have no relation to Islam, such as cinema, theater, dance, and immoral clubs. In doing so, we blindly imitate Europeans."[30] The language of time wasting and value owed much to the discourse it criticized, and it is directly related to the turn-of-the-century "value of time" discussions described in the introduction. It mimicked the very Europe al-Bannā attacked as a source of blind imitation.[31] As students of colonialism have pointed out, metropolitan categories often define the spectrum of possibilities for anticolonial resistance.[32] Yet the derivative nature of anticolonial politics did not foreclose the new critical space they opened up. Al-Bannā's critique, its many intellectual successors,[33] and the antagonistic temporality it promoted, were at once colonial *and* anticolonial. Islamic punctuality was a simulation that discarded its source, a replica that retroactively projected itself as origin.

At the moment of writing these lines, when the Brothers have significantly advanced toward taking over the Egyptian state, their Islamic neoclassical modernism oscilates between these two poles. On the one hand, it promises a transformative vision based on counterhegemonic valuations of human life that takes the community as the proper subject of politics. On the other hand, rather than fulfilling this elusive potential, the Brothers have so far done little beyond putting Islamic garb on dated versions of neoliberalism, for which they appropriate the name *Nahḍa,* or Renaissance Project. We are yet to see them revive something more than Mubarak-era forms of governance.

Regardless of where they turn from here, the emergence of Islamists as key players in Egyptian formal politics reshapes this playing field, vitalizing familiar modes of backward-looking legitimation. As we have seen, Islamism is only one manifestation of the basic procedure of weaving the social fabric by interlacing historical and quotidian times. A catalog of ideological and cultural formations that similarly evoked spheres newly seen as "classic" would include Egyptian nationalism, its various reincarnations in the 1920s and 1930s as Pharaonism and "the return of the spirit," traditional singing conventions and the corresponding dispositions of Sufi audition, and the reemergence of epics such as *A Thousand and One Nights* and *Majnūn Laylā* or the printed travelogue of Ibn Batutah.

The return to the past was obviously not only about retrieving. Such movements along the diachronic axis were animated by, and in turn created, various synchronic effects. Contemporary forms of togetherness and competing imaginaries of the social were developed and contested by retrospectively turning to the ʿAbbasid "golden age," the authenticity of the fellah, or even pre-Islamic periods. In this kind of tug-of-war, predicated on evoking times past while concealing the historicity of one's agenda, historians may take quite an active role. The time travel we ourselves have just completed, in whose wake the familiar, straight lines of technology and homogenous time have disappeared, may offer one possible trajectory.

NOTES

INTRODUCTION

1. For example, a popular 2009 time-management manual opens with a contrast between "their reality"—taking the example of a U.S. medical center that compensates patients waiting more than twenty minutes for a doctor by forfeiting the money from the doctor's salary—to "our reality," wherein "27% of workers arrive late to work, 21% leave before the official time, 27% are lazy in performing their tasks." Ibrāhīm al-Fiqī, *Idārat al-Waqt* (Manūfīyah: Ibdāʿ liʾl-Iʿlām waʾl-Nashr, 2009), 11–12.

2. Dan Richardson, *Rough Guide to Egypt* (New York: Rough Guides, 2003), 80. And here is another example: "A more relaxed attitude to time which reaches its height in that most elastic of Egyptian words *shuwayyah*—'a little.' If this is used to refer to a period of time, it can actually mean anything from 'five minutes' to 'tomorrow.'" Eva Ambros, *Nelles Guide to Egypt* (Hunter, NJ: Hunter, 2001), 231.

3. The historical interface of Egyptian and Western discourses on indigenous indolence is examined in chapter 3. Yet the tendency to point to culture as a primary context for perceived Egyptian and Arab laxity is alive and well even today. See Fadwa El Guindi's *By Noon Prayer: The Rhythm of Islam* (Oxford: Berg, 2008); and Dan Diner, *Lost in the Sacred: Why the Muslim World Stood Still,* trans. Steven Rendall (Princeton, NJ: Princeton University Press, 2009). This form of explanation is dominant in popular culture. The 2009 film *Cairo Time,* by director Ruba Nadda, tells the story of Juliette, a middle-aged American who arrives in Cairo for the first time and falls for Tareq, an Egyptian man. But the real love story is Juliette's falling for the Orient and its temporality, which she at first abhors. Gradually, this workaholic magazine editor gets accustomed to Cairo and its lax time. She embraces lazy awakenings in the middle of the day and the fact that she can pop unannounced into Tareq's café, always finding him playing chess and ready to leave work to spend his day with her. Things are slower and more relaxed in Cairo, a megalopolis that resists the tyranny of the clock.

4. See M. Adas, *Machines as the Measure of Men: Science, Technology, and Ideologies of Western Dominance* (Ithaca, NY: Cornell University Press, 1990).

5. This approach complements, rather than contradicts, the study of Orientalism, which has exposed a much longer history and various other mechanisms of exoticizing the Orient.

6. On Egypt in the first wave of globalization, see R. Owen, *The Middle East in the World Economy,* 1800–1914 (London: Methuen, 1981).

7. P. Chatterjee, *The Nation and Its Fragments: Colonial and Postcolonial Histories* (Princeton, NJ: Princeton University Press, 1993); G. Prakash, *Another Reason: Science and the Imagination of Modern India* (Princeton, NJ: Princeton University Press, 1999).

8. Aaron Jakes, "The Scales of Public Utility: Agricultural Roads and State Space in the Era of the British Occupation," in *The Long* 1890*s in Egypt: Colonial Quiescence, Subterranean Resistance,* ed. Marilyn Booth and Anthony Gorman (Edinburgh: Edinburgh University Press, 2013).

9. Qasim Amin, *The Liberation of Women, and, The New Woman: Two Documents in the History of Egyptian Feminism,* trans. Samiha Sidhom Peterson (Cairo: American University in Cairo Press, 2000), 190–191.

10. [Mahatma] Gandhi, *Hind Swaraj and Other Writings,* ed. Anthony Parel (Cambridge: Cambridge University Press, 1997), 47–48. On the Egyptian interest in Gandhi and his rejection of industrial society, see Noor-Aiman Khan, *Egyptian-Indian Nationalist Collaboration and the British Empire* (New York: Palgrave-Macmillan, 2011).

11. Nile Green, *Bombay Islam: The Religious Economy of the West Indian Ocean,* 1840–1915 (Cambridge: Cambridge University Press, 2011).

12. See Eric Hobsbawm and Terence Ranger, eds., *The Invention of Tradition* (Cambridge: Cambridge University Press, 1992).

13. Talal Asad, *Formations of the Secular: Christianity, Islam, Modernity* (Stanford, CA: Stanford University Press, 2003), chapter 7.

14. As Lewis Mumford famously put it in an often repeated statement, "The clock is not merely a means of keeping track of the hours, but of synchronizing the actions of men. The clock, not the steam-engine, is the key-machine of the modern industrial age." See Lewis Mumford, *Technics and Civilization* (New York: Harcourt, Brace & World, 1963). Quoted, for example, in D. Landes, *Revolution in Time: Clocks and the Making of the Modern World* (Cambridge: Harvard University Press, 1983); and S. Tanaka, *New Times in Modern Japan* (Princeton, NJ: Princeton University Press, 2004).

15. The term *countertempo* is inspired by the neologism *counterpublic,* which Charles Hirschkind borrows from Michael Warner to account for the fact that collectives often develop not simply as one among a horizontal constellation of social groups, but as explicitly articulated alternatives to other publics that exclude them or mark their members as substandard or nonnormative. A countertempo is how a counterpublic is synchronized, how its members position themselves vis-à-vis what in the process becomes the standard public. See C. Hirschkind, *The Ethical Soundscape: Cassette Sermons and Islamic Counterpublics* (New York: Columbia University Press, 2006); and M. Warner, *Publics and Counterpublics* (New York: Zone Books, 2002).

16. D. Chakrabarty, *Provincializing Europe: Postcolonial Thought and Historical Difference* (Princeton, NJ: Princeton University Press, 2000).

17. B. Latour, *Reassembling the Social: An Introduction to Actor-Network-Theory* (Oxford: Oxford University Press, 2005), 81.

18. *Al-Ittiḥād al-Miṣrī,* January 20, 1898. Translations are mine unless otherwise noted.

19. See *Al-Muṣawwar,* May 3, 1902.

20. K. Marx, *Grundrisse: Foundations of the Critique of Political Economy* (New York: Vintage Books, 1973); Mumford, *Technics and Civilization;* A. Chandler, *The Visible Hand: The Managerial Revolution in American Business* (Cambridge, MA: Belknap Press, 1977); D. Harvey, "Between Space and Time: Reflections on the Geographical Imagination," *Annals of the Association of American Geographers* 80, no. 3 (1990): 418.

21. Tawfīq al-Ḥakīm, *Return of the Spirit: Tawfiq al-Hakim's Classic Novel of the* 1919 *Revolution,* trans. William M. Hutchins (Washington, DC: Three Continents Press, 1990), 156–157.

22. *Al-Tankīt wa' l-Tabkīt,* August 7, 1881.

23. Avner Wishnitzer, *Reading Clocks,* Alla Turca: *Ottoman Temporal Culture and Its Transformation during the Long Nineteenth Century* (Chicago: Chicago University Press, forthcoming).

24. *Al-Hilāl,* January 15, 1895.

25. *Majallat al-Muṣawwar al-Ḥadīthah al-Muṣawwarah,* December 11, 1929.

26. *Ḍiyā' al-Sharq,* May 4, 1908. See also Muḥammad 'Umar, *Kitāb Ḥāḍir al-Miṣrīyīn* (Cairo: Maṭba'at al-Muqtaṭaf, 1902), 241–244.

27. I borrow this term from Bruno Latour's *On the Modern Cult of Factish Gods* (Durham, NC: Duke University Press, 2010), to indicate the fabricated nature of objective facts and scientific standards, akin to the fetish objects of "the primitives."

28. "Wait Just Five Minutes," in *Al-Ṣiḥāfah,* December 29, 1907.

29. Max Weber, *The Protestant Ethic and the Spirit of Capitalism,* trans. Talcott Parsons (New York: Courier Dover Publications, 2003), 49–51. Weber was quoting Benjamin Franklin, whom his Egyptians contemporaries were reading in Arabic and Ottoman Turkish translations.

30. Ibid.

31. S. Smiles, *'Alayka: Naṣā'iḥ li-Tabaṣur al-Shubbān bi-Muqtaḍayāt al-'Aysh wa-Asrār al-Najāḥ,* trans. Ibrāhīm Ramzī (Cairo, 1914), 9. The author was the great popularizer of British railway engineering, the biographer of the Stephensons and writer of self-help books, several of which were translated into Arabic.

32. See, for example, the transcript of a lecture given at al-Azhar titled "Indolence Is the Essence of Death," printed in *Al-Majallah al-Miṣrīyah,* November 15, 1900.

33. See, for example, *Ḍiyā' al-Sharq,* May 4, 1908; and *Al-Muqaṭṭam,* January 1, 1920. Unlike the Christian Sunday and Jewish Sabbath, the Islamic Friday was traditionally a day of communal worship, not a rest day, and some Islamic theologians even disapproved of Muslims not returning to work after the Friday

noon prayer, in imitation of non-Islamic practices. *Encyclopedia of Islam*, CD-ROM edition, v.1.0., quoted in T. Atabaki, *The State and the Subaltern: Modernization, Society and the State in Turkey and Iran* (London: I.B. Tauris, 2007), 9. The first reference to the introduction of Friday as a day off goes back to the 1830s, when Ibrahim Pasha included this measure in a labor regulation in Çukurova. See ibid., 10.

34. See Marwa S. Elshakry, "Darwin's legacy in the Arab East: Science, Religion and Politics, 1870–1914" (PhD diss., Princeton University, 2003).

35. See Lewis Mumford, "The Monastery and the Clock," in *The Human Prospect*, ed. Harry T. Moore and Karl W. Deutsch (Boston: Beacon Press, 1956); Malcolm Miles and Tim Hall, with Iain Borden, eds., *The City Cultures Reader* (New York: Routledge, 2000), 121; Eviatar Zerubavel, *Hidden Rhythms: Schedules and Calendars in Social Life* (Berkeley: University of California Press, 1985), 31–70.

36. Indeed, mechanical clocks, introduced into Egypt long before the arrival of trains and telegraphs, were mainly used by religious scholars to coordinate the call for prayer, on whose wings time radiated outward from the mosque (*jāmiʿ*, from whose root the words for "gathering" and "togetherness" are derived). Daniel Stolz, "Correcting the Clock: Mechanical Timekeeping and Islamic Astronomical Tradition in 18th/19th-Century Egypt" (paper presented to the Princeton Islamic Studies Colloquium, Princeton, NJ, spring 2012).

37. E.P. Thompson, "Time, Work-Discipline and Industrial Capitalism," *Past and Present* 38 (December 1967): 56–97; cf. J. May and N. Thrift, *TimeSpace: Geographies of Temporality* (London: Routledge, 2001).

38. Graham Burchill, Colin Gordon, and Peter Miller, eds., *The Foucault Effect: Studies in Governmentality* (London: Harvester Wheatsheaf, 1991).

39. See Chandler, *The Visible Hand.*

40. M. Savage, "Discipline, Surveillance and the 'Career': Employment on the Great Western Railway 1833–1914," in *Foucault, Management and Organization Theory*, ed. Alan McKinlay and Ken Starkey (London: Sage Publications, 1998), 65–93.

41. Even when Thompson wrote his article in 1967, he used Evans-Pritchard's study of the contemporary Sudanese Nuer and Bourdieu's work on the Algerian Kabyle as living illustrations of England's past.

42. Jean Vallet, "Contribution à l'étude de la condition des ouvriers de la grande industrie au Caire" (PhD diss., Valence, 1911), 86–94; Egyptian State Railway, Report, October 19, 1910; Joel Beinin and Zachary Lockman, *Workers on the Nile: Nationalism, Communism, Islam, and the Egyptian Working Class,* 1882–1954 (Cairo: American University in Cairo Press, 1998), 74.

43. *Majallat ʿUmmāl al-Sikkah al-Ḥadīd* (Cairo, 1909).

44. *Al-Ahrām,* October 18, 1910; Vallet, "Contribution," 42–43; ESR 1 Report, October 19, 1910; Beinin and Lockman, *Workers on the Nile,* 74. According to the account in *Al-Ahrām,* the toilet regulation allowed ten minutes of toilet time rather than five.

45. A similar claim about slaves in the antebellum U.S. South appears in Mark Michael Smith, *Mastered by the Clock: Time, Slavery, and Freedom in the American South* (Chapel Hill: University of North Carolina Press, 1997).

46. "Regulations of the Egyptian School in Paris, October 1844," quoted in Timothy Mitchell, *Colonising Egypt* (Cambridge: Cambridge University Press, 1988), 72.

47. Clot Bey, *Lamḥah ʿĀmmah Ilā Miṣr,* trans. Muḥammad Masʿūd (Cairo: Dar al-Mawqif al-ʿArabī, 1981), 4:85.

48. Fīlīb b. Yūsuf Jallād, "Madrasa," chapter 5, article 68, in *Qāmūs al-Idārah waʾl-Qaḍāʾ* (Alexandria: al-Maṭbaʿah al-Tijārīyah, 1900).

49. Salāma Mūsā, *The Education of Salāma Mūsā,* trans. L.O. Schuman (Leiden: Brill, 1961), 28.

50. Al-Ḥakīm, *Return of the Spirit,* 272; Al-Ḥakīm, *ʿAwdat al-Rūḥ* (Cairo: Dar al-Maʿārif, 1946), 214.

51. Giorgio Agamben, *Infancy and History: The Destruction of Experience,* trans. Liz Heron (London: Verso, 1993), 91.

52. Al-Ḥakīm, *Return of the Spirit,* 225.

53. Such an "aporia of time" was discussed by Jacques Derrida in "No Apocalypse, Not Now (Full Speed Ahead, Seven Missiles, Seven Missives)," *Diacritics* 14, no. 2 (Summer 1984): 20–31.

54. Lila Abu-Lughod, "The Marriage of Feminism and Islamism in Egypt: Selective Repudiation as a Dynamic of Postcolonial Cultural Politics," in *Remaking Women: Feminism and Modernity in the Middle East,* ed. Lila Abu-Lughod (Princeton, NJ: Princeton University Press, 2001), 243–270.

55. V. Danielson, *"The Voice of Egypt": Umm Kulthūm, Arabic Song, and Egyptian Society in the Twentieth Century* (Chicago: University of Chicago Press, 1997), 94–95.

56. F. Lagrange, "Women in the Singing Business, Women in Songs," *History Compass* 7, no. 1 (2009): 229.

57. Wishnitzer, *Reading Clocks,* Alla Turca.

58. For Bergson's influence in Egypt, particularly on Muḥammad Ḥusayn Haykal, see Charles Smith, *Islam and the Search for Social Order in Modern Egypt: A Biography of Muhammad Husayn Haykal* (Albany: SUNY Press, 1983).

59. See Suzanne Guerlac, *Thinking in Time: An Introduction to Henri Bergson* (Ithaca, NY: Cornell University Press, 2006).

CHAPTER 1

Epigraph: Rudyard Kipling, "The Deep-Sea Cables," in *The White Man's Burdens: An Anthology of British Poetry of the Empire,* ed. Chris Brooks and Peter Faulkner (Exeter: Exeter University Press, 1996), 293.

1. Roderic H. Davidson, "Where Is the Middle East?" *Foreign Affairs* 38 (1960): 665–675; Clayton R. Koppes, "Captain Mahan, General Gordon, and the Origins of the Term 'Middle East,'" *Middle Eastern Studies* 12, no. 1 (January 1976): 95–98.

2. Ahmad Ibn Majid, *Arab Navigation in the Indian Ocean before the Coming of the Portuguese,* trans. G.R. Tibbetts (London: Royal Asiatic Society of Great Britain

and Ireland, 1971), 10. See also A. W. Crosby, *Ecological Imperialism: The Biological Expansion of Europe* (Cambridge: Cambridge University Press, 2004).

3. K. Pomeranz, *The Great Divergence: China, Europe, and the Making of the Modern World Economy* (Princeton, NJ: Princeton University Press, 2000).

4. See, for example, L. Colley, *Britons: Forging the Nation,* 1707–1837 (New Haven, CT: Yale University Press, 2009); M. Goswami, *Producing India: From Colonial Economy to National Space* (Chicago: University of Chicago Press, 2004).

5. C. Murray, *Victorian Narrative Technologies in the Middle East* (New York: Routledge, 2008).

6. Pomeranz, *The Great Divergence,* 43–68.

7. J. Seaward, *Observations on the Advantages of Successfully Employing Steam Power in Navigating Ships between This Country and the East Indies* (London, 1829), 10.

8. T. F. Waghorn, *Steam Navigation to India by the Cape of Good Hope: Documents and Papers* (London: C. Whittingham, 1929).

9. T. F. Waghorn, *Particulars of an Overland Journey from London to Bombay by Way of the Continent, Egypt, and the Red Sea* (London: Parbury, Allen, 1831).

10. J. H. Wilson, *Facts Connected with the Origin and Progress of Steam Communication between India and England* (London, 1850), 131. See also Captain James Barber, *The Overland Guide-Book: A Complete Vade-Mecum for the Overland Taveller* (London: W. H. Allen, 1845).

11. Lieut. Waghorn, T. F., *The Acceleration of Mails between England and the East Indies* (London, 1843), 19; and J. A. Galloway, *Observations on the Proposed Improvements in the Overland Route via Egypt with Remarks on the Ship Canal, the Boulac Canal, and the Suez Railroad* (London, 1844), 7.

12. See, for example, Waghorn, *The Acceleration of Mails.*

13. "He who leaves India on the 100th day (2nd March) is a sound man, he who leaves on the 110th will be alright. However, he who leaves on the 120th is stretching the bounds of possibility and he who leaves on the 130th is inexperienced and an ignorant gambler." See Ibn Majid, *Arab Navigation in the Indian Ocean,* 231.

14. See Janet Abu-Lughod, *Before European Hegemony: A.D.* 1250–1350 (New York: Oxford University Press, 1989), 242.

15. F. Arrow, "On the Influence of the Suez Canal on Trade with India," *Journal of the Society of the Arts,* March 11, 1870, 363

16. For a biography of Mehmet ʿAli, see K. Fahmy, *Mehmed Ali: From Ottoman Governor to Ruler of Egypt* (Oxford: Oneworld, 2009).

17. J. Cole, *Napoleon's Egypt: Invading the Middle East* (New York: Palgrave Macmillan, 2007), 12–16.

18. M. A. Ḥassūnah, *Miṣr waʾl-Ṭuruq al-Ḥadīdīyah* (Cairo, 1938), 61–62.

19. The British support for the Porte during this crisis was partially the result of a desire to divide the risk of closure of all overland routes to India. Confining Mehmet ʿAli to Egypt guaranteed that if he closed the Egyptian route, the Euphrates route, under Istanbul's control, might still be open. See H. L. Hoskins, *British Routes to India* (New York: Longmans, Green, 1928), 286.

20. For example, in October 1839, the Pasha rushed the news about the First Anglo-Afghan War with his personal steamer. Waghorn, *The Acceleration of Mails,* 16.

21. See F.R. Chesney, *Narrative of the Euphrates Expedition* (London: Longmans, Green, 1868), 172–173, 179, 404, 468.

22. Galloway, *Observations,* 4.

23. Hoskins, *British Routes to India,* 231–32.

24. Galloway, *Observations,* 13.

25. In fact, its status as the key highway to India was not secure even after the inauguration of the canal. See, for example, G. Latham, *Proposed New Overland Route via Turkish Arabia* (Calcutta, 1870).

26. "Local Intelligence," *Manchester Times and Gazette,* September 27, 1834.

27. "News of the Week," *Aberdeen Journal,* October 18, 1837.

28. F. Scheer, *The Cape of Good Hope versus Egypt; or, Political and Commercial Consideration on the Proper Line of Steam Communication with the East Indies* (London, 1839).

29. For example, see Hoskins, *British Routes to India,* 285.

30. Quoted in *The Egyptian Railway; or, The Interest of England in Egypt* (London: Hope, 1852), 36. It is unlikely that the Egyptian ruler actually used such strong language, but what is important for me here is the way his own agenda was translated to and converged with British imperialism.

31. T.F. Waghorn, *Egypt as It Is in* 1837 (London, 1837).

32. R. Owen, *Cotton and the Egyptian Economy,* 1820–1914*: A Study in Trade and Development* (Oxford: Clarendon, 1969).

33. It was Waghorn who started transporting coal in camel caravans across Egypt between these different stations. See Ḥassūnah, *Miṣr wa᾿l-ṭuruq,* 53–54.

34. R.C. Taylor, *Statistics of Coal: The Geographical and Geological Distribution of Mineral Combustibles or Fossil Fuel* (Philadelphia: J.W. Moore, 1848), 622.

35. Ibid., 623.

36. U.S. Bureau of Foreign Commerce, "Foreign Markets for American Coal," in *Special Consular Reports* 21, no. 1 (Washington, D.C.: Government Printing Office, 1900), 272.

37. See O. Barak, "Scraping the Surface: The Techno-Politics of Modern Streets in Turn-of-the-Twentieth-Century Alexandria," *Mediterranean Historical Review* 24, no. 2 (December 2009): 187–205.

38. For a review of the literature on cotton and capitalism, see K. Caliskan, *Market Threads: How Cotton Farmers and Traders Create a Global Commodity* (Princeton, NJ: Princeton University Press, 2010).

39. The high price of coal in Egypt pushed engineers to look for substitutions, one of which was the oil contained in refuse of cotton and cotton seed, making cotton both a raw material and a processed product of itself. See R.C. Taylor, *Statistics,* 623.

40. During this decade, a system of telegraphs and railroads was laid out also in India, under Governor-General Dalhousie, a coincidence that demonstrates and

contextualizes the colonial nature of the Egyptian undertaking. See B. Metcalf and T. Metcalf, *A Concise History of India* (Cambridge: Cambridge University Press, 2002), 93–98.

41. See Ḥassūnah, *Miṣr wa' l-Ṭuruq*, 113.

42. *The Egyptian Railway*, 29.

43. Adas, *Machines*, 226–227.

44. Hoskins, *British Routes*, 400.

45. Ibid., 401.

46. *Irish University Press Series of British Parliamentary Papers*, vol. 1858, no. 382 (Shannon: Irish University Press, 1968-), 220, 227, quoted in Hoskins, *British Routes*, 403.

47. Amīn Sāmī, *Taqwīm al-Nīl* (Cairo: Maṭba'at Dār al-Kutub al-Miṣrīyah, 1936), 1:340.

48. Hoskins, *British Routes*, 404–405.

49. *British Parliamentary Papers*, vol. 1866, no. 428, pp. 75–76, quoted in Hoskins, *British Routes*, 405.

50. Hoskins, *British Routes*, 406.

51. G. W. Wheatley, "Some Accounts of the Late Lieut. Waghorn, R.N., The Originator of the Overland Route," *Bentley's Miscellany* 27 (1850): 356.

52. See R. Hyde, *Panoramania!* (London: Trefoil, 1988).

53. *Graham's Magazine* (1852), 100–101.

54. A. Miller, "The Panorama, the Cinema, and the Emergence of the Spectacular," *Wide Angle* 18, no. 2 (April 1996): 34–69.

55. *Manchester Times*, April 21, 1852.

56. *Daily News*, January 8, 1859.

57. Hyde, *Panoramania!*, 144.

58. After attracting millions in London, the Overland Route diorama visited almost every central city in England during most of the 1850s, accompanied by a massive press campaign, probably one of the first appearances of mass advertisement. It was shown so many times that the canvases wore out and needed occasional replacement. (Worn originals were frequently put on sale. See, for example, a sale notice in *The Era*, September 20, 1857.) The inauguration of the Suez Canal provided the pretext for the making of a sequel—the Grand Diorama of the New Overland Route to India, in 1876.

59. *The Patrician* (London, 1847), 486.

60. J. Crary, *Techniques of the Observer: On Vision and Modernity in the Nineteenth Century* (Cambridge: MIT Press, 1992), 112.

61. Charles Marshall, *Historical and Statistic Description of Mr. Charles Marshall's Great Moving Diorama Illustrating the Grand Routes of a Tour through Europe* (London: n.p., 1848), 3.

62. The *Times*, quoted in Hyde, *Panoramania!*, 143.

63. *The Musical World*, March 30, 1850 (my emphasis).

64. "Some Stage Effects: Their Growth and History," *Gentleman's Magazine* (1888), pp. 85–87.

65. S. Oettermann, *The Panorama: History of a Mass Medium,* trans. D. Schneider (New York: Zone Books, 1997).

66. P. Virilio, "Cinema Isn't I See, It's I Fly: The Imposture of Immediacy and Traveling Shot," in *War and Cinema: the Logistics of Perception,* trans. Patrick Camiller (London: Verso, 1989), 11–30, 46–51, 69–95.

67. J. Crary, *Techniques of the Observer: On Vision and Modernity in the Nineteenth Century* (Cambridge, MA: MIT Press, 1992), 14.

68. See S. Lane-Poole, *Life of William Edward Lane* (London: Williams and Norgate, 1877), 36.

69. E. Said, *Orientalism* (New York: Vintage Books, 1979).

70. Lane's interest in Egypt was ignited after an exhibition in the Egyptian Hall. See Derek Gregory, "Performing Cairo: Orientalism and the City of the Arabian Nights," in *Making Cairo Medieval,* ed. N. AlSayyad, I. A. Bierman, and N. Rabbat (Lanham, MD: Lexington Books, 2005), 69–93.

71. Mitchell, *Colonising Egypt.*

72. J. L. Stephens, *Incidents of Travel in Egypt, Arabia Petræa, and the Holy Land* (Harper & Brothers, 1853), 181.

73. P. R. Salmon, *The Wonderland of Egypt* (London: Religious Tract Society, 1915), 90.

74. W. Schivelbusch, *The Railway Journey: The Industrialization of Time and Space* (Berkeley: University of California Press, 1987).

75. D. B. W. Sladen, *Queer Things about Egypt* (London: Hurst & Blackett, 1910), 185–186.

76. C. D. Warner, *Mummies and Moslems* (Hartford, CT: American Publishing, 1876), 45.

77. F. J. Jobson, *Australia: With Notes by the Way, on Egypt, Ceylon, Bombay, and the Holy Land* (London: Hamilton, Adams, 1862), 24–25.

78. Warner, *Mummies and Moslems,* 46.

79. F. W. Fairholt, *Up the Nile, and Home Again: A Handbook for Travellers, and a Travel-book for the Library* (London: Chapman and Hall, 1862), 34.

80. "We have been assured by a man who knows Egypt well, that mummies have been frequently used as fuel for locomotives." G. Farrer Rodwell, *South by East: Notes of Travel in Southern Europe* (London: M. Ward, 1877), 266. See also A. C. Aufderheide, *The Scientific Study of Mummies* (Cambridge: Cambridge University Press, 2003), 524; *Church Review* (1886), p. 76; E. P. Whipple, *Lectures on Subjects Connected with Literature and Life* (Boston: Ticknor and Fields, 1859), 135.

81. J. D. Henry, *Baku: An Eventful History* (North Stratford, NH: Ayer Publishing, 1977), 18.

82. T. Wallace Knox, *Underground: Gambling and Its Horrors* (Hartford: J. B. Burr, 1876), 285.

83. Mark Twain jested, "The fuel [Egyptian trains] use for the locomotive is composed of mummies three thousand years old, purchased by the ton or by the graveyard for that purpose, and . . . sometimes one hears the profane engineer call out pettishly, 'D—n these plebeians, they don't burn worth a cent—pass out a

King!" Mark Twain, *Innocents Abroad; or, The New Pilgrims' Progress* (Scituate, MA: Digital Scanning, 2001 [1869]), 632. Like the symbolic temporal contrast between the train and the pyramid, seen as the pharaonic legacy passed on to imperial Britain, past and present seemed to be fused together: "It is a curious fact that the bodies of the most enlightened nation in its time, many years ago, are now made to aid in getting up steam in the present fast age. On the new railway in Egypt, the first locomotive run used mummies for fuel. The bituminous matter used to embalm them and to seal the wrappings makes them very inflammable." *The Peninsular and Independent Medical Journal, Devoted to Medicine, Surgery, and Pharmacy* 1–2 (April 1858–March 1860): 496.

84. *New Monthly Magazine* (1850), p. 141.

85. H. S. Polehampton, *A Memoir, Letters and Diary of Henry S. Polehampton,* (London: Richard Bentley, 1859), 58.

86. D. Sandeman, *Memoir of the Life and Brief Ministry of David Sandeman* (London: J. Nisbet, 1861), 268.

87. H. Puckler-Muskau, *Egypt under Mehmet Ali,* trans. H. Evans Lloyd (London: H. Colburn, 1845), 155.

88. Exiting the theater, spectators were surprised to discover that they were not in the East and that people rode horses rather than camels (camels being *the* markers of the East). *Punch* reviewer (18 [1850]: 208) quoted in Hyde, *Panoramania!,* 143.

89. Ibid.

90. George Francis Train, *An American Merchant in Europe, Asia and Australia: A Series of Letters from Java, Singapore* (New York: G. P. Putnam, 1857), 273. Alongside camels, such unruly semiosis characterized also the visualization of other "typical" segments of the Egyptian landscape. As another railway passenger wrote about the pyramids of Giza, "I try to shake off the impression of their solemn antiquity. . . . But that is impossible. The imagination always prompts the eye." Such accounts join the aforementioned disorientations and suggest that new techniques of representation placed the landscape inside observers, making this uncanny fusion key to the Egyptian railway journey. See Warner, *Mummies and Moslems,* 46.

91. "The picture seemed to be real; one felt on looking on it that it was no mere imaginary scene." *Juvenile Missionary Herald* (July 1845), 160.

92. E. C. Brewer, *Authors and Their Works* (London: Chatto & Windus, 1884), 1345.

93. S. Wilks, "The Ethics of Vivisection," *Popular Science Monthly* 21, no. 19 (1882): 346.

94. For example, an article preceding the British invasion argues that the objections of the Turkish sultan to British policy in Egypt would lead to a takeover by the Turkish governor, "who alights upon the country as a vulture alights on a dying camel." See *Bristol Mercury and Daily Post,* January 18, 1882.

95. See Hoskins, *British Routes,* 242–243.

96. Stephenson designed rail ties (sleepers) with the camel's foot in mind. See Richard Allen, *Letters from Egypt, Syria and Greece* (Dublin: Gunn & Cameron,

1869), 17. For subsequent designs based on this principle, see William Charles Francis Molyneux, *Campaigning in South Africa and Egypt* (London: Macmillan, 1896), 250.

97. See, for example, *Newcastle Courant,* May 25, 1883; and Sladen, *Queer Things about Egypt,* 68.

98. F. B. Perkins, *Scrope; or, The Lost Library* (Boston: Roberts, 1874), 13.

99. See, for example, *Tashrīʿāt wa-Manshūrāt,* 1880–1882 (1), pp. 83–84; 1880–1883, pp. 55–56, 94–97, 108–111; 1884, p. 135.

100. Such as Tawfīq al-Ḥakīm. See his *Yawmīyāt Nāʾib fī al-Aryāf,* published in English as *Maze of Justice: Diary of a Country Prosecutor: An Egyptian Novel,* trans. Abba Eban (Austin: University of Texas Press, 1989).

101. This issue will be dealt with in depth in chapter 3.

102. See, for example, Crosbie Smith and M. Norton Wise, *Energy and Empire: A Biographical Study of Lord Kelvin* (Cambridge: Cambridge University Press, 1989); Prakash, *Another Reason*; David Arnold, *Science, Technology, and Medicine in Colonial India* (Cambridge: Cambridge University Press, 2000); Arnold, *The Tropics and the Traveling Gaze: India, Landscape, and Science* 1800–1856 (Seattle: University of Washington Press, 2005); John Reider, *Colonialism and the Emergence of Science Fiction* (Middletown, CT: Wesleyan University Press, 2008); Lucile H. Brockway, *Science and Colonial Expansion: The Role of the British Royal Botanic Gardens* (New Haven, CT: Yale University Press, 2002).

103. The deployment of the Malta-Alexandria line, for example, required corrections in the existing maps that proved to be incorrect and insufficient. See Hoskins, *British Routes,* 377–387.

104. See Smith and Wise, *Energy and Empire,* 740–754.

105. *Encyclopedia Britannica,* 1910 ed., s.v. "Gutta-percha."

106. D. R. Headrick, *Tools of Empire: Technology and European Imperialism in the Nineteenth Century* (New York: Oxford University Press, 1981), 158.

107. Hoskins, *British Routes,* 395–407.

108. It was extracted through incisions in the tree bark, particularly in the rainy season, when the latex is more fluid and abundant. Malays usually felled the tree, chopped off the branches, and removed circles of the bark, forming cylindrical channels in various points down the trunk, through which the latex exudes and flows. The process was eventually mechanized after the discovery of the commercial value of the material. See *Encyclopedia Britannica,* 1910 ed., s.v. "Gutta-percha."

109. C. Bright, *Submarine Telegraphs: Their History, Construction and Work* (C. Lockwood, 1898), 2.

110. See D. R. Headrick, *The Invisible Weapon: Telecommunications and International Politics,* 1851–1945 (New York: Oxford University Press, 1991).

111. Bright, *Submarine Telegraphs,* 174.

112. Land telegraphy was used already in the Crimean War in 1853.

113. M. Perkins, *The Reform of Time: Magic and Modernity* (Sterlin, VA: Pluto Press, 2001), 19.

114. *Electrical Review,* June 15, 1882.

115. See S. Schaffer, "Late Victorian Metrology and Its Instrumentation," in *The Science Studies Reader,* ed. Mario Biagioli (New York: Routledge, 1999), 460.

116. As shown in Schaffer's article that bears this name (ibid.).

117. Thompson, 1871, quoted in ibid., 460.

118. Ibid.

119. See Smith and Wise, *Energy and Empire.*

120. See also B. Hunt, "Scientists, Engineers, and Wildman Whitehouse: Measurement and Credibility in Early Cable Telegraphy," *British Journal for the History of Science* 29, no. 2 (June 1996), 155–169.

121. C. Bright, *Submarine Telegraphs: Their History, Construction and Work* (London: C. Lockwood, 1898), 63.

122. A famous example of such a cover-up is the history of the meter. See Ken Alder, *The Measure of All Things: The Seven-Year Odyssey and Hidden Error That Transformed the World* (New York: Free Press, 2002).

123. R. Kipling, "The Deep-Sea Cables," quoted in Smith and Wise, *Energy and Empire,* 650.

124. The following account is based on Hoskins, *British Routes to India,* 377–378.

125. Ibid., 378.

126. K. Reise, S. Gollasch, and W.J. Wolff, "Introduced Marine Species of the North Sea Coasts," *Helgoländer Meeresuntersuchungen* 52 (1999), 219–234.

127. K.N. Hoppe, "Teredo Navalis—The Cryptogenic Shipworm," in *Invasive Aquatic Species of Europe: Their Distribution, Impacts and Management,* ed. E. Leppakoski (London: Kluwer, 2002), 116–120.

128. An 1865 novel by Mary Mapes Dodge, *Hans Brinker,* based on published sources about Dutch life and the memories of a Dutch couple living in the United States, produced what is probably one of the most lasting images of the Dutch, "the hero of Haarlem"—the little boy who saved Holland from being flooded by sticking his finger in a hole in the wooden dike. Art historian Annette Stott argues that "the fanciful tale of a finger in the dike, which was repeated by other authors of juvenile literature, undoubtedly went some distance toward establishing in young American minds a belief in the courage, independence and trustworthiness of the Dutch." Annette Stott, *Holland Mania: The Unknown Dutch Period in American Art and Culture* (Woodstock, NY: Overlook Press, 1998), 241. Since the hole in the wooden dike was a fictional one, there is no point in attempting to identify its actual cause. However, the anxieties about leaky wooden dikes, which eventually led to the replacement of wood with stone, also generated local mythologies and heroes. Could the *Teredo navalis* have helped shape the international image of its Dutch hosts?

129. Thereby demonstrating the percolation of knowledge between "biology" and "engineering" and between an Eastern worm and a Victorian engineer.

130. J.L. Warden, *The Coasts of Devon and Lundy Island: Their Towns, Villages, Scenery, Antiquates, and Legends* (London: Cox, 1895), 88.

131. H. Frith, *The Romance of Engineering: The Stories of the Highway, the Waterway, the Railway, and the Subway* (London: Ward, Lock, Bowden, 1895), 315.

132. Beyond boring, Brunel's tunneling shield was important to the work of physicist Michael Faraday on the visual effects of motion after Brunel's son described to him a system of two wheels used inside the tunnel, turning at such velocity as to give the impression of motionlessness. Such observations led to the development of the phenakistoscope (literally, "deceptive view"), a disk with figures representing different stages of motion, which, as a result of retinal persistence, gives the impression of continuous motion when spinning rapidly. Combined with the work of Daguerre on camera lucidas and dioramas and the photographic camera, such optical devices as the phenakistoscope were cornerstones in the emergence of cinema. See M. Faraday, "On a Peculiar Class of Optical Deceptions," in *Experimental Researches in Chemistry and Physics* (London: R. Taylor & W. Francis, 1859), 291.

133. T. Peters, *Building the Nineteenth Century* (Cambridge, MA: MIT Press, 1996), 15.

134. Ibid., 20.

135. See, for example, N. William, *Conversations with M. Thiers, M. Guizot, and Other Distinguished Persons during the Second Empire,* vol. 2 (London: Hurst and Blackett, 1878), 187. See also T. Peters, *Building the Nineteenth Century.*

136. F. D. Por, *Lessepsian Migration: The Influx of Red Sea Biota into the Mediterranean by Way of the Suez Canal* (Berlin: Springer-Verlag, 1978).

137. T. Mitchell, "Can the Mosquito Speak?" in *Rule of Experts: Egypt, Techno-Politics, Modernity* (Berkeley: University of California Press, 2002), 19–54.

138. "Tanẓīm al-Barīd fī al-Shām ibbān al-Ḥukm al-Miṣrī, 1831–1840," *Al-Majallah al-Tārīkhīyah al-Miṣrīyah* 40 (1997–1999): 185–207.

139. Ibid., 190.

140. Ibid., 191, 195. This system allowed the creation of a postal price structure based on distance measured by travel time. See Maṣlaḥat al-Barīd, *Tārīkh al-Barīd fī Miṣr* (Cairo: Wizārat al-Muwāṣalāt, 1934), 47.

141. "Tanẓīm al-Barīd," 188.

142. Ibid., 194.

143. See J. C. Scott, *Seeing like a State: How Certain Schemes to Improve the Human Condition Have Failed* (New Haven, CT: Yale University Press, 1988).

144. "Tanẓīm al-Barīd," 201. See also K. Fahmy, *All the Pasha's Men: Mehmed Ali, His Army, and the Making of Modern Egypt* (Cambridge: Cambridge University Press, 1998), 171.

145. Indeed, vision played an important role in the development of time discipline. See M. J. Sauter, "Clockwatchers and Stargazers: Time Discipline in Early Modern Berlin," *American Historical Review* 112, no. 3 (June 2007), 685–710.

146. Maṣlaḥat al-Barīd, *Tārīkh al-Barīd fī Miṣr* (Cairo: Wizārat al-Muwāṣalāt, 1934), 46n1; and Hoskins, *British Routes,* 230.

147. W. B. Dana, "The Semaphoric and Marine Telegraph Flags," *Merchant's Magazine and Commercial Review* (1844), 337. The semaphoric telegraph was invented and introduced into Europe by Arab scientists. See J. V. Marmery, *Progress of Science: Its Origin, Course, Promoters, and Results* (London: Chapman and Hall, 1895), 42.

148. Hoskins, *British Routes,* 230.

149. Waghorn, *The Acceleration of Mails,* 13.

CHAPTER 2

Epigraph: Walter Benjamin, "Theses on the Philosophy of History," in *Illuminations,* ed. Hannah Arendt, trans. Harry Zohn (New York: Harcourt, Brace & World, 1968), 253.

1. Mitchell, *Colonising Egypt,* chapter 3.

2. Ḥassūnah, *Miṣr wa' l-Ṭuruq,* 146.

3. Ibid., 151.

4. F. Ayrton, *Railways in Egypt: Communication with India* (London: Ridgway, 1857) 39; Ḥassūnah, *Miṣr wa'l-Ṭuruq,* 150–51.

5. Waiting as a political principle is discussed in A. Hammoudi, *A Season in Mecca: Narrative of a Pilgrimage* (Cambridge: Polity, 2006).

6. Ḥassūnah, *Miṣr wa' l-Ṭuruq,* 147–149.

7. Quoted in A. Omar, "Anglo-Egyptian Relations and the Construction of the Alexandria-Cairo-Suez Railway, 1833–1858" (PhD diss., University of London, 1966), 266.

8. "A Lady's Visit to the Khedive," *Ladies' Repository,* September 1871, p. 203.

9. See Ḥassūnah, *Miṣr wa' l-Ṭuruq,* 139–140.

10. *Mudhakkirāt Iskandar Bāshā Fahmī,* quoted in ibid., 140–141.

11. A reputation problematized by Ehud Toledano. See *State and Society in Mid-Nineteenth-Century Egypt* (Cambridge: Cambridge University Press, 1990).

12. P. Virilio, *The Virilio Reader,* ed. J. Der Derian (Malden, MA: Blackwell, 1998), 13. According to Virilio, every technology anticipates its own accident. Accidents exist only vis-à-vis a purpose or structure, and vice versa: the system and its accidents are mutually constitutive.

13. Latour, *Reassembling the Social,* 81. While this might be true, accidents also help produce the black box itself and facilitate its closure.

14. Fairholt, *Up the Nile,* 35–36.

15. Ayrton, *Railways in Egypt,* 40.

16. A. E. Garwood, *Forty Years of an Engineer's Life at Home and Abroad* (Newport, Monmouthshire: A. W. Dawson, 1903), 100.

17. See, for example, "Manshūr bi-Sha'n al-Intibāh li-'Adam Tamakkun al-Ashqiyā' min al-Saṭw 'alā Quṭūrāt al-Wābūrāt," *Tashrī'āt wa-Manshūrāt,* 1880–1882, p. 83; "Manshūr Niẓārat al-Dākhilīyah bi'l-Ta'kīd 'alā man Yulzam bi-Man' Ramy al-Aḥjār 'alā Quṭūrāt Wābūrāt Sikkat al-Ḥadīd," *Tashrī'āt wa-Manshūrāt,* 1880–1883, p. 55.

18. *Newcastle Courant,* February 25, 1889.

19. Ibid.

20. The design was credited to Stephenson himself. See Ḥassūnah, *Miṣr wa'l-Ṭuruq,* 122–124.

21. T. Sopwith, *Notes of a Visit to Egypt, by Paris, Lyons, Nismes, Marseilles and Toulon* (London, 1857), 112–135.

22. See, for example, Train, *An American Merchant in Europe,* 286–290.

23. *Daily News,* May 29, 1858.

24. Ayrton, *Railways in Egypt,* 39–40.

25. Subsequent accounts may be found in Jerrold Blanchard, *Egypt under Ismail Pacha: Being Some Chapters of Contemporary History* (London: S. Tinsley, 1879); James Bland, *Prince Ahmed of Egypt* (London: S. Paul, 1939); and Nubar Pasha, *Mémoires de Nubar Pacha* (Beirut: Librairie du Liban,1983).

26. *Morning Chronicle,* May 28, 1858.

27. See Blanchard, *Egypt under Ismail Pacha,* 19–23. See also Samir Raafat, "The Much Debated Royal Death on the Nile," *Egyptian Mail,* June 11, 1994.

28. *Glasgow Herald,* June 9, 1858.

29. Ibid.

30. Omar, "Anglo-Egyptian Relations," 212.

31. Green to Nūbār, April 21, 1858, in FO 142/22, quoted in ibid., 275.

32. Ibid., 275–277.

33. Sladen, *Queer Things about Egypt,* 73.

34. See Ḥassūnah, *Miṣr wa' l-Ṭuruq,* 125.

35. See, for example, *Tashrī'āt wa-Manshūrāt,* 1880–1882, p. 83; and *Tashrī'āt wa-Manshūrāt,* 1880–1883, pp. 96–97, 108–111.

36. Ismā'īl tripled the railroad during his reign. See Ḥassūnah, *Miṣr wa' l-Ṭuruq,* 155. This was one of the key projects that led to the Egyptian insolvency and eventual colonization. See Ḥassūnah, *Miṣr wa' l-Ṭuruq,* 166–167.

37. See, for example, Edwin De Leon, *The Khedive's Egypt; or, The Old House of Bondage under New Masters* (London: S. Low, Marston, Searle & Rivington, 1877), 154–157.

38. Memorial of April 26, 1864, enclosed in Colquhoun, May 3, 1864: FO 78/1818, quoted in Owen, *Cotton and the Egyptian Economy,*112.

39. Ḥassūnah, *Miṣr wa' l-Ṭuruq,* 158.

40. Ibid.

41. 'Alī Bāshā Mubārak, *Ḥayātī: Sīrat al-Marḥūm 'Alī Mubārak Bāshā,* ed. 'Abd al-Raḥīm Yūsuf al-Jamal (Cairo: Maktabat al-Ādāb, 1989), 25–26.

42. A.E.C. De Cosson, "Notes on the Early History of the Egyptian State Railways," *Egyptian State Railways Magazine,* September 1932, p. 10.

43. Sikak Ḥadīd Miṣr, *Egyptian Railways in* 125 *Years,* 1852–1977 (Cairo, 1977), 233.

44. *Wādī al-Nīl,* October 16, 1870.

45. Omar, "Anglo-Egyptian Relations," 238–239.

46. See Ḥassūnah, *Miṣr wa' l-Ṭuruq,*115–117.

47. Ibid., 155.

48. De Lesseps had planned to open the canal by the end of 1868 but had to delay the inauguration to November 1869 as a result of cholera and a labor shortage. See

C. W. Hallberg, *The Suez Canal: Its History and Diplomatic Importance* (New York: Octagon Books, 1974), 214.

49. Mitchell, *Colonising,* 63–94

50. See Schivelbusch, *The Railway Journey,* chapter 11.

51. ʿAlī Mubārak, *Al-Khiṭaṭ al-Tawfīqīyah al-Jadīdah li-Miṣr al-Qāhirah wa-Mudunihā wa-Bilādihā al-Qadīmah wa-al-Shahīrah* (Bulaq: al-Maṭbaʿah al-Kubrā al-Amīrīyah, 1304–1305 [1886–1889]), 7:259.

52. Decree of 25 Jumādā II, 1288, quoted in R. Peters, "Administrators and Magistrates: The Development of a Secular Judiciary in Egypt," *Die Welt des Islams* 39, no. 3 (November 1999): 390–391.

53. J. A. Kilby (Alexandria Divisional Locomotive Superintendent), "Notes on the Economical Operation of Locomotives," *Egyptian State Railways Magazine* (May 1932), 7.

54. Ḥassūnah, *Miṣr waʾl-Ṭuruq,* 151–152.

55. *Wādī al-Nīl,* December 12, 1870.

56. Mubārak, *Al-Khiṭaṭ,* 7:253.

57. Garwood, *Forty Years,* 100.

58. *Wādī al-Nīl,* December 12, 1870.

59. Mubārak, *Al-Khiṭaṭ,* 7:257, 260.

60. Ibid., 258–289.

61. Omar, "Anglo-Egyptian Relations," 288.

62. *Wādī al-Nīl,* December 12, 1870; and W. D. Knight, "Failures," *Egyptian State Railways Magazine* (May 1932), p. 7.

63. *Majallat Sikak Ḥadīd wa-Tilighrāfāt wa-Tilifūnāt al-Ḥukūma al-Miṣrīyah* (November–December 1941) gives a brief history of the use of these models.

64. Maṣlaḥat al-Barīd, *Tārīkh al-Barīd,* 107.

65. W. Cronon, *Nature's Metropolis: Chicago and the Great West* (New York: Norton, 1992), 84.

66. *British Parliamentary Papers,* Transport and Communication 12, "Report from Select Committee on Railway Companies Amalgamation" (1872).

67. Bruce Podobnik, *Global Energy Shifts: Fostering Sustainability in a Turbulent Age* (Philadelphia: Temple University Press, 2006), 38–39.

68. R. Owen, *Lord Cromer: Victorian Imperialist, Edwardian Proconsul* (Oxford: Oxford University Press, 2005), 95.

69. Ibid., 97.

70. A. Vale, "The Railway System in Egypt," *Railway Magazine* 11 (1902): 237.

71. "International jealousies have, however to be satisfied; and the result is that the work is badly done, the trains are few, slow, and unpunctual, the fares are high, the carriages dirty." I. Taylor, *Leaves from an Egyptian Note-Book* (London: Kegan Paul, Trench, 1888), 94.

72. Knight, "Failures," 7.

73. Ibid.

74. Ibid., 8.

75. Ibid.

76. Ibid.

77. See R. A. Buchanan, "The Diaspora of British Engineering," *Technology and Culture* 27, no. 3 (July 1986): 501–524.

78. P. Doyle, *Indian Engineering* 32 (August 9, 1902): 85.

79. Vale, "The Railway System in Egypt," 239–240.

80. Knight, "Failures," 10.

81. See De Cosson, "Notes on the Early History of the Egyptian State Railways," 10.

82. Garwood, *Forty Years of an Engineer's Life,* 98–102.

83. Mubārak, *Al-Khiṭaṭ,* 7:255.

84. Knight, "Failures," 8–9.

85. Vale, "The Railway System in Egypt," 239–240.

86. See, for example, H. R. Hall, *A Handbook for Egypt and the Sudan* (London: E. Stanford, 1907), 10.

87. Vale, "The Railway System in Egypt," 128.

88. Ibid., 122.

89. See, for example, Danielson, *The Voice of Egypt,* 33.

90. See Sopwith, *Notes,* 112–135; and H.H. Ayrout, *The Egyptian Peasant* (Boston: Beacon Press, 1963 [1938]), 143.

91. A.B. Zahlan, "The Impact of Technology Change on the Nineteenth-Century Arab World," in *Between the State and Islam,* ed. C.E. Butterworth and I.W. Zartman (Cambridge: Cambridge University Press, 2001), 31–59.

92. This will be discussed in chapter 6.

93. Garwood, *Forty Years of an Engineer's Life,* 98–102.

94. Vale, "The Railway System of Egypt," 239.

95. D. Harvey, *The Condition of Postmodernity: An Enquiry into the Origins of Cultural Change* (Cambridge, MA: Blackwell, 1990); May and Thrift, *TimeSpace.*

96. May and Thrift, *TimeSpace,* 7. See also S. Kern, *The Culture of Time and Space* (Cambridge, MA: Harvard University Press, 1983).

97. Salmon, *The Wonderland of Egypt,* 87.

98. Fairholt, *Up the Nile,* 35–36.

99. According to Schivelbusch, 20–30 mph was the speed of the earliest English trains, before 1845, when the fastest express reached 46 mph. See Schivelbusch, *The Railway Journey,* 34n2.

100. Mubārak, *Al-Khiṭaṭ,* 7:262.

101. See Harvey, "Between Space and Time," 418–434.

102. See P. Galison, *Einstein's Clocks, Poincaré's Maps: Empires of Time* (New York: Norton, 2003), 38.

103. See Latour, *Reassembling the Social,* 213n286.

104. B. Latour, "A Relativistic Account of Einstein's relativity," *Social Studies of Science* 18, no. 1 (February 1988): 3–44.

105. See Galison, *Einstein's Clocks,* on the importance of Switzerland's railway and telegraph systems for the development of the theory of relativity.

106. Evelyn Baring, Earl of Cromer, *Modern Egypt* (New York: Macmillan, 1908), 56.

107. Ibid., 72.

108. Ibid., 327.

109. Mitchell, *Colonising Egypt,* 157–159.

110. Cromer, *Modern Egypt,* 260.

111. Ibid., 261.

112. B. Latour, *Science in Action: How to Follow Scientists and Engineers through Society* (Cambridge, MA: Harvard University Press, 1988), 130.

113. See, for example, D. Lardner, *The Steam Engine Familiarly Explained and Illustrated,* 8th ed. (London: Taylor, Walton, and Maberly, 1851), 53–54.

114. A. Smith, *An Inquiry into the Nature and Causes of the Wealth of Nations,* ed. Edwin Cannan (London: Methuen, 1904).

115. Karl Marx, *Capital: A Critique of Political Economy,* trans. David Fernbach (New York: Penguin Classics, 1976), 507.

116. For the automaton as an emblem of this tradition, see Minsoo Kang, *Sublime Dreams of Living Machines: The Automaton in the European Imagination* (Cambridge, MA: Harvard University Press, 2011).

117. Cromer, *Modern Egypt,* 2:148.

118. See, for example, B. St. John, *Village Life in Egypt: With Sketches of the Saïd* (Boston: Ticknor, Reed, and Fields, 1853), 2–3; Sarah Atkins and Giovanni Battista Belzoni, *Fruits of Enterprize Exhibited in the Adventures of Belzoni in Egypt and Nubia: With an Account of His Discoveries in the Pyramids, among the Ruins of Cities, and in the Ancient Tombs* (New York: Charles S. Francis, 1850), 47–49.

119. P. J. Hartog, *Examinations and Their Relation to Culture and Efficiency with a Speech by the Late Earl of Cromer* (London: Constable, 1918), 41.

120. Cromer, *Modern Egypt,* 155.

121. Ibid.

122. Ibid., 477.

123. Ibid., 241.

124. Ibid., 240.

125. Ibid., 242. These incidents were already cited by Cromer in his report for the year 1903.

126. In this year, one of the head engineers in the railway authority promised that the wages of day workers who did not enjoy the improvement in the salary scale would still be raised, because productivity had improved due to the calmness of the workforce. See *Al-Muqaṭṭam,* August 24, 1923.

127. Sladen, *Queer Things about Egypt,* 69.

128. See, for example, his article in *Al-Tilighrāfāt al-Jadīdah,* June 10, 1899.

129. See *Al-Muʾayyad,* August 12, 1908.

130. We have seen how ʿAlī Mubārak's reforms included opening educational institutions for local train drivers and engineers. Saʿīd likewise endeavored to

increase the number of the Arab workers, albeit to avoid paying the inflated salaries of European workers. See Omar, "Anglo-Egyptian Relations," 282–283. In 1856, the Egyptian transportation sector employed 2,535 "Turkish and Arab workers" earning an annual total of 448,274 piasters, and 127 Europeans earning 154,944 piasters. See Omar, "Anglo-Egyptian Relations," 265.

131. Beinin and Lockman, *Workers on the Nile,* 72.

132. "Extract from Lord Cromer's Report for 1906," in *Documents Collected for the Information of the Special Committee Appointed to Enquire the Situation in Egypt,* vol. 1, p. 23.

133. Vale, "The Railway System in Egypt," 242.

134. Ibid., 243.

135. See Chandler, *The Visible Hand.*

136. See R. Williams, *Keywords: A Vocabulary of Culture and Society* (New York: Oxford University Press, 1983); see also Savage, "Discipline," 66.

137. Savage, "Discipline," 65–93.

138. M. Reynolds, *Engine-Driving Life* (London: Crosby Lockwood, 1881), quoted in ibid., 79.

139. Ibid., 65–93.

140. Omar, "Anglo-Egyptian Relations," 273.

141. As discussed in chapter 5.

142. Mark Smith makes a similar claim about slaves in the antebellum U.S. South. Mark Smith, *Mastered by the Clock.*

143. *Al-Niẓām,* July 4, 1909.

144. D. Quataert, "Ottoman Workers and the State, 1826-1914," in *Workers and Working Classes in the Middle East: Struggles, Histories, Historiographies,* ed. Zachary Lockman (Albany, 1994), 32–35; quoted in Atabaki, *The State and the Subaltern,* 10.

145. I. Khuri-Makdisi, *The Eastern Mediterranean and the Making of Global Radicalism,* 1860–1914 (Berkeley: University of California Press, 2010).

146. See, for example, *Al-Ṣiḥāfah,* June 11, 1905.

147. For the Indian case, see D. R. Headrick, *Tools of Empire: Technology and European Imperialism in the Nineteenth Century* (New York: Oxford University Press, 1981).

148. *Majallat ʿUmmāl al-Sikkah al-Ḥadīd,* 1909.

149. Vallet, "Contribution," 86–94; ESR 1 Report, October 19, 1910; Beinin and Lockman, *Workers on the Nile,* 74.

150. E. P. Thompson, *The Making of the English Working Class* (London: Vintage Books, 1963), 201.

151. Thompson, "Time, Work-Discipline and Industrial Capitalism."

152. *Wādī al-Nīl,* September 16, 1870.

153. These hours are called "temporal hours." See Atabaki, *The State and the Subaltern,* 6.

154. See the explanation in *Al-Hilāl,* November 1, 1902.

155. See Wishnitzer, "Reading Clocks, *Alla Turca.*"

156. Mubārak, *Al-Khiṭaṭ,* 7:252.

157. Vale, "The Railway System in Egypt," 243.

158. As early as 1881, ʿAbd Allāh al-Nadīm raised the issue and connected language purity to cultural and political identity. See *Al-Tankīt waʾl-Tabkīt,* September 18, 1881.

159. *Al-Kawkab,* October 16, 1905.

160. "Extract from Lord Cromer's Report for 1906," 23–30.

161. *Wādī al-Nīl,* January 22, 1916.

162. Ayrton, *Railways in Egypt,* 54.

163. Quoted in Vale, "The Railway System in Egypt," 242.

164. Cromer, *Modern Egypt,* 2:148.

165. See Ziad Fahmy, *Ordinary Egyptians: Creating the Modern Nation through Popular Culture* (Stanford, CA: Stanford University Press, 2011), 51–60.

166. "Muzzling the Egyptian Press," *Nation,* January 12, 1882.

167. See, for example, *Al-Qāhirah,* which regularly reported matters such as train accidents, delays, and dysfunctional equipment during this period.

168. A list of the newspaper's distributers/correspondents and their addresses was published on *Al-Ahrām*'s first page during its early years.

169. Incidentally, newspapers sent for distribution in the countryside traveled second class, with the effendis who read them. See *Tashrīʿāt wa-Manshūrāt,* 1889, pp. 58–85.

170. See A. Hunter, *Power and Passion in Egypt: A Life of Sir Eldon Gorst, 1861–1911* (London: I.B. Tauris, 2007), 165.

171. The incident is described in the introduction to her memoir. See Hudā Shaʿrāwī, *Harem Years: The Memoirs of an Egyptian Feminist* (1879–1924), trans. Margot Badran (New York: Feminist Press, 1987).

172. M. Taymūr, "Fī al-Qiṭār," in *Mā Tarāhu al-ʿUyūn* (Cairo: al-Dār al-Qawmīyah liʾl-Ṭibāʿah waʾl-Nashr, 1964).

173. *Al-Muṣawwar,* May 3, 1902.

174. Ibid. Other articles complained, for example, about the futility of press critique regarding the speed of inner-city transportation. See, for example, *Diyāʾ al-Sharq,* May 6, 1908.

175. Amīn al-Ḥaddād, "Ḥubb al-Surʿah," in *Muntakhabāt* (Alexandria: Maṭbaʿat Jurjī Gharzūzī, 1913), 202–206.

176. Jakes, "The Scales of Public Utility."

177. "Extract from Sir Eldon Gorst's Report for 1908," *Documents Collected,* vol. 1, pp. 43–45.

178. The more diplomatic Gorst strove for a rapprochement between the British and Khedive ʿAbbās Ḥilmī II, pushing Egyptian nationalists (who had just formed the Nationalist Party in 1907) to seek new alliances and constituencies—with workers and the masses in particular—in order to build a more broadly based independence movement. In doing so, they responded in disillusioned fashion to the 1904 Anglo-French *entente cordiale* securing European recognition of Britain's entrenchment in Egypt. See Beinin and Lockman, *Workers on the Nile,* 66–69; and Ziad Fahmy, *Ordinary Egyptians,* 98–104.

179. *African Times and Orient Review,* March 31, 1914, pp. 37–38.

CHAPTER 3

Epigraph: J. Derrida, *Specters of Marx,* trans. Peggy Kamuf (New York: Routledge, 1994), 4.

1. Taymūr, "Fī al-Qiṭār."

2. As demonstrated also by Yaḥyā Haqqī's short story "Al-Qiṭār" (The train) as well as Tawfīq al-Ḥakīm's *Song of Death.* In al-Ḥakīm's later plays (*The Tree Climber* [1962] and *A Train Journey* [1964]), the train is a metaphor for life (in the former) or society (in the latter) and for the conflicts characterizing them. For a discussion of these plays, see Muḥammad Muṣṭafá Badawī, *Modern Arabic Drama in Egypt* (Cambridge: Cambridge University Press, 1987).

3. See *ESR Statistical Yearbook for the Year* 1909, p. 128.

4. Ibid., 130.

5. Lewis R. Freeman, "The Railroad Conquest of Africa," *American Review of Reviews* 50 (July–December 1914): 68.

6. Danielson, *The Voice of Egypt,* 33, 33n54; M. Goldman, *Umm Kulthum: A Voice Like Egypt,* Arab Film Distribution, 1996.

7. See, for example, Goswami, *Producing India;* and Rudolf Mrázek, *Engineers of Happy Land: Technology and Nationalism in a Colony* (Princeton, NJ: Princeton University Press, 2002). For a history of the Ḥijāz railway, see William Ochsenwald, *The Hijaz Railroad* (Charlottesville: University Press of Virginia, 1980).

8. A symptomatic example, using the Egyptian railway as an emblem for secular globalization, is provided in Thomas L. Friedman, "One Country, Two Worlds," *New York Times,* January 28, 2000, p. A23.

9. See C. Taylor, *A Secular Age* (Cambridge, MA: Harvard University Press, 2007); Jacques Le Goff, "Merchant's Time and Church's Time in the Middle Ages," in *Time, Work and Culture in the Middle Ages,* trans. Arthur Goldhammer (Chicago: University of Chicago Press, 1980), 29–42.

10. Max Weber, "Science as a Vocation" in *From Max Weber: Essays in Sociology,* trans. and ed. H.H. Gerth and C. Wright Mills (New York: Oxford University Press, 1946), 129–156. Benjamin's theory of the "mortification" of the work of art offers a similar image of technology. Walter Benjamin, *The Work of Art in the Age of Its Technological Reproduction and Other Writings on Media,* trans. Edmund Jephcott et al., ed. Michael Jennings, Brigid Doherty, and Thomas Levin (Cambridge: Harvard University Press, 2008).

11. See Karl Marx, "The British Rule in India," *New York Daily Tribune,* June 25, 1853; and Marx, "The Future Results of British Rule in India," *New York Daily Tribune,* August 8, 1853. See Mia Carter and Barbara Harlow, eds., *Archives of Empire: From the East India Company to the Suez Canal* (Durham, NC: Duke University Press, 2003), 117–131. Marx's thinking on the non-West evolved over the coming decades, eschewing many of these assumptions. See Kevin Anderson, *Marx on the Margins: Nationalism, Ethnicity, and Non-Western Societies* (Chicago: University of Chicago Press, 2010).

12. Metcalf and Metcalf, *A Concise History of India,* 93–98; Mrázek, *Engineers of Happy Land;* Goswami, *Producing India,* particularly chapter 3.

13. See Thompson, "Time, Work-Discipline and Industrial Capitalism"; Douglas A. Reid, "The Decline of Saint Monday 1766–1876," *Past and Present* 71 (May 1976): 76–101; and Reid, "Weddings, Weekdays, Work and Leisure in Urban England 1791–1911: The Decline of Saint Monday Revisited," *Past and Present* 153 (November 1996): 135–163.

14. Green, *Bombay Islam,* effectively pursues this avenue.

15. On Hamlet in Arabic, see Margaret Litvin, *Hamlet's Arab Journey: Shakespeare's Prince and Nasser's Ghost* (Princeton, NJ: Princeton University Press, 2011).

16. Derrida, *Specters of Marx,* 10.

17. Muḥammad Rashīd Riḍā, *Fatāwā al-Imām Muḥammad Rashīd Riḍā,* ed. Ṣalāḥ al-Dīn al-Munajjid and Yūsuf Khūrī (Beirut: Dār al-kitāb al-jadīd, 1970), 1:180 (see *Al-Manār* 7 [1904], 416–417). Another fatwā, from 1906, addressed the special license of a railway traveler to combine two prayers in case it was impossible to perform one of them onboard. The incessant motion of the train collapsed and folded prayer time upon itself. See *Al-Manār* 9 (1906), in *Fatāwā al-Imām,* 2:534–535.

18. Galloway, *Observations on the Proposed Improvements,* 4.

19. Omar, *Anglo-Egyptian Relations,* 326.

20. "The Ship of the Desert," *Eclectic Magazine of Foreign Literature, Science, and Art* 54 (September–December 1861): 451. This shift in turn brought about an etymological shift in the meaning of the expression *Qiṭār al-Ḥajj* (the pilgrimage camel train). For earlier uses of this expression in Ottoman Egypt, see Jane Hathaway, *The Politics of Households in Ottoman Egypt: The Rise of the Qazdağlis* (Cambridge: Cambridge University Press, 2002). For a description of the *maḥmal*'s route, the ceremonies along the way, and the protocols for weaving the *kiswa,* see Mubārak, *Al-Khiṭaṭ,* 9:57–88.

21. See *Al-Tankīt wa'l-Tabkīt,* August 15, 1881. See also "Maḥmal" in J. Christoph Brugel, *Der Islam im Spiegel zeigenössischer Literatur der islamischen Welt: Vorträge eines Internationalen Symposiums an der Universität Bern, 11.-14. Juli* 1983 (Leiden: E. J. Brill, 1985), 45. Between 1910 and 1913 the route was changed again: via railway from Cairo to Alexandria, from there by steamer to Haifa, and then to Medina by the Ḥijāz railway.

22. See, for example, *Al-Qāhira,* October 10, 1887.

23. See, for example, *Al-Ṣiḥāfa,* February 5, 1905, on the theft of *Surat al-Maḥmal,* the funds meant to be distributed to Mecca's poor. Or *Al-Ṣiḥāfa,* May 7, 1905, about Bedouin attacks against the convoy. In 1895, twenty-one of the *maḥmal*'s guards died of cholera. See *Al-Waṭan,* August 2, 1895.

24. Michael Christopher Low, "Empire and the *Ḥajj:* Pilgrims, Plagues, and Pan-Islam under British Surveillance, 1865–1908," *International Journal of Middle East Studies* 40, no. 2 (May 31, 2008): 269–290; see also David Arnold, *Colonizing the Body: State Medicine and Epidemic Disease in Nineteenth-Century India* (Berkeley: University of California Press, 1993), 186–189.

25. F. Peters, *The Hajj: The Muslim Pilgrimage to Mecca and the Holy Places* (Princeton, NJ: Princeton University Press, 1995), 301.

26. *Tashrīʿāt wa-Manshūrāt,* 1889, pp. 34–35.

27. According to the Ottoman traveler Evliya Çelebi, the beggars' guild regularly attended the *maḥmal* procession in seventeenth-century Cairo. See Gabriel Baer, *Egyptian Guilds in Modern Times* (Jerusalem: Israel Oriental Society, 1964), 117. Begging was later completely forbidden in train stations. See *Tashrīʿāt wa-Manshūrāt,* 1907, pp. 90–94.

28. Esther Peskes, "The Wahhabiyya and Sufism in the Eighteenth Century," in *Islamic Mysticism Contested: Thirteen Centuries of Controversies and Polemics,* ed. Frederick de Jong and Bernd Radtke (Leiden: Brill, 1999), 158.

29. S. H. Leeder, *Veiled Mysteries of Egypt and the Religion of Islam* (New York: Charles Scribner's Sons, 1913), 216. For the anti-Sufi campaign during the late nineteenth century, see Frederick de Jong, "Opposition to Sufism in Twentieth-Century Egypt, 1900–1970: A Preliminary Survey," in *Islamic Mysticism Contested: Thirteen Centuries of Controversies and Polemics,* ed. F. de Jong and B. Radtke (Leiden: Brill, 1999), 310–311.

30. *Tashrīʿāt wa-Manshūrāt,* 1891, p. 669.

31. *Al-Waṭan,* August 2, 1895.

32. *Al-Ṣiḥāfa,* May 7, 1905.

33. See *Al-Ahrām,* June 24, 1926.

34. Michael Winter, *Egyptian Society under Ottoman Rule,* 1517–1798 (New York: Routledge, 2004), 164–184. On *mawlid*s in Egypt and their times, see Winter, "The Mawlids in Egypt from the Eighteenth Century until the Middle of the Twentieth Century," in *The ʿUlama and Problems of Religion in the Muslim World: Studies in Memory of Professor Uriel Heyd* (Hebrew), ed. G. Baer (Jerusalem: Israel Oriental Society, 1971), 79–103.

35. Ayrton, *Railways in Egypt,* 39; Ḥassūnah, *Miṣr waʾl-Ṭuruq,* 150–151.

36. Alexander Wallace, *The Desert and the Holy Land* (Edinburgh: William Oliphant, 1868), 69, quoted in *Evangelical Repository* 1 (1868): 194.

37. See *Wādī al-Nīl,* 10 Muḥaram 1286, and 22 Jumādā al-Awwal 1287.

38. See ʿAlī Mubārak, *ʿAlam al-Dīn* (Alexandria: Maṭbaʿat Jarīdat al-Maḥrūsah, 1882), 159–162; and Mubārak, *Al-Khiṭaṭ,* 7:259.

39. *Al-Barīd,* April 4, 1895.

40. *Al-Waṭan,* August 20, 1895.

41. *Al-Barīd,* June 26, 1895.

42. Ibid.

43. ʿUmar, *Kitāb Ḥāḍir al-Miṣrīyīn,* 245nn1,2.

44. See, for example, announcements regarding special railway readiness for a Jewish grave visitation in *Al-Ahrām,* October 4, 1913.

45. ʿUmar, *Kitāb Ḥādir al-Miṣrīyīn,* 1, where the author indicates his debt to Zaghlūl's translation of Demolins's book.

46. Aḥmad Fatḥī Zaghlūl, *Sirr Taqaddum al Inkilīz al-Saksūnīyīn* (Cairo: Maṭbaʿāt al-Taraqqī, 1898), 20. Evoking indolence, Zaghlūl redeployed one of the

key conceptual filters for European understanding of the Orient. Indolence was so thoroughly associated with the Orient that even Demolins's book, dealing entirely with Europe, rhetorically conjured up the "indolence of the Oriental" as the diametrical opposite of the initiative fostered by education. See E. Demolins, *Anglo-Saxon Superiority: To What It Is Due,* trans. Louis Bertram Lavigne (London: Leadenhall Press, 1899), 209.

47. See, for example, Chesney, *Narrative of the Euphrates Expedition,* 405; B. St. John, *Village Life in Egypt,* 2–3; Sarah Atkins Wilson and Giovanni Battista Belzoni, *Fruits of Enterprize Exhibited in the Adventures of Belzoni in Egypt and Nubia: With an Account of His Discoveries in the Pyramids, Among among the Ruins of Cities, and in the Ancient Tombs* (New York: Charles S. Francis, 1850), 47–49; J. A. St. John, *Egypt and Nubia* (London: Chapman and Hall, 1845), 336.

48. Significant parts of Demolins's examination are predicated on analyzing timetables of British schools in a way that allowed the pedagogue to quantify and calculate the distribution of personal time and guided work, and physical and intellectual activity. See, for example, *Anglo-Saxon Superiority,* p. 47. In the nineteenth century, rigid timetables became an increasingly important element in modern Egyptian schooling and military training, following the adoption of the "Lancaster method" during the first half of the century. Gradually, fixed timetables became effective means of pedagogic supervision, allowing school inspectors to compare what they observed in class to the official timetables issued as regulation and printed in the official newspaper. See such timetables in, for example, Fīlīb b. Yūsuf Jallād, *Qāmūs al-Idāra wa'l-Qaḍā'*, 2084, 2120. On military schedules, see Fahmy, *All the Pasha's Men,* 108. On the Lancaster system, see Mitchell, *Colonising Egypt,* 69; and Paul Sedra, *From Mission to Modernity: Evangelicals, Reformers, and Education in Nineteenth Century Egypt* (London: I. B. Tauris, 2011).

49. See Z. Lockman, "Imagining the Working Class: Culture, Nationalism, and Class Formation in Egypt, 1899–1914," Poetics Today 15, no. 2 (Summer 1994): 157–190, for an analysis of this new mapping of Egyptian society.

50. See Lucie Razova, "Egyptionizing Modernity through the 'New Effendiya': Social and Cultural Constructions of the Middle Class in Egypt under the Monarchy," in *Re-envisioning Egypt* 1919–1952, ed. Barak A. Salmoni and Amy J. Johnson (Cairo: American University in Cairo Press, 2005), pp. 124–164.

51. On effendi character and its relation to strict time management, see Wilson Chacko Jacob, *Working Out Egypt: Effendi Masculinity and Subject Formation in Colonial Modernity,* 1870–1940 (Durham, NC: Duke University Press, 2011).

52. ʿUmar, *Kitāb Ḥāḍir al-Miṣrīyīn,* 244.

53. Ibid., 246.

54. See, for example, "Egyptian Holidays—An Impermissible Innovation," *Al-Ṣiḥāfa,* March 5, 1905.

55. See, for example, ʿAbd al-Raḥmān al-Jabartī, *ʿAjāʾib al-Āthār fī al-Tarājim wa'l-Akhbār* (Cairo: Maṭbaʿat Dār al-Kutub al-Miṣrīyah, 1997–1998), 1:220.

56. ʿUmar, *Kitāb Ḥāḍir al-Miṣrīyīn,* 247.

57. Ibid., 248–249.

58. For example, see Muḥammad Ḥilmī Zayn al-Dīn, *Maḍarr al-Zār* (Cairo: Maṭbaʿat Dīwām ʿUmūm al-Awqāf, 1903), 54.

59. See Samuli Schielke, "Snacks and Saints: Mawlid Festivals and the Politics of Festivity and Modernity in Contemporary Egypt" (PhD diss., Amsterdam University, 2006), pp. 57–58, 84–85.

60. ʿUmar, *Kitāb Ḥāḍir al-Miṣrīyīn,* 244. Most of Mubārak's discussion of *mawlids* is concentrated in volume 1 of *Al-Khiṭaṭ,* yet *mawlid* mentions and accounts of other popular festivals are scattered throughout the other volumes. See, for example, *Al-Khiṭaṭ,* 10:67 (ll. 1–8), 12:66 (ll. 31–32), 12:97 (ll. 18–19), 12:103 (ll. 25–30), and 18:34 (l. 14).

61. Michael Winter, *Society and Religion in Early Ottoman Egypt: Studies in the Writings of ʿAbd Al-Wahhāb Al-Shaʿrānī* (New Brunswick, NJ: Transaction, 2006), 138.

62. ʿAlī Mubārak's daily schedule during the late 1860s is described in his autobiography, *Ḥayātī,* p. 43. The busy official divided his day so that he would be able to attend to schooling and public works during the first part of the day and to railway issues, which required the better part of his day, from the afternoon until the evening.

63. Wen-chin Ouyang, "Fictive Mode, 'Journey to the West,' and Transformation of Space: ʿAli Mubarak's Discourses of Modernization," *Comparative Critical Studies* 4, no. 3 (2007): 331–358.

64. Mubārak, *ʿAlam al-Dīn,* 159–160.

65. Ibid, 162–163.

66. For the emergence of this ethnography within the social sciences in Egypt, see Omnia El Shakry, *The Great Social Laboratory: Subjects of Knowledge in Colonial and Postcolonial Egypt* (Stanford, CA: Stanford University Press, 2007).

67. See especially chapters 24–27.

68. E. W. Lane, *An Account of the Manners and Customs of the Modern Egyptians* (Cairo: American University of Cairo Press, 2003), 446–447.

69. Clot Bey, *Lamḥah ʿĀmmah ilā Miṣr,* 3:62.

70. Ibid., 63.

71. Ibid., 59–60.

72. Ibid., 60.

73. Notably, the term *ethnography* was probably first coined in Georges Bernard Depping's 1817 *Evening Entertainments; or, Delineations of the Manners and Customs of Various Nations* (London: N. Hailes, 1817), as a science that would offer an educational aid revealing the moral aspects of the "prejudices among people of the world" (p. vi). Lane's own *Manners and Customs* was published in 1836 as part of "The Library of Entertaining Knowledge," a popular alternative to "The Library of Useful Knowledge." During that year, the library published such books as *The Chinese: A Description of the Empire of China and Its Inhabitants.*

74. El Shakry, *The Great Social Laboratory,* 23–53.

75. Aḥmad Amīn, *Qāmūs al-ʿĀdāt waʾl-Taqālīd waʾl-Taʿābīr al-Miṣrīyah* (Cairo: Maktabat al-Nahḍah al-Miṣrīyah, 1982 [1953]), 112, 159.

76. Ibid., 117.

77. See Michael Gasper, *The Power of Representation: Publics, Peasants, and Islam in Egypt* (Stanford, CA: Stanford University Press, 2009).

78. Weber, "Science as a Vocation," 129–156.

79. See Talal Asad, *Formations of the Secular: Christianity, Islam, Modernity* (Stanford, CA: Stanford University Press, 2003), chapter 1.

80. Mubārak studied engineering in Egypt and France. See Mubārak, *Ḥayātī,* 15–16.

81. Mubārak, *ʿAlam al-Dīn,* 89–90.

82. E. De Leon, "How I Introduced the Telephone into Egypt," *Fraser's Magazine* 106 (1882): 522.

83. As Gyan Prakash showed for colonial India, modern science in Egypt, "staged to conquer ignorance and superstition, became enmeshed in the very effects that were meant for elimination." Prakash, *Another Reason,* 34.

84. Jamāl Badawī, *Miṣr min Nāfidhat al-Tārīkh* (Cairo: Dār al-Shurūq, 1994), 196–198; Muḥammad Sayyid Kīlānī, *Trām al-Qāhira* (Cairo: al-Hayʾa al-ʿĀmmah li-Quṣūr al-Thaqāfa, 2010), 14.

85. Ḥasan Tawfīq al-Dajawī, *Al-Risālah al-ʿIlmīyah fī al-Tirāmawīyah wa-Shurūḥihi wa-Kayfiyat Sayrihi* (Cairo: Maṭbaʿat al-Adab waʾl-mufid, 1314/1896), 2.

86. Winifred S. Blackman, *The Fellahin of Upper Egypt* (Cairo: American University of Cairo Press, 2000), 236.

87. *Al-Fukāhah,* October 31, 1928.

88. Printed in ʿAbd al-ʿAzīz al-Bishrī, *Al-Mukhtār* (Cairo: Dār al-Maʿārif, 1959), 188.

89. *Wādī al-Nīl,* January 30, 1916.

90. Blackman, *Fellahin,* 101–102.

91. Ibid., 237.

92. Muhammad Hussein Haikal, *Zaynab,* trans. John Mohammad Grinsted (London: Darf, 1989), 131.

93. Ibid.

94. Sayyid Quṭb, *A Child from the Village,* trans. and ed. John Calvert and William E. Shepard (Syracuse, NY: Syracuse University Press, 2004), 66.

95. Muḥammad ʿAbduh, *Tafsīr al-Qurʾān al-Ḥakim al-Mushtahar bi-Ism Tafsīr al-Manār* (Cairo: al-Manār, 1947), 8:366. Quṭb later rejected this view in *Fī Ẓilāl al-Qurʾān.* See Olivier Carré, Carol Artigues, and W. Shepard, *Mysticism and Politics: A Critical Reading of Fī Ẓilāl al-Qurʾān by Sayyid Quṭb* (1906–1966) (Leiden: Brill, 2003), 73.

96. *Al-Manār* 8 (1904): 159; Riḍā, *Fatāwā,* 1:117.

97. Ibid.

98. Ibid.

99. Periodicals such as *Al-Manār,* in which Riḍā's *fatwā*s were printed, were pioneering media for what Brinkley Messick has diagnosed as a change in the function of *fatwās*. From being private interchanges between questioner and mufti (normally on commercial or personal matters), *fatwā*s became a medium of public exchange. Many of the questioners writing to Riḍā directly commented on this new function of *Al-Manār,* indicating their desire to publish their question in the news-

paper so that a large readership would benefit from the answer (see, for example, *Al-Manār* 7 (1904): 416–417. See also B. Messick, *The Calligraphic State: Textual Domination and History in a Muslim Society* (Berkeley: University of California Press, 1992), chapter 7; and Jakov Skovgaard Petersen, *Defining Islam for the Egyptian State: Muftis and Fatwas of the Dār al-Iftā* (Leiden: Brill, 1997).

100. Umar Ryad, *Islamic Reformism and Christianity* (Leiden: Brill, 2009), 84.

101. On Abbate, see El Shakry, *The Great Social Laboratory,* 30–41. The following account is based on this section.

102. Muḥammad Farīd Wajdī, *Al-Madanīyah wa'l-Islām* (Cairo: al-Maṭba'a al-Hindīyah, 1901). Wajdī was another member of 'Abduh's circle, and Riḍā greatly admired his book, deeming it second only to 'Abduh's *Risālat al-Tawḥīd.* See *Al-Manār* 2: 110, 111.

103. Wajdī, *Al-Madanīyah wa'l-Islām,* 74–76.

104. For mentions of the *qarīnah,* see G. Sengers, *Women and Demons: Cult Healing in Islamic Egypt* (Leiden: Brill, 2003), 40–42.

105. *Al-Manār* 7 (1904): 702–707; Riḍā, *Fatāwā,* 1:252. On Riḍā's approach to positivism and materialism, see Daniel Stolz, "'By Virtue of Your Knowledge': Scientific Materialism and the Fatwās of Rashīd Riḍā," *Bulletin of the School of Oriental and African Studies* 75, no. 2 (June 2012): 223–247.

106. *Al-Manār* 6 (1903): 267.

107. *Al-Manār* 7 (1904): 702–707; Riḍā, *Fatāwā,* 1:255.

108. See, for example, "Electricity and Life," *Al-Ṣiḥāfah,* December 15, 1907. This association was deliberately and laboriously created by Edison as a business strategy. See Thomas Parke Hughes, *Networks of Power: Electrification in Western Society, 1880–1930* (Baltimore, MD: Johns Hopkins University Press, 1993).

109. See *Al-Ṣiḥāfah,* December 15, 1907; "Al-Ṭibb bi'l-Kahrabā'" (Medical Treatment with Electricity), *Ṭabīb al-'Ā'ilah,* April 15, 1896.

110. See, for example, *Al-Manār* 7 (1904): 54; Riḍā, *Fatāwā,* 1:86.

111. *Ṭawāli' al-Mulūk,* January 1907.

112. Ibid., October 1907.

113. *Al-Mufīd,* April 16, 1916.

114. Alison Winter, *Mesmerized: Powers of Mind in Victorian Britain* (Chicago: University of Chicago Press, 1998), chapter 8; P. van der Veer, *Imperial Encounters: Religion and Modernity in India and Britain* (Princeton, NJ: Princeton University Press, 2001), chapter 3; Janet Oppenheim, *The Other World: Spiritualism and Psychical Research in England,* 1850–1914 (Cambridge: Cambridge University Press, 1988).

115. Steven Connor, "The Machine in the Ghost: Spiritualism, Technology, and the 'Direct Voice,'" in *Ghosts: Deconstruction, Psychoanalysis, History,* ed. Peter Buse and Andrew Stott (New York: St. Martin's Press, 1999), 203–226.

116. Ibid., 211.

117. Zayn al-Dīn, *Maḍarr al-Zār,* 44–45.

118. K. Fahmy, "Modernizing Cairo," in *Making Cairo Medieval,* ed. N. AlSayyad (Lanham, MD: Lexington Books, 2005). See also Mubārak, *Al-Khiṭaṭ,* 1:98 (l. 26)–1:99 (l. 9), 1:99 (ll. 19–24), 1:103 (l. 33)–1:104 (l. 6).

119. See, for example, the Wizārat al-Dākhilīyah decree in *Tashrī'āt wa-Manshūrāt,* September 27, 1883.

120. *Al-Waṭan,* July 1895.

121. On the introduction of autopsy and its relation to law, see Khaled Fahmy, "The Anatomy of Justice: Forensic Medicine and Criminal Law in Nineteenth-Century Egypt," *Islamic Law and Society* 6, no. 2 (1999): 224–271.

122. The decree was published in *Wādī al-Nīl,* 16 Rabī' al-Ākhar 1287.

123. Joanna Bourke, *Fear: A Cultural History* (Berkeley, CA: Counterpoint Press, 2007), 33–37.

124. Ibid., 36.

125. Nadīm used the custom of quick burial in the early 1880s to demonstrate the difference between Easterners and Westerners. See *Al-Tankīt,* August 7, 1881.

126. *Al-Manār* 13 (1910): 100–102; Riḍā, *Fatāwā,* 851.

127. Ibid.

128. Leor Halevi, *Muhammad's Grave: Death Rites and the Making of Islamic Society* (New York: Columbia University Press, 2011), 202–207. See also Christian Lange, "Barzakh," *Encyclopedia of Islam* 3, ed. Gudrun Krämer et al. (Leiden: Brill, 2011).

129. Halevi, *Muhammad's Grave,* chapter 7.

130. 'Abd al-Raḥmān al-mashhūr bi-Jalāl al-Dīn al-Suyūṭī, *Kitāb KSharḥ al-Ṣudūr bi-Sharḥ Ḥāl al-Mawtā wa'l-Qubūr, wa-bi-Hāmishihi: Bushrā al-Ka'īb bi-Liqā' al-Ḥabīb* (Cairo: al-Maṭba'ah al-Maymanīyah, 1309/1892); *Sharḥ al-Ṣudūr bi-Sharḥ Ḥāl al-Mawtā wa'l-Qubūr* (Maṭba'at Dār Iḥyā' al-Kutub al-'Arabīyah, 1900); *Sharḥ al-Suḍūr bi-Sharḥ Ḥāl al-Mawtā wa'l-Qubūr* (Cairo 1329/1911).

131. Leah Kinberg, "Interaction between This World and the Afterworld in Early Islamic Tradition," *Oriens* 29/30 (1986): 285–308.

132. *Al-Manār* 8 (1904); Riḍā, *Fatāwā,* 1:112.

133. Al-Suyūṭī, *Sharḥ al-Ṣudūr* (Jeddah: Dār al-Madanī, 1985), 94–97.

134. See Lange, "Barzakh"; and Halevi, *Muhammad's Grave,* chapter 2.

135. Al-Suyūṭī, *Sharḥ al-Ṣudūr,* p. 144.

136. Fahmy, "The Anatomy of Justice," 236.

137. Ibid., 243.

138. Al-Hakīm, *Maze of Justice,* 87.

139. El Shakry, *The Great Social Laboratory,* especially chapter 1, on the notion of "survivals."

140. Muḥammad al-Muwayliḥī, *Ḥadīth 'Īsā ibn Hishām, aw Fatrah min al-Zamān, li-Munshi'ihi Muḥammad al-Muwayliḥī* (Cairo: al-Dār al-Qawmīyah li'l-Ṭibā'ah wa'l-Nashr, 1964); Roger Allen, *A Period of Time: A Study and Translation of Ḥadīth 'Īsā ibn Hishām by Muḥammad al-Muwayliḥī* (Reading: Ithaca Press, 1992).

141. This transcript of a lecture given in al-Azhar by Shaykh Yūsuf Effendi al-Dagawī introduced British admonitory discourses about lazy Egyptians to a new religious context. Printed in *Al-Majallah al-Miṣrīyah,* November 15, 1900.

142. *Al-Ṣiḥāfah,* March 26, 1905.

143. *Al-Muṣawwar,* November 1, 1902.

144. See, for example, *Al-Ṣiḥāfah,* March 19, 1905.

145. See Lisa Pollard, "Working by the Book: Constructing New Homes and the Emergence of the Modern Egyptian State under Muhammad Ali," in *Transitions in Domestic Consumption and Family Life in the Modern Middle East: Houses in Motion,* ed. Relli Shechter (New York: Palgrave Macmillan, 2003), 18. See also Mitchell, *Colonising Egypt,* 106–108.

146. Depping, *Evening Entertainments,* 2.

147. Mubārak, *ʿAlam al-Dīn,*7.

148. Sleeping hours and the appropriate time to go to bed became an important domain of measurement and scientific observation in the first decade of the twentieth century. Popular psychology journals such as *Al-Nafs al-Barīʾah* (The healthy spirit) mapped sleeping and dreaming patterns, discussing, for example, the specific moments in which dreaming occurred during a night's sleep. Oftentimes, discussions of sleep and rest were imbedded in more general concerns regarding the proper distribution of work and leisure deemed necessary for mental, physical, and even national health. See *Al-Muqtaṭaf* 35 (January 1909): 65. Articles in *Al-Sāʿah* linked sleeping eight hours a night to the ability to make a fortune. See, for example, August 12, 1923; and *Al-Nafs al-Barīʾah,* June 5, 1930.

149. On these columns, see Omnia El-Shakry, "Schooled Mothers and Structured Play: Child-Rearing in Turn of the Century Egypt," in *Remaking Women: Feminism and Modernity in the Middle East,* ed. Lila Abu-Lughod (Princeton, NJ: Princeton University Press, 1998); Lisa Pollard, *Nurturing the Nation: The Family Politics of Modernizing, Colonizing, and Liberating Egypt,* 1805–1923 (Berkeley: University of California Press, 2005); and Jacob, *Working Out Egypt.*

150. *Al-Muqtaṭaf* 28 (February 1903): 170. See also *Al-Muṣawwar,* January 23, 1925, 2, for a comparison of child rearing in Egypt and abroad. The article complains about the Egyptian habit of giving children to uneducated servants who fill their minds with talk of jinn and *ʿafārīt* and the "stories of Sitt Ḥasan."

151. Ibid.

152. See Blackman, *The Fellahin of Upper Egypt,* 235.

153. On whether Amin should be seen as a feminist, see L. Ahmed, *Women and Gender in Islam: Historical Roots of a Modern Debate* (New Haven, CT: Yale University Press, 1992).

154. Qasim Amin, *The Liberation of Women,* 26–27.

155. As Izutsu defined *taqwā.* See Toshihiko Izutsu, *God and Man in the Qurʾān* (Karachi: Royal Book, 2002), 234–238.

156. Jane Idleman Smith and Yvonne Yazbeck Haddad, *The Islamic Understanding of Death and Resurrection* (Oxford: Oxford University Press, 2002), 105–113.

157. Hirschkind, *Ethical Soundscape,* 185.

158. It was thought that the fear of *ʿafārīt* hampers children's sleep (*Al-Muqtaṭaf* 28 [February 1903]: 170). Another text suggested that children's irregular sleeping hours instilled the fear of *ʿafārīt* in them (see *Al-Muṣawwar,* March 27, 1925, p. 3;

and *Al-Sufur,* July 3, 1918, on servants and their role in raising the children of landlords). For Wajdī, superstitions increased one's susceptibility to cowardice, and at other times the *'afārīt* themselves were deemed responsible for children's fear and nightmares. If a child suffered from bad dreams or sleepwalked, this was taken to indicate that an *'ifrīt* had entered his body (see Blackman, *The Fellahin of Upper Egypt,* 237).

159. See Charles Turner, *Modernity and Politics in the Work of Max Weber* (New York: Routledge, 1992), 126n33, for another possible reading of Weber's disenchantment thesis in tandem with Adorno and Horkheimer.

160. Schielke, *Snacks and Saints,* 38.

CHAPTER 4

Epigraph: Jalāl al-Dīn Rūmī, "The Man Who Fancied He Saw the New Moon," in *Tales of Mystic Meaning: Selections from the Mathnawī of Jalāl-ud-Dīn Rūmī,* trans. Reynold Alleyne Nicholson (Oxford: Oneworld, 1995), 27.

1. For a history of the Arab press, see A. Ayalon, *The Press in the Arab Middle East: A History* (Oxford: Oxford University Press, 1995).

2. I am grateful to Michael Cook for suggesting this analogy.

3. There was one textual genre, astronomy, in which the Coptic calendar had a high status, and this was the genre in which calendar and timekeeping were traditionally studied.

4. According to Mikhail Bakhtin, a chronotope is a spatiotemporal matrix that defines a narrative. See M. Bakhtin, *The Dialogic Imagination: Four Essays,* ed. Michael Holquist, trans. Caryl Emerson and Michael Holquist (Austin: University of Texas Press, 1981).

5. On the connection between the daily schedule and the monthly calendar, see Zerubavel, *Hidden Rhythms.*

6. B. Van Dalen et al., "Ta'rīkh," in *The Encyclopedia of Islam,* 2nd ed. (Leiden: Brill, 1955–2005).

7. See 'Abd al-Raḥmān al-Jabartī, *Napoleon in Egypt: Al-Jabartī's Chronicle of the First Seven Months of the French Occupation,* 1798, trans. Shmuel Moreh (Princeton, NJ: M. Wiener, 2004), 49.

8. See *Wādī al-Nīl,* 1 Ṣafar 1287, on these changes.

9. On the culture of book copying, see N. Hanna, *In Praise of Books: A Cultural History of Cairo's Middle Class, Sixteenth to the Eighteenth Century* (Cairo: American University in Cairo Press, 2004).

10. According to al-Jabartī—see *Napoleon in Egypt,* 27.

11. According to Joseph Marie Moiret—see J. M. Moiret, *Memoirs of Napoleon's Egyptian Expedition,* 1798–1801, ed. and trans. Rosmary Brindle (London: Greenhill Books, 2001), 42.

12. Between 1822 and 1842, three such calendars were printed in Būlāq. See J. Heyworth-Dunne, "Printing and Translations under Muḥammad 'Alī of Egypt:

The Foundation of Modern Arabic," *Journal of the Royal Asiatic Society of Great Britain and Ireland,* no. 3 (July 1940): 325–349.

13. For example, in a decree launching a wave of reforms in the printing house during 1860, its performance is measured vis-à-vis foreign printing houses. See Sāmī, *Taqwīm al-Nīl,* 1:356–357; Lane, *An Account of the Manners and Customs,* 226–227.

14. Hanna, *In Praise of Books,* 94–6.

15. ʿAbd al-Raḥmān al-Jabartī, *Al-Jabartī's History of Egypt,* ed. Jane Hathaway (Princeton, NJ: Markus Wiener, 2006), 1:276, 2:298, 2:279–290. See also Hanna, *In Praise of Books,* 90.

16. See Ibn Baṭūṭah, *Kitāb Riḥlat Ibn Baṭūṭah al-Musammāh Tuḥfat al-Nuẓẓār fī Gharāʾib al-Amṣār wa-ʿAjāʾib al-Asfār* (Cairo: Maṭbaʿat Wādī al-Nīl, 1287 (–1288) [1870–1871]).

17. The agenda of reintroducing the classics of Arabic literature in print form was avidly promoted by al-Ṭahṭāwī during this period. See A. Hourani, *Arabic Thought in the Liberal Age,* 1798–1939 (Cambridge: Cambridge University Press, 1983), 72.

18. *Wādī al-Nīl,* 10 Muḥarram 1286.

19. J. Fabian, *Time and the Other: How Anthropology Makes its Object* (New York: Columbia University Press, 2002).

20. E. Povinelli, "Radical Worlds: The Anthropology of Incommensurability and Inconceivability," *Annual Review of Anthropology* 30 (October 2001): 327–328.

21. Van Dalen et al, "Taʾrīkh."

22. An example of such an almanac is printed in S. M. Zwemer, "The Clock, the Calendar, the Koran," *Moslem World* 3 (1913): 270.

23. Sāmī, *Taqwīm al-Nīl,* 3:1251.

24. Mubārak, *Ḥayātī,* 57.

25. Le Goff, "Merchant Time and Church's Time in the Middle Ages," 29–42. For a critique of this thesis, see Gerhard Dohrn-van Rossum, *History of the Hour: Clocks and Modern Temporal Orders,* trans. Thomas Dunlap (Chicago: University of Chicago Press, 1996), 138–71.

26. See "Al-Sāʿāt al-ʿArabīyah waʾl-Ajnabīyah," *Al-Muqtaṭaf* 52 (1918): 128; and "Al-Sāʿāh al-ʿArabīyah waʾl-Ifranjīyah," *Al-Muqtaṭaf* 32 (1907): 132.

27. See, for example, *Wādī al-Nīl,* September 16, 1870.

28. K. Baedeker, *Egypt: Handbook for Travelers* (Leipsig: K. Baedeker, 1902), lxvii.

29. See the explanation in *Al-Hilāl,* November 1, 1902.

30. See, for example, *Al-Hilāl,* November 1, 1902, and November 15, 1901.

31. Nādīyah al-Sanhūrī and Tawfīq al-Shāwī, eds., *Al-Sanhūrī min Khilāl Awrāqihi al-Shakhṣīyah* (Cairo: Dar al-Shurūq, 2005), 54. The word *Mīlādī* denotes the birth of Christ.

32. Other examples are Ḥasan al-Bannā's father (a watch repairer)—see Jamāl al-Bannā, *Khiṭābāt Ḥasan al-Bannā al-Shābb ilā Abīhi: Maʿ Tarjamah Musahhabah wa-Muwaththaqah li-Ḥayāt wa-ʿAmal al-Wālid al-Shaykh Aḥmad al-Bannā* (Cairo:

Dār al-Fikr al-Islāmī, 1990); Muṣṭafā Kāmil's father (an engineer who built railway stations)—see ʿAlī Fahmī Kāmil, *Muṣṭafá Kāmil Bāshā fī Thalāthah wa-Arbaʿīn Rabīʿ: Sīratuhu wa-Aʿmāluhu min Khuṭab wa-Aḥādīth wa-Rasāʾil Siyāsīyah wa-ʿUmrānīyah* (Cairo: Maṭbaʿat al-Liwāʾ, 1908); and Tawfīq al-Ḥakīm's father—see Tawfīq al-Ḥakīm, *The Prison of Life,* trans. Pierre Cachia (Cairo: American University in Cairo Press, 1992), 140. See also Jacob, *Working Out Egypt,* 55, 142.

33. Galāl Amīn, *Whatever Happened to the Egyptians? Changes in Egyptian Society from 1950 to the Present* (Cairo: American University in Cairo Press, 2000).

34. Cromer, *Modern Egypt,* 152.

35. B. Anderson, *The Specter of Comparisons: Nationalism, Southeast Asia and the World* (London: Verso, 1998), 69.

36. Abdelfattah Kilito, *Thou Shalt Not Speak My Language,* trans. Waïl S. Hassan (Syracuse, NY: Syracuse University Press, 2008), 8–9.

37. Asad, *Formations of the Secular,* 205–257.

38. Stanley Lane-Poole, *Studies in a Mosque* (London: Eden, Remington, 1883), 101; and Cromer, *Modern Egypt,* 134.

39. *Al-Manār* 6 (1903): 705; Riḍā, *Fatāwā,* 1:45.

40. See Zayn al-ʿĀbidīn Shams al-Dīn Najm, *Būr Saʿīd: Tārīkhuha wa-Taṭawwuruha Mundhu Nashʾatihā* 1859 *Ḥatā ʿĀm* 1882 (Cairo: al-Hayʾa al-ʿĀmma al-Miṣriyya liʾl-Kitāb, 1987, 94.

41. *Al-Manār* 6 (1903): 862; Riḍā, *Fatāwā,* 1:67.

42. Ahmad Dallal makes a similar argument about how the nation-state framed Riḍā's legal thought. See "Appropriating the Past: Twentieth-Century Reconstruction of Pre-Modern Islamic Thought," *Islamic Law and Society* 7, no. 1 (2000): 357.

43. See *Al-Manār* 7 (1904): 575–576.

44. Shaykh Muḥammad Bakhīt al-Muṭīʿī, *Kitāb Irshād Ahl al-Millah ilā Ithbāt al-Ahillah* (Beirut: Dār Ibn Ḥazm, 2000), 144–169.

45. Al-Muṭīʿī appended al-Subkī's manuscript on the verification of Hijrī months in printed form to his own guide. See Taqī al-Dīn Al-Subkī, *Kitāb al-ʿIlm al-Manshūr fī Ithbāt al-Shuhūr* (Cairo: Maṭbaʿat Kurdistān al-ʿIlmīyah, 1329 A.H. [1911]).

46. Probably Aḥmad Mūsā al-Zarqāwī, author of *Al-Adillah al-Islāmiyyah ʿAlā Taḥarruk al-Kurah al-Arḍīyah* (Cairo: Maṭbaʿat al-Hilāl, 1913).

47. S. W. Zwemer, "The Clock, the Calendar, and the Koran," *Moslem World* 3 (1913): 262–274.

48. Aḥmad Muḥammad Shākir, *Awāʾil al-Shuhūr al-ʿArabīyah: Hal Yajūz Shar ʿAn ʿIthbātuha biʾl-Ḥisāb al-Falakī?* (Giza: Maktabat Ibn Taymīyah, 1986), 3–4.

49. E. Moosa, "Shaykh Ahmad Shakir and the Adoption of a Scientifically-Based Lunar Calendar," *Islamic Law and Society* 5, no. 1 (1998): 69.

50. *Al-Waqāʾiʿ al-Miṣrīyah,* 23 Rabīʿ al-Awwal / July 25, 1867; see also Sāmī, *Taqwīm,* 2:713.

51. Sāmī, *Taqwīm,* 2:713.

52. G. Storey, *Reuters: The Story of a Century of News-Gathering* (New York: Crown, 1951), 95.

53. Allocating to it 20,000 francs a year. See Sāmī, *Taqwīm,* 2:782.

54. Sāmī, *Taqwīm,* 1:240

55. *Wādī al-Nīl,* 18 Jumādā al-Ūlā 1287.

56. Ibid., May 9, 1870.

57. Ibid., December 29, 1870.

58. D. Read, *The Power of News: The History of Reuters,* 2nd ed. (Oxford: Oxford University Press, 1999), 18.

59. See *Al-Tankīt wa'l-Tabkīt,* June 6, 1881.

60. Ibrāhīm ʿAbduh, *Jarīdat al-Ahrām, Tārīkh wa-Fann* 1875–1964 (Cairo: Muʾassasat Sijill al-ʿArab, 1964), 23.

61. Storey, *Reuters,* 95.

62. "Gisborne Concession for Landlines in Egypt, 27th February 1856," in *Egyptian Telegraph Agreements* (ESR, 1927), 6. A similar clause also appears in other telegraph agreements. See FO 881/4979x for a similar stipulation in 1884. In 1866, the British Consulate in Alexandria requested the Foreign Office to include the town of Port Said in its contract with the British telegraph company. According to this arrangement, all British consular telegraphic communication between Alexandria, Cairo, and Suez was conducted free of charge. Telegraphers automatically stamped such telegrams "Consular" instead of "Paid" and gave them the highest priority. Communication with Port Said, by contrast, was not included in this arrangement. Without a stipulation in which the route defined the category of the telegram, telegraphers resorted to reading the telegrams to and from Port Said and deciding whether they were "consular" or "private" based on their content. The telegram's substance, not the identity of its sender or recipient, determined its category, and hence its speed. See FO 78/1941.

63. This is discussed in chapter 6.

64. *Tashrīʿāt wa-Manshūrāt,* 1880–1882 (1), pp. 81, 227–228.

65. The date of the decree stipulating the transmission of these daily reports reveals the temporal (in)commensurability this chapter explores. In was published in *Tashrīʿāt wa-Manshūrāt,* 1880–1882 (1) on 28 Shaʿbān 1298, according to the Ministry of Public Works calendar, and on July 25, 1881, according to the calendar used by the railway and telegraphs authority.

66. *Tashrīʿāt wa-Manshūrāt,* 1880–1883, p. 69.

67. Ibid., 1880–1882 (1), pp. 81, 227–228.

68. Manshūr Niẓārat al-Ashghāl no. 28 from 23 Ramaḍān 1298, August 18, 1881, in ibid. (2).

69. "*Tilighrāf,*" decree from April 12, 1880, in *Qāmūs al-Idārah wa'l-Qaḍāʾ,* 662.

70. *Tashrīʿāt wa-Manshūrāt,* 1880–1882 (1), pp. 81, 227–228.

71. Ibid. See also Qarār Majlis al-Nuẓẓār no. 15, 23 Rabīʿ al-Ākhir 1298.

72. *Tashrīʿāt wa-Manshūrāt,* 1880–1883, p. 70, 11 Shawwāl 1300.

73. Ibid.

74. Ibid.

75. "*Tilighrāf,*" October 21, 1884, in Jallād, *Qāmūs al-Idārah.*

76. *Tashrīʿāt wa-Manshūrāt,* 1892, p. 456.

77. Ibid., 1880–1882 (1), p. 81.

78. Ibid.

79. See, for example, ibid., 1880–1883, pp. 409–410.

80. In 1880 the Criminal Law was changed to allow meting out harsh sentences to people tampering with the telegraph poles and wires. Jallād, *Qāmūs al-Idārah,* 662.

81. See *Tashrī'āt wa-Manshūrāt,* 1884, p. 37.

82. See ibid., 1890, pp. 659, 668–670.

83. *Al-Barīd,* June 26, 1895.

84. *Tashrī'āt wa-Manshūrāt,* 1891, pp. 217, 225–234, 569–575.

85. Subscription fares appeared on the header of every newspaper.

86. *Tashrī'āt wa-Manshūrāt,* May 19, 1889, p. 414.

87. Ibid.

88. Baedeker, *Egypt,* xxxiii.

89. On the importance of colloquial Arabic during this period, see Ziad Fahmy, *Ordinary Egyptians.*

90. Ṭāhā Ḥusayn, *Ḥāfiẓ wa-Shawqī,* 4th ed. (Cairo, 1958), 4–5.

91. Ṭāhā Ḥusayn, "Fī al-jaw," *Al-Risālah,* January 8, 1934, p. 404.

92. *Wādī al-Nīl,* 3 Rabī' al-Awwal 1287.

93. Ziad Fahmy, *Ordinary Egyptians,* 74.

94. Niloofar Haeri, *Sacred Language, Ordinary People: Dilemmas of Culture and Politics in Egypt* (New York: Palgrave Macmillan, 2003).

95. See Samah Selim, *The Novel and the Rural Imaginary in Egypt,* 1880–1985 (New York: Routledge Curzon, 2004), 25; 'Abd al-'Azīz 'Abd al-Majīd, *The Modern Arabic Story: Its Emergence, Development, and Form* (Cairo, Dār al-Ma'ārif, 1956); S. Hafez, *The Genesis of Arabic Narrative Discourse* (London: Saqi Books, 1993), 120–129; S. Sheehi, *Foundations of Modern Arab Identity* (Gainesville: University Press of Florida, 2004), 112.

96. The following description is based on 'Alī al-Ḥadīdī, *'Abdallah al-Nadīm: Khaṭīb al-Waṭanīyah* (Cairo: al-Mu'assasah al-Miṣrīyah al-'Āmmah, n.d.), 14–46.

97. *Al-Tankīt wa'l-Tabkīt,* June 6, 1881, quoted in Selim, *The Novel,* 32.

98. For a new appreciation of al-Nadīm's language reform, see John C. Baskerville, Jr., "From Tahdhiib al-Amma to Tahmiish al-Ammiyya: In Search of Social and Literary Roles for Standard and Colloquial Arabic in Late 19th Century Egypt" (PhD diss., University of Texas at Austin, 2009).

99. See Peter Gran, *Islamic Roots of Capitalism: Egypt,* 1760–1840 (Austin: University of Texas Press, 1979), 155–159.

100. *Al-Tankīt wa'l-Tabkīt,* September 4, 1881.

101. Ibid., June 6, 1881. See also Ziad Fahmy, *Ordinary Egyptians,* 82.

102. Mūsā, *The Education of Salāma Mūsā,* 38.

103. Salāmah Mūsā, "Al-Lughah al-Fuṣhah wa'l-Lughah al-'Āmmīyah," *Al-Hilāl,* Sept. 1, 1926: 1073–1077.

104. *Al-Nīl,* January 2, 1892, and January 5, 1892.

105. Ibid., January 2, 1892.

106. Ibid.

107. Ibid., January 9, 1892.

108. Ibid.

109. The following description is based on ibid.

110. Ibid., January 11, 1892.

111. Salīm Khalīl al-Naqqāsh, *Misr lil-Misriyin* (Alexandria: Maṭbaʿat Jarīdat al-Maḥrūsah, 1884), 6–8.

CHAPTER 5

Epigraphs: A. Lyttelton, ed., *Italian Fascisms, From Pareto to Gentile* (London: Jonathan Cape, 1973), p. 209; M. Bayram al-Tūnisī, *Al-Aʿmāl al-Kāmilah* (Cairo: al-Hayʾah al-Miṣrīyah al-ʿĀmmah liʾl-Kitāb, 1976), 3:51–52.

1. According to the Google Ngram phrase-usage graphing tool, between 1905 and 1935, the term *age of speed* climbs by about 300 percent.

2. A series of articles in that spirit appeared in *Al-Tilighrāfāt al-Jadīdah* in June 1899. See also al-Ḥaddād, "Ḥubb al-Surʿah," 202–206; F. A. ʿAbd al-Waḥīd, *Taṭawwur al-Naql waʾl-Muwāṣalāt al-Dākhilīyah fī Miṣr fī ʿAhd al-Iḥtilāl al-Bariṭānī,* 1882–1914 (Cairo: al-Hayʾah al-Miṣrīyah al-ʿĀmmah liʾl-Kitāb, 1989); and *Al-Hilāl,* August 1930, p. 1162, where Tawfīq Dūs, Egyptian minster of transportation, used these terms. The problem of speed was addressed in almost every issue of the motor vehicle magazine *Al-Otombīl* in 1928. On the "age of speed" and the history of aviation in Egypt, see Yoav Di-Capua, "Common Skies Divided Horizons: Aviation, Class and Modernity in Early Twentieth Century Egypt," *Journal of Social History* 41, no. 4 (Summer 2008): 917–942.

3. This view of modernity usually traces its origins to Georg Simmel's 1903 "The Metropolis and Mental Life," based on which Siegfried Kracaur, Walter Benjamin, and others developed a neurological conception of modernity. For a useful introduction, see Ben Singer, "Modernity, Hyperstimulus, and the Rise of Popular Sensationalism," in *Cinema and the Invention of Modern Life,* ed. Leo Charney and Vanessa Schwartz (Berkeley: University of California Press, 1995), 72–103.

4. Sayyid Quṭb, "Al-ʿĀlam Yajrī," *Al-Risālah,* September 15, 1933, pp. 12–13.

5. *Al-Majallah al-Miṣrīyah,* January 1, 1902; see, for example, *Ḍiyāʾ al-Sharq,* May 1, 1908; *Ḍiyāʾ al-Sharq,* May 4, 1908; *Ḍiyāʾ al-Sharq,* May 20, 1908.

6. "Our Jobs and Their Effect on Our Personal Lives," *Egyptian State Railways Magazine,* February 1932.

7. Ibid.

8. See, for example, Ḥaddād, "Ḥubb al-Surʿah."

9. Quṭb, "Al-ʿĀlam Yajrī," 13.

10. Ibid.

11. On indolence and the Egyptian character, see Mitchell, *Colonising Egypt,* 104–114.

12. See R. Bulliet, *The Camel and the Wheel* (New York: Columbia University Press, 1990), 10.

13. See, for example, a poem addressing this feature of trams in *Al-Muqaṭṭam,* February 18, 1914, quoted in Kīlānī, *Trām al-Qāhirah,* 97.

14. Bayram al-Tunisi, "Mudīr al-Trām," in *Al-Aʿmāl al-Kāmilah,* 4:65–66.

15. This is increasingly the case even in non-Western settings. For an account of changes in timekeeping in the Ottoman Empire, see Avner Wishnitzer, *Reading Clocks,* Alla Turca (Chicago: Chicago University Press, forthcoming). See also Fred Cooper, "Colonizing Time: Work Rhythms and Labor Conflict in Colonial Mombassa," in *Colonialism and Culture,* ed. Nicholas B. Dirks (Ann Arbor: University of Michigan Press, 1992), 209–247; Prathama Banerjee, *Politics of Time: 'Primitives' and History-Writing in a Colonial Society* (New Delhi: Oxford University Press, 2006).

16. See P. Virilio, *Speed and Politics: An Essay on Dromology,* trans. Mark Polizzotti (New York: Semiotexte, 1986); J. T. Schnapp, "Crash (Speed as Engine of Individuation)," *Modernism/Modernity* 6, no. 1 (1999): 1–49.

17. See, for example, *Ḍiyāʾ al-Sharq,* May 6, 1908.

18. *Al-Sharq,* June 10, 1896, quoted in Kīlānī, *Trām,* 76–77 (my translation).

19. *Al-Ṣiḥāfah,* July 2, 1905.

20. Ibid., July 23, 1905.

21. Sayyid Quṭb, "Fī Mustaqbal Āmāl wa-Furaṣ: Muhayyaʾah li-Istiqlāl," *Majallat al-Shuʾūn al-Ijtimāʿīyah* 4 (January 1943): 30, quoted in John Calvert, *Sayyid Qutb and the Origins of Radical Islamism* (New York: Columbia University Press, 2010), 89.

22. Kīlānī, *Trām,* 14.

23. *Al-Muqaṭṭam,* August 1, 1896, quoted in Kīlānī, *Trām,* 4, and in al-Shaykh Ḥasanayn Makhlūf, *Mudhakkirāt al-Shaykh Ḥasanayn Makhlūf,* 4–15, http://modernegypt.bibalex.org/DocumentViewer/TextViewer.aspx?w = 1258&h = 902&type = document&id = 20822&s = 1, my translation.

24. "Cairo Tramway Company," January 5, 1928, FO 141/817.

25. See *Ifādah min al-Misyū Paul Ilā Niẓārat al-Ashghāl al-ʿUmūmīyah bi-Shaʾn Minḥat Imtiyāz bi-Iqāmat Khuṭūṭ al-Trāmway bi-Madīnat al-Qāhirah,* December 4, 1982, Dār al-Wathāʾiq al-Qawmīyah, OuD no. 0075–008605–0001; "Tramways in Cairo," in *Paving and Municipal Engineering* 5 (November 1893): 228; and "Cairo—Who Will Get There First?," *Electrical Engineer* 16 (October 25, 1893): 377.

26. For the concession, see "Acte de concession de tramways pour la ville du Caire" at http://modernegypt.bibalex.org/DocumentViewer/TextViewer.aspx?w = 1258&h = 902&type = document&id = 5682&s = 1; al-Dajawī, *Al-Risālah al-ʿIlmīyah fī al-Trāmawīyah wa-Shurūḥihi wa-Kayfīyat Sayrihi,* 15; for the confiscation acts, see *Al-Waṭan,* August 9, 1895.

27. See Janet L. Abu-Lughod, *Cairo:* 1001 *Years of the City Victorious* (Princeton, NJ: Princeton University Press, 1971), 138.

28. Kīlānī, *Trām,* 14; Janet Abu-Lughod, *Cairo,* 133–137.

29. André Raymond, *Cairo,* trans. Willard Wood (Cambridge, MA: Harvard University Press, 2000), 324.

30. William Hausman, Peter Hertner, and Mira Wilkins, *Global Electrification: Multinational Enterprise and International Finance in the History of Light and*

Power, 1878–2007 (Cambridge: Cambridge University Press, 2008), 104. For Belgian investment in Egypt, see Robert Tignor, "The Economic Activities of Foreigners in Egypt, 1920–1950: From Millet to Haute Bourgeoisie," *Comparative Studies in Society and History* 22, no. 3 (July 1980): 416–449.

31. Hausman, Hertner, and Wilkins, *Global Electrification,* 102–103.

32. Kīlānī, *Trām,* 77, 30.

33. W. Garstin, *Report upon the Administration of the Public Works Department in Egypt for* 1904 (Cairo: National Printing Department, 1905), 281.

34. W. Garstin, *Report upon the Administration of the Public Works Department in Egypt for* 1903 (Cairo: National Printing Department, 1904), 323–324.

35. See Barak, "Scraping the Surface."

36. Janet Abu-Lughod, *Cairo,* chapter 8.

37. Kīlānī, *Trām,* 16.

38. J. Chalcraft, *The Striking Cabbies of Cairo and Other Stories: Crafts and Guilds in Egypt,* 1863–1914 (Albany: SUNY Press, 2004), 135.

39. Khaled Fahmy, "An Olfactory Tale of Two Cities: Cairo in the Nineteenth Century," in *Historians in Cairo: Essays in Honor of George Scanlon,* ed. Jill Edwards (Cairo: American University Press, 2002), 155–202.

40. Janet Abu-Lughod, *Cairo,* 133; Raymond, *Cairo,* 324.

41. See, for example, *Al-Ṣiḥāfah,* July 21, 1907, mentioning previous complaints.

42. N. Al-Sayyad, I. A. Bierman, and N. Rabbat, eds, *Making Cairo Medieval* (Lanham, MD: Lexington Books, 2005).

43. See *Al-Muqaṭṭam,* June 17, 1911, and February 22, 1912, quoted in Kīlānī, *Trām,* 35–36.

44. Heliopolis's relation to Cairo was a contentious matter. In 1908, when the Egyptian government demanded payment of property tax from the Heliopolis Company, its claim was rejected on the grounds that a foreign company was exempt from such land taxation under the capitulations—the notorious tax exemptions granted to foreigners throughout the Ottoman Empire. A year later the government extended the borders of Cairo to include Heliopolis—until that time an independent town—in its metropolitan area and repeated the demand for taxation. It was rejected again. The matter was settled only in 1912 by the Mixed Court of Appeal, in a well-publicized ruling in favor of the government. See Mark S. W. Hoyle, "The Mixed Courts of Egypt 1906–1915," *Arab Law Quarterly* 2, no. 2 (May 1987): 166–184.

45. For a history of the timeline and of conceiving of time as a line, see Daniel Rosenberg and Anthony Grafton, *Cartographies of Time: A History of the Timeline* (New York: Princeton Architectural Press, 2010).

46. Taha Hussien, *A Man of Letters,* trans. Mona El-Zayyat (Cairo: American University in Cairo Press, 1994), 11.

47. See *Al-Ṣiḥāfah,* July 23, 1905; Kīlānī, *Trām,* 30–31; and Janet Abu-Lughod, *Cairo,* 135–136.

48. Tignor, "The Economic Activities of Foreigners," 428.

49. Robert Tignor, "Nationalism, Economic Planning, and Development Projects in Interwar Egypt," *International Journal of African Historical Studies* 10, no. 2 (1977): 185–208, 188.

50. Kīlānī, *Trām,* 39, 102.

51. During the last decade of the nineteenth century, the number of cafes, bars, and gaming rooms in Cairo more than tripled—from 2,316 to 7,475. According to Egypt's official census, a similar increase is detectable in the number of workers in such institutions. In 1907 there were 11,772 males and 301 females employed in hotels, coffeehouses, restaurants, and bars. By 1917 this number increased to 25,433 and 1,777 respectively. See Mitchell, *Colonising Egypt,* 116; and Maṣlaḥat ʿUmūm al-Iḥṣāʾ, *The Census of Egypt Taken in* 1917 (Cairo: Government Press, 1920–21), 2:386.

52. For example, in 1898 jurist and public intellectual Aḥmad Fatḥī Zaghlūl blamed coffeehouses for spreading indolence and stifling the ability to think and act creatively. See Aḥmad Fatḥī Zaghlūl, *Sirr Taqaddum al-Inkilīz,* 20.

53. The tramway extended the Egyptian railway into the urban spheres of Cairo, Alexandria, and Port Said, at the same time changing patterns of horse-drawn carriage movement. There were various interfaces between these systems. Already in 1895, the ESR started cooperating with the Suez Canal Company, which operated a tram line in Port Said. Passengers could buy train tickets that also covered the tram ride and vice versa. See *Al-Barīd,* April 20, 1895. Gradually, tramways and railways were connected also by donkey boys or cabbies who waited for passengers outside central train or tram stations. In this respect, trains and trams contributed to the proliferation of preexisting modes of transportation. See Garstin, 1904 *Report,* 282, on the interface between the Cairo tramway and the ESR central station in Bāb al-Ḥadīd. See *Al-Waṭan,* August 9, 1895, on connections of the tramway and railway in Port Said.

54. A. W. Meyers, "The Trams of the World," *Cassell's Magazine* 8 (1901): 561; Garstin, 1904 *Report,* 279.

55. Maḥmūd Khayrat, *Al-Marʾah bayn al-Māḍī waʾl-Ḥāḍir* (Cairo: Idārat Majallat al-Ikhāʾ, 1928), 23.

56. See Beth Baron, "Unveiling in Early Twentieth Century Egypt: Practical and Symbolic Considerations," in *Middle Eastern Studies* 25, no. 3 (July 1989): 370–386, 378.

57. Egyptian feminist Hudā al-Shaʿrāwī famously unveiled at the Cairo central train station after being convinced to do so onboard the train from Alexandria. Another feminist, Nabawīya Mūsā, recounted such conversations in trams. See Nabawīya Mūsā in Anwar al-Jundī, *Adab al-Marʾah al-ʿArabīyah* (Cairo, n.d.), 71, quoted in Baron, "Unveiling," 381.

58. See Kīlānī, *Trām,* 23.

59. *Al-Muqaṭṭam,* August 19, 1898, quoted in Kīlānī, *Trām,* 22–23.

60. Baron, "Unveiling," 376.

61. I. ʿAbd al-Quddūs, "I Am Free," in *I Am Free and Other Stories,* trans. Trevor J. Le Gassick (Cairo: General Egyptian Book Organization, 1978), 127–223.

62. See Barak, "Scraping the Surface"; and Will Hanley, "Foreignness and Localness in Alexandria, 1880–1914" (PhD diss., Princeton University, 2007).

63. Barak, "Scraping the Surface," 195–196.

64. The company also announced that a third-class ticket in all lines would cost one *qirsh* (which was much cheaper than most cab rides) and promised that passengers would be able to transfer among lines without additional cost. *Al-Ittiḥād al-Miṣrī,* February 3, 1898.

65. Ibid., February 13, 1898.

66. See, for example, *Al-Tilighrāfāt al-Jadīdah,* June 29, 1899.

67. *Tashrī'āt wa-Manshūrāt,* 1899, pp. 45–51.

68. See Garstin, 1904 *Report,* 323–324, about a series of lethal electrocution accidents in Alexandria during 1901.

69. *Al-Ṣiḥāfah,* October 29, 1905.

70. Kīlānī, *Trām,* 92.

71. Like "The Electrical Tram" by Elias Hanikati, a poem describing chopped limbs that was published in *Al-Muqaṭṭam,* March 25, 1898, quoted in Kīlānī, *Trām,* 94.

72. See Singer, "Modernity," 80–83.

73. Barak, "Scraping the Surface," 195.

74. *Al-Muqaṭṭam,* August 30, 1896; and Kīlānī, *Tram,* 92.

75. See Singer, "Modernity," 80–83.

76. W. Garstin, *Report upon the Administration of the Public Works Department in Egypt for* 1905 (Cairo: National Printing Department, 1906), 35. Emphasis added.

77. P. E. H. Hair, "Death from Violence in Britain: A Tentative Secular Survey," *Population Studies* 25, no. 1 (March 1971): 5–24, 6.

78. Singer, "Modernity," 82.

79. *Al-Sharq,* December 26, 1896, quoted in Kīlānī, *Trām,* 93 (my translation).

80. *Al-Akhbār,* December 12, 1896, quoted in Kīlānī, *Trām,* 92 (my translation).

81. *Al-Ṣiḥāfah,* July 30, 1905.

82. *Al-Tilighrāfāt al-Jadīdah,* June 29, 1899.

83. Scott Molloy, *Trolley Wars: Streetcar Workers on the Line* (Washington, DC: Smithsonian Institution Press, 1996), 98–104.

84. Ibid.

85. Bayram al-Tunisi, "Mudīr al-Trām," in *Al-A'māl al-Kāmilah,* 4:65–66.

86. What was true in 1899 became all the more true in subsequent years. News items covering the 1908 tramway strike describe how difficult it was to move around the streets, which suddenly seemed packed with pedestrians, also citing the damage to businesses and the upkeep of public order. See, for example, *Al-Liwā',* November 20, 1908.

87. See *Al-Ṣiḥāfah,* July 2, 1905.

88. Garstin, 1904 *Report,* p. 279.

89. Ads for this brand of watches could be found in *Al-Ahrām* (see, for example, March 10, 1919) and *Al-Muqaṭṭam* (see August 24, 1923).

90. See Chalcraft, *Striking Cabbies.*

91. *Al-Khalā'a,* November 12, 1904, quoted in Kīlānī, *Tram,* 98–99.

92. Michel Foucault, *Discipline and Punish: The Birth of the Prison* (New York: Random House, 1977).

93. *Wādī al-Nīl,* January 18, 1916.

94. Ahmad Amin, *My Life: The Autobiography of an Egyptian Scholar, Writer, and Cultural Leader,* trans. Issa J. Boullata (Leiden: Brill Archive, 1978), 80.

95. Ibid.

96. Hanley, *Foreignness and Localness in Alexandria,* 66.

97. See *Al-Ṣiḥāfah,* July 30, 1905.

98. Indeed, whereas this translation is based on actual travel time when using the meter, the ticket is predicated on an impersonal calculus of average time.

99. *Wādī al-Nīl,* January 10, 1916.

100. D. Sladen, *Egypt and the English* (London: Hurst and Blackett, 1908).

101. Cromer, *Modern Egypt,* 421; Sladen, *Queer Things about Egypt,* 184.

102. *Al-Ṣiḥāfah,* July 21, 1907.

103. Kīlānī, *Tram,* 112–113.

104. Ibid., 92.

105. Martin Shaw Briggs, *Through Egypt in War Time* (London: T. Fisher Unwin, 1918), 39.

106. *Ḍiyā' al-Sharq,* May 14, 1908.

107. Ibid.

108. Ṭal'at Ḥarb, *Majmū'at Khuṭub* (Cairo, 1938), 3:63–67, quoted in Tignor, "Nationalism, Economic Planning, and Development Projects in Interwar Egypt," 188. See also R. Tignor, "The Egyptian Revolution of 1919: New Directions in the Egyptian Economy," *Middle East Studies* 12, no.3 (October 1976): 53–54.

109. *Taqrīr min Nāẓir al-Mālīyyah ilā Majlis al-Nuzzār 'An Dirāsat 'Aqd Ta'sīs Sharikat Trām al-Qāhirah,* DWQ, UoD no. 0075–008607–0006.

110. Kīlānī, *Trām,* 17.

111. FO 141/748.

112. Following al-'Adl's premature death, Forster described the beginning of their affair in a long love letter never meant to be read. He wrote it between 1922 and 1929, and it was finally published in 2004. See E. M. Forster, "Letter to Mohammed el Adl," in *Alexandria: A History and a Guide and Pharos and Pharillon,* ed. Miriam Allott (Cairo: American University in Cairo Press, 2004). Unless otherwise noted, the account here is based on this letter.

113. Forster to Florence Barger, October 16, 1917, quoted in M. Haag, *Alexandria: City of Memory* (New Haven, CT: Yale University Press, 2004), 32.

114. The courting continued into April and May, in accidental encounters, until one time al-'Adl asked Forster why Englishmen dislike Mohammadens so much. "They don't," said Forster. "They do, because I heard one soldier say to another in the tram 'That's a mosque for fucking (I beg your pardon) Mohammadens.'" But there was no time to settle the issue, and Forster got al-'Adl to give him his schedule.

115. See, for example, a series of articles in that spirit in *Al-Tilighrāfāt al-Jadīdah* in June 1899.

116. As we saw in the above 1899 *Al-Tilighrāfāt al-Jadīdah* article. See also *Al-Ṣiḥāfah*, July 2, 1905.

117. *Tashrī'āt wa-Manshūrāt*, 1900, pp. 243–247.

118. *Al-Kawkab*, October 16, 1905.

119. See, for example, *Al-Ṣiḥāfah*, July 2, 1905.

120. Ibid., July 30, 1905.

121. *Tashrī'āt wa-Manshūrāt*, 1899, pp. 45–51.

122. *Al-Ṣiḥāfah*, August 28, 1905.

123. Ibid July 30, 1905.

124. Bayram al-Tunisi, "Al-Trām," in *Al-A'māl al-Kāmilah*, 4:63–64.

125. See Philip Nicholas Furbank, *E. M. Forster: A Life* (New York: Harcourt Brace, 1994), 39. See also Hala Halim, "Forster in Alexandria: Gender and Genre in Narrating Colonial Cosmopolitanism," in *Hawwa* 4 (November 17, 2006): 237–273.

126. *Al-Ṣiḥāfah*, July 2, 1905.

127. See, for example, ibid., July 23, 1905.

128. *Majallat al-Dunyā al-Jadīdah*, October 28, 1904, quoted in Kīlānī, *Trām*, 139.

129. *Ḍiyā' al-Sharq*, May 6, 1908. Bayram al-Tunisi, "Mudīr al-Trām," in *Al-A'māl al-Kāmilah*, 65–66.

130. "Note on the Strike of the Cairo Electric Tramways," 1919, in FO 141/748.

131. *Al-Waqā'i' al-Miṣrīyah*, January 11, 1904.

132. *Ḍiyā' al-Sharq*, May 6, 1908.

133. *Mukātabah min Majlis Shūrā al-Qawānīn ilā Majlis al-Nuẓẓār bi-Sha'n Taklīf Sharikat al-Trām bi'Ittikhādh al-Asbāb al-Mūjibah li-Talāshī al-Aḥdāth allatī Talḥaq bi'l-Ahālī*, April 23, 1898, DWQ, UoD no. 0075–0086050003; *Mukātabah min Ra'īs Majlis al- Shūrā ilā Ra'īs Majlis al-Nuẓẓār Iqtirāḥ min 'Aḍw Madīnat al-Maḥrūsah 'an Talab Milaffāt al-Aḍrār al-Nāshi'ah 'An 'Arabāt al-Trām wa-'Arabāt al-Otombīl*, April 28, 1907, DWQ UoD no. 0075–016018–0001.

134. U. Beck, *Risk Society: Towards a New Modernity*, trans. Mark Ritter (London: Sage Publications, 1992), 21.

CHAPTER 6

Epigraph: Walter Benjamin, "Preparatory Notes to the 'Theses on the Philosophy of History,'" quoted in *Walter Benjamin and the Demands of History*, ed. M. Steinberg (Ithaca, NY: Cornell University Press, 1996), 92.

1. Karl Marx, "On Bruno Bauer's *On the Jewish Question* (1843)," in *The Broadview Anthology of Social and Political Thought: From Plato to Nietzsche*, ed. Andrew Bailey (Peterborough, Ontario: Broadview Press, 2008), 994.

2. Jonathan Wolff, "Karl Marx," in *The Stanford Encyclopedia of Philosophy*, Summer 2011 edition, ed. Edward N. Zalta, available at http://plato.stanford.edu/archives/sum2011/entries/marx/.

3. Beinin and Lockman, *Workers on the Nile;* Z. Lockman, "Imagining the Working Class: Culture, Nationalism, and Class Formation in Egypt, 1899–1914," *Poetics Today* 15, no. 2 (Summer 1994): 157–190.

4. Lockman, "Imagining the Working Class," 161.

5. Ilham Khuri-Makdisi, "Levantine Trajectories: The Formulation and Dissemination of Radical Ideas in and between Beirut, Cairo, and Alexandria, 1860–1914" (PhD diss., Harvard University, 2003), particularly chapter 4.

6. Ibid., p. 284.

7. See Omar, *Anglo-Egyptian Relations,* 278, on an 1867 strike by English train drivers fighting for increased compensation and lighter workloads.

8. Khuri-Makdisi, "Levantine Trajectories," 309.

9. Beinin and Lockman, *Workers on the Nile,* 57.

10. Chalcraft, *Striking Cabbies.*

11. As we saw in the previous chapter, the transition to collective action among the workers of the Cairo Tram Company was made possible by changes in the holding structure and stock distribution of the company, making individual subversion less legitimate (if not less pervasive).

12. Beinin and Lockman, *Workers on the Nile,* 57–61.

13. "[Workers] had accepted the categories of their employers and learned to fight back within them. They had learned their lesson, that time is money, only too well." Thompson, "Time, Work-Discipline, and Industrial Capitalism," 38.

14. Historians have shown that Thompson incorrectly identified the historical origins of time discipline, which predated industrialization, emerging in early modern Europe in spheres unrelated to the factory system. However, in Egypt clock time and modern capitalist technology were introduced together. For a critique of Thompson in the European context, see, for example, Sauter, "Clockwatchers and Stargazers."

15. *Al-Liwāʾ,* November 20, 1908.

16. Beinin and Lockman, *Workers on the Nile,* 61.

17. Khuri-Makdisi, "Levantine Trajectories," 306.

18. Beinin and Lockman, *Workers on the Nile,* 62.

19. Kīlānī, *Trām,* 66–68.

20. *Al-ʿĀlam,* August 1, 1911, quoted in Beinin and Lockman, *Workers on the Nile,* 63.

21. Beinin and Lockman, *Workers on the Nile,* 64.

22. *Al-Liwāʾ,* August 5, 1911, quoted in Lockman, "Imagining the Working Class," 177. The theme of technological coordination in the building of the Egyptian national home was not new; what was new was the identity of the participants in the project. Already in the first years of British military presence, protonationalists compared the Egyptian reaction to foreign occupation to the actions of a man unaware of the principles of engineering trying to rectify his house, only to be buried under its debris. Salīm Ḥalīl al-Naqqāsh, *Miṣr liʾl-Miṣrīyīn* (Alexandria: Maṭbaʿat Jarīdat al-Maḥrūsa, 1884), p. 6.

23. Khuri-Makdisi, "Levantine Trajectories," 307n66, and see also 315n92.

24. The water company relied on coal gas to fuel its steam pumps, while the railway relied on the company's water for boiler cooling, as did the electric company, whose energy powered the tram.

25. Khuri-Makdisi, "Levantine Trajectories," 317.

26. "Cairo Tramway Co. Relations with its Employees," FO 141/748.

27. Andrew Pickering, *The Mangle of Practice: Time, Agency, and Science* (Chicago: University of Chicago Press, 1995), 16.

28. *The Egyptian State Railways Magazine,* February 1932 (my translation).

29. Ibid.

30. *Wādī al-Nīl,* January 22, 1916.

31. Ibid., January 2, 1916.

32. Ibid., January 1, 1916. In this case, British alarm had much to rely on. Several months earlier, villagers in Minyā province uprooted the rail track near their village, causing the passing express train to derail, resulting in several deaths and many injuries. See *Al-Ahrām,* August 26, October 6, and November 27, 1915, discussed in N. Brown, *Peasant Politics in Modern Egypt: The Struggle against the State* (New Haven, CT: Yale University Press, 1990), 92.

33. *Wādī al-Nīl,* January 4, 1916.

34. Germany's submarine campaign in the Atlantic failed to stop U.S. oil imports to Britain and France, and eventually resulted in dragging the United States into the war, after the May 1915 sinking of the steamship *Lusitania.*

35. Podobnik, *Global Energy Shifts,* 69–71.

36. Great Britain, Dept. of Overseas Trade, "Report on Economic and Commercial Conditions in Egypt," 1920, p. 22.

37. *Wādī al-Nīl,* January 2, 1916.

38. Ibid., January 20, 1916.

39. Ibid., January 3, 1916.

40. Ibid., January 10, 1916.

41. G. A. Roush, ed., *The Mineral Industry: Its Statistics, Technology and Trade during* 1916 (London: McGraw-Hill, 1917), 142.

42. *Wādī al-Nīl,* January 4, 1916.

43. Ibid., January 10, 1916.

44. Ibid., January 22, 1916.

45. Ibid., January 20, 1916.

46. Ibid., January 30, 1916. In Cairo and Alexandria, electrical street illumination was provided by the municipal tram companies using coal-burning generators.

47. Latour, *Reassembling the Social,* 81.

48. *Popular Mechanics,* July 1918.

49. "Cottonseed News," in *Flour & Feed: Devoted to the Interests of the Flour and Feed Trade,* June 1918, p. 45.

50. Erez Manela, *The Wilsonian Moment: Self-Determination and the International Origins of Anticolonial Nationalism* (Oxford: Oxford University Press, 2007), 41.

51. See ibid.

52. "The President at the Peace Table," *Literary Digest* 59 (November 30, 1918): 14.

53. In April 1917, within a week after the United States entered the war, the president created a new organ tasked with war propaganda and with advertising his peace plan around the globe, the Committee on Public Information. Manela, *The Wilsonian Moment,* 48.

54. Ibid., 48–51.

55. "The Making of Common Will," *Century Illustrated Monthly Magazine* 103 (November 1921).

56. Erez Manela has shown how the "Wilsonian moment" simultaneously enveloped many places in the colonial world that responded to the powerful messages coming from the United States, igniting a wave of anticolonial revolts in 1919.

57. David Paull Nickles, *Under the Wire: How Telegraphy Changed Diplomacy* (Cambridge, MA: Harvard University Press, 2003), 2.

58. Alfred Dennis, "The Indian Problem and Imperial Politics," *Journal of Race Development* 1 (1910–1911): 187–209.

59. Sir Eldon Gorst, "Lord Cromer in Egypt," in *The Empire and the Century: A Series of Essays on Imperial Problems and Possibilities* (London: John Murray, 1905): 767.

60. J.M. Robertson, *House of Commons, Parliamentary Debates,* vol. 162, August 4, 1906, p. 1825.

61. Lord Milner comments on this state of affairs in the *Report of the Special Mission to Egypt* (London: London: H.M. Stationery Office, 1921), 9.

62. J. Terry, *The Wafd* 1919–1952*: Cornerstone of Egyptian Political Power* (Beirut: Third World Centre, 1982), 77.

63. Ibid., 79.

64. Milner, *Report of the Special Mission to Egypt,*13–14.

65. Terry, *The Wafd,* 90; Milner, *Report of the Special Mission to Egypt,* 13.

66. Abd al-ʿAẓīm Ramaḍān, *Taṭawwur al-Ḥarakah al-Waṭanīyah fī Miṣr,* 1918–1936 (Cairo: al-Hayʾa al-Miṣrīyah al-ʿĀmmah Liʾl-kitāb, 1998), 1:88–94.

67. Wingate to Balfour, telegram from Nov. 25, 1918, in *Documents Collected for the Information of the Special Mission,* 2:4.

68. Saʿd Zaghlūl, *Mudhakkirāt Saʿd Zaghlūl* (Cairo: al-Hayʾa al-Miṣrīyah al-ʿĀmmah Liʾl-kitāb, 1988–), 7:177.

69. The Bibliotheca Alexandrina has a large collection of petitions for the release the Dinshaway prisoners.

70. The ostensibly benign and licit nature of the gesture proved productive. Zaghlūl noted in his diary that one thing that favored the campaign with students was the fact that the Wafd did not call for demonstrations or any action that would threaten public safety, but would be satisfied simply with a signature. Saʿd Zaghlūl, *Mudhakkirāt,* 7:183.

71. Ibid., 7:177–9.

72. Terry, *Wafd,* 89.

73. Ibid., 86–87.

74. The intricate deal was quickly tailored and brokered telegraphically during the last months of that year among the British colonial officials in Egypt, the Foreign Office in London, the French, and the pro-British faction in the khedival family.

75. Telegram, Cheetham to Grey, December 8, 1914, in Great Britain, Foreign Office, *Reply to Charges Brought against British Troops by Egyptian Delegation in Paris during Egyptian Disturbances* (London, 1919), 1:136. The exchange of telegrams between August and December 1914 documenting the formation of this deal can be found in *Reply to Charges,* 1:95–143.

76. Fu'ād indeed seized the first opportunity he had and replaced *sultan* with *king* in 1922.

77. See James E. Baldwin, "Petitioning the Sultan in Ottoman Egypt," *Bulletin of the School of Oriental and African Studies* 75 (2012): 499–524.

78. Israel Gershoni and James P. Jankowski, *Egypt, Islam, and the Arabs: The Search for Egyptian Nationhood,* 1900–1930 (Oxford: Oxford University Press, 1986), 40–50.

79. Cheetham to Curzon, March 6, 1919, in *Documents Collected for the Information of the Special Mission,* p. 79.

80. See Manela, *The Wilsonian Moment,* 142, for telegrams in American archives; for telegrams housed in the Bibliotheca Alexandrina, see http://modernegypt.bibalex.org/Collections/Documents/DocumentsLucene.aspx.

81. See Ziad Fahmy, *Ordinary Egyptians,* 137–138, on Zaghlūl's telegram of February 16, 1919, to Wilson, intercepted by British intelligence. On January 13, 1919, Zaghlūl sent the first telegram (see Sa'd Zaghlūl, *Mudhakkirāt,* 9:21). A telegram from January 3, 1919, complained about two previous telegrams that were not acknowledged.

82. Sa'd Zaghlūl, *Mudhakkirāt,* 9:35.

83. Cheetham to Curzon, March 6, 1919, *Documents Collected for the Information of the Special Mission,* p. 79.

84. Allenby to Curzon, March 28, 1919, *Documents Collected for the Information of the Special Mission,* 2:112; Curzon to British Delegation in Paris, March 30, 1919, 2:116.

85. Manela, *The Wilsonian Moment,* 146–149.

86. Muḥammad Ḥusayn Haykal, *Mudhakkirāt fī al-Sīyāsah al-Miṣrīyah* (Cairo: Maktabat al-Nahḍah al-Miṣrīyah, 1951–1933), 1:81, quoted in Manela, *The Wilsonian Moment,* 149.

87. A memorandum sent by a group of Egyptian university students, quoted in Manela, *The Wilsonian Moment,* 150.

88. Allenby to Curzon, April 15, 1919, in *Documents Collected for the Information of the Special Mission,* 2:135.

89. The Residency of the British High Commissioner regularly received daily updates from the Public Security Department, including verbatim copies of telegrams and commentary on their contents. Many are filed in FO 141/780.

90. "Press Criticism of General Allenby," April 4, 1919, quoted in Ziad Fahmy, *Ordinary Egyptians,* 139.

91. Telegrams were sent by student organizations in dozens of educational institutions. They are housed in the Bibliotheca Alexandrina and are accessible online at http://modernegypt.bibalex.org/Collections/Documents/DocumentsLucene.aspx. Many of the telegrams sent to the United States or to American officials in Europe are kept in archives in the United States. See Manela, *The Wilsonian Moment,* 265nn8,9.

92. Foreign Office, *Reply to Charges.* See also M. Badrawi, *Isma'il Sidqi,* 1875–1950*: Pragmatism and Vision in Twentieth Century Egypt* (Richmond, Surrey: Curzon, 1996), 15; Manela, *Wilsonian Moment,* 143.

93. Such telegrams are filed in FO 141/780/1.

94. Beinin and Lockman, *Workers on the Nile,* 96.

95. 'Abd al-Raḥmān al-Rāfi'ī, *Thawrat* 1919 (Cairo: Maktabat al-Nahḍah al-Miṣrīyah, 1946), 193.

96. The student demonstrators insisted on the peaceful nature of their protests, and these claims were repeated daily in *Al-Ahrām* between March 9 and March 15, 1919. See also al-Rāfi'ī, *Thawrat* 1919, 196.

97. Al- Rāfi'ī, *Thawrat* 1919, 200.

98. FO 141/748

99. Al-Rāfi'ī, *Thawrat* 1919, 216.

100. Ramaḍān, *Taṭawwur,* 136.

101. Foreign Office, *Reply to Charges,* 4.

102. Ibid.

103. See Ramaḍān, *Taṭawwur,* 137.

104. FO 141/745; and *Al-Ahrām,* March 16, 1919.

105. Al-Rāfi'ī, *Thawrat* 1919, 209.

106. Ibid.

107. As described also by another participant in these events, Naguib Mahfouz, in *Palace Walk,* trans. William Maynard Hutchins (New York: Random House, 1991), 373.

108. T. Abāẓah, "Fog," in *Cairo Literary Atlas: One Hundred Years on the Streets of the City,* ed. Samia Mehrez (Cairo: American University in Cairo Press, 2010), 292–294.

109. Al-Rāfi'ī, *Thawrat* 1919, 220.

110. Guy Debord, *The Society of the Spectacle* (New York: Zone Books, 1995).

111. Al-Hakim, *Return of the Spirit,* 272; al-Hakim, *'Awdat al-Rūḥ,* 214.

112. Reinhart Koselleck, *Futures Past: On the Semantics of Historical Time,* trans. Keith Tribe (New York: Columbia University Press, 2004).

113. Al-Rāfi'ī, *Thawrat* 1919, 223.

114. Ramaḍān, *Taṭawwur,* 135.

115. F. Abāẓah, *Al-Ḍāḥik al-Bākī* (Cairo: Dār al-Hilāl, 1991), 52.

116. *Al-Muqaṭṭam,* January 15, 1920.

117. Mahfouz, *Palace Walk,* 376–377.

118. Abāẓah, *Al-Ḍāḥik,* 65–66.

119. "Official Reports of the House of Commons," March 20, 1919, p. 2350, quoted in Ellis Goldberg, "Peasants in Revolt—Egypt 1919," *International Journal of Middle East Studies* 24, no. 2 (May 1992): 275.

120. A Reuter's telegram from March 24, 1919, quoted in "Egyptian Unrest under British Rule," *Current History: A Monthly Magazine of The New York Times* 10 (April–September 1919): 259.

121. Abāẓah, *Al-Ḍāḥik,* 63.

122. Ḥāfiẓ Ibrāhīm's *qasīdah* about the 1919 revolution, quoted in Mūsā, *The Education of Salāma Mūsā,* 106.

123. Partly because many of the necessary materials had to be imported from Europe and partly because repair trains were regularly ambushed. See FO 141/745. From the end of March, railway tickets were only sold to holders of a special permit that was issued to British citizens and other foreigners, government servants carrying written authorization from their British department heads, or persons connected to the military authorities. FO 141/745. Regular passenger-transportation only resumed in mid-May. Al-Rāfiʿī, *Thawrat* 1919, 332.

124. FO 141/745.

125. Kenneth Cuno, *The Pasha's Peasants: Land, Society and Economy in Lower Egypt,* 1740–1858 (Cambridge: Cambridge University Press, 1992), 5.

126. Cuno, *The Pasha's Peasants,* 139.

127. See Khaled Fahmy, *All the Pasha's Men,* 95, about a Shaykh Riḍwān declaring himself *mahdī* in Upper Egypt in 1824, joined by over 30,000 peasants. During the 1820s, several peasant revolts and attacks against government storehouses were led by a *mahdī* and characterized by an eschatological ideology. P. M. Holt, "Egypt and the Nile Valley," in *The Cambridge History of Africa,* ed. John E. Flint, vol. 5, *From c.* 1790 *to c.* 1870 (London: Cambridge University Press, 1976), 30. See also J. Berque, *Egypt: Imperialism and Revolution,* trans. Jean Stewart (London: Faber, 1972), 137.

128. In 1865, a millenarian Sufi mystic provoked riots in several small towns in Upper Egypt; an anti-Greek riot in Ṭanṭā was sparked in 1872 on similar grounds. See Juan Cole, *Colonialism and Revolution in the Middle East*(Princeton, NJ: Princeton University Press, 1993), 211. In 1875, several villages in Upper Egypt rose at the bidding of Aḥmad al-Ṭayyib, a new *mahdī,* who sought to reform the entire province. See Berque, *Egypt,* 137.

129. In 1906, 90 percent of the families in the countryside were no longer in control of their land. See Beinin and Lockman, *Workers on the Nile,* 24.

130. See Khaled Fahmy, "Justice and Pain in Khedival Egypt," in *Standing Trial: Law and the Person in the Modern Middle East,* ed. Baudouin Dupres (London: I. B. Tauris, 2004), 85–116.

131. Judith Tucker, *Women in Nineteenth-Century Egypt* (Cambridge: Cambridge University Press, 1985), 174–175. See also Eve Troutt Powell, *A Different Shade of Colonialism: Egypt, Great Britain, and the Mastery of the Sudan,* Berkeley: University of California Press, 2003), chapter 4.

132. Cromer, *Modern Egypt,* 2:406–419.

133. Ibid., 2:416.

134. *Al-Mu'ayyad,* July 11, 1894, quoted in Gasper, *The Power of Representation,* 141.

135. See Saidiya Hartman, *Scenes of Subjection: Terror, Slavery, and Self-Making in Ninteenth-Century America* (New York: Oxford University Press, 1997); Douglas Blackmon, *Slavery by Another Name: The Re-Enslavement of Black Americans from the Civil War to World War II* (New York: Random House, 2009).

136. Brown, *Peasant Politics,* 92.

137. Ibid.

138. Such incidents are described in Tawfīq al-Hakīm's *Yawmīyāt Nā'ib fī al-Aryāf.* See al-Hakīm, *Maze of Justice,* 46.

139. As Yūsuf Naḥḥās put it in 1902, unlike European workers, Egyptian peasants, and especially daily workers, could not be pushed into striking or revolution and could resist only by slacking off. See Brown, *Peasant Politics,* 93.

140. Alan Mikhail, *Nature and Empire in Ottoman Egypt* (Cambridge: Cambridge University Press, 2011), 10.

141. Quṭb, *A Child from the Village,* 25.

142. Goldberg, "Peasants in Revolt," 262.

143. Haikal, *Zaynab,* 3–5. Michael Gaspar firmly anchors the novel in the conventions of middle-class representations of the peasantry between 1906 and 1919. See Gasper, *The Power of Representation,* chapter 5.

144. Robert Tignor, "The Egyptian Revolution of 1919: New Directions in the Egyptian Economy," *Middle East Studies* 12, no. 3 (October 1976): 42.

145. Brown, *Peasant Politics,* 199.

146. Ibid., 200.

147. Tignor, "The Egyptian Revolution of 1919," 42–43.

148. Brown, *Peasant Politics,* 196–201.

149. Fertilizers came mainly from Chile. In 1902, Egypt imported 2,152 tons of chemical manure. By 1906 the amount rose to 12,725 tons. "Fertilizers in Egypt," in *American Fertilizer,* February 26, 1910.

150. Timothy Mitchell described the later effects of this newly introduced set of techniques and devices in *Rule of Experts,* 19–54.

151. FO 368/1905/98508, quoted in Goldberg, "Peasants in Revolt," 265.

152. Goldberg, "Peasants in Revolt," 268. According to Salāmah Mūsā, the Australian horses used by the British required twice as much fodder as Egyptian horses, resulting in reclamation of crops and heavy taxation. See Mūsā, *The Education of Salāma Mūsā,* 93.

153. Goldberg, "Peasants in Revolt," 268.

154. Allenby to Curzon, May 14, 1919, quoted in Brown, *Peasant Politics,* 205.

155. ESR Manager to High Commissioner, March 22, 1919, in FO 141/780.

156. Ibid.

157. Report by Mr. Selby, April 17, 1919, in FO 141/745.

158. See William Willcocks and J. I. Craig, *Egyptian Irrigation* (London: E. and F. N. Spon, 1913) for an account of the transition from basin to perennial irrigation.

159. R. Schulze, *Die Rebellion der ägyptischen Fallahin, 1919: Zum Konflikt zwischen d. agrar.-oriental. Gesellschaft u. d. kolonialen Staat in Ägypten,* 1820–1919 (Berlin: Baalbek Verlag, 1981), 79.

160. Schulze, *Die Rebellion,* 304.

161. Cloth merchants in Manṣūrah, for example, denied red cloth to European women because this textile would be needed for ʿAbbās's return. FO 371/3711/12827, quoted in Goldberg, "Peasants in Revolt," 276n8. Goldberg also cites millenarian mentions of ʿAbbās in popular poetry. For a discussion of millenarianism in a colonial context, see Michael Adas, *Prophets of Rebellion: Millenarian Protest Movements against the European Colonial Order* (Chapel Hill: University of North Carolina Press, 1979).

162. *Al-Ahrām,* March 9, 1919.

163. Goldberg, "Peasants in Revolt," 273.

164. Events like the famous "Women's Demonstration" of March 16, 1919, at the beginning of the revolution, or a 1922 women's boycott of British goods dovetailing with it, were coordinated in this fashion. See Shaʿrāwī, *Harem Years,* 112–113; and Mona Russell, *Creating the New Egyptian Women* (New York: Palgrave Macmillan, 2004), 90.

165. FO 141/780/1.

166. FO 141/748.

167. See Brown, *Peasant Politics,* 204. The surprising character of the revolt is repeated in al-Rāfiʿī's *Thawrat* 1919 and in al-Hakīm's *Return of the Spirit.*

168. Berque, *Egypt,* 306.

169. FO 608/213/5.

170. FO 141/745. For a description from the ground of Asyūṭ bombarded from the air, see Abāẓah, *Al-Ḍāḥik,* 57–62.

171. During March, the Air Intelligence Summary was issued thrice daily. It reveals that the two main tasks of planes were dropping bombs on rioters and messages to disconnected British outposts and hovering over the key rail lines, noting any Egyptian presence in the vicinity. Airplanes were also used to register the whereabouts and condition of trains on these lines. See FO 141/745.

172. FO 141/753/3.

173. Curzon to Allenby, April 12, 1919, in *Documents Collected for the Information of the Special Mission,* 2:131–132.

174. Milner, *Report of the Special Mission to Egypt,* 6–10.

175. Speaking of martyrdom and the arousing nationalist mass funeral processions that helped spread the revolt, Fahmy comments: "Is it really a revolution? Let them kill as many as their savagery dictates. Death only invigorates us." Mahfouz, *Palace Walk,* 373.

176. See Mūsā, *The Education of Salāma Mūsā,* 103. I retranslated the end of the statement in a way that more accurately conveys the original meaning.

177. I. Gershoni, *Piramidah La-umah: Hantsaḥah, Zikaron u-Leʾumiyut be-Mitsrayim ba-Meʾah ha-ʿEśrim* (Tel Aviv: ʿAm ʿOved, 2006), 78, 89.

178. Ibid., 94.

179. *Al-Kashkūl,* September 25, 1921. Reproduced in Gershoni, *Piramidah La-umah,* 99.

180. FO 141/745.

181. Such views were expressed in one of Tawfīq Diyāb's "Glimpses" columns in *Al-Ahrām* during the fall of 1919. See Yunan Labib Rizk, "The Prince of Wit," *Al-Ahram Weekly,* December 16–22, 1999, http://weekly.ahram.org.eg/1999/460/chrncls.htm. High school year-end exams were postponed already in March 1919. The first institution to have done so was al-Azhar, which cancelled its exams on March 16—see *Al-Ahrām* for that day—and other institutions followed. Presumably such measures facilitated students' sustained demonstrations.

182. Fikrī Abāẓah, *Al-Ahrām,* June 13, 1922. The translation of the first few lines is taken from Yunan Labib Rizk, "The Prince of Wit."

183. Fikrī Abāẓah, *Al-Ahrām,* June 13, 1922.

CHAPTER 7

Epigraph: Gilles Deleuze and Claire Parnet, *Dialogues,* trans. H. Tomlinson and B. Habberjam (New York: Columbia University Press, 1987), 96, 70. See also p. 103.

1. De Leon, "How I Introduced the Telephone," 529.

2. For example, during the Nile inundation, the rising water loosened telegraph poles from the ground, and peasants took advantage of the situation to reposition them away from their fields. See *Tashrīʿāt wa-Manshūrāt,* 1880–1882 (1), p. 81.

3. De Leon, "How I Introduced the Telephone," 529; *Al-Tilighrāfāt al-Jadīdah,* June 29, 1899.

4. See, for example, *Al-Muqaṭṭam,* August 24, 1923, on a long-standing dispute regarding rent for 843 telephone poles standing on *waqf* real estate.

5. De Leon, "How I Introduced the Telephone," 529.

6. See *American Architect and Architecture* 75–78 (1902).

7. De Leon, "How I Introduced the Telephone," 529–530.

8. Ibid., 531.

9. Ibid., 531–532.

10. Ibid., 532. Other men were more proactive: for example, on August 13, 1881, less than a week after the inauguration of the service, ten phone lines were deliberately cut on the roof of the main offices of the newspaper *L'Égypte* in Alexandria. See *Al-Ahrām,* August 16, 1881.

11. *Al-Fukāhah,* June 20, 1928.

12. *Kull Shayʾ waʾl-ʿĀlam,* no. 4 (December 7, 1925): 13.

13. See David Harvey, *Paris, Capital of Modernity* (Psychology Press, 2003), 47.

14. See Shaʿarāwī, *Harem Years,* 112–113; and Russell, *Creating the New Egyptian Women,* 90.

15. Saba Mahmood, *Politics of Piety: The Islamic Revival and the Feminist Subject* (Princeton, NJ: Princeton University Press, 2005). See especially chapter 1.

16. See Jacob, *Working out Egypt.*

17. See April Middeljans, "On the Wire with Death and Desire: The Telephone and Lovers' Discourse in the Short Stories of Dorothy Parker," *Arizona Quarterly* 62, no. 4 (2006): 47–70.

18. Of course, such a gendered division of the "caller" and "answerer" roles may also be indicative of the higher risk that women receiving calls from men were exposed to, compared to men receiving calls from women.

19. *Mudhākarah min Niẓārat al-Ashghāl al-ʿUmūmīyah ilā Majlis al-Nuẓẓār Bishaʾn al-Taṣrīḥ Li-Sharikat al-Tilifūn al-Sharqīyah,* October 6, 1889, DWQ UoD. no. 0075–033351.

20. *Al-Barīd,* May 14, 1895

21. *Al-Muqtaṭaf* 28 (1902), p. 406.

22. "Al-Tilifūn: Niẓāmuhu wa-Taqaddumuhu fī Miṣr," *Miṣr al-Ḥadīthah al-Muṣawwarah,* April–May 1928.

23. W. H. Moreton Cameron and Walter Feldwich, *Ports and Cities of the World* (Globe Encyclopedia Company, 1927), 17.

24. Eli M. Noam, *Telecommunications in Africa* (Oxford: Oxford University Press, 1999), 40.

25. Cameron and Feldwich, *Ports and Cities,* 17.

26. See Galāl Amīn, *Whatever Else Happened to the Egyptians: From the Revolution to the Age of Globalization* (Cairo: American University in Cairo Press, 2004), 57–71.

27. *Al-Dalīl al-Miṣrī* (Cairo, 1917). See also Government of Egypt, *Almanac for the Year* 1915 (Cairo, 1915).

28. *Al-Ahrām,* August 11, 1881.

29. De Leon, "How I Introduced the Telephone," 531.

30. In 1926, for example, residents of the Ramal suburb in Alexandria who wanted to join the network could not due to a shortage of numbers. See *Al-Ahrām,* October 24, 1926.

31. "We in the East tend to fault those in charge of anything that at first glance seems to be not working properly. But the issue we address [delays in being connected to the phone network] is not difficult to explain." See "Al-Tilifūn: Niẓāmuhu wa-taqaddumuhu fī Miṣr," 7.

32. Ibid., 3.

33. Ibid., 9.

34. Ibid., 5.

35. Noam, *Telecommunications in Africa,* 40.

36. Ibid.

37. *Al-Muqtaṭaf* 81 (1932): 70; see also FO 141/706/2.

38. *Al-Ahrām,* January 4, 1934.

39. Ibid.

40. Bayram al-Tūnisī even composed a humoresque about this experience. See "Daftar al-Tilifūn," in *Al-Aʿmāl al-Kāmilah li-Bayram al-Tūnisī,* ed. Rushdī Ṣāliḥ (Cairo: al-Hayʾah al-Miṣrīyah al-ʿĀmmah liʾl-Kitāb, 1975), 4:58.

41. *Al-Ahrām,* January 4, 1934.

42. "Al-Tilifūn: Niẓāmuhu wa-Taqaddumuhu fī Miṣr," 6.

43. See B. Latour, *Pandora's Hope: Essays on the Reality of Science Studies* (Cambridge, MA: Harvard University Press, 1999).

44. Noam, *Telecommunications in Africa,* 40.

45. Al-Ḥakīm, *Return of the Spirit,* 85.

46. See Donna Haraway, "A Cyborg Manifesto: Science, Technology, and Socialist-Feminism in the Late Twentieth Century," in *Simians, Cyborgs and Women: The Reinvention of Nature* (London: Free Association, 1991).

47. See Michele Martin, *"Hello, Central?" Gender, Technology, and Culture in the Formation of Telephone Systems* (Montreal: McGill-Queen's University Press, 1991).

48. "Al-Tilifūn: Niẓāmuhu wa-Taqaddumuhu fī Miṣr," 4.

49. From a poem by Ḥāfiẓ Ibrāhīm, a neoclassical poet whose technological poems are discussed in chapter 5, published in *Al-Majallah al-Miṣrīyah,* September 30, 1900.

50. Telephony was often unfavorably compared to the telegraph. For example, a 1912 article in the daily newspaper *Al-Waṭanīyah* (see March 29, 1912) complained about the decision of the Amīrīyah railway company to replace telegraphy with telephony in its stations. People now had to read or give their messages to operators, who read them out loud over the phone, divulging merchants' secrets exactly when prices should be kept confidential. Unlike telephone operators, telegraphers were familiar figures. The names of the graduates of the telegraph school were regularly published in the Official Newspaper, and every so often they featured in the news. For lists of graduates, see *Tashrīʿāt wa-Manshūrāt,* 1885, pp. 165–167; 1888, p. 132; 1902, p. 383. For telegraphers in the news, see, for example, *Al-Waṭan,* July 5, 1895, and August 16, 1895.

51. See *Al-Fukāhah,* June 6, 1928. Compare this image to the one in chapter 5, of a woman sitting in a tramcar with a lipstick and hand mirror. These recurring tropes in the depiction of women suggest that the new visual language developing in Egyptian periodicals stressed the masculine gaze, which even women were directing toward themselves. On Eros and the phone operator, see John Durham Peters, *Speaking into the Air: A History of the Idea of Communication* (Chicago: University of Chicago Press, 1999), 196–197.

52. *Al-Ṣiḥāfah,* November 21, 1905, quoted the story from *Al-Muqaṭṭam.*

53. See Barak, "Times of *Tamaddun:* Gender, Urbanity and Temporality in Modern Egypt," in "Women and the City, Women in the City: A Gendered Perspective for Ottoman Urban History," ed. Nazan Maksudyan (unpublished manuscript).

54. Cameron and Feldwich, *Ports and Cities,* 17; "Al-Tilifūn: Niẓāmuhu wa-Taqaddumuhu fī Miṣr," 6.

55. "Al-Tilifūn: Niẓāmuhu wa-Taqaddumuhu fī Miṣr," 9.

56. "Al-Marʾah al-Miṣrīyah waʾl-ʿAmal," in *Rūz al-Yūsuf,* November 16, 1925. Ads were published in venues like the railway guide.

57. *Al-Fukāhah,* June 20, 1928.

58. *Al-Mar'ah al-Miṣrīyah,* May 1, 1923.

59. Cameron and Feldwich, *Ports and Cities,* 17. According to another account, in 1923 there were already 202 public phone booths. See "Al-Tilifūn: Niẓāmuhu wa-Taqaddumuhu fī Miṣr," 3.

60. "Al-Tilifūn: Niẓāmuhu wa-Taqaddumuhu fī Miṣr," 3.

61. *Kull Shay' wa'l-Dunyā,* March 27, 1935.

62. For middle-class women's role in facilitating their husbands' and sons' abstract routines by simultaneously supporting them and playing the role of a constitutive "other," see Barak, "Times of *Tamaddun.*"

63. And indeed, *Rūz al-Yūsuf* identified press attacks against female telephone operators as backlashes by a reactionary patriarchal movement against women's labor. See *Rūz al-Yūsuf,* November 16, 1925.

64. *Al-Fukāhah,* June 20, 1928.

65. "Tilifūnī al-Majnūn," *Al-Fukāhah,* June 6, 1928.

66. Walter Gam Nkwi, "From the Elitist to the Commonality of Voice Communication: The History of the Telephone in Buea, Cameroon," in *Mobile Phones, the New Talking Drums of Everyday Africa,* ed. Mirjam de Bruijn et al. (Bamenda, Cameroon: Langaa RPCIG, 2009).

67. Benjamin, *The Work of Art in the Age of Its Technological Reproduction,* 77–78 (my emphasis).

68. See De Leon, "How I Introduced the Telephone," 532.

69. Printed in al-Bishrī, *Al-Mukhtār,* 188.

70. See Yunan Labib Rizk, "I Conjure Thee," *Al-Ahram: A Diwan of Contemporary Life* (536), http://weekly.ahram.org.eg/2004/680/chrncls.htm.

71. See, for example, *Al-Manār,* 1906–1907, p. 35.

72. M. K. Al-Khula'ī, *Kitāb al-Musīqā al-Sharqī* (Cairo: Maṭba'at al-Taqaddum, 1902).

73. Ḥāfiẓ Abū al-Faraj 'Abd al-Raḥmān ibn al-Jawzī, *Naqd al-'Ilm wa'l-'Ulamā', aw, Talbīs Iblīs* (Cairo: Maṭba'at al-Sa'ādah, 1922). See, for example, Khaled al-Berry's account of the importance of this text in *Life Is More Beautiful Than Paradise: A Jihadist's Own Story,* trans. Humphrey Davies (London: Haus, 2009), 12–13.

74. See Ḥāfiẓ Abū al-Faraj 'Abd al-Raḥmān ibn al-Jawzī, *Mukhtaṣar Kitāb Talbīs Iblīs,* ed. 'Alī al-Sharbajī (Beirut: Mu'assasat al-Risālah, 1992), 192–193.

75. See Karin van Nieuwkerk, *A Trade like Any Other: Female Singers and Dancers in Egypt* (Austin: University of Texas Press, 1995), 129–130, for a repudiation of the female use of the telephone.

76. Khayrat, *Al-Mar'ah,* 95.

77. Ibid., 30–31. See also M. Doles, *Majnūn: The Madman in Medieval Islamic Society* (Oxford: Clarendon Press, 1992), esp. chapter 6.

78. Khayrat, *Al-Mar'ah,* 34–35.

79. Ibid., 23.

80. Jacques Derrida, "Autoimmunity: Real and Symbolic Suicides," in *Philosophy in a Time of Terror: Dialogues with Jürgen Habermas and Jacques Derrida,* by Giovanna Barradori (Chicago: University of Chicago Press, 2004), 85–137.

81. Muḥammad ʿAbd al-Wahhāb, vocal performance of *Majnūn Laylā* by Aḥmad Shawqī, cassette tape, Soutelphan, n.d.

82. Umm Kulthūm sang many of Shawqī's poems, yet persistent rumors about her participation in a *Majnūn and Laylā* production did not materialize. See Danielson, *"The Voice of Egypt,"* 171. However, she eventually did sing a Mursī Jamīl ʿAzīz adaptation of *Alf Laylā wa-Laylā.*

83. See the discussion of *dahr* in I. Izutsu, *God and Man in the Koran* (Karachi: Royal Book Company, 2002).

84. See Ahmad Shawqī, *Majnūn Laylā* (Cairo: Muʾassasat Fann al-Ṭibāʿah, 1958), for example, p. 26.

85. *Kull Shayʾ waʾl-ʿĀlam,* October 11, 1933, pp. 6–7.

86. Tawfīq al-Ḥakīm, *Shahrazad,* in *Plays, Prefaces and Postscripts of Tawfiq al-Hakim,* trans. W. M. Hutchins (Washington, DC: Three Continents Press, 1981), 148.

87. Ibid., 134.

88. Ibid., 146.

89. Bayram al-Tūnisī, "Al-Maqāmah al-Tilifūnīyah," in *Maqāmāt Bayram al-Tūnisī,* ed. Ṭāhir Abū Fashā (Cairo: Maktabat Madbūlī, 1975), 48–52.

90. Doles, *Majnūn,* 221n53.

91. Wāʾil Abū Hindī, *Al-Waswās al-Qahrī Bayn al-Dīn waʾl-Ṭibb al-Nafsī* (Giza: Nahḍat Miṣr, 2002).

92. This happened first in Western Europe and North America. See Laura Otis, *Networking: Communicating with Bodies and Machines in the Nineteenth Century* (Ann Arbor: University of Michigan Press, 2001).

93. *Kull Shayʾ waʾl-ʿĀlam,* June 25, 1928.

94. The German *Nervenzentrale* of the original better captures the connotation of a telephone central.

95. See his five-volume magnum opus, *Das Leben des Menschen: Eine Volkstümliche Anatomie, Biologie, Physiologie und Entwicklungsgeschichte des Menschen* (Stuttgart: Franckh'sche Verlagshandlung, 1922–31).

96. Gilles Deleuze and Felix Guattari, *Anti-Oedipus* (London: Penguin Classics, 2009), chapter 1.

97. *Al-Muṣawwar,* November 1, 1902. The French names of the series' characters suggest that these conversations were translated or inspired by skits in the French press, but also that these themes resonated with the Egyptian effendi readership.

98. Ibid.

99. A. Rabinbach, *The Human Motor: Energy, Fatigue, and the Origins of Modernity* (New York: Basic Books, 1990).

100. Such as the two competitors for the title "the first Egyptian novel," Haykal's 1913 *Zaynab,* and the earlier *ʿAdhrāʾ Dinshuwāy* (1906). Naguib Mahfouz later developed the trend further in various novels. The political implications of gendering the nation feminine are analyzed by Beth Baron in *Egypt as a Woman: Nationalism, Gender, and Politics* (Berkeley: University of California Press, 2005).

101. Al-Ḥakīm, *Return of the Spirit,* 261–262.

102. Beyond several similar scenes in *'Awdat al-Rūḥ,* the timing of romantic encounters under the moon was a familiar trope in other media in early 1930s Egypt. *Taḥt Ḍaw' al-Qamar* (Under the moonlight), the first silent Egyptian film (1930, later released with a soundtrack), revolved around such an encounter, as did *Jināyat Niṣf al-Layl* (Crime in the middle of the night, 1930). The trope of waiting under the moon also featured prominently Umm Kulthūm's lyrics during the 1930s. See Maḥmūd Qāsim et al., eds., *Dalīl al-Aflām fī al-Qarn al-'ishrīn fī Miṣr wa' l-'Ālam al-'Ārabi* (Cairo: Maktabat Madbūlī, 2002), 16–17. See also Danielson, "*The Voice of Egypt,*" especially chapter 5.

103. Al-Ḥakīm, *Return of the Spirit,* 262–271.

104. These deferrals are similar to the professor's practice of being fifteen minutes late, often encouraged as a means of producing his or her magisterial discourse. See Jacques-Alain Miller, *Ha-Eroṭika shel ha-Zeman* (Tel Aviv: Resling, 2008), 121.

105. Al-Ḥakīm, *Return of the Spirit,* 97.

106. Ibid., 99. Emphasis added.

107. Al-Khula'ī, *Kitāb al-Musīqā al-Sharqī,* 90. In Muḥammad Mutwallī's *Al-Wardah al-Bayḍā'* (The white rose) (Cairo: Maṭba'at Ḥijāzī), a couple of musicians similarly postpone the beginning of a concert. See pp. 227–229.

108. A. J. Racy, "Musical Aesthetics in Present Day Cairo," *Ethnomusicology* 26, no. 3 (September 1982): 397.

109. *Al-Ahrām,* January 3, 1934.

110. See Danielson, *"The Voice of Egypt,"* 77, 88.

111. Changes in the rhythms, themes, and instruments of Arabic music were at the center of a more general debate about modernity itself. Those who supported musical modernization claimed that Arabic music is excessively engaged with sexual love, perhaps as the result of a flamboyant Eastern imagination subjected to veiling practices and hot climate. It was accused of being monotonous and non-harmonic, leading to boredom and stirring repressed anxieties. See, for example, Niqūlā Yūsuf, *Al-Ḥayāt al-Jadīdah* (Cairo: Maṭba'at al-Majallah al-Jadīdah, 1936), 180–181.

112. *Al-Rādiyō,* December 4, 1937.

113. Qāsim, *Dalīl,* 28.

114. Lesley Kitchen Lababidi, *Cairo Street Stories: Exploring the City's Statues, Squares, Bridges, Gardens, and Sidewalk Cafés* (Cairo: American University in Cairo Press, 2008), 112.

115. Danielson, *"The Voice of Egypt,"* 86.

116. Richard Nidel, *World Music: The Basics* (New York: Routledge, 2005), 189.

117. Danielson, *"The Voice of Egypt,"* 94–95.

118. On this tradition of logocentrism, see Messick, *Calligraphic State.*

119. Racy, *Musical Aesthetics,* 392–394.

120. Ibid., 394.

121. *Rūz al-Yūsuf,* October 27, 1926, quoted in Danielson, *"The Voice of Egypt,"* 62.

122. Immanuel Kant, *Critique of Practical Reason,* trans. Mary J. Gregor (Cambridge: Cambridge University Press, 1997), 27.

123. Slavoj Žižek, "Kant and Sade: The Ideal Couple," *Lacanian Ink* 13 (Fall 1998), http://www.egs.edu/faculty/zizek/zizek-kant-and-sade-the-ideal-couple .html.

124. The process is described with great sadness in Naguib Mahfouz, *Midaq Alley, Cairo,* trans. Trevor Le Gassick (Beirut: Khayats, 1966). See, for example: "We know all the stories you tell by heart and we don't need to run through them again. People today don't want a poet. They keep asking me for a radio and there's one over there being installed now. So go away and leave us alone" (p. 5).

125. The connective effect of radio schedules has a complex history in Egypt. As the radio program was relatively complex and irregular—a consequence of its balancing different interest groups in the country—it was hard to anticipate what would be broadcast at which time. For a history of the Egyptian radio, see Anwar al-Samālūṭī et al., *Tārīkh Ḥayāt al-Idhāʿah Mundhu Nashāʾihā Ḥattā al-Ān* (Cairo: Idhāʿat al-Jumhūrīyah al-ʿArabīyah al-Muttaḥidah, 1969).

126. See Robert Winston Witkin, *Adorno on Music* (London: Routledge, 1998), chapter 9.

127. Shawqī, *Majnūn,* 25.

128. Izutsu, *God and Man in the Koran,* 67–68.

129. Hirschkind, *The Ethical Soundscape,* 36–37, 51–54.

130. For example, ʿAbd al-Ḥalīm Ḥāfiẓ, famous for his prosthetic connection to the microphone, replaced this device with a telephone in the film *Al-Wisādah al-Khālīyah* (singing "Awwal Marrah").

131. Lagrange, "Women in the Singing Business, Women in Songs."

132. See Robert St. John, *The Boss: The Story of Gamal Abdel Nasser* (London: McGraw-Hill, 1960), 84. See also Jehan Sadat, *A Woman of Egypt* (New York: Simon and Schuster, 1987), 65.

133. Amin, *Whatever Else Happened to the Egyptians,* 57–71.

134. John Waterbury, *Egypt: Burdens of the Past/Options for the Future* (Bloomington: Indiana University Press, 1978), 239.

135. This tradition consists of at least two Egyptian films titled *A Thousand and One Nights,* in 1941 and 1964. See Qāsim, *Dalīl,* 49, 405.

136. Naguib Mahfouz, "Shahrazād," in *God's World: An Anthology of Short Stories,* trans. Akef Abadir and Roger Allan (Minneapolis, MN: Bibliotheca Islamica, 1973), 63–75.

137. *Al-Wisādah al-Khālīyah* (The empty cushion, 1957), *Al-Ṭarīq al-Masdūd* (Dead-end / The closed way, 1958), *Anā Ḥurrah* (I am free, 1959), and *Lā Tuṭfi al-Shams* (Don't extinguish the sun, 1960).

CONCLUSION

Epigraph: *Al-Majallah al-Miṣrīyah,* December 15, 1900 (my translation from the Arabic and Susan Stewart's from my tongue-tied English).

1. Mumford, *Technics and Civilization,* 14.

2. For an insightful account of clocks in Ottoman Egypt, see Stolz, "Correcting the Clock."

3. To use Bergson's term for qualitative temporal multiplicity, which he juxtaposed with empty homogeneous time.

4. Wishnitzer, *Reading Clocks,* Alla Turca.

5. Stolz, "Correcting the Clock," 23.

6. This agenda was set forth by Timothy Mitchell, who has attended to how abstract routines promoted by such institutions as the school or city planning were introduced into Egypt. Beyond new techniques of discipline, these processes ushered in a new metaphysics, resulting in "the appearance of order," of which abstract time and space were part. See Mitchell, *Colonising Egypt.*

7. See, for example, the critique of Mitchell's account of the introduction of the Lancaster system in Sedra, *From Mission to Modernity,* chapter 2.

8. See, for example, Sauter, "Clockwatchers and Stargazers."

9. Formal notice was given in *Al-Jarīdah al-Rasmīyah* on August 20, 1900. On Greenwich time, see M. Perkins, *The Reform of Time: Magic and Modernity* (Sterlin, VA: Pluto Press, 2001), 19; and A. Barrows, *The Cosmic Time of Empire: Modern Britain and World Literature* (Berkeley: University of California Press, 2011).

10. ʿAbd al-Rāziq ʿĪsā and ʿAbīr Ḥasan, eds., *Miṣr wa-Mīlād al-Qarn al-ʿIshrīn: Ṣūrat Miṣr ʿĀm* 1900, *Dirāsah Taḥlīlīyah* (Cairo: al-ʿArabī, 2001).

11. Maṣlaḥat ʿUmūm al-Iḥṣāʾ, *Census of Egypt Taken in* 1917.

12. Elsewhere, I take issue with E. P. Thompson's classic distinction between task-oriented time and abstract clock time. In the domestic sphere, for example, it was the task-oriented time of feminine labor that allowed husbands to keep regular schedules. See Barak, "Times of *Tamaddun.*"

13. See, for example, *Al-Ghazālah,* June 2, 1986, quoted in Baskerville, *From Tahdhiib al-Amma to Tahmiishh al-Ammiyya,* 9.

14. Mahmud Tahir Haqqi, "The Maiden of Dinshway," in *Three Pioneering Egyptian Novels,* trans. Saad El-Gabalawy (Fredericton, Canada: York Press, 1986), 40.

15. *Majallat al-Muṣawwar al-Ḥadīthah al-Muṣawwarah,* December 11, 1929.

16. Ḥāfiẓ Ibrāhīm, *Dīwān Ḥāfiẓ Ibrāhīm,* ed. Aḥmad Amīn et al. (Cairo: Al-Hayʾah al-Miṣrīyah al-ʿĀmmah liʾl-Kitāb, 1980), 2:37–42.

17. Fredric Jameson, *A Singular Modernity* (London: Verso Books 2002), 12.

18. Slavoj Žižek, *Less Than Nothing: Hegel and the Shadows of Dialectical Materialism* (London: Verso, 2012), Loc. 17512.

19. M. M. Badawi, *A Critical Introduction to Modern Arabic Poetry* (Cambridge: Cambridge University Press, 1975), 14–21.

20. S. Somekh, "The Neo-Classical Arabic Poets," in *Modern Arabic Literature,* ed. M. M. Badawi (Cambridge: Cambridge University Press, 1993), 56.

21. *Al-Majallah al-Miṣrīyah,* July 1900, p. 85, quoted in ibid., 39.

22. Fransīs Fatḥ Allāh Marrāsh, quoted in S. Moreh, "The Neoclassical Qasida: Modern Poets and Critics," in *Studies in Modern Arabic Prose and Poetry* (Leiden: Brill, 1988), 34.

23. Al-Khulaʿī, *Kitāb al-Musīqā al-Sharqī,* 12; "ʿArūḍ," *Encyclopaedia of Islam,* 2nd ed. (Leiden: Brill, 2012); D. Frolov, *Classical Arabic Verse: History and Theory of ʿArud* (Leiden: Brill, 2000), 12–13.

24. Marwa S. Elshakry, "Knowledge in Motion: The Cultural Politics of Modern Science Translations in Arabic," *Isis* 99, no. 4 (December 2008): 701–730.

25. Aḥmad Shawqī, quoted in ʿAbd al-Fattāḥ Abū Ghuddah, *Qīmat al-Zaman ʿInd al-ʿUlamāʾ* (Beirut: Maktabat al-Maṭbūʿāt al-Islāmīyah, 1974), 59.

26. Ḥasan ibn Aḥmad al-Bannā, *Mudhakkirāt al-Daʿwā wa'l-Dāʿīyah* (Cairo: Dār al-Kitāb al-ʿArabī, 1951).

27. Abū Ghuddah, *Qīmat al-Zamān,* 59.

28. S. M. Ḥasan al-Bannā, *Imām Shahīd Ḥasan Al-Bannā: From Birth to Martyrdom* (Milpitas, CA: Awakening, 2002), 36.

29. Ḥasan al-Bannā, "Letter to a Muslim Student," *Jannah.org,* http://www.jannah.org/articles/letter.html

30. Ḥasan al-Bannā, *Ḥadīth al-Thulathāʾ,* ed. Aḥmad ʿĪsā ʿĀshūr (Cairo: Maktabat al-Qurʾān, 1985), 449.

31. Another example is the theme of "time is life," found in S. Smiles, *ʿAlayka: Naṣāʾiḥ li-Tabaṣur al-Shubbān bi-Muqtaḍayāt al-ʿAysh wa-Asrār al-Najāḥ,* trans. Ibrāhīm Ramzī (Cairo, 1914), 10. Al-Bannā's aforementioned letters and lectures, and numerous later discussions, all echo Marx's claim, already in *The Poverty of Philosophy* from 1847, that in capitalism man is "at the most an incarnation of time. Quality no longer matters. Quantity alone decides everything: hour for hour, day for day." Yet it is exactly this generic temporality that is inflected when it is translated into local situations, languages, and settings.

32. See Nicholas B. Dirks, "Colonialism and Culture," in *Colonialism and Culture* (Ann Arbor: University of Michigan Press, 1992), 1–27.

33. See, for example, Abū Ghuddah, *Qīmat al-Zamān;* Riḍā ʿAlawī Sayyid Aḥmad, *Kayfa Tastamirr Awqātuka?* (Beirut: Dar al-Bayān al-ʿArabī, 1993); Majdī Muḥammad Abū al-ʿAṭā, *Idārat al-Waqt* (Cairo, 2010).

BIBLIOGRAPHY

PERIODICALS

Aberdeen Journal
African Times and Orient Review
Al-Ahrām
Al-Akhbār
Al-ʿĀlam
American Fertilizer
Al-Barīd
Bentley's Miscellany
Bristol Mercury and Daily Post
Century Illustrated Monthly Magazine
Church Review
Connecticut Magazine: An Illustrated Monthly
Daily News
Al-Dalīl al-Miṣrī
Ḍiyāʾ al-Sharq
Eclectic Magazine of Foreign Literature, Science, and Art
Egyptian Mail
Egyptian State Railways Magazine
Electrical Engineer
Electrical Review
Era
Evangelical Repository
Flour & Feed
Al-Fukāhah
Gentleman's Magazine
Glasgow Herald
Graham's Magazine
Graphic

Al-Hilāl
Illustrated London News
Al-Ittiḥād al-Miṣrī
Journal of the Society of the Arts
Juvenile Missionary Herald
Al-Kashkūl
Al-Kawkab
Kull Shayʾ waʾl-ʿĀlam
Ladies' Repository
Literary Digest
Al-Liwāʾ
London Times
Al-Majallah al-Miṣrīyah
Majallat al-Muṣawwar al-Ḥadīthah al-Muṣawwarah
Majallat Ramsīs
Majallat Sikak Ḥadīd wa-Tilighrāfāt wa-Tilifūnāt al-Ḥukūmah al-Miṣrīyah
Majallat ʿUmmāl al-Sikkah al-Ḥadīd
Manchester Times and Gazette
Al-Marʾah al-Miṣrīyah
Merchant's Magazine and Commercial Review
Miṣr al-Ḥadīthah al-Muṣawwarah
Morning Chronicle
Al-Muʾayyad
Al-Mufīd
Al-Muqaṭṭam
Al-Muqtaṭaf
Al-Muṣawwar
Musical World
Al-Nafs al-Barīʾah
Nation
Newcastle Courant
New Monthly Magazine
New York Daily Tribune
Al-Nīl
Al-Niẓām
Patrician
Paving and Municipal Engineering
Peninsular and Independent Medical Journal, Devoted to Medicine, Surgery, and Pharmacy
Popular Science Monthly
Punch
Al-Qāhirah
Al-Rādiyō
Railway Magazine

Al-Risālah
Rūz al-Yūsuf
Al-Sāʿah
Al-Sharq
Al-Ṣiḥāfah
Al-Sufūr
Ṭabīb al-ʿĀʾilah
Al-Tankīt waʾl-Tabkīt
Tashrīʿāt wa-Manshūrāt
Ṭawāliʿ al-Mulūk
Al-Tilighrāfāt al-Jadīdah
Wādī al-Nīl
Al-Waqāʾiʿ al-Miṣrīyah
Al-Waṭan
Al-Waṭanīyah

WORKS CITED IN ARABIC

Abāẓah, F. *Al-Ḍāḥik al-Bākī*. Cairo: Dār al-Hilāl, 1991.

ʿAbd al-Waḥīd, F. A. *Taṭawwur al-Naql waʾl-Muwāṣalāt al-Dākhilīyah fī Miṣr fī ʿAhd al-Iḥtilāl al-Bariṭānī, 1882–1914*. Cairo: al-Hayʾah al-Miṣrīyah al-ʿĀmmah liʾl-Kitāb, 1989.

ʿAbduh, Ibrāhīm. *Jarīdat al-Ahrām, Tārīkh wa-Fann* 1875–1964. Cairo: Muʾassasat Sijill al-ʿArab, 1964.

ʿAbduh, Muḥammad. *Tafsīr al-Qurʾān al-Ḥakim al-Mushtahar bi-Ism Tafsīr al-Manār*. Cairo: al-Manār, 1947.

Abū al-ʿAṭā, Majdī Muḥammad. *Idārat al-Waqt*. Cairo, 2010.

Abū Ghuddah, ʿAbd al-Fattāḥ. *Qīmat al-Zamān ʿInd al-ʿUlamāʾ*. Beirut: Maktabat al-Maṭbūʿāt al-Islāmīyah, 1974.

Abū Hindī, Wāʾil. *Al-Waswās al-Qahrī Bayna al-Dīn waʾl-Ṭibb al-Nafsī*. Giza: Nahḍat Miṣr, 2002.

Aḥmad, Riḍā ʿAlawī Sayyid. *Kayfa Tastamirr Awqātuka?* Beirut: Dar al-Bayān al-ʿArabī, 1993.

Amīn, Aḥmad. *Qāmūs al-ʿĀdāt waʾl-Taqālīd waʾl-Taʿābīr al-Miṣrīyah*. Cairo: Maktabat al-Nahḍah al-Miṣrīyah, 1982 [1953].

Badawī, Jamāl. *Miṣr min Nāfidhat al-Tārīkh*. Cairo: Dār al-Shurūq, 1994.

Bannā, Ḥasan al-. *Ḥadīth al-Thulathāʾ*. Edited by Aḥmad ʿĪsā ʿĀshūr. Cairo: Maktabat al-Qurʾān, 1985.

Bannā, Ḥasan ibn Aḥmad al-. *Mudhakkirāt al-Daʿwā waʾl-Dāʿiyah*. Cairo: Dār al-Kitāb al-ʿArabī, 1951.

Bannā, Jamāl al-. *Khiṭābāt Ḥasan al-Bannā al-Shābb ilā Abīhi: Maʿ Tarjamah Musahhabah wa-Muwaththaqah li-Ḥayāt wa-ʿAmal al-Wālid al-Shaykh Aḥmad al-Bannā*. Cairo: Dār al-Fikr al-Islāmī, 1990.

Bishrī, ʿAbd al-ʿAzīz al-. *Al-Mukhtār.* Cairo: Dār al-Maʿārif, 1959.
Clot Bey. *Lamḥah ʿĀmmah ilā Miṣr.* Translated by Muḥammad Masʿūd. Cairo: Dār al-Mawqif al-ʿArabī, 1981–1984.
Dajawī, Ḥasan Tawfīq al-. *Al-Risālah al-ʿIlmīyah fī al-Trāmawīyah wa-Shurūḥihi wa-Kayfīyat Sayrihi.* Cairo: Maṭbaʿat al-Adab waʾl-Mufīd, 1314/1896.
Fiqī, Ibrāhīm al-. *Idārat al-Waqt.* Manūfīyah: Ibdāʿ liʾl-Iʿlām waʾl-Nashr, 2009.
Gabalawy, Saad el-, trans. *Three Pioneering Egyptian Novels.* Fredericton, Canada: York Press, 1986.
Ḥaddād, Amīn al-. "Ḥubb al-Surʿah." In *Muntakhabāt.* Alexandria: Maṭbaʿat Jurjī Gharzūzī, 1913.
Ḥadīdī, ʿAlī al-. *ʿAbdallah al-Nadīm: Khaṭīb al-Waṭanīyah.* Cairo: al-Muʾassasah al-Miṣrīyah al-ʿĀmmah, n.d.
Ḥakīm, Tawfīq al-. *ʿAwdat al-Rūḥ.* Cairo: Dar al-Maʿārif, 1946.
Ḥarb, Ṭalʿat. *Majmūʿat Khuṭub.* Cairo, 1938.
Ḥassūnah, M. A. *Miṣr waʾl-Ṭuruq al-Ḥadīdīyah.* Cairo, 1938.
Haykal, Muḥammad Ḥusayn. *Mudhakkirāt fī al-Sīyāsah al-Miṣrīyah.* Cairo: Maktabat al-Nahḍah al-Miṣrīyah, 1951–1933.
Ḥusayn, Ṭāhā. *"Fī al-Jaw." Al-Risālah,* January 8, 1934: 404.
———. *Ḥāfiẓ wa-Shawqī.* 4th ed. Cairo, 1958.
Ibn al-Jawzī, Ḥāfiẓ Abū al-Faraj ʿAbd al-Raḥmān. *Mukhtaṣar Kitāb Talbīs Iblīs.* Edited by ʿAlī al-Sharbajī. Beirut: Muʾassasat al-Risālah, 1992.
———. *Naqd al-ʿIlm waʾl-ʿUlamāʾ, aw, Talbīs Iblīs.* Cairo: Maṭbaʿat al-Saʿādah, 1922.
Ibn Baṭūṭah. *Kitāb Riḥlat Ibn Baṭūṭah al-Musammāh Tuḥfat al-Nuẓẓār fī Gharāʾib al-Amṣār wa-ʿAjāʾib al-Asfār.* Cairo: Maṭbaʿat Wādī al-Nīl, 1287(-1288) [1870–71].
Ibrāhīm, Ḥāfiẓ. *Dīwān Ḥāfiẓ Ibrāhīm.* Edited by Aḥmad Amīn et al. Cairo: Al-Hayʾah al-Miṣrīyah al-ʿĀmmah liʾl-Kitāb, 1980.
ʿĪsā, ʿAbd al-Rāziq, and ʿAbīr Ḥasan, eds. *Miṣr wa-Mīlād al-Qarn al-ʿIshrīn: Ṣūrat Miṣr ʿĀm* 1900*: Dirāsah Taḥlīlīyah.* Cairo: al-ʿArabī, 2001.
Jabartī, ʿAbd al-Raḥmān al-. *ʿAjāʾib al-Āthār fī al-Tarājim waʾl-Akhbār.* Cairo: Maṭbaʿat Dār al-Kutub al-Miṣrīyah, 1997–1998.
Jallād, Fīlīb b. Yūsuf. *Qāmūs al-Idārah waʾl-Qaḍāʾ.* Alexandria: al-Maṭbaʿah al-Tijārīyah, 1900.
Jundī, Anwar al-. *Adab al-Marʾah al-ʿArabīyah.* Cairo, n.d.
Kāmil, ʿAlī Fahmī. *Muṣṭafá Kāmil Bāshā fī Thalāthah wa-Arbaʿīn Rabīʿ: Sīratuhu wa-Aʿmāluhu min Khuṭab wa-Aḥādīth wa-Rasāʾil Siyāsīyah wa-ʿUmrānīyah.* Cairo: Maṭbaʿat al-Liwāʾ, 1908.
Khayrat, Maḥmūd. *Al-Marʾah bayn al-Māḍī waʾl-Ḥāḍir.* Cairo: Idārat Majallat al-Ikhāʾ, 1928.
Khulaʿī, M. K al-. *Kitāb al-Musīqā al-Sharqī.* Cairo: Maṭbaʿat al-Taqaddum, 1902.
Kīlānī, Muḥammad Sayyid. *Trām al-Qāhirah.* Cairo: al-Hayʾa al-ʿĀmma li-Quṣūr al-Thaqāfah, 2010.
Makhlūf, Al-Shaykh Ḥasanayn. *Mudhakkirāt al-Shaykh Ḥasanayn Makhlūf.* http://modernegypt.bibalex.org/DocumentViewer/TextViewer.aspx?w = 1258&h = 902&ty pe = document&id = 20822&s = 1

Maṣlaḥat al-Barīd. *Tārīkh al-Barīd fī Miṣr.* Cairo: Wizārat al-Muwāṣalāt, 1934.
Maṣlaḥat ʿUmūm al-Iḥṣāʾ. *The Census of Egypt Taken in 1917.* Cairo: Government Press, 1920–21.
Mubārak, ʿAlī. *ʿAlam al-Dīn.* Alexandria: Maṭbaʿat Jarīdat al-Maḥrūsah, 1882.
———. *Ḥayātī: Sīrat al-Marḥūm ʿAlī Mubārak Bāshā.* Edited by ʿAbd al-Raḥīm Yūsuf al-Jamal. Cairo: Maktabat al-Ādāb, 1989.
———. *Al-Khiṭaṭ al-Tawfīqīyah al-Jadīdah li-Miṣr al-Qāhirah wa-Mudunihā wa-Bilādihā al-Qadīmah wa-al-Shahīrah.* Bulaq: al-Maṭbaʿah al-Kubrā al-Amīrīyah, 1304–1305 [1886–1889].
Mutawallī, Muḥammad. *Al-Wardah al-Bayḍāʾ.* Cairo: Maṭbaʿat Ḥijāzī.
Muṭīʿī, Shaykh Muḥammad Bakhīt al-. *Kitāb Irshād ahl al-Millah ilā Ithbāt al-Ahillah.* Beirut: Dār Ibn Ḥazm, 2000.
Muwayliḥī, Muḥammad al-. *Ḥadīth ʿĪsā ibn Hishām, aw Fatrah min al-Zamān, li-Munshiʾihi Muḥammad al-Muwayliḥī.* Cairo: al-Dār al-Qawmīyah liʾl-Ṭibāʿah waʾl-Nashr, 1964.
Najm, Zayn al-ʿĀbidīn Shams al-Dīn. *Būr Saʿīd: Tārīkhuha wa-Taṭawwuruha Mundhu Nashʾatihā* 1859 *Ḥatā ʿĀm* 1882. Cairo: al-Hayʾa al-ʿĀmma al-Miṣriyya liʾl-Kitāb, 1987.
Naqqāsh, Salīm Khalīl al-. *Miṣr liʾl-Miṣrīyīn.* Alexandria: Maṭbaʿat Jarīdat al-Maḥrūsah, 1884.
Qāsim, Maḥmūd, et al., eds. *Dalīl al-Aflām fī al-Qarn al-ʿIshrīn fī Miṣr waʾl-ʿĀlam al-ʿArabī.* Cairo: Maktabat Madbūlī, 2002.
Quṭb, Sayyid . "Fī Mustaqbal Āmāl wa-Furaṣ: Muhayyaʾa li-Istiqlāl." *Majallat al-Shuʾūn al-Ijtimāʿīyah* 4 (January 1943).
Rāfiʿī, ʿAbd al-Raḥmān al-. *Thawrat* 1919. Cairo: Maktabat al-Nahḍah al-Miṣrīyah, 1946.
Ramaḍān, Abd al-ʿAẓīm. *Taṭawwur al-Ḥarakah al-Waṭanīyah fī Miṣr,* 1918–1936. Cairo: al-Hayʾa al-Miṣrīyah al-ʿĀmmah liʾl-Kitāb, 1998.
Riḍā, Muḥammad Rashīd. *Fatāwā al-Imām Muḥammad Rashīd Riḍā.* Edited by Ṣalāḥ al-Dīn al-Munajjid and Yūsuf Khūrī. Beirut: Dār al-Kitāb al-Jadīd, 1970.
Samālūṭī, Anwar al-, et al. *Tārīkh Ḥayāt al-Idhāʿah Mundhu Nashāʾihā Ḥattā al-Ān.* Cairo: Idhāʿat al-Jumhūrīyah al-ʿArabīyah al-Muttaḥidah, 1969.
Sāmī, Amīn. *Taqwīm al-Nīl.* Cairo: Maṭbaʿat Dār al-Kutub al-Miṣrīyah, 1936.
Sanhūrī, Nādīyah al-, and Tawfīq al-Shāwī, eds. *Al-Sanhūrī min Khilāl Awrāqihi al-Shakhṣīyah.* Cairo: Dar al-Shurūq, 2005.
Shākir, Aḥmad Muḥammad. *Awāʾil al-Shuhūr al-ʿArabīyah: Hal Yajūz Sharʿan ʿIthbātuha biʾl-Ḥisāb al-Falakī?* Giza: Maktabat Ibn Taymīyah, 1986.
Shawqī, Ahmad. *Majnūn Laylā.* Cairo: Muʾassasat Fann al-Ṭibāʿah, 1958.
Sikak Ḥadīd Miṣr. *Egyptian Railways in 125 Years,* 1852–1977. Cairo, 1977.
Smiles, S. *ʿAlayka: Naṣāʾiḥ li-Tabaṣur al-Shubbān bi-Muqtaḍayāt al-ʿAysh wa-Asrār al-Najāḥ.* Translated by Ibrāhīm Ramzī. Cairo, 1914.
Subkī, Taqī al-Dīn al-. *Kitāb al-ʿIlm al-Manshūr fī Ithbāt al-Shuhūr.* Cairo: Maṭbaʿat Kurdistān al-ʿIlmīyah, 1329 A.H. [1911].

Suyūṭī, ʿAbd al-Raḥmān al-Mashhūr bi-Jalāl al-Dīn al-. *Kitāb Sharḥ al-Ṣudūr bi-Sharḥ Ḥāl al-Mawtā waʾl-Qubūr, wa-bi-Hāmisihi: Bushrā al-Kaʾīb bi-Liqāʾ al-Ḥabīb.* Cairo: al-Maṭbaʿah al-Maymanīyah, 1309/1892.

———. *Sharḥ al-Ṣudūr bi-Sharḥ Ḥāl al-Mawtā wa-al-Qubūr.* Maṭbaʿat Dār Iḥyāʾ al-Kutub al-ʿArabīyah, 1900.

———. *Sharḥ al-Ṣudūr bi-Sharḥ Ḥāl al-Mawtā wa-l-Qubūr.* Cairo, 1329/1911.

Ṭahṭāwī, Rifāʿa Rāfiʿ al-. *Takhlīṣ al-Ibrīz fī Talkhīṣ Bārīs.* Cairo, 1834.

"Tanẓīm al-Barīd fī al-Shām Ibān al-Ḥukm al-Miṣrī, 1831–1840." *Al-Majallah al-Tārīkhīyah al-Miṣrīyah* 40 (1997–1999): 185–207.

Taymūr, M. "Fī al-Qiṭār." In *Mā Tarāhu al-ʿUyūn.* Cairo: al-Dār al-Qawmīyah liʾl-Ṭibāʿah waʾl-Nashr, 1964.

Tūnisī, M. Bayram al-. *Al-Aʿmāl al-Kāmilah.* Cairo: Al-Hayʾah al-Miṣrīyah al-ʿĀmmah liʾl-Kitāb, 1976.

———. "Al-Maqāmah al-Tilifūnīyah." *Maqāmāt Bayram al-Tūnisī.* Edited by Ṭāhir Abū Fashā. Cairo: Maktabat Madbūlī, 1975.

ʿUmar, Muḥammad. *Kitāb Ḥāḍir al-Miṣrīyīn.* Cairo: Maṭbaʿat al-Muqtaṭaf, 1902.

Wajdī, Muḥammad Farīd. *Al-Madanīyah waʾl-Islām.* Cairo: al-Maṭbaʿah al-Hindīyah, 1901.

Yūsuf, Niqūlā. *Al-Ḥayāt al-Jadīdah.* Cairo: Maṭbaʿat al-Majallah al-Jadīdah, 1936.

Zaghlūl, Aḥmad Fatḥī. *Sirr Taqaddum al-Inkilīz al-Saksūnīyīn.* Cairo: Maṭbaʿāt al-Taraqqī, 1898.

Zaghlūl, Saʿd. *Mudhakkirāt Saʿd Zaghlūl.* Cairo: al-Hayʾah al-Miṣrīyah al-ʿĀmmah liʾl-kitāb, 1988–.

Zarqāwī, Aḥmad Mūsā al-. *Al-Adillah al-Islāmiyyah ʿAlā Taḥarruk al-Kurah al-Arḍīyah.* Cairo: Maṭbaʿat al-Hilāl, 1913.

Zayn al-Dīn, Muḥammad Ḥilmī. *Maḍarr al-Zār.* Cairo: Maṭbaʿat Dīwān ʿUmūm al-Awqāf, 1903.

WORKS CITED IN OTHER LANGUAGES

Abāẓah, T. "Fog." In *Cairo Literary Atlas: One Hundred Years on the Streets of the City.* Edited by Samia Mehrez. Cairo: American University in Cairo Press, 2010.

ʿAbd al-Majīd, ʿAbd al-ʿAzīz. *The Modern Arabic Story: Its Emergence, Development, and Form.* Cairo, Dār al-Maʿārif, 1956.

ʿAbd al-Quddūs, I. "I Am Free." In *I Am Free and Other Stories.* Translated by Trevor J. Le Gassick. Cairo: General Egyptian Book Organization, 1978.

Abu-Lughod, Janet L. *Before European Hegemony: A.D. 1250–1350.* New York: Oxford University Press, 1989.

———. *Cairo: 1001 Years of the City Victorious.* Princeton, NJ: Princeton University Press, 1971.

Abu-Lughod, Lila. "The Marriage of Feminism and Islamism in Egypt: Selective Repudiation as a Dynamic of Postcolonial Cultural Politics." In *Remaking*

Women: Feminism and Modernity in the Middle East. Edited by Lila Abu-Lughod. Princeton, NJ: Princeton University Press, 2001.
Adas, M. *Machines as the Measure of Men: Science, Technology, and Ideologies of Western Dominance.* Ithaca, NY: Cornell University Press, 1990.
———. *Prophets of Rebellion: Millenarian Protest Movements against the European Colonial Order.* Chapel Hill: University of North Carolina Press, 1979.
Agamben, Giorgio. *Infancy and History: The Destruction of Experience.* Translated by Liz Heron. London: Verso, 1993.
Ahmed, L. *Women and Gender in Islam: Historical Roots of a Modern Debate.* New Haven, CT: Yale University Press, 1992.
Alder, Ken. *The Measure of All Things: The Seven-Year Odyssey and Hidden Error That Transformed the World.* New York: Free Press, 2002.
Allen, Richard. *Letters from Egypt, Syria and Greece.* Dublin: Gunn & Cameron, 1869.
Allen, Roger. *A Period of Time: A Study and Translation of Ḥadīth ʿĪsā ibn Hishām by Muḥammad al-Muwayliḥī.* Reading: Ithaca Press, 1992.
Ambros, Eva. *Nelles Guide to Egypt.* Hunter, NJ: Hunter, 2001.
Amin, Ahmad. *My Life: The Autobiography of an Egyptian Scholar, Writer, and Cultural Leader.* Translated by Issa J. Boullata. Leiden: Brill Archive, 1978.
Amīn, Galāl. *Whatever Else Happened to the Egyptians: From the Revolution to the Age of Globalization.* Cairo: American University in Cairo Press, 2004.
———. *Whatever Happened to the Egyptians? Changes in Egyptian Society from 1950 to the Present.* Cairo: American University in Cairo Press, 2000.
Amin, Qasim. *The Liberation of Women, and, The New Woman: Two Documents in the History of Egyptian Feminism.* Translated by Samiha Sidhom Peterson. Cairo: American University in Cairo Press, 2000.
Anderson, B. *The Specter of Comparisons: Nationalism, Southeast Asia and the World.* London: Verso, 1998.
Anderson, Kevin. *Marx on the Margins: Nationalism, Ethnicity, and Non-Western Societies.* Chicago: University of Chicago Press, 2010.
Arnold, David. *Colonizing the Body: State Medicine and Epidemic Disease in Nineteenth-Century India.* Berkeley: University of California Press, 1993.
———. *Science, Technology, and Medicine in Colonial India.* Cambridge: Cambridge University Press, 2000.
———. *The Tropics and the Traveling Gaze: India, Landscape, and Science* 1800–1856. Seattle: University of Washington Press, 2005.
Arrow, F. "On the Influence of the Suez Canal on Trade with India." *Journal of the Society of the Arts,* March 11, 1870.
Asad, Talal. *Formations of the Secular: Christianity, Islam, Modernity.* Stanford, CA: Stanford University Press, 2003.
Atabaki, T. *The State and the Subaltern: Modernization, Society and the State in Turkey and Iran* London: I.B. Tauris, 2007.
Aufderheide, A.C. *The Scientific Study of Mummies.* Cambridge: Cambridge University Press, 2003.

Ayalon, A. *The Press in the Arab Middle East: A History.* Oxford: Oxford University Press, 1995.

Ayrout, H. H. *The Egyptian Peasant.* Boston: Beacon Press, 1963 [1938].

Ayrton, F. *Railways in Egypt: Communication with India.* London: Ridgway, 1857.

Badawi, M. M. *A Critical Introduction to Modern Arabic Poetry.* Cambridge: Cambridge University Press, 1975.

———. *Modern Arabic Drama in Egypt.* Cambridge: Cambridge University Press, 1987.

Badiou, Alain. "The Passion for the Real and the Montage of Semblance." In *The Century.* Translated by Alberto Toscano. Cambridge: Polity Press, 2007.

Badrawi, M. *Isma'il Sidqi,* 1875–1950*: Pragmatism and Vision in Twentieth Century Egypt.* Richmond, Surrey: Curzon, 1996.

Baedeker, K. *Egypt: Handbook for Travelers.* Leipzig: K. Baedeker, 1902.

Baer, Gabriel. *Egyptian Guilds in Modern Times.* Jerusalem: Israel Oriental Society, 1964.

Bakhtin, M. *The Dialogic Imagination: Four Essays.* Edited by Michael Holquist. Translated by Caryl Emerson and Michael Holquist. Austin: University of Texas Press, 1981.

Baldwin, James E. "Petitioning the Sultan in Ottoman Egypt." *Bulletin of the School of Oriental and African Studies* 75 (2012): 499–524.

Banerjee, Prathama. *Politics of Time: 'Primitives' and History-Writing in a Colonial Society.* New Delhi: Oxford University Press, 2006.

Bannā, Ḥasan al-. "Letter to a Muslim Student in the West." *Jannah.org.* www.jannah.org/articles/letter.html.

Bannā, S. M. Ḥasan al-. *Imām Shahīd Ḥasan Al-Bannā: From Birth to Martyrdom.* Milpitas, CA: Awakening, 2002.

Barak, On. "Scraping the Surface: The Techno-Politics of Modern Streets in Turn-of-the-Twentieth-Century Alexandria." *Mediterranean Historical Review* 24, no. 2 (December 2009): 187–205.

———. "Times of *Tamaddun:* Gender, Urbanity and Temporality in Modern Egypt." In "Women and the City, Women in the City: A Gendered Perspective for Ottoman Urban History." Edited by Nazan Maksudyan. Unpublished manuscript.

Barber, Captain James. *The Overland Guide-Book: A Complete Vade-Mecum for the Overland Traveller.* London: W. H. Allen, 1845.

Baron, Beth. *Egypt as a Woman: Nationalism, Gender, and Politics.* Berkeley: University of California Press, 2005.

———. "Unveiling in Early Twentieth Century Egypt: Practical and Symbolic Considerations." *Middle Eastern Studies* 25, no. 3 (July 1989): 370–386.

Barrows, A. *The Cosmic Time of Empire: Modern Britain and World Literature.* Berkeley: University of California Press, 2011.

Barthes, R. *Camera Lucida: Reflections on Photography.* New York: Hill and Wang, 1981.

Baskerville, John C., Jr. "From Tahdhiib al-Amma to Tahmiish al-Ammiyya: In Search of Social and Literary Roles for Standard and Colloquial Arabic in Late 19th Century Egypt." PhD diss., University of Texas at Austin, 2009.

Beck, U. *Risk Society: Towards a New Modernity.* Translated by Mark Ritter. London: Sage Publications, 1992.

Beinin, Joel, and Zachary Lockman. *Workers on the Nile: Nationalism, Communism, Islam, and the Egyptian Working Class,* 1882–1954. Cairo: American University in Cairo Press, 1998.

Bell, Charles Frederic Moberly. *From Pharaoh to Fellah.* London: Wells Gardner, Darton, 1888.

Benjamin, Walter. "Theses on the Philosophy of History." In *Illuminations.* Edited by Hannah Arendt. Translated by Harry Zohn. New York: Harcourt, Brace & World, 1968.

———. *The Work of Art in the Age of Its Technological Reproduction and Other Writings on Media.* Edited by Michael Jennings, Brigid Doherty, and Thomas Levin. Translated by Edmund Jephcott et al. Cambridge, MA: Harvard University Press, 2008.

Berque, J. *Egypt: Imperialism and Revolution.* Translated by Jean Stewart. London: Faber, 1972.

Berry, Khaled al-. *Life Is More Beautiful Than Paradise: A Jihadist's Own Story.* Translated by Humphrey Davies. London: Haus, 2009.

Blackman, Winifred S. *The Fellahin of Upper Egypt.* Cairo: AUC Press, 2000.

Blackmon, Douglas. *Slavery by Another Name: The Re-Enslavement of Black Americans from the Civil War to World War II.* New York: Random House, 2009.

Blanchard, Jerrold. *Egypt under Ismail Pacha: Being Some Chapters of Contemporary History.* London: S. Tinsley, 1879.

Bland, James. *Prince Ahmed of Egypt.* London: S. Paul, 1939.

Bonar, A. *Memoir of the Life and Brief Ministry of David Sandeman.* London: J. Nisbet, 1861.

Booth, Marilyn, and Anthony Gorman, eds. *The Long* 1890s *in Egypt: Colonial Quiescence, Subterranean Resistance.* Edinburgh: Edinburgh University Press, 2013.

Bourke, Joanna. *Fear: A Cultural History.* Berkeley, CA: Counterpoint Press, 2007.

Brewer, E. C. *Authors and Their Works.* London: Chatto & Windus, 1884.

Briggs, Martin Shaw. *Through Egypt in War Time.* London: T. Fisher Unwin, 1918.

Bright, C. *Submarine Telegraphs: Their History, Construction and Work.* London: C. Lockwood, 1898.

Brockway, Lucile H. *Science and Colonial Expansion: The Role of the British Royal Botanic Gardens.* New Haven, CT: Yale University Press, 2002.

Brooks, Chris, and Peter Faulkner. *The White Man's Burdens: An Anthology of British Poetry of the Empire.* Exeter: Exeter University Press, 1996.

Brown, N. *Peasant Politics in Modern Egypt: The Struggle against the State.* New Haven, CT: Yale University Press, 1990.

Brugel, J. Christoph. *Der Islam im Spiegel zeigenössischer Literatur der islamischen Welt: Vorträge eines Internationalen Symposiums an der Universität Bern,* 11.-14. *Juli* 1983. Leiden: E. J. Brill, 1985.

Buchanan, R. A. "The Diaspora of British Engineering." *Technology and Culture* 27, no. 3 (July 1986): 501–524.

Bulliet, R. *The Camel and the Wheel.* New York: Columbia University Press, 1990.
Burchill, Graham, Colin Gordon, and Peter Miller, eds. *The Foucault Effect: Studies in Governmentality.* London: Harvester Wheatsheaf, 1991.
Caliskan, K. "Making a Global Commodity: The Production of Markets and Cotton in Egypt, Turkey, and the United States." PhD diss., New York University, 2005.
———. *Market Threads: How Cotton Farmers and Traders Create a Global Commodity.* Princeton, NJ: Princeton University Press, 2010.
Calvert, John. *Sayyid Qutb and the Origins of Radical Islamism.* New York: Columbia University Press, 2010.
Cameron, W. H. Moreton, and Walter Feldwich. *Ports and Cities of the World.* N.p.: Globe Encyclopedia, 1927.
Carré, Olivier, Carol Artigues, and W. Shepard. *Mysticism and Politics: A Critical Reading of Fī Ẓilāl al-Qurʾān by Sayyid Quṭb* (1906–1966). Leiden: Brill, 2003.
Carter, Mia, and Barbara Harlow, eds. *Archives of Empire: From the East India Company to the Suez Canal.* Durham, NC: Duke University Press, 2003.
Chakrabarty, D. *Provincializing Europe: Postcolonial Thought and Historical Difference.* Princeton, NJ: Princeton University Press, 2000.
Chalcraft, J. *The Striking Cabbies of Cairo and Other Stories: Crafts and Guilds in Egypt,* 1863–1914 Albany: SUNY Press, 2004.
Chandler, A. *The Visible Hand: The Managerial Revolution in American Business.* Cambridge, MA: Belknap Press, 1977.
Chatterjee, P. *The Nation and Its Fragments: Colonial and Postcolonial Histories.* Princeton, NJ: Princeton University Press, 1993.
Chesney, F. R. *Narrative of the Euphrates Expedition.* London: Longmans, Green, 1868.
Cole, Juan. *Colonialism and Revolution in the Middle East.* Princeton, NJ: Princeton University Press, 1993.
———. *Napoleon's Egypt: Invading the Middle East.* New York: Palgrave Macmillan, 2007.
Colley, L. *Britons: Forging the Nation,* 1707–1837. New Haven, CT: Yale University Press, 2009.
Connor, Steven. "The Machine in the Ghost: Spiritualism, Technology, and the 'Direct Voice.'" In *Ghosts: Deconstruction, Psychoanalysis, History.* Edited by Peter Buse and Andrew Stott. New York: St. Martin's Press, 1999.
Cooper, Fred. "Colonizing Time: Work Rhythms and Labor Conflict in Colonial Mombassa." In *Colonialism and Culture,* edited by Nicholas B. Dirks, pp. 209–247. Ann Arbor: University of Michigan Press, 1992.
Crary, J. *Techniques of the Observer: On Vision and Modernity in the Nineteenth Century.* Cambridge, MA: MIT Press, 1992.
Cromer, Evelyn Baring, Earl of. *Modern Egypt.* New York: Macmillan, 1908.
Cronon, W. *Nature's Metropolis: Chicago and the Great West.* New York: Norton, 1992.
Crosby, A. W. *Ecological Imperialism: The Biological Expansion of Europe.* Cambridge: Cambridge University Press, 2004.

Cuno, Kenneth. *The Pasha's Peasants: Land, Society and Economy in Lower Egypt, 1740–1858*. Cambridge: Cambridge University Press, 1992.

Dallal, Ahmad. "Appropriating the Past: Twentieth-Century Reconstruction of Pre-Modern Islamic Thought." *Islamic Law and Society* 7, no. 1 (2000).

Danielson, V. *"The Voice of Egypt": Umm Kulthūm, Arabic Song, and Egyptian Society in the Twentieth Century*. Chicago: University of Chicago Press, 1997.

Davidson, Roderic H. "Where Is the Middle East?" *Foreign Affairs* 38 (1960): 665–675.

Debord, Guy. *The Society of the Spectacle*. New York: Zone Books, 1995.

De Jong, Frederick. "Opposition to Sufism in Twentieth-Century Egypt, 1900–1970: A Preliminary Survey." In *Islamic Mysticism Contested: Thirteen Centuries of Controversies and Polemics*, edited by F. de Jong and B. Radtke. Leiden: Brill, 1999.

Deleuze, Gilles, and Claire Parnet. *Dialogues*. Translated by H. Tomlinson and B. Habberjam. New York: Columbia University Press, 1987.

Deleuze, Gilles, and Felix Guattari. *Anti-Oedipus*. London: Penguin Classics, 2009.

De Leon, E. "How I Introduced the Telephone into Egypt." *Fraser's Magazine* 106 (1882).

———. *The Khedive's Egypt; or, The Old House of Bondage under New Masters*. London: S. Low, Marston, Searle & Rivington, 1877.

Demolins, E. *Anglo-Saxon Superiority: To What It Is Due*. Translated by Louis Bertram Lavigne. London: Leadenhall Press, 1899.

Dennis, Alfred. "The Indian Problem and Imperial Politics." *Journal of Race Development* 1 (1910–1911): 187–209.

Department of Overseas Trade, United Kingdom. "Report on Economic and Commercial Conditions in Egypt." 1920.

Depping, Georges Bernard. *Evening Entertainments; or, Delineations of the Manners and Customs of Various Nations*. London: N. Hailes, 1817.

Derrida. Jacques. "Autoimmunity: Real and Symbolic Suicides." In *Philosophy in a Time of Terror: Dialogues with Jürgen Habermas and Jacques Derrida*, by Giovanna Barradori. Chicago: University of Chicago Press, 2004.

———. "No Apocalypse, Not Now (Full Speed Ahead, Seven Missiles, Seven Missives)." *Diacritics* 14, no. 2 (Summer 1984): 20–31.

———. *Specters of Marx*. Translated by Peggy Kamuf. New York: Routledge, 1994.

Di-Capua, Yoav. "Common Skies Divided Horizons: Aviation, Class and Modernity in Early Twentieth Century Egypt." *Journal of Social History* 41, no. 4 (Summer 2008): 917–942.

Diner, Dan. *Lost in the Sacred: Why the Muslim World Stood Still*. Translated by Steven Rendall. Princeton, NJ: Princeton University Press, 2009.

Dirks, Nicholas B. "Colonialism and Culture." In *Colonialism and Culture*, edited by N. Dirks. Ann Arbor: University of Michigan Press, 1992.

Dohrn-van Rossum, Gerhard. *History of the Hour: Clocks and Modern Temporal Orders*. Translated by Thomas Dunlap. Chicago: University of Chicago Press, 1996.

Doles, M. *Majnūn: The Madman in Medieval Islamic Society.* Oxford: Clarendon Press, 1992.

The Egyptian Railway; or, The Interest of England in Egypt. London: Hope, 1852.

"Egyptian Unrest under British Rule." *Current History: A Monthly Magazine of the New York Times* 10 (April-September 1919): 259.

El Guindi, Fadwa. *By Noon Prayer: The Rhythm of Islam.* Oxford: Berg, 2008.

Elshakry, Marwa S. "Darwin's Legacy in the Arab East: Science, Religion and Politics, 1870–1914." PhD diss., Princeton University, 2003.

———. "Knowledge in Motion: The Cultural Politics of Modern Science Translations in Arabic." *Isis* 99, no. 4 (December 2008).

El Shakry, Omnia. *The Great Social Laboratory: Subjects of Knowledge in Colonial and Postcolonial Egypt.* Stanford, CA: Stanford University Press, 2007.

———. "Schooled Mothers and Structured Play: Child-Rearing in Turn of the Century Egypt." In *Remaking Women: Feminism and Modernity in the Middle East,* edited by Lila Abu-Lughod. Princeton, NJ: Princeton University Press, 1998.

ESR Statistical Yearbook for the Year 1909.

Fabian, J. *Time and the Other: How Anthropology Makes Its Object.* New York: Columbia University Press, 2002.

Fahmy, Khaled. *All the Pasha's Men: Mehmed Ali, His Army, and the Making of Modern Egypt.* Cambridge: Cambridge University Press, 1998.

———. "The Anatomy of Justice: Forensic Medicine and Criminal Law in Nineteenth-Century Egypt." *Islamic Law and Society* 6, no. 2 (1999): 224–271.

———. "Justice and Pain in Khedival Egypt." In *Standing Trial: Law and the Person in the Modern Middle East,* edited by Baudouin Dupres. London: I. B. Tauris, 2004.

———. "An Olfactory Tale of Two Cities: Cairo in the Nineteenth Century." In *Historians in Cairo: Essays in Honor of George Scanlon.* Edited by Jill Edwards. Cairo: American University in Cairo Press, 2002.

———. *Mehmed Ali: From Ottoman Governor to Ruler of Egypt.* Oxford: Oneworld, 2009.

———. "Modernizing Cairo." In *Making Cairo Medieval,* edited by N. Al-Sayyad, I. A. Bierman, and N. Rabbat. Lanham, MD: Lexington Books, 2005.

Fahmy, Ziad. *Ordinary Egyptians: Creating the Modern Nation through Popular Culture.* Stanford, CA: Stanford University Press, 2011.

Fairholt, F. W. *Up the Nile, and Home Again: A Handbook for Travellers and a Travel-book for the Library.* London: Chapman and Hall, 1862.

Faraday, M. "On a Peculiar Class of Optical Deceptions." In *Experimental Researches in Chemistry and Physics.* London: R. Taylor & W. Francis, 1859.

Foreign Office, Great Britain. *Reply to Charges Brought against British Troops by Egyptian Delegation in Paris during Egyptian Disturbances.* London, 1919.

Forster, E. M. "Letter to Mohammed el Adl." In *Alexandria: A History and a Guide and Pharos and Pharillon,* edited by Miriam Allott. Cairo: American University in Cairo Press, 2004.

Foucault, Michel. *Discipline and Punish: The Birth of the Prison.* New York: Random House, 1977.
Freeman, Lewis R. "The Railroad Conquest of Africa." *American Review of Reviews* 50 (July-December 1914): 64–80.
Friedman, Thomas L. "One Country, Two Worlds." *New York Times,* January 28, 2000: A23
Frith, H. *The Romance of Engineering: The Stories of the Highway, the Waterway, the Railway, and the Subway.* London: Ward, Lock, Bowden, 1895.
Frolov, D. *Classical Arabic Verse: History and Theory of ʿArud.* Leiden: Brill, 2000.
Furbank, Philip Nicholas. *E. M. Forster: A Life.* New York: Harcourt Brace, 1994.
Galison, P. *Einstein's Clocks, Poincaré's Maps: Empires of Time.* New York: Norton, 2003.
Galloway, J. A. *Observations on the Proposed Improvements in the Overland Route via Egypt with Remarks on the Ship Canal, the Boulac Canal, and the Suez Railroad.* London, 1844.
Gandhi, [Mahatma]. *Hind Swaraj and Other Writings.* Edited by Anthony Parel. Cambridge: Cambridge University Press, 1997.
Garstin, W. *Report upon the Administration of the Public Works Department in Egypt for* 1903. Cairo: National Printing Department, 1904.
———. *Report upon the Administration of the Public Works Department in Egypt for* 1904. Cairo: National Printing Department, 1905.
———. *Report upon the Administration of the Public Works Department in Egypt for* 1905. Cairo: National Printing Department, 1906.
Garwood, A. E. *Forty Years of an Engineer's Life at Home and Abroad.* Newport, Monmouthshire: A. W. Dawson, 1903.
Gasper, Michael. *The Power of Representation: Publics, Peasants, and Islam in Egypt.* Stanford, CA: Stanford University Press, 2009.
Gershoni, Israel. *Piramidah La-umah: Hantsaḥah, Zikaron u-Leʾumiyut be-Mitsrayim ba-Meʾah ha-ʿEśrim.* Tel Aviv: ʿAm ʿOved, 2006.
Gershoni, Israel, and James P. Jankowski. *Egypt, Islam, and the Arabs: The Search for Egyptian Nationhood,* 1900–1930. Oxford: Oxford University Press, 1986.
Goldberg, Ellis. "Peasants in Revolt—Egypt 1919." *International Journal of Middle Eastern Studies* 24, no. 2 (May 1992): 261–280.
Goldman, M. *Umm Kulthum: A Voice like Egypt.* Arab Film Distribution, 1996.
Gorst, Sir Eldon. "Lord Cromer in Egypt." In *The Empire and the Century: A Series of Essays on Imperial Problems and Possibilities.* London: John Murray, 1905.
Goswami, M. *Producing India: From Colonial Economy to National Space.* Chicago: University of Chicago Press, 2004.
Government of Egypt. *Almanac for the Year* 1915. Cairo, 1915.
Gran, Peter. *Islamic Roots of Capitalism: Egypt,* 1760–1840. Austin: University of Texas Press, 1979.
Green, Nile. *Bombay Islam: The Religious Economy of the West Indian Ocean,* 1840–1915. Cambridge: Cambridge University Press, 2011.

Gregory, Derek. "Performing Cairo: Orientalism and the City of the Arabian Nights." In *Making Cairo Medieval,* edited by N. Al-Sayyad, I. A. Bierman, and N. Rabbat. Lanham, MD: Lexington Books, 2005.

Guerlac, Suzanne. *Thinking in Time: An Introduction to Henri Bergson.* Ithaca, NY: Cornell University Press, 2006.

Haag, M. *Alexandria: City of Memory.* New Haven, CT: Yale University Press, 2004.

Haeri, Niloofar. *Sacred Language, Ordinary People: Dilemmas of Culture and Politics in Egypt.* New York: Palgrave Macmillan, 2003.

Hafez, S. *The Genesis of Arabic Narrative Discourse.* London: Saqi Books, 1993.

Haikal, Mohammad Hussein. *Zaynab.* Translated by John Mohammad Grinsted. London: Darf, 1989.

Hair, P. E. H. "Death from Violence in Britain: A Tentative Secular Survey." *Population Studies* 25, no. 1 (March 1971): 36–43.

Ḥakīm, Tawfīq al-. *Maze of Justice: Diary of a Country Prosecutor: An Egyptian Novel.* Translated by Abba Eban. Austin: University of Texas Press, 1989.

———. *The Prison of Life.* Translated by Pierre Cachia. Cairo: American University in Cairo Press, 1992

———. *Return of the Spirit: Tawfiq al-Hakim's Classic Novel of the* 1919 *Revolution.* Translated by William M. Hutchins. Washington, DC: Three Continents Press, 1990.

———. "Shahrazad." In *Plays, Prefaces and Postscripts of Tawfiq al-Hakim,* translated by W. M. Hutchins. Washington, DC: Three Continents Press, 1981.

Halevi, Leor. *Muhammad's Grave: Death Rites and the Making of Islamic Society.* New York: Columbia University Press, 2011.

Halim, Hala. "Forster in Alexandria: Gender and Genre in Narrating Colonial Cosmopolitanism." *Hawwa* 4 (November 17, 2006): 237–273.

Hall, H. R. *A Handbook for Egypt and the Sudan.* London: E. Stanford, 1907.

Hallberg, C. W. *The Suez Canal: Its History and Diplomatic Importance.* New York: Octagon Books, 1974.

Hammoudi, A. *A Season in Mecca: Narrative of a Pilgrimage.* Cambridge: Polity, 2006.

Hanley, Will. "Foreignness and Localness in Alexandria, 1880–1914." PhD diss., Princeton University, 2007.

Hanna, N. *In Praise of Books, A Cultural History of Cairo's Middle Class, Sixteenth to the Eighteenth Century.* Cairo: American University in Cairo Press, 2004.

Haraway, Donna. "A Cyborg Manifesto: Science, Technology, and Socialist-Feminism in the Late Twentieth Century." In *Simians, Cyborgs and Women: The Reinvention of Nature.* London: Free Association, 1991.

Hartman, Saidiya. *Scenes of Subjection: Terror, Slavery, and Self-Making in Nineteenth-Century America.* New York: Oxford University Press, 1997.

Hartog, P. J. *Examinations and Their Relation to Culture and Efficiency with a Speech by the Late Earl of Cromer.* London: Constable, 1918.

Harvey, David. "Between Space and Time: Reflections on the Geographical Imagination." *Annals of the Association of American Geographers* 80, no. 3 (1990): 418–434.

———. *The Condition of Postmodernity: An Enquiry into the Origins of Cultural Change.* Cambridge, MA: Blackwell, 1990.

———. *Paris, Capital of Modernity.* New York: Psychology Press, 2003.

Hathaway, Jane. *The Politics of Households in Ottoman Egypt: The Rise of the Qazdağlis.* Cambridge: Cambridge University Press, 2002.

Hausman, William, Peter Hertner, and Mira Wilkins. *Global Electrification: Multinational Enterprise and International Finance in the History of Light and Power, 1878–2007.* Cambridge: Cambridge University Press, 2008.

Headrick, D. R. *The Invisible Weapon: Telecommunications and International Politics,* 1851–1945. New York: Oxford University Press, 1991.

———. *Tools of Empire: Technology and European Imperialism in the Nineteenth Century.* New York: Oxford University Press, 1981.

Henry, J. D. *Baku: An Eventful History.* Stratford, NH: Ayer, 1905.

Heyworth-Dunne, J. "Printing and Translations under Muḥammad ʿAlī of Egypt: The Foundation of Modern Arabic." *Journal of the Royal Asiatic Society of Great Britain and Ireland,* no. 3 (July 1940): 325–349.

Hirschkind, Charles. *The Ethical Soundscape: Cassette Sermons and Islamic Counterpublics.* New York: Columbia University Press, 2006.

Hobsbawm, Eric, and Terence Ranger, eds. *The Invention of Tradition.* Cambridge: Cambridge University Press, 1992.

Holt, P. M. "Egypt and the Nile Valley." In *The Cambridge History of Africa.,* edited by John E. Flint, volume 5, *From c.* 1790 *to c.* 1870. London: Cambridge University Press, 1976.

Hoppe, K. N. "Teredo Navalis—The Cryptogenic Shipworm." In *Invasive Aquatic Species of Europe: Their Distribution, Impacts and Management,* edited by E. Leppakoski. London: Kluwer, 2002.

Hoskins, H. L. *British Routes to India.* New York: Longmans, Green: 1928.

Hourani, A. *Arabic Thought in the Liberal Age,* 1798–1939. Cambridge: Cambridge University Press, 1983.

Hoyle, Mark S. W. "The Mixed Courts of Egypt 1906–1915." *Arab Law Quarterly* 2, no. 2 (May 1987): 166–184.

Hughes, Thomas Parke. *Networks of Power: Electrification in Western Society,* 1880–1930. Baltimore, MD: Johns Hopkins University Press, 1993.

Hunt, B. "Scientists, Engineers, and Wildman Whitehouse: Measurement and Credibility in Early Cable Telegraphy." *British Journal for the History of Science* 29, no. 2 (June 1996): 155–170.

Hunter, A. *Power and Passion in Egypt: A Life of Sir Eldon Gorst,* 1861–1911. London: I. B. Tauris, 2007.

Hussien, Taha. *A Man of Letters.* Translated by Mona El-Zayyat. Cairo: American University in Cairo Press, 1994.

Hyde, R. *Panoramania!* London: Trefoil, 1988.

Ibn Majid, Ahmad. *Arab Navigation in the Indian Ocean before the Coming of the Portuguese.* Translated by G. R. Tibbetts. London: Royal Asiatic Society of Great Britain and Ireland, 1971.

Izutsu, Toshihiko. *God and Man in the Qur'ān.* Karachi: Royal Book Company, 2002.

Jabartī, ʿAbd al-Raḥmān al-. *Al-Jabartī's History of Egypt.* Edited by Jane Hathaway. Princeton, NJ: Markus Wiener, 2006.

———. *Napoleon in Egypt: Al-Jabartī's Chronicle of the First Seven Months of the French Occupation,* 1798. Translated by Shmuel Moreh. Princeton, NJ: M. Wiener, 2004.

Jacob, Wilson Chacko. *Working Out Egypt: Effendi Masculinity and Subject Formation in Colonial Modernity,* 1870–1940. Durham, NC: Duke University Press, 2011.

Jakes, Aaron. "The Scales of Public Utility: Agricultural Roads and State Space in the Era of the British Occupation." In *The Long* 1890*s in Egypt: Colonial Quiescence, Subterranean Resistance,* edited by Marilyn Booth and Anthony Gorman. Edinburgh: Edinburgh University Press, 2013.

Jameson, Fredric. *A Singular Modernity.* London: Verso Books 2002.

Jobson, F.J. *Australia: With Notes by the Way, on Egypt, Ceylon, Bombay, and the Holy Land.* London: Hamilton, Adams, 1862.

Kang, Minsoo. *Sublime Dreams of Living Machines: The Automaton in the European Imagination.* Cambridge, MA: Harvard University Press, 2011.

Kant, Immanuel. *Critique of Practical Reason.* Translated by Mary J. Gregor. Cambridge: Cambridge University Press, 1997.

Kennedy, Philip. *Abu Nuwas: A Genius of Poetry.* Oxford: Oneworld, 2005.

Kern, S. *The Culture of Time and Space.* Cambridge, MA: Harvard University Press, 1983.

Khan, Fritz. *Das Leben des Menschen: Eine Volkstümliche Anatomie, Biologie, Physiologie und Entwicklungsgeschichte des Menschen.* Stuttgart: Franckh'sche Verlagshandlung, 1922–31.

Khan, Noor-Aiman. *Egyptian-Indian Nationalist Collaboration and the British Empire.* New York: Palgrave-Macmillan, 2011.

Khuri-Makdisi, Ilham. *The Eastern Mediterranean and the Making of Global Radicalism,* 1860–1914. Berkeley: University of California Press, 2010.

———. "Levantine Trajectories: The Formulation and Dissemination of Radical Ideas in and between Beirut, Cairo, and Alexandria, 1860–1914." PhD diss., Harvard University, 2003.

Kilito, Abdelfattah. *Thou Shalt Not Speak My Language.* Translated by Waïl S. Hassan. Syracuse, NY: Syracuse University Press, 2008.

Kinberg, Leah. "Interaction between This World and the Afterworld in Early Islamic Tradition." *Oriens* 29/30 (1986): 285–308.

Kirby, L. *Parallel Tracks: The Railroad and Silent Cinema.* Durham, NC: Duke University Press, 2007.

Knox, T. Wallace. *Underground: Gambling and Its Horrors.* Hartford: J.B. Burr, 1876.

Koppes, Clayton R. "Captain Mahan, General Gordon, and the Origins of the Term 'Middle East.'" *Middle Eastern Studies* 12, no. 1 (January 1976): 95–98.

Koselleck, Reinhart. *Futures Past: On the Semantics of Historical Time.* Translated by Keith Tribe. New York: Columbia University Press, 2004.

Lababidi, Lesley Kitchen. *Cairo Street Stories: Exploring the City's Statues, Squares, Bridges, Gardens, and Sidewalk Cafés.* Cairo: American University in Cairo Press, 2008.

Lacan, J. "Seminar on the Purloined Letter." In *The Purloined Poe,* edited by John P. Muller and William R. Richardson. Baltimore, MD: Johns Hopkins University Press, 1988.

Lagrange, F. "Women in the Singing Business, Women in Songs." *History Compass* 7/1 (2009): 226–250.

Landes, D. *Revolution in Time: Clocks and the Making of the Modern World.* Cambridge: Harvard University Press, 1983.

Lane, E. W. *An Account of the Manners and Customs of the Modern Egyptians.* Cairo: American University of Cairo Press, 2003.

Lane-Poole, S. *Life of William Edward Lane.* London: Williams and Norgate, 1877.

———. *Studies in a Mosque.* London: Eden, Remington, 1883.

Lange, Christian. "Barzakh." In *Encyclopedia of Islam* 3, edited by Gudrun Krämer et al. Leiden: Brill, 2011.

Lardner, D. *The Steam Engine Familiarly Explained and Illustrated.* 8th ed. London: Taylor, Walton, and Maberly, 1851.

Latham, G. *Proposed New Overland Route via Turkish Arabia.* Calcutta, 1870.

Latour, Bruno. *On the Modern Cult of Factish Gods.* Durham, NC: Duke University Press, 2010.

———. *Pandora's Hope: Essays on the Reality of Science Studies.* Cambridge, MA: Harvard University Press, 1999.

———. *Reassembling the Social: An Introduction to Actor-Network-Theory.* Oxford: Oxford University Press, 2005.

———. "A Relativistic Account of Einstein's Relativity." *Social Studies of Science* 18, no. 1 (February 1988): 3–44.

———. *Science in Action: How to Follow Scientists and Engineers through Society.* Cambridge, MA: Harvard University Press, 1988.

Leeder, S. H. *Veiled Mysteries of Egypt and the Religion of Islam.* New York: Charles Scribner's , 1913.

Le Goff, Jacques. "Merchant's Time and Church's Time in the Middle Ages." In *Time, Work and Culture in the Middle Ages,* translated by Arthur Goldhammer, 29–42. Chicago: University of Chicago Press, 1980.

Litvin, Margaret. *Hamlet's Arab Journey: Shakespeare's Prince and Nasser's Ghost.* Princeton, NJ: Princeton University Press, 2011.

Lockman, Z. "Imagining the Working Class: Culture, Nationalism, and Class Formation in Egypt, 1899–1914." Poetics Today 15, no. 2 (Summer 1994): 157–190.

Low, Michael Christopher. "Empire and the *Ḥajj:* Pilgrims, Plagues, and Pan-Islam under British Surveillance, 1865–1908." *International Journal of Middle East Studies* 40, no. 2 (May 31, 2008): 269–290.

Mahfouz, Naguib. *God's World: An Anthology of Short Stories.* Translated by Akef Abadir and Roger Allan. Minneapolis, MN: Bibliotheca Islamica, 1973.

———. *Midaq Alley, Cairo.* Translated by Trevor Le Gassick. Beirut: Khayats, 1966.

———. *Palace Walk.* Translated by William Maynard Hutchins. New York: Random House, 1991.

Mahmood, Saba. *Politics of Piety: The Islamic Revival and the Feminist Subject.* Princeton, NJ: Princeton University Press, 2005.

Manela, Erez. *The Wilsonian Moment: Self-Determination and the International Origins of Anticolonial Nationalism.* Oxford: Oxford University Press, 2007.

Marmery, J.V. *Progress of Science: Its Origin, Course, Promoters, and Results.* London: Chapman and Hall, 1895.

Marshall, Charles. *Historical and Statistic Description of Mr. Charles Marshall's Great Moving Diorama Illustrating the Grand Routes of a Tour through Europe.* London, n.p., 1848.

Martin, Michele. *"Hello, Central?" Gender, Technology, and Culture in the Formation of Telephone Systems.* Montreal: McGill-Queen's University Press, 1991.

Marx, Karl. "On Bruno Bauer's *On the Jewish Question* (1843)." In *The Broadview Anthology of Social and Political Thought: From Plato to Nietzsche,* edited by Andrew Bailey. Peterborough, Ontario: Broadview Press, 2008.

———. *Capital: A Critique of Political Economy.* Translated by David Fernbach. New York: Penguin Classics, 1976.

———. *Grundrisse: Foundations of the Critique of Political Economy.* New York: Vintage Books, 1973.

———. *The Poverty of Philosophy.* Moscow: Foreign Languages, [1973].

May, J., and N. Thrift. *TimeSpace: Geographies of Temporality.* London: Routledge, 2001.

Messick, B. *The Calligraphic State: Textual Domination and History in a Muslim Society.* Berkeley: University of California Press, 1992.

Metcalf, B., and T. Metcalf. *A Concise History of India.* Cambridge: Cambridge University Press, 2002.

Meyers, A.W. "The Trams of the World." *Cassell's Magazine* 8 (1901): 559–567.

Middeljans, April. "On the Wire with Death and Desire: The Telephone and Lovers' Discourse in the Short Stories of Dorothy Parker." *Arizona Quarterly* 62, no. 4 (2006): 47–70.

Mikhail, Alan. *Nature and Empire in Ottoman Egypt.* Cambridge: Cambridge University Press, 2011.

Miles, Malcolm, and Tim Hall, with Iain Borden, eds. *The City Cultures Reader.* New York: Routledge, 2000.

Miller, Angela. "The Panorama, the Cinema, and the Emergence of the Spectacular." *Wide Angle* 18, no. 2 (April 1996): 34–69.

Miller, Jacques-Alain. *Ha-Eroṭiḳa shel ha-zman.* Tel Aviv: Resling, 2008.

Milner, Alfred. *Report of the Special Mission to Egypt.* London: H.M. Stationery Office, 1921.

Mitchell, Timothy. *Colonising Egypt.* Cambridge: Cambridge University Press, 1988.

———. *Rule of Experts: Egypt, Techno-Politics, Modernity.* Berkeley: University of California Press, 2002.

Moiret, J.M. *Memoirs of Napoleon's Egyptian Expedition,* 1798–1801. Edited and translated by Rosmary Brindle. London: Greenhill Books, 2001.

Molloy, Scott. *Trolley Wars: Streetcar Workers on the Line.* Washington, DC: Smithsonian Institution Press, 1996.

Molyneux, William Charles Francis. *Campaigning in South Africa and Egypt.* London: Macmillan, 1896.

Moore, Harry T., and Karl W. Deutsch, eds. *The Human Prospect.* Boston: Beacon Press, 1956.

Moosa, E. "Shaykh Ahmad Shakir and the Adoption of a Scientifically-Based Lunar Calendar." *Islamic Law and Society* 5, no. 1 (1998): 57–89.

Moreh, S. "The Neoclassical Qasida: Modern Poets and Critics." In *Studies in Modern Arabic Prose and Poetry.* Leiden: Brill, 1988.

Mrázek, Rudolf. *Engineers of Happy Land: Technology and Nationalism in a Colony.* Princeton, NJ: Princeton University Press, 2002.

Mumford, Lewis. "The Monastery and the Clock." In *The Human Prospect,* edited by Harry T. Moore and Karl W. Deutsch. Boston: Beacon Press, 1956.

———. *Technics and Civilization.* New York: Harcourt, Brace & World, 1963.

Murray, C. *Victorian Narrative Technologies in the Middle East.* New York: Routledge, 2008.

Mūsā, Salāma. *The Education of Salāma Mūsā.* Translated by L.O. Schuman. Leiden: Brill, 1961.

Nickles, David Paull. *Under the Wire: How Telegraphy Changed Diplomacy.* Cambridge, MA: Harvard University Press, 2003.

Nidel, Richard. *World Music: The Basics.* New York: Routledge, 2005.

Nkwi, Walter Gam. "From the Elitist to the Commonality of Voice Communication: The History of the Telephone in Buea, Cameroon." In *Mobile Phones, the New Talking Drums of Everyday Africa,* edited by Mirjam de Bruijn et al. Bamenda, Cameroon: Langaa RPCIG, 2009.

Noam, Eli M. *Telecommunications in Africa.* Oxford: Oxford University Press, 1999.

Nubar Pasha. *Mémoires de Nubar Pacha.* Beirut: Librairie du Liban, 1983.

Ochsenwald, William. *The Hijaz Railroad.* Charlottesville: University Press of Virginia, 1980.

Oettermann, S. *The Panorama: History of a Mass Medium.* Translated by D. Schneider. New York: Zone Books, 1997.

Omar, A. "Anglo-Egyptian Relations and the Construction of the Alexandria-Cairo-Suez Railway, 1833–1858." PhD diss., University of London, 1966.

Oppenheim, Janet. *The Other World: Spiritualism and Psychical Research in England, 1850–1914*. Cambridge: Cambridge University Press, 1988.

Otis, Laura. *Networking: Communicating with Bodies and Machines in the Nineteenth Century*. Ann Arbor: University of Michigan Press, 2001.

Ouyang, Wen-chin. "Fictive Mode, 'Journey to the West,' and Transformation of Space: ʿAli Mubarak's Discourses of Modernization." *Comparative Critical Studies* 4, no. 3 (2007): 331–358.

Owen, R. *Cotton and the Egyptian Economy, 1820–1914: A Study in Trade and Development*. Oxford: Clarendon, 1969.

———. *Lord Cromer: Victorian Imperialist, Edwardian Proconsul*. Oxford: Oxford University Press, 2005.

———. *The Middle East in the World Economy*, 1800–1914. London: Methuen, 1981.

Perkins, F. B. *Scrope; or, The Lost Library*. Boston: Roberts, 1874.

Perkins, M. *The Reform of Time: Magic and Modernity*. Sterlin, VA: Pluto Press, 2001.

Peskes, Esther. "The Wahhabiyya and Sufism in the Eighteenth Century." In *Islamic Mysticism Contested: Thirteen Centuries of Controversies and Polemics*, edited by Frederick de Jong and Bernd Radtke. Leiden: Brill, 1999.

Peters, F. *The Hajj: The Muslim Pilgrimage to Mecca and the Holy Places*. Princeton, NJ: Princeton University Press, 1995.

Peters, John Durham. *Speaking into the Air: A History of the Idea of Communication*. Chicago: University of Chicago Press, 1999.

Peters, R. "Administrators and Magistrates: The Development of a Secular Judiciary in Egypt." *Die Welt des Islams* 39, no. 3 (November 1999): 378–397.

Peters, T. *Building the Nineteenth Century*. Cambridge, MA: MIT Press, 1996.

Pickering, Andrew. *The Mangle of Practice: Time, Agency, and Science*. Chicago: University of Chicago Press, 1995.

Podobnik, Bruce. *Global Energy Shifts: Fostering Sustainability in a Turbulent Age*. Philadelphia: Temple University Press, 2006.

Polehampton, H. S. *A Memoir, Letters and Diary of Henry S. Polehampton*. London: Richard Bentley, 1859.

Pollard, Lisa. *Nurturing the Nation: The Family Politics of Modernizing, Colonizing, and Liberating Egypt*, 1805–1923. Berkeley: University of California Press, 2005.

———. "Working by the Book: Constructing New Homes and the Emergence of the Modern Egyptian State under Muhammad Ali." In *Transitions in Domestic Consumption and Family Life in the Modern Middle East: Houses in Motion*, edited by Relli Shechter. New York: Palgrave Macmillan, 2003.

Pomeranz, K. *The Great Divergence: China, Europe, and the Making of the Modern World Economy*. Princeton, NJ: Princeton University Press, 2000.

Por, F. D. *Lessepsian Migration: The Influx of Red Sea Biota into the Mediterranean by Way of the Suez Canal*. Berlin: Springer-Verlag, 1978.

Povinelli, E. "Radical Worlds: The Anthropology of Incommensurability and Inconceivability." *Annual Review of Anthropology* 30 (October 2001): 319–334.

Powell, Eve Troutt. *A Different Shade of Colonialism: Egypt, Great Britain, and the Mastery of the Sudan.* Berkeley: University of California Press, 2003.

Prakash, G. *Another Reason: Science and the Imagination of Modern India.* Princeton, NJ: Princeton University Press, 1999.

Puckler-Muskau, H. *Egypt under Mehmet Ali.* Translated by H. Evans Lloyd. London: H. Colburn, 1845.

Quṭb, Sayyid. *A Child from the Village.* Translated and edited by John Calvert and William E. Shepard. Syracuse, NY: Syracuse University Press, 2004.

Rabinbach, A. *The Human Motor: Energy, Fatigue, and the Origins of Modernity.* New York: Basic Books, 1990.

Racy, A.J. "Musical Aesthetics in Present Day Cairo." *Ethnomusicology* 26, no. 3 (September 1982): 391–406.

Raymond, André. *Cairo.* Translated by Willard Wood. Cambridge, MA: Harvard University Press, 2000.

Razova, Lucie. "Egyptionizing Modernity through the 'New Effendiya': Social and Cultural Constructions of the Middle Class in Egypt under the Monarchy." In *Re-envisioning Egypt* 1919–1952, edited by Barak A. Salmoni and Amy J. Johnson. Cairo: American University in Cairo Press, 2005.

Read, D. *The Power of News: The History of Reuters.* 2nd ed. Oxford: Oxford University Press, 1999.

Reid, Douglas A. "The Decline of Saint Monday, 1766–1876." *Past and Present* 71 (May 1976): 76–101.

———. "Weddings, Weekdays, Work and Leisure in Urban England 1791–1911: The Decline of Saint Monday Revisited." *Past and Present* 153 (November 1996): 135–163.

Reider, John. *Colonialism and the Emergence of Science Fiction.* Middletown, CT: Wesleyan University Press, 2008.

Reise, K., S. Gollasch, and W. J. Wolff. "Introduced Marine Species of the North Sea Coasts." *Helgoländer Meeresuntersuchungen* 52 (1999): 219–234.

Reynolds, M. *Engine-Driving Life.* London: Crosby Lockwood, 1881.

Richardson, Dan. *Rough Guide to Egypt.* New York: Rough Guides, 2003.

Rizk, Yunan Labib. "I Conjure Thee." *Al-Ahram: A Diwan of Contemporary Life,* March 4–10, 2004. http://weekly.ahram.org.eg/2004/680/chrncls.htm

———. "The Prince of Wit." *Al-Ahram Weekly.* December 16–22, 1999. http://weekly.ahram.org.eg/1999/460/chrncls.htm

Rodwell, G. Farrer. *South by East: Notes of Travel in Southern Europe.* London: M. Ward, 1877.

Rosenberg, Daniel, and Anthony Grafton. *Cartographies of Time: A History of the Timeline.* New York: Princeton Architectural Press, 2010.

Roush, G. A., ed. *The Mineral Industry: Its Statistics, Technology and Trade during 1916.* London: McGraw-Hill, 1917.

Rūmī, Jalāl al-Dīn. "The Man Who Fancied He Saw the New Moon." In *Tales of Mystic Meaning: Selections from the Mathnawī of Jalāl-ud-Dīn Rūmī.* Translated by Reynold Alleyne Nicholson. Oxford: Oneworld, 1995.

Russell, Mona. *Creating the New Egyptian Women.* New York: Palgrave Macmillan, 2004.
Ryad, Umar. *Islamic Reformism and Christianity.* Leiden: Brill, 2009.
Saba, Mahmoud. *Egyptian Telegraph Agreements.* Cairo: ESR, 1927.
Sadat, Jehan. *A Woman of Egypt.* New York: Simon and Schuster, 1987.
Said, E. *Orientalism.* New York: Vintage Books, 1979.
Salmon, P. R. *The Wonderland of Egypt.* London: Religious Tract Society, 1915.
Sandeman, D. *Memoir of the Life and Brief Ministry of David Sandeman.* London: J. Nisbet, 1861.
Sauter, M. J. "Clockwatchers and Stargazers: Time Discipline in Early Modern Berlin." *American Historical Review* 112, no. 3 (June 2007): 685–710.
Savage, M. "Discipline, Surveillance and the 'Career': Employment on the Great Western Railway 1833–1914." In *Foucault, Management and Organization Theory,* edited by Alan McKinlay and Ken Starkey. London: Sage Publications, 1998.
Sayyad, N. al-, I. A. Bierman, and N. Rabbat, eds. *Making Cairo Medieval.* Lanham, MD: Lexington Books, 2005.
Schaffer, S. "Late Victorian Metrology and Its Instrumentation." In *Science Studies Reader,* edited by Mario Biagioli. New York: Routledge, 1999.
Scheer, F. *The Cape of Good Hope versus Egypt; or, Political and Commercial Consideration on the Proper Line of Steam Communication with the East Indies.* London, 1839.
Schielke, Samuli. "Snacks and Saints: Mawlid Festivals and the Politics of Festivity and Modernity in Contemporary Egypt." PhD diss., Amsterdam University, 2006.
Schivelbusch, W. *The Railway Journey: The Industrialization of Time and Space.* Berkeley: University of California Press, 1987.
Schnapp, J. T. "Crash (Speed as Engine of Individuation)." *Modernism/Modernity* 6, no. 1 (1999): 1–49.
Schulze, R. *Die Rebellion der ägyptischen Fallahin,* 1919*: Zum Konflikt zwischen d. agrar. -oriental. Gesellschaft u. d. kolonialen Staat in Ägypten,* 1820–1919. Berlin: Baalbek Verlag, 1981.
Scott, J. C. *Seeing like a State: How Certain Schemes to Improve the Human Condition Have Failed.* New Haven, CT: Yale University Press, 1988.
Seaward, J. *Observations on the Advantages of Successfully Employing Steam Power in Navigating Ships between This Country and the East Indies.* London, 1829.
Sedra, Paul. *From Mission to Modernity: Evangelicals, Reformers, and Education in Nineteenth Century Egypt.* London: I. B. Tauris, 2011.
Selim, Samah. *The Novel and the Rural Imaginary in Egypt,* 1880–1985. New York: Routledge Curzon, 2004.
Sengers, G. *Women and Demons: Cult Healing in Islamic Egypt.* Leiden: Brill, 2003.
Shaʿrāwī, Hudā. *Harem Years: The Memoirs of an Egyptian Feminist* (1879–1924). Translated by Margot Badran. New York: Feminist Press, 1987.
Sheehi, S. *Foundations of Modern Arab Identity.* Gainesville: University Press of Florida, 2004.

Singer, Ben. "Modernity, Hyperstimulus, and the Rise of Popular Sensationalism." In *Cinema and the Invention of Modern Life,* edited by Leo Charney and Vanessa Schwartz. Berkeley: University of California Press, 1995.

Skovgaard Petersen, Jakov. *Defining Islam for the Egyptian State: Muftis and Fatwas of the Dār al-Iftā.* Leiden: Brill, 1997.

Sladen, D. *Egypt and the English.* London: Hurst and Blackett, 1908.

———. *Queer Things about Egypt.* London: Hurst & Blackett, 1910.

Smith, A. *An Inquiry into the Nature and Causes of the Wealth of Nations.* Edited by Edwin Cannan London: Methuen, 1904.

Smith, Charles. *Islam and the Search for Social Order in Modern Egypt: A Biography of Muhammad Husayn Haykal.* Albany: SUNY Press, 1983.

Smith, Crosbie, and M. Norton Wise. *Energy and Empire: A Biographical Study of Lord Kelvin.* Cambridge: Cambridge University Press, 1989.

Smith, Jane Idleman, and Yvonne Yazbeck Haddad. *The Islamic Understanding of Death and Resurrection.* Oxford: Oxford University Press, 2002.

Smith, Mark Michael. *Mastered by the Clock: Time, Slavery, and Freedom in the American South.* Chapel Hill: University of North Carolina Press, 1997.

Somekh, S. "The Neo-Classical Arabic Poets." In *Modern Arabic Literature,* edited by M. M. Badawi. Cambridge: Cambridge University Press, 1993.

Sopwith, T. *Notes of a Visit to Egypt, by Paris, Lyons, Nismes, Marseilles and Toulon.* London, 1857.

St. John, B. *Village Life in Egypt: With Sketches of the Saïd.* Boston: Ticknor, Reed, and Fields, 1853.

St. John, J. A. *Egypt and Nubia.* London: Chapman and Hall, 1845.

St. John, Robert. *The Boss: The Story of Gamal Abdel Nasser.* London: McGraw-Hill, 1960.

Steinberg, M., ed. *Walter Benjamin and the Demands of History.* Ithaca, NY: Cornell University Press, 1996.

Stephens, J. L. *Incidents of Travel in Egypt, Arabia Petræa, and the Holy Land.* Harper & Brothers, 1853.

Stolz, Daniel A. "'By Virtue of Your Knowledge': Scientific Materialism and the Fatwās of Rashīd Riḍā." *Bulletin of the School of Oriental and African Studies* 75, no. 2 (June 2012): 223–247.

———. "Correcting the Clock: Mechanical Timekeeping and Islamic Astronomical Tradition in 18th/19th-Century Egypt." Paper presented to the Princeton Islamic Studies Colloquium, Princeton, NJ, Spring 2012.

Storey, G. *Reuters: The Story of a Century of News-Gathering.* New York: Crown, 1951.

Stott, Annette. *Holland Mania: The Unknown Dutch Period in American Art and Culture.* Woodstock, NY: Overlook Press, 1998.

Tanaka, S. *New Times in Modern Japan.* Princeton, NJ: Princeton University Press, 2004.

Taylor, C. *A Secular Age.* Cambridge, MA: Harvard University Press, 2007.

Taylor, I. *Leaves from an Egyptian Note-Book.* London: Kegan Paul, Trench, 1888.

Taylor, R. C. *Statistics of Coal: The Geographical and Geological Distribution of Mineral Combustibles or Fossil Fuel.* Philadelphia: J. W. Moore, 1848.
Terry, J. *The Wafd 1919–1952: Cornerstone of Egyptian Political Power.* Beirut: Third World Centre, 1982.
Thompson, E. P. *The Making of the English Working Class.* London: Vintage Books, 1963.
———. "Time, Work-Discipline and Industrial Capitalism." *Past and Present* 38 (December 1967): 56–97.
Tignor, Robert. "The Economic Activities of Foreigners in Egypt, 1920–1950: From Millet to Haute Bourgeoisie." *Comparative Studies in Society and History* 22, no. 3 (July 1980): 416–449.
———. "The Egyptian Revolution of 1919: New Directions in the Egyptian Economy." *Middle East Studies* 12, no. 3 (October 1976): 41–67.
———. "Nationalism, Economic Planning, and Development Projects in Interwar Egypt." *International Journal of African Historical Studies* 10, no. 2 (1977): 185–208.
Toledano, Ehud. *State and Society in Mid-Nineteenth-Century Egypt.* Cambridge: Cambridge University Press, 1990.
Train, George Francis. *An American Merchant in Europe, Asia and Australia: A Series of Letters from Java, Singapore.* New York: G. P. Putnam, 1857.
Tucker, Judith. *Women in Nineteenth-Century Egypt.* Cambridge: Cambridge University Press, 1985.
Turner, Charles. *Modernity and Politics in the Work of Max Weber.* New York: Routledge, 1992.
Twain, Mark. *Innocents Abroad; or, the New Pilgrims' Progress.* Scituate, MA: Digital Scanning, 2001 [1869].
U.S. Bureau of Foreign Commerce. "Foreign Markets for American Coal." *Special Consular Reports* 21, no. 1. Washington, D.C.: Government Printing Office, 1900.
Vallet, Jean. "Contribution à l'étude de la condition des ouvriers de la grande industrie au Caire." PhD diss., Université de Grenoble, Valence, 1911.
Van Dalen, B., et al. "Taʾrīkh." In *Encyclopedia of Islam.* 2nd ed. Leiden: Brill, 1955–2005.
Van der Veer, P. *Imperial Encounters: Religion and Modernity in India and Britain.* Princeton, NJ: Princeton University Press, 2001.
Van Nieuwkerk, Karin. *A Trade like Any Other: Female Singers and Dancers in Egypt.* Austin: University of Texas Press, 1995.
Virilio, P. "Cinema Isn't I See, It's I Fly: The Imposture of Immediacy and Traveling Shot." In *War and Cinema: The Logistics of Perception,* translated by Patrick Camiller. London: Verso, 1989.
———. "The Last Vehicle." In *The Paul Virilio Reader,* edited by Steve Redhead. New York: Columbia University Press, 2004: 109–121.
———. *Speed and Politics: An Essay on Dromology.* Translated by Mark Polizzotti. New York: Semiotexte, 1986.
———. *The Virilio Reader.* Edited by J. Der Derian. Malden, MA: Blackwell, 1998.

Waghorn, T.F. *The Acceleration of Mails between England and the East Indies.* London, 1843.

———. *Egypt as It Is in* 1837. London, 1837.

———. *Particulars of an Overland Journey from London to Bombay by Way of the Continent, Egypt, and the Red Sea.* London: Parbury, Allen, 1831.

———. *Steam Navigation to India by the Cape of Good Hope: Documents and Papers.* London: C. Whittingham, 1929.

Wallace, Alexander. *The Desert and the Holy Land.* Edinburgh: William Oliphant, 1868.

Warden, J.L. *The Coasts of Devon and Lundy Island: Their Towns, Villages, Scenery, Antiquates, and Legends.* London: Cox, 1895.

Warner, C.D. *Mummies and Moslems.* Hartford, CT: American Publishing, 1876.

Warner, M. *Publics and Counterpublics.* New York: Zone Books, 2002.

Waterbury, John. *Egypt: Burdens of the Past/Options for the Future.* Bloomington: Indiana University Press, 1978.

Weber, Max. *The Protestant Ethic and the Spirit of Capitalism.* Translated by Talcott Parsons. New York: Courier Dover, 2003.

———. "Science as a Vocation." In *From Max Weber: Essays in Sociology,* translated and edited by H.H. Gerth and C. Wright Mills. New York: Oxford University Press, 1946.

Whipple, E.P. *Lectures on Subjects Connected with Literature and Life.* Boston: Ticknor and Fields, 1859.

Wilson, J.H. *Facts Connected with the Origin and Progress of Steam Communication between India and England.* London, 1850.

Wilson, Sarah Atkins, and Giovanni Battista Belzoni. *Fruits of Enterprize Exhibited in the Adventures of Belzoni in Egypt and Nubia: With an Account of His Discoveries in the Pyramids, among the Ruins of Cities, and in the Ancient Tombs.* New York: Charles S. Francis, 1850.

Willcocks, William, and J.I. Craig. *Egyptian Irrigation.* London: E. and F.N. Spon, 1913.

William, N. *Conversations with M. Thiers, M. Guizot, and Other Distinguished Persons during the Second Empire.* London: Hurst and Blackett, 1878.

Williams, R. *Keywords: A Vocabulary of Culture and Society.* New York: Oxford University Press, 1983.

Winter, Alison. *Mesmerized: Powers of Mind in Victorian Britain.* Chicago: University of Chicago Press, 1998.

Winter, Michael. *Egyptian Society under Ottoman Rule,* 1517–1798. New York: Routledge, 2004.

———. "The Mawlids in Egypt from the Eighteenth Century until the Middle of the Twentieth Century." In *The ʿUlama and Problems of Religion in the Muslim World: Studies in Memory of Professor Uriel Heyd* (Hebrew), edited by G. Baer. Jerusalem: Israel Oriental Society, 1971.

———. *Society and Religion in Early Ottoman Egypt: Studies in the Writings of ʿAbd Al-Wahhāb Al-Shaʿrānī.* New Brunswick, NJ: Transaction, 2006.

Wishnitzer, Avner. *Reading Clocks,* Alla Turca: *Ottoman Temporal Culture and Its Transformation during the Long Nineteenth Century.* Chicago: Chicago University Press, forthcoming.

———. "The Transformation of Ottoman Temporal Culture during the Long Nineteenth Century." PhD diss., Tel Aviv University, 2009.

Witkin, Robert Winston. *Adorno on Music.* London: Routledge, 1998.

Wolff, Jonathan. "Karl Marx." In *The Stanford Encyclopedia of Philosophy.* Summer 2011 edition. Edited by Edward N. Zalta, http://plato.stanford.edu/archives/sum2011/entries/marx/

Zahlan, A. B. "The Impact of Technology Change on the Nineteenth-Century Arab World." In *Between the State and Islam,* edited by C. E. Butterworth and I. W. Zartman. Cambridge: Cambridge University Press, 2001.

Zerubavel, Eviatar. *Hidden Rhythms: Schedules and Calendars in Social Life.* Berkeley: University of California Press, 1985.

Žižek, Slavoj. "Kant and Sade: The Ideal Couple." *Lacanian Ink* 13 (Fall 1998), http://www.egs.edu/faculty/zizek/zizek-kant-and-sade-the-ideal-couple.html

———. *Less Than Nothing: Hegel and the Shadows of Dialectical Materialism.* London: Verso, 2012.

———. *The Puppet and the Dwarf: The Perverse Core of Christianity.* Cambridge, MA: MIT Press, 2003.

Zwemer, S. M. "The Clock, the Calendar, the Koran." *Moslem World* 3 (1913): 262–274.

INDEX